Study Guide

for

Introduction to Psychology:
Gateways to Mind and Behavior

Tenth Edition

Dennis Coon

THOMSON

WADSWORTH

Australia • Canada • Mexico • Singapore • Spain • United Kingdom • United States

For more information about our products,
contact us at:
Thomson Learning Academic Resource Center
1-800-423-0563

For permission to use material from this text,
contact us by:
Phone: 1-800-730-2214
Fax: 1-800-731-2215
Web: http://www.thomsonrights.com

Wadsworth/Thomson Learning
10 Davis Drive
Belmont, CA 94002-3098
USA

Asia
Thomson Learning
5 Shenton Way #01-01
UIC Building
Singapore 068808

Australia/New Zealand
Thomson Learning
102 Dodds Street
Southbank, Victoria 3006
Australia

Canada
Nelson
1120 Birchmount Road
Toronto, Ontario M1K 5G4
Canada

Europe/Middle East/South Africa
Thomson Learning
High Holborn House
50/51 Bedford Row
London WC1R 4LR
United Kingdom

Latin America
Thomson Learning
Seneca, 53
Colonia Polanco
11560 Mexico D.F.
Mexico

Spain/Portugal
Paraninfo
Calle/Magallanes, 25
28015 Madrid, Spain

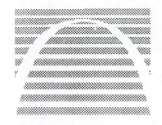

CONTENTS

Introduction

How to Use this Study Guide

 This *Study Guide* for *Introduction to Psychology: Gateways to Mind and Behavior* is designed to help you learn more, study efficiently, and get better grades. The exercises in this guide are closely coordinated with text chapters so that you can practice and review what you have read.

Each *Study Guide* chapter contains the following sections:

- **Chapter Overview**
- **Learning Objectives**
- **Recite and Review**
- **Connections**
- **Check Your Memory**
- **Final Survey and Review**
- **Mastery Test**
- **Answers**

A brief description of each section follows, along with suggestions for using them.

Chapter Overview

The Chapter Overview is a highly focused summary of major ideas in the text. By boiling chapters down to their essence, the Chapter Overview will give you a framework to build on as you learn additional ideas, concepts, and facts. Before you work on any other sections of this guide, read the Chapter Overview. In fact, it would be a good idea to re-read the Chapter Overview each time you use the *Study Guide*.

Learning Objectives

The Learning Objectives will show you, in detail, if you have mastered a reading assignment. To use them, you may want to write brief responses for each objective after you finish reading a chapter of the text. As an alternative, you may want to just read the Learning Objectives, pausing after each to see if you can respond in your own words. Then, after you have completed all of the other exercises in the *Study Guide* you can return to the Learning Objectives. At that time, you can either respond verbally or in writing. In either case, give special attention to any objectives you can't complete.

Recite and Review

This section will give you a chance to review major terms and concepts. Recite and Review is organized with the same Survey Questions found in the textbook chapters. This exercise will help you actively process information, so that it becomes more meaningful. Recite and Review also gives you a chance to practice recalling ideas from your reading, after you've closed the book.

As you work through Recite and Review, don't worry if you can't fill in all of the blanks. All of the answers are listed at the end of each *Study Guide* chapter. Filling in missing terms with the help of the answer key will focus your attention on gaps in your knowledge. That way, you can add new information to what you *were* able to remember. Page numbers are provided for each section of Recite and Review so you can return to the text to clarify any points that you missed.

Connections

This section contains matching-type items. It will help you build associations between related terms, facts, concepts, and ideas. Where appropriate, art is reproduced from the text so that you can match to images, rather than words. This is a good way to add links to your memory networks. Again, answers are listed at the end of the chapter.

Check Your Memory

The true-false statements in Check Your Memory highlight facts and details that you may have overlooked when you read the text. It's easy to fool yourself about how much you are remembering as you read. If you answered wrong for any of the items in Check Your Memory, you should return to the textbook to find out why. Page numbers listed for each group of items will make it easy for you to locate the relevant information in the textbook.

Final Survey and Review

This exercise might seem like a repeat of the Recite and Review section, but it's not. This time, you must supply a different set of more difficult terms and concepts to complete the review. The Final Survey and Review challenges you to consolidate your earlier learning and to master key concepts from the text. The Final Survey and Review is not a test. Don't be upset if you can't fill in some of the blanks. But do give missing ideas extra practice when you check your answers. Indeed, try to learn more each time you complete a *Study Guide* exercise, check your answers, or return to the text for review and clarification.

Mastery Test

The multiple-choice items of the Mastery Test are at least as difficult as those found on typical in-class tests. If you do well on the Mastery Test, you can be confident that you are prepared for in-class tests. On the other hand, a low score is a clear signal that further study and review are needed. However, don't expect to always get perfect scores on the Mastery Tests. In some cases the questions cover information that was not reviewed in any of the preceding *Study Guide* sections. The Mastery Tests are designed to continue the learning process, as well as to give you feedback about your progress.

Answers

Answers for all of the preceding exercises are listed at the end of each *Study Guide* chapter. Answers for the Mastery Test include page numbers so you can locate the source of the question in the textbook.

Language Development Guide

It's a good idea to read with a dictionary close at hand. Looking up words you don't know will add to your general vocabulary, as well as your understanding of the textbook. However, it can be difficult to find the meaning of idioms, slang, and refences to history, literature, and popular culture. If you come across an unfamiliar word or phrase in the text, a separate *Language Guide* is available with your text. Ask you professor about obtaining the guide if you would like to use it for clarification as you read.

A FIVE-DAY STUDY PLAN

There is no single "best" way to use this guide. Getting the most out of the *Study Guide* depends greatly on your personal learning style and study habits. Nevertheless, as a starting point, you might want to give the following plan a try.

Days 1 and 2   Read the assigned chapter in the textbook. As you do, be sure to make use of the Learning Checks and all the steps of the SQ4R method described in the textbook.

Day 3   Review the textbook chapter and any notes you made as you read it. Read the Chapter Overview in the *Study Guide* and read the Learning Objectives. Now do the Recite and Review section.

Day 4   Read the margin definitions in the textbook and the Chapter Overview in the *Study Guide*. Do the Connections and Check Your Memory sections of the *Study Guide*. Return to the textbook and make sure you understand why any items you missed were wrong.

Day 5   Review the textbook chapter and any notes you made as you read it. Read the Chapter Overview in the *Study Guide*. Then do the Final Survey and Review section, and check your answers. Return to the textbook and clarify any items you missed. Now take the Mastery Test. If you miss any questions, review appropriate sections of the textbook again. To really consolidate your learning, say or write responses to all of the Learning Objectives.

Summary

The close ties between *Introduction to Psychology* and the *Study Guide* make it possible for the *Study Guide* to be used in a variety of ways. You may prefer to turn to the *Study Guide* for practice and review after you have completed a reading assignment, as suggested in the Five-Day Plan. Or, you might find it more helpful to treat the *Study Guide* as a reading companion. In that case, you would complete appropriate *Study Guide* sections from each type of exercise as you progress through the text. In any event, it is nearly certain that if you use the *Study Guide* conscientiously, you will retain more, learn more efficiently, and perform better on tests. Good luck.

Chapter 1
Introduction to Psychology and Research Methods

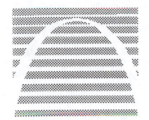

CHAPTER OVERVIEW

Psychology is the scientific study of behavior and mental processes. Psychology's goals are to describe, understand, predict, and control behavior. Psychologists answer questions about behavior by applying the scientific method and gathering empirical evidence.

Psychology grew out of philosophy. The first psychological laboratory was established by Wilhelm Wundt, who studied conscious experience. The first school of thought in psychology was structuralism, a kind of "mental chemistry." Structuralism was followed by the rise of functionalism, behaviorism, Gestalt psychology, psychoanalytic psychology, and humanistic psychology. Five main streams of thought in modern psychology are behaviorism, humanism, the psychodynamic approach, biopsychology, and cognitive psychology.

The training of psychologists differs from that of psychiatrists, psychoanalysts, counselors, and social workers. Clinical and counseling psychologists specialize in doing psychotherapy. Other specialties are industrial-organizational, educational, consumer, school, developmental, engineering, medical, environmental, forensic, psychometric, and experimental psychology.

Scientific investigation involves observing, defining a problem, proposing a hypothesis, gathering evidence/testing the hypothesis, publishing results, and forming a theory.

Many psychological investigations begin with naturalistic observation, which is informative despite its limitations. In the correlational method, the strength of the relationship between two measures is investigated. Correlations allow predictions, but they do not demonstrate cause-and-effect connections.

Experiments show whether an independent variable has an effect on a dependent variable. This allows cause-and-effect connections to be identified.

The clinical method employs detailed case studies of single individuals. In the survey method, people in a representative sample are asked a series of questions. This provides information on the behavior of large groups of people.

A key element of critical thinking is an ability to weigh the evidence bearing on a claim and to evaluate the quality of that evidence.

Belief in various pseudo-psychologies is based in part on uncritical acceptance, the fallacy of positive instances, and the Barnum effect.

Information in the popular media varies greatly in quality and accuracy. It is wise to approach such information with skepticism regarding the source of information, uncontrolled observation, correlation and causation, inferences, over-simplification, single examples, and unrepeatable results.

LEARNING OBJECTIVES

To demonstrate mastery of this chapter, you should be able to:

1. List two reasons for studying psychology.
2. Define *psychology*.
3. Describe what behavior is and differentiate overt from covert behavior.
4. Explain what empirical evidence is and give an example of it.
5. Identify when psychology became a science and what sets it apart from other fields.
6. Give two reasons why it is difficult to study some topics in psychology.
7. Write a brief summary of each of the following areas of specialization in psychology.

    a. developmental   f. comparative
    b. learning   g. biopsychology
    c. personality   h. social
    d. cognitive   i. cultural
    e. sensation and perception   j. industrial

8. Explain why and how animals are used in research and define the term *animal model* in your discussion. List a way in which psychological research may benefit animals.
9. List and explain the four goals of psychology and its ultimate goal, including why the word *control* has a special meaning for psychologists that is distinct from the everyday meaning of the word.
10. Use the following schools of psychology to answer the five questions below: structuralism, functionalism, behaviorism, Gestalt psychology, psychodynamic school, and humanism.

    a. its founder
    b. reasons it was founded
    c. its goal
    d. its impact on modern psychology
    e. its possible value in psychotherapy

11. Characterize the representation of the sexes in early psychology research and explain the reason for the discrepancy. State the ratio of the sexes receiving doctorates in psychology today. Name the first woman to receive a doctorate in psychology.
12. Describe the eclectic approach.
13. List and briefly describe the five major perspectives in modern psychology.
14. Explain how understanding human diversity may help us better understand ourselves and the behavior of others. Define the terms *cultural relativity* and *norms*.
15. Characterize the differences in training, emphasis, and/or expertise between psychologists, psychiatrists, psychoanalysts, counselors, and psychiatric social workers. Describe the roles of clinical and counseling psychologists, and define the term *scientist-practitioner model*.
16. List three points in the professional code for psychologists established by the APA.
17. Identify the largest areas of specialization among psychologists. Name the major source of employment for psychologists.
18. Differentiate basic from applied research.
19. List and define the six steps of the scientific method.
20. Define the term *hypothesis* and be able to identify a hypothesis. Explain what an operational definition is.
21. Explain the purpose of theory formulation and the importance of publication.

22. Identify three advantages and two disadvantages of the experimental method. (Table 1.2).

23. Describe the technique of naturalistic observation including three advantages and four disadvantages of this method. (See Table 1.2 in text.) Include the terms *observer effect* and *observer bias*. Explain what the anthropomorphic fallacy is and how it can lead to problems in psychological research. Define the term *observation record*.

24. Describe what a correlational study is and list three advantages and disadvantages of such a method. Explain what a correlation coefficient is, how it is expressed, what it means, and how it is related to causation. (See Table 1.2 in text.)

25. List and describe the three variables in the experimental method.

26. Explain the nature and the purpose of the control group and the experimental group in an experiment.

27. Explain the purpose of randomly assigning subjects to either the control or the experimental group.

28. Explain what statistically significant results are. Describe the technique of meta-analysis.

29. Explain the value of replication of results in science.

30. Explain what a placebo is and its role in an experiment.

31. Explain what single-blind and double-blind experimental approaches are and which sets up a better controlled experiment.

32. Explain the nature of the experimenter effect and how it is related to the self-fulfilling prophecy.

33. Briefly describe the clinical method of research including two advantages and three disadvantages. (See Table 1.2.) Give an example of a case in which the clinical method would be used.

34. Briefly describe the survey method of investigation including two advantages and three disadvantages. (See Table 1.2.) Define the terms *gender bias, courtesy bias,* and *my-side bias* and explain how they may make evidence less useful.

35. Indicate the foundations and fallacies of each of the following pseudo-psychologies:

    a. palmistry

    b. phrenology

    c. graphology

    d. astrology

36. List and explain the three reasons why pseudo-psychologies continue to thrive even though they have no scientific basis.

The following objectives are related to the material in the "Psychology in Action" and "A Step Beyond" sections of your text.

37. Define the term *critical thinking* and describe its four basic principles. List and then apply six questions which should be considered when evaluating information.

38. List seven suggestions that the author gives to help you become a more critical reader of psychological information in the popular press.

39. List and describe the three areas of ethical concern in psychological experiments, and explain the position of the APA in terms of ethical guidelines.

40. Briefly describe the polarity that exists in the debate concerning animal research. Describe the middle ground of the debate.

RECITE AND REVIEW

● *What is psychology? What are its goals?*

Recite and Review: Pages 12-18

1. Psychology is both a science and a _____.
2. Psychology is defined as the scientific study of behavior and _____ processes.
3. Psychologists study overt and covert _____.
4. Psychologists seek empirical _____ based on scientific observation.
5. Scientific observation is _____ so that it answers questions about the world.
6. Answering psychological questions requires a valid research _____.
7. Critical thinking is the ability to _____, compare, analyze, critique, and synthesize information.
8. Developmental psychologists study the course of human _____.
9. Learning theorists study how and why _____ occurs.
10. Personality _____ study personality traits and dynamics.
11. Sensation and perception psychologists study the _____ organs and perception.
12. Comparative psychologists study different species, especially _____.
13. Biopsychologists study the connection between biological processes and _____.
14. Cognitive psychologists are mainly interested in _____.
15. Gender psychologists study differences between _____ and _____.
16. Social psychologists study _____ behavior.
17. Cultural psychologists study the ways that culture affects _____.
18. Evolutionary psychologists are interested in patterns of behavior that were shaped by _____.
19. Other species are used as _____ models in psychological research to discover principles that apply to human behavior.
20. Psychology's goals are to describe, _____, predict, and control behavior.
21. Positive psychology focuses on topics that relate to _____ human functioning.

● *How did psychology emerge as a field of knowledge?*

Recite and Review: Pages 18-23

22. Historically, psychology is an outgrowth of philosophy, the study of _____, reality, and human nature.
23. The first psychological _____ was established in Germany by Wilhelm Wundt.
24. Wundt tried to apply scientific methods to the study of conscious _____.
25. Functionalism was concerned with how the mind helps us _____ to our environments.
26. Behaviorism was launched by John B. _____.
27. Behaviorists objectively study the relationship between stimuli and _____.
28. The modern behaviorist B. F. Skinner believed that most behavior is controlled by _____ reinforcers.

29. Cognitive behaviorism combines _____, reinforcement, and environmental influences to explain behavior.
30. Gestalt psychology emphasizes the study of _____ units, not pieces.
31. According to the Gestalt view, in psychology the whole is often _____ than the sum of its parts.
32. The psychoanalytic approach emphasized the _____ origins of behavior.
33. Psychoanalytic psychology, developed by Austrian physician Sigmund _____, is an early psychodynamic approach.
34. Humanistic psychology emphasizes free will, subjective experience, human potentials, and personal _____.
35. Psychologically, humanists believe that self-_____ and self-evaluation are important elements of personal adjustment.
36. Humanists also emphasize a capacity for self-actualization—the full development of personal _____.

● *What are the major trends and specialties in psychology?*

Recite and Review: Pages 23-30

37. Five main streams of thought in modern psychology are behaviorism, _____, the psychodynamic approach, biopsychology, and cognitive psychology.
38. Much of contemporary psychology is an eclectic _____ of the best features of various viewpoints.
39. To fully understand behavior, psychologists must be aware of human _____ as well as human universals.
40. Our behavior is greatly affected by cultural _____ and by social norms (_____ that define acceptable behavior).
41. Psychologists who treat emotional problems specialize in _____ or counseling psychology.
42. Psychiatrists typically use both _____ and psychotherapy to treat emotional problems.
43. Freudian psychoanlysis is a specific type of _____.
44. Both counselors and psychiatric social workers have _____ degrees.
45. Some major _____ in psychology are clinical, counseling, industrial-organizational, educational, consumer, school, developmental, engineering, medical, environmental, forensic, psychometric, and experimental psychology.
46. Scientific research in psychology may be either _____ or applied.

● *How do psychologists collect information?*

Recite and Review: Pages 30-36

47. Scientific investigation in psychology is based on reliable evidence, accurate description and _____, precise definition, controlled observation, and repeatable results.
48. The scientific method involves observing, defining a _____, proposing a hypothesis, gathering evidence/testing the hypothesis, publishing _____, and forming a theory.
49. To be scientifically _____ a hypothesis must be testable.
50. Psychological concepts are given operational _____ so that they can be observed.
51. A _____ is a system of ideas that interrelates facts and concepts.

52. Published research reports usually include the following sections: an _____, an introduction, a methods section, a _____ section, and a final discussion.
53. The tools of psychological research include naturalistic observation, the correlational method, the experimental method, the _____ method, and the survey method.
54. Naturalistic observation refers to actively observing behavior in _____ settings.
55. Two problems with naturalistic studies are the effects of the observer on the observed (the observer _____) and _____ bias.
56. The anthropomorphic fallacy is the error of attributing human qualities to _____.
57. Problems with naturalistic studies can be minimized by keeping careful observational _____.
58. In the correlational method, the _____ between two traits, responses, or events is measured.
59. Correlation coefficients range from +1.00 to –1.00. A correlation of _____ indicates that there is no relationship between two measures.
60. Correlations of +1.00 and –1.00 reveal that _____ relationships exist between two measures.
61. The closer a correlation coefficient is to plus or _____ 1, the stronger the measured relationship is.
62. A positive correlation shows that _____ in one measure correspond to increases in a second measure.
63. In a negative correlation, _____ in one measure correspond to decreases in a second measure.
64. Correlations allow us to make _____, but correlation does not demonstrate causation.
65. _____-and-effect relationships in psychology are best identified by doing a controlled experiment.
66. Graphing a linear relationship between two measures forms a straight line. When curvilinear relationships are graphed, a _____ line results.

● *How is an experiment performed?*

Recite and Review: Pages 37-40

67. In an experiment, conditions that might affect behavior are intentionally _____. Then, changes in behavior are observed and recorded.
68. In an experiment, a variable is any condition that can _____, and that might affect the outcome of the experiment (the behavior of subjects).
69. Experimental conditions that are intentionally varied are called _____ variables.
70. _____ variables measure the results of the experiment.
71. Extraneous variables are conditions that a researcher wishes to _____ from affecting the outcome of the experiment.
72. Extraneous variables are controlled by making sure that they are the same for all _____ in an experiment.
73. Subjects exposed to the independent variable are in the experimental _____. Those not exposed to the independent variable form the control _____.
74. Extraneous variables that involve personal _____, such as age or intelligence, can be controlled by randomly assigning subjects to the experimental and control groups.

75. If all extraneous variables are _____ for the experimental group and the control group, any differences in behavior must be caused by differences in the independent variable.
76. The results of an experiment are statistically significant when they would occur very rarely by _____ alone.
77. Meta-analysis is a statistical technique to _____ the results of many studies.
78. Experiments involving drugs must control for the placebo _____.
79. In a single-_____ study, subjects don't know if they are getting a drug or a placebo. In a double-_____ study, neither experimenters nor subjects know who is receiving a real drug.
80. Researchers must minimize the experimenter effect (the tendency for people to do what is _____ of them).
81. In many situations, the experimenter effect leads to self-fulfilling _____.

● *What other research methods do psychologists use?*

Recite and Review: Pages 41-44

82. Clinical psychologists frequently gain information from _____ studies.
83. Case studies may be thought of as _____ clinical tests.
84. In the survey method, information about large populations is gained by asking people in a representative _____ a series of carefully worded questions.
85. The value of surveys is lowered when the sample is biased and when replies to questions are _____.

● *How does psychology differ from false explanations of behavior?*

Recite and Review: Pages 44-47

86. In psychology, _____ thinking skills help evaluate claims about human behavior.
87. Critical thinking involves a willingness to _____ evaluate _____.
88. Scientific observations usually provide the highest quality _____ about various claims.
89. Palmistry, phrenology, graphology, and astrology are _____ systems or pseudo-psychologies.
90. Belief in pseudo-psychologies is encouraged by uncritical acceptance, the fallacy of positive instances, and the _____ effect, named after a famous showman who had "something for everyone."

● *How good is psychological information found in the popular media?*

Recite and Review: PSYCHOLOGY IN ACTION

91. _____ and critical thinking are called for when evaluating claims in the popular media.
92. You should be on guard for _____ or biased sources of information in the media.
93. Many claims in the media are based on unscientific observations that lack control _____.
94. In the popular media, a failure to distinguish between correlation and _____ is common.
95. Inferences and opinions may be reported as if they were _____ observations.
96. Single cases, unusual _____, and testimonials are frequently reported as if they were valid generalizations.

● *What ethical questions does psychological research raise?*

Recite and Review: A STEP BEYOND

97. Psychological researchers must be cautious and responsible with respect to moral or _____ issues.

98. Three ethical issues in research are _____, invasion of privacy, and lasting harm.

99. Deception may be necessary in psychological research, but its use should be _____, and subjects should be debriefed after participating.

100. The _____ and confidentiality of human subjects must be respected.

101. Ethical researchers treat participants with dignity and respect and ensure that they are not _____.

102. In addition to human subjects, _____ used in behavioral studies must be treated humanely.

CONNECTIONS

1. _____ biopsychology   a. hidden from view
2. _____ psychology   b. brain waves
3. _____ personality theorist   c. systematic observation
4. _____ empirical evidence   d. animal behavior
5. _____ covert behavior   e. detailed record
6. _____ scientific observation   f. human and animal behavior
7. _____ EEG   g. "why" questions
8. _____ comparative psychology   h. brain and behavior
9. _____ description   i. direct observation
10. _____ understanding   j. traits, dynamics, individual differences

11. _____ psychometrics   a. father of psychology
12. _____ control   b. natural selection
13. _____ Wundt   c. behaviorism
14. _____ Titchener   d. mental measurement
15. _____ James   e. functionalism
16. _____ Darwin   f. conditioned responses
17. _____ Skinner   g. Gestalt
18. _____ Pavlov   h. color vision
19. _____ Wertheimer   i. introspection
20. _____ Ladd-Franklin   j. influencing behavior

21. _____	Freud	a.	self-actualization
22. _____	Maslow	b.	self-image
23. _____	psychodynamic view	c.	psychoanalysis
24. _____	behavioristic view	d.	information processing
25. _____	humanistic view	e.	Ph.D., Psy.D., Ed.D.
26. _____	biopsychology	f.	M.D.
27. _____	cognitive view	g.	internal forces
28. _____	psychologist	h.	physiological processes
29. _____	psychiatrist	i.	controlled observation
30. _____	scientific method	j.	environmental forces

31. _____	common sense	a.	tentative explanation
32. _____	hypothesis	b.	formal log
33. _____	operational definition	c.	specific procedures
34. _____	Clever Hans	d.	related traits, behaviors
35. _____	observational record	e.	math error
36. _____	correlational study	f.	head signals
37. _____	correlation of +3.5	g.	effect on behavior
38. _____	identify causes of behavior	h.	experimental method
39. _____	independent variable	i.	unscientific information
40. _____	dependent variable	j.	varied by experimenter

41. _____	extraneous variables	a.	Phineas Gage
42. _____	control group	b.	done by using chance
43. _____	random assignment to groups	c.	participation is voluntary
44. _____	lobotomy	d.	excluded by experimenter
45. _____	placebos	e.	clinical method
46. _____	endorphins	f.	representative of population
47. _____	case studies	g.	inaccurate answers
48. _____	valid sample	h.	opiate-like
49. _____	courtesy bias	i.	reference for comparison
50. _____	ethical research	j.	sugar pills

CHECK YOUR MEMORY

Check Your Memory: Pages 12-18

1. Psychology can best be described as a profession, not a science. T or F?
2. Psychology is defined as the scientific study of human behavior. T or F?
3. Although it is a covert activity, dreaming is a behavior. T or F?
4. The term *empirical evidence* refers to the opinion of an acknowledged authority. T or F?
5. The term *data* refers to a systematic procedure for answering scientific questions. T or F?
6. Naming and classifying are the heart of psychology's second goal, understanding behavior. T or F?

Check Your Memory: Pages 18-23

7. In 1879, Wundt established a lab to study the philosophy of behavior. T or F?
8. Wundt used introspection to study conscious experiences. T or F?
9. Edward Titchener is best known for promoting functionalism in America. T or F?
10. The functionalists were influenced by the ideas of Charles Darwin. T or F?
11. Behaviorists define psychology as the study of conscious experience. T or F?
12. Watson used Pavlov's concept of conditioned responses to explain most behavior. T or F?
13. The "Skinner Box" is used primarily to study learning in animals. T or F?
14. Cognitive behaviorism combines thinking and Gestalt principles to explain human behavior. T or F?
15. Margaret Washburn was the first woman in America to be awarded a Ph.D. in psychology. T or F?
16. Mary Calkins did early research on memory. T or F?
17. According to Freud, repressed thoughts are held out of awareness, in the unconscious. T or F?
18. Humanists generally reject the determinism of the behavioristic and psychodynamic approaches. T or F?

Check Your Memory: Pages 23-30

19. The five major perspectives in psychology today are behaviorism, humanism, functionalism, biopsychology, and cognitive psychology. T of F?
20. Humanism offers a positive, philosophical view of human nature. T or F?
21. The cognitive view explains behavior in terms of information processing. T or F?
22. To understand behavior, psychologists must be aware of the cultural relativity of standards for evaluating behavior. T or F?
23. Most psychologists work in private practice. T or F?
24. The differences between clinical and counseling psychology are beginning to fade. T or F?
25. To enter the profession of psychology today you would need to earn a doctorate degree. T or F?
26. The Psy.D. degree emphasizes scientific research skills. T or F?
27. More than half of all psychologists specialize in clinical or counseling psychology. T or F?
28. Clinical psychologists must be licensed to practice legally. T or F?
29. Over 40 percent of all psychologists are employed by the military. T or F?
30. Studying ways to improve the memories of eyewitnesses to crimes would be an example of applied research. T or F?

Check Your Memory: Pages 30-36

31. The scientific method involves testing a proposition by systematic observation. T or F?

32. An operational definition states the exact hypothesis used to represent a concept. T or F?
33. Clever Hans couldn't do math problems when his owner left the room. T or F?
34. Operational definitions link concepts with concrete observations. T or F?
35. Most research reports begin with an abstract. T or F?
36. Jane Goodall's study of chimpanzees made use of the clinical method. T or F?
37. Concealing the observer helps reduce the observer effect. T or F?
38. A correlation coefficient of +.100 indicates a perfect positive relationship. T or F?
39. Strong relationships produce positive correlation coefficients; weak relationships produce negative correlations. T or F?
40. Perfect correlations demonstrate that a causal relationship exists. T or F?
41. The best way to identify cause-and-effect relationships is to perform a case study. T or F?

Check Your Memory: Pages 37-40

42. Extraneous variables are those that are varied by the experimenter. T or F?
43. Independent variables are suspected causes for differences in behavior. T or F?
44. In an experiment to test whether hunger affects memory, hunger is the dependent variable. T or F?
45. Independent variables are randomly assigned to the experimental and control groups. T or F?
46. A person who takes a drug may be influenced by his or her expectations about the drug's effects. T or F?
47. Placebos appear to reduce pain because they cause a release of endogenous dexedrine. T or F?
48. In a single-blind experiment, the experimenter remains blind as to whether she or he is administering a drug. T or F?
49. Subjects in psychology experiments can be very sensitive to hints about what is expected of them. T or F?

Check Your Memory: Pages 41-44

50. Phineas Gage is remembered as the first psychologist to do a case study. T or F?
51. Case studies may be inconclusive because they lack formal control groups. T or F?
52. Representative samples are often obtained by randomly selecting people to study. T or F?
53. A tendency to give socially desirable answers to questions can lower the accuracy of surveys. T or F?

Check Your Memory: Pages 44-47

54. Critical thinking is the ability to make good use of intuition and mental imagery. T or F?
55. Critical thinkers actively evaluate claims, ideas, and propositions. T or F?
56. A key element of critical thinking is evaluating the quality of evidence related to a claim. T or F?
57. Critical thinkers recognize that the opinions of experts and authorities should be respected without question. T or F?
58. Pseudo-scientists test their concepts by gathering data. T or F?
59. Phrenologists believe that lines on the hands reveal personality traits. T or F?
60. Graphology is only valid if a large enough sample of handwriting is analyzed. T or F?
61. Astrological charts consisting of positive traits tend to be perceived as "accurate" or true, even if they are not. T or F?
62. The Barnum effect refers to our tendency to remember things that confirm our expectations. T or F?

Check Your Memory: PSYCHOLOGY IN ACTION

63. The existence of dermo-optical perception was confirmed by recent experiments. T or F?

64. Psychological courses and services offered for profit may be misrepresented, just as some other products are. T or F?

65. At least some psychic ability is necessary to perform as a stage mentalist. T or F?

66. Successful firewalking requires neurolinguistic programming. T or F?

67. Violent crime rises and falls with lunar cycles. T or F?

68. If you see a person crying, you must infer that he or she is sad. T or F?

69. Individual cases and specific examples tell us nothing about what is true in general. T or F?

Check Your Memory: A STEP BEYOND

70. The Stanford prison experiment raised questions about the mistreatment of animals. T or F?

71. Deception is necessary to create realistic conditions in some psychology experiments. T or F?

72. Most of the subjects in Milgram's study of obedience to authority felt positive about their participation. T or F?

73. As a subject in a psychological study you have the right to expect that research results will be made available to you. T or F?

74. Ethical researchers accurately describe risks to potential subjects. T or F?

FINAL SURVEY AND REVIEW

● *What is psychology? What are its goals?*

1. Psychology is both a _____ and a _____.

2. Psychology is defined as the scientific study of _____ and _____ _____.

3. Psychologists study both overt and _____ behavior.

4. Psychologists seek _____ evidence based on scientific observation. They settle disputes by collecting _____.

5. _____ observation is structured and systematic.

6. Answering psychological questions requires a valid _____ _____.

7. Critical thinking is the ability to evaluate, compare, analyze, _____, and _____ information.

8. _____ psychologists study the course of human development.

9. Learning _____ study how and why learning occurs.

10. _____ theorists study personality traits and dynamics.

11. _____ and perception psychologists study the sense organs and perception.

12. _____ psychologists study different species, especially animals.

13. _____ study biological processes and behavior.

14. _____ psychologists are mainly interested in thinking and mental processes.

15. _____ psychologists study differences between males and females.

16. Social psychologists study _____ _____.

17. _____ psychologists study the ways that culture affects behavior.

18. _____ psychologists are interested in patterns of behavior that were shaped by natural selection.

19. Other species are used as _____ _____ in psychological research to discover principles that apply to human behavior.

20. Psychology's goals are to describe, understand, _____, and _____ behavior.

21. _____ psychology focuses on topics that relate to optimal human functioning.

● *How did psychology emerge as a field of knowledge?*

22. Historically, psychology is an outgrowth of _____.

23. The first psychological laboratory was established in Germany by _____
_____.

24. His goal was to apply scientific methods to the study of _____
_____.

25. The first school of thought in psychology was _____, a kind of "mental chemistry."

26. _____ was concerned with how the mind helps us adapt to our environments. William _____ was one of its proponents.

27. _____ was launched by John B. Watson, who wanted to study the relationship between _____ and responses.

28. The modern behaviorist B. F. _____ believed that most behavior is controlled by positive
_____.

29. _____ behaviorism combines thinking and environmental influences to explain behavior.

30. _____ psychology emphasizes the study of whole experiences, not elements or pieces.

31. According to Max _____ and other _____ psychologists, the whole is often greater than the _____ of its parts.

32. The _____ approach emphasizes the unconscious origins of behavior.

33. The Austrian physician, Sigmund _____, developed a psychodynamic system called
_____.

34. _____ psychology emphasizes free will, subjective experience, human _____, and personal growth.

35. Psychologically, humanists believe that _____, self-evaluation, and one's _____ of reference are important elements of personal adjustment.

36. Humanists also emphasize a capacity for _____—the full development of personal potential.

● *What are the major trends and specialties in psychology?*

37. Five main streams of thought in modern psychology are _____,
_____, the psychodynamic approach, _____, and cognitive psychology.

38. Much of contemporary psychology is an _____ blend of the best features of various viewpoints.

39. To fully understand behavior, psychologists must be aware of human _____, as reflected in personal and _____ differences.

40. Our behavior is greatly affected by _____ values and by social _____ (rules that define acceptable behavior).

41. Psychologists who treat emotional problems specialize in _____ or _____ psychology.

42. _____ are medical doctors who typically use both drugs and _____ to treat emotional problems.

43. Freudian _____ is a specific type of psychotherapy.

44. Both counselors and _____ _____ workers have Master's degrees.

45. _____ psychologists specialize in the growth of children; _____ psychologists help design machinery; _____ psychologists study classroom dynamics.

46. Scientific research in psychology may be either basic or _____.

● *How do psychologists collect information?*

47. Scientific investigation in psychology is based on reliable _____, accurate description and _____, precise definition, controlled observation, and repeatable results.

48. The scientific method involves observing, defining a problem, proposing a _____, gathering evidence/testing the hypothesis, publishing results, and forming a _____.

49. To be _____ valid a hypothesis must be _____.

50. Psychological concepts are given _____ definitions so that they can be observed. Such definitions state the exact _____ used to represent a concept.

51. A _____ is a system of ideas that interrelates facts and concepts. In general, good _____ summarize existing _____, explain them, and guide further research.

52. The results of scientific studies are _____ in professional _____ so they will be publicly available.

53. The tools of psychological research include naturalistic observation, the correlational method, the _____ method, the clinical method, and the _____ method.

54. Naturalistic observation refers to actively observing behavior in _____ _____, which are the typical _____ in which people and animals live.

55. Two problems with naturalistic observation are the effects of the observer on the _____ and observer _____.

56. The _____ fallacy is the error of attributing human qualities to animals.

57. Problems with naturalistic observation can be minimized by keeping careful _____ _____.

58. In the _____ method, the strength of the relationship between two traits, responses, or events is measured.

59. Correlation _____ range from +1.00 to −1.00.

60. A correlation of _____ indicates that there is no relationship between two measures. Correlations of +1.00 and −1.00 reveal that _____ relationships exist between two measures.

61. The _____ a correlation coefficient is to plus or minus 1.00, the stronger the measured relationship is.

62. A _____ correlation or relationship shows that increases in one measure correspond to increases in a second measure.

63. In a negative correlation, _____ in one measure correspond to _____ in a second measure.

64. Correlations allow prediction, but correlation does not demonstrate _____.

65. Cause-and-effect relationships in psychology are best identified by doing a _____ _____.

66. Graphing a _____ relationship between two measures forms a straight line. When _____ relationships are graphed, a curved line results.

● *How is an experiment performed?*

67. In an experiment, conditions that might affect behavior are intentionally varied. Then, changes in behavior are _____ and _____.

68. In an experiment a _____ is any condition that can change, and that might affect the outcome of the experiment.

69. Experimental conditions that are intentionally varied are called _____ variables; they are potential _____ of changes in behavior.

70. _____ variables measure the results of the experiment; they reveal any _____ on behavior.

71. _____ variables are conditions that a researcher wishes to prevent from affecting the _____ of the experiment.

72. Extraneous variables are _____ by making sure that they are the same for all subjects in an experiment.

73. Subjects exposed to the independent variable are in the _____ group. Those not exposed to the independent variable form the _____ group.

74. Extraneous variables that involve _____ characteristics, such as age or intelligence, can be controlled by _____ assigning subjects to the experimental and control groups.

75. If all extraneous variables are identical for the experimental group and the control group, any differences in behavior must be caused by differences in the _____ variable.

76. The results of an experiment are _____ significant when they would occur very rarely by chance alone.

77. _____ is a statistical technique for combining the results of many studies.

78. Experiments involving drugs must control for the _____ effect.

79. In a _____ study, subjects don't know if they are getting a drug or a placebo. In a _____ study, neither experimenters nor subjects know who is receiving a real drug.

80. Researchers must also minimize the _____ _____ (the tendency for people to do what is expected of them).

81. In many situations, the experimenter effect leads to _____ prophecies.

● *What other research methods do psychologists use?*

82. Clinical psychologists frequently gain information from _____ _____, which focus on all aspects of a single _____.
83. Case studies may be thought of as natural _____ _____ of the effects of brain tumors, accidental poisonings, and other unusual conditions.
84. In the survey method, information about large _____ is gained by asking people in a _____ sample a series of carefully worded questions.
85. The value of surveys is lowered when the sample is _____ and when replies to _____ are inaccurate or untruthful.

● *How does psychology differ from false explanations of behavior?*

86. In psychology, critical thinking skills help _____ claims about human behavior.
87. Critical thinking involves evaluating the quality of the _____ used to support various claims.
88. _____ observations usually provide the highest quality evidence about various claims.
89. Palmistry, _____, graphology, and astrology are _____-psychologies.
90. Belief in false psychologies is encouraged by _____ acceptance, the fallacy of _____ instances, and the _____ effect.

● *How good is psychological information found in the popular media?*

91. _____ and _____ thinking are called for when evaluating claims in the popular media.
92. You should be on guard for unreliable or _____ sources of information in the media.
93. Many claims in the media are based on unscientific observations that lack _____ groups.
94. _____ does not demonstrate causation. In the popular media, a failure to distinguish between _____ and causation is common.
95. Inferences and opinions may be reported as if they were objective _____.
96. Single _____, unusual examples, and testimonials are frequently reported as if they were valid _____.

● *What ethical questions does psychological research raise?*

97. Three _____ issues in psychological research are deception, invasion of privacy, and lasting _____.
98. Deception may be necessary in psychological research, but its use should be minimized and subjects should be _____ after participating.
99. The privacy of human subjects and _____ of results must be respected.
100. Ethical researchers treat participants with dignity and respect and ensure that they are not _____.

101. Animals used in behavioral studies must be treated _____.

MASTERY TEST

1. Data in psychology are typically gathered to answer questions about
   a. clinical problems   b. human groups   c. human cognition   d. overt or covert behavior

2. Who among the following would most likely study the behavior of gorillas?
   a. developmental psychologist   b. comparative psychologist   c. environmental psychologist
   d. forensic psychologist

3. An engineering psychologist helps redesign an airplane to make it safer to fly. The psychologist's work reflects which of psychology's goals?
   a. understanding   b. control   c. prediction   d. description

4. Who among the following placed the greatest emphasis on introspection?
   a. Watson   b. Wertheimer   c. Washburn   d. Wundt

5. Which pair of persons had the most similar ideas?
   a. Titchener—Skinner   b. James—Darwin   c. Watson—Rogers   d. Wertheimer—Maslow

6. The behaviorist definition of psychology clearly places great emphasis on
   a. overt behavior   b. conscious experience   c. psychodynamic responses   d. introspective analysis

7. As a profession, psychology is fully open to men and women, a fact that began with the success of
   a. O'Sullivan-Calkins   b. Tyler-James   c. Ladd-Franklin   d. Neal-Collins

8. The idea that threatening thoughts are sometimes repressed would be of most interest to a
   a. structuralist   b. psychoanalyst   c. humanist   d. Gestaltist

9. "A neutral, reductionistic, mechanistic view of human nature." This best describes which viewpoint?
   a. psychodynamic   b. cognitive   c. psychoanalytic   d. biopsychological

10. Which of the following professional titles usually requires a doctorate degree?
    a. psychologist   b. psychiatric social worker   c. counselor   d. all of the preceding

11. Who among the following is most likely to treat the physical causes of psychological problems?
    a. scientist-practitioner   b. psychoanalyst   c. forensic psychologist   d. psychiatrist

12. More than half of all psychologists specialize in what branches of psychology?
    a. counseling and comparative   b. applied and counseling   c. psychodynamic and clinical
    d. counseling and clinical

13. When critically evaluating claims about behavior it is important to also evaluate
    a. the source of anecdotal evidence   b. the credentials of an authority   c. the quality of the evidence
    d. the strength of one's intuition

14. Which of the following pairs is most different?
    a. pseudo-psychology—critical thinking   b. graphology—pseudo-psychology
    c. palmistry—phrenology   d. psychology—empirical evidence

15. The German anatomy teacher Franz Gall popularized
    a. palmistry   b. phrenology   c. graphology   d. astrology

16. A tendency to believe flattering descriptions of oneself is called
    a. the Barnum effect   b. the astrologer's dilemma   c. the fallacy of positive instances
    d. uncritical acceptance

17. Descriptions of personality that contain both sides of several personal dimensions tend to create
    a. an illusion of accuracy   b. disbelief and rejection   c. the astrologer's dilemma
    d. a system similar to phrenology

18. If an entire population is surveyed, it becomes unnecessary to obtain a
    a. control group   b. random comparison   c. random sample   d. control variable

19. Control groups are most often used in
    a. naturalistic observation   b. the clinical method   c. parascience   d. experiments

20. Concealing the observer can be used to minimize the
    a. observer bias effect   b. double-blind effect   c. observer effect   d. effects of extraneous correlations

21. A psychologist studying lowland gorillas should be careful to avoid the
    a. anthropomorphic error   b. Gestalt fallacy   c. psychodynamic fallacy
    d. fallacy of positive instances

22. Testing the hypothesis that frustration encourages aggression would require
    a. a field study   b. operational definitions   c. adult subjects   d. perfect correlations

23. In experiments involving drugs, experimenters remain unaware of who received placebos in a
    _____ arrangement
    a. zero-blind   b. single-blind   c. double-blind   d. control-blind

24. The idea that Clever Hans's owner might be signaling him was an informal
    a. research hypothesis   b. self-fulfilling prophecy   c. operational definition   d. dependent variable

25. In psychology, the _____ variable is a suspected cause of differences in

    _____.
    a. independent, the control group   b. dependent, the experimenter effect   c. independent, behavior
    d. dependent, correlations

26. A person who is observed crying may not be sad. This suggests that it is important to distinguish
    between
    a. individual cases and generalizations   b. correlation and causation   c. control groups and
    experimental groups   d. observation and inference

27. In an experiment on the effects of hunger on the reading scores of elementary school children, reading scores are the
    a. control variable   b. independent variable   c. dependent variable   d. reference variable

28. Which of the following correlation coefficients indicates a perfect relationship?
    a. 1.00   b. 100.0   c. –1   d. both a and c

29. Jane Goodall's studies of chimpanzees in Tanzania are good examples of
    a. field experiments   b. experimental control   c. correlational studies   d. naturalistic observation

30. To equalize the intelligence of members of the experimental group and the control group in an experiment, you could use
    a. extraneous control   b. random assignment   c. independent control   d. subject replication

31. Which method would most likely be used to study the effects of tumors in the frontal lobes of the brain?
    a. sampling method   b. correlational method   c. clinical method   d. experimental method

32. The release of endorphins by the pituitary gland helps explain the
    a. experimenter effect   b. placebo effect   c. multiple-personality effect   d. gender-bias effect

33. Cause is to effect as _____ variable is to _____ variable.
    a. extraneous, dependent   b. dependent, independent   c. independent, extraneous
    d. independent, dependent

34. The specific procedures used to gather data are described in which section of a research report?
    a. introduction   b. abstract   c. method   d. discussion

35. Which of the following correlations demonstrates a cause-effect relationship?
    a. .980   b. 1.00   c. .50   d. none of the preceding

36. A graph of a perfect negative relationship would form a
    a. straight line   b. circle   c. horizontal line   d. U-shaped line

37. A researcher statistically combines the results of all of the published results concerning the effects of sugar on hyperactive behavior in children. In order to draw a conclusion about the effects of sugar on hyperactivity, the researcher has used
    a. the double-blind technique   b. experimental replication   c. natural clinical trials   d. meta-analysis

ANSWERS

Recite and Review

1. profession
2. mental
3. behavior
4. evidence
5. planned or structured
6. method
7. evaluate
8. development
9. learning
10. theorists
11. sense (or sensory)
12. animals
13. behavior
14. thinking
15. males, females
16. social
17. behavior
18. evolution
19. animal
20. understand
21. optimal
22. knowledge
23. laboratory
24. experience
25. adapt
26. Watson
27. responses
28. positive
29. thinking
30. whole
31. greater
32. unconscious
33. Freud
34. growth
35. image
36. potentials
37. humanism
38. blend
39. diversity (or differences)
40. values, rules
41. clinical
42. drugs
43. psychotherapy
44. Master's

45. specialties
46. basic
47. measurement
48. problem, results
49. valid (or useful)
50. definitions
51. theory
52. abstract, results
53. clinical
54. natural
55. effect, observer
56. animals
57. records
58. correlation (or relationship)
59. zero
60. perfect
61. minus
62. increases
63. increases
64. predictions
65. Cause
66. curved
67. varied
68. change
69. independent
70. Dependent
71. prevent
72. subjects
73. group, group
74. characteristics
75. identical
76. chance
77. combine
78. effect
79. blind, blind
80. expected
81. prophecies
82. case
83. natural
84. sample
85. untruthful (or inaccurate)
86. critical
87. actively, ideas
88. evidence
89. false
90. Barnum

91. Skepticism
92. unreliable (or inaccurate)
93. groups
94. causation
95. valid (or scientific)
96. examples
97. ethical
98. deception
99. minimized
100. privacy
101. harmed
102. animals

Connections

1. h
2. f
3. j
4. i
5. a
6. c
7. b
8. d
9. e
10. g
11. d
12. j
13. a
14. i
15. e
16. b
17. c
18. f
19. g
20. h
21. c
22. a
23. g
24. j
25. b
26. h
27. d
28. e
29. f
30. i

31. i
32. a
33. c
34. f
35. b
36. d
37. e
38. h
39. j
40. g
41. d
42. i
43. b
44. a
45. j
46. h
47. e
48. f
49. g
50. c

Check Your Memory

1. F
2. F
3. T
4. F
5. F
6. F
7. F
8. T
9. F
10. T
11. F
12. T
13. T
14. F
15. T
16. T
17. T
18. T
19. F
20. T
21. T
22. T
23. F
24. T
25. F
26. F

27. T
28. T
29. F
30. T
31. T
32. F
33. F
34. T
35. T
36. F
37. T
38. F
39. F
40. F
41. F
42. F
43. T
44. F
45. F
46. T
47. F
48. F
49. T
50. F
51. T
52. T
53. T
54. F
55. T
56. T
57. F
58. F
59. F
60. F
61. T
62. F
63. F
64. T
65. F
66. F
67. F
68. F
69. T
70. F
71. T
72. T
73. T
74. T

Final Survey and Review

1. science, profession
2. behavior, mental, processes
3. covert
4. empirical, data
5. scientific
6. research method
7. critique, synthesize
8. Developmental
9. theorists
10. Personality
11. Sensation
12. Comparative
13. Biopsychologists
14. Cognitive
15. Gender
16. social behavior
17. Cultural
18. Evolutionary
19. animal models
20. predict, control
21. Positive
22. philosophy
23. Wilhelm Wundt
24. conscious experience
25. structuralism
26. Functionalism, James
27. Behaviorism, stimuli
28. Skinner, reinforcers
29. Cognitive
30. Gestalt
31. Wertheimer, Gestalt, sum
32. Psychoanalytic (or psychodynamic)
33. Freud, psychoanalysis
34. Humanistic, potentials
35. self-image, frame
36. self-actualization
37. behaviorism, humanism, biopsychology
38. eclectic
39. diversity, cultural
40. cultural, norms
41. clinical, counseling
42. Psychiatrists, psychotherapy
43. psychoanalysis
44. psychiatric social

45. Developmental, engineering, educational
46. applied
47. evidence, measurement
48. hypothesis, theory
49. scientifically, testable
50. operational, procedures
51. theory, theories, observations
52. published, journals
53. experimental, survey
54. natural settings, environments
55. observed, bias
56. anthropomorphic
57. observational records
58. correlational
59. coefficients
60. zero, perfect
61. closer
62. positive
63. increases, decreases
64. causation
65. controlled experiment
66. linear, curvilinear
67. observed, recorded
68. variable
69. independent, causes
70. Dependent, effects
71. Extraneous, outcome
72. controlled
73. experimental, control
74. personal, randomly
75. independent
76. statistically
77. Meta-analysis
78. placebo
79. single-blind, double-blind
80. experimenter effect
81. self-fulfilling
82. case studies, subject
83. clinical tests
84. populations, representative
85. biased, questions
86. evaluate
87. evidence
88. Scientific
89. phrenology, pseudo

90. uncritical, positive, Barnum
91. Skepticism, critical
92. biased
93. control
94. Correlation, correlation
95. observations
96. cases, generalizations
97. ethical, harm
98. debriefed
99. confidentiality
100. harmed
101. humanely

Mastery Test

1. d (p. 14)
2. b (p. 15)
3. b (p. 18)
4. d (p. 18)
5. b (p. 19)
6. a (p. 20)
7. c (p. 22)
8. b (p. 21)
9. d (p. 25)
10. a (p. 28)
11. d (p. 28)
12. d (p. 30)
13. c (p. 44)
14. a (p. 45)
15. b (p. 45)
16. d (p. 46)
17. a (p. 47)
18. c (p. 42)
19. d (p. 37)
20. c (p. 34)
21. a (p. 34)
22. b (p. 31)
23. c (p. 40)
24. a (p. 31)
25. c (p. 37)
26. d (p. 50)
27. c (p. 37)
28. d (p. 34)
29. d (p. 33)
30. b (p. 38)
31. c (p. 41)
32. b (p. 40)

33. d (p. 38)
34. c (p. 32)
35. d (p. 35)
36. a (p. 36)
37. d (p. 39)

Chapter 2
The Brain, Biology, and Behavior

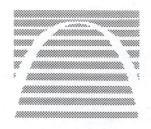

CHAPTER OVERVIEW

The brain and nervous system are made up of networks of neurons. Nerve impulses are basically electrical. Communication between neurons is chemical in that neurons release neurotransmitters which affect other neurons. Rather than merely carrying messages, neuropeptides regulate the activity of neurons in the brain.

The nervous system includes the central nervous system (CNS), consisting of the brain and spinal cord, and the peripheral nervous system (PNS). The PNS includes the somatic system and the autonomic system, with its sympathetic and parasympathetic branches.

Conventional brain research relies on dissection, staining, ablation, deep lesioning, electrical recording, electrical stimulation, micro-electrode recording, EEG recording, and clinical studies. Newer methods make use of computer-enhanced images of the brain and its activities.

The basic functions of the lobes of the brain are as follows: occipital lobes—vision; parietal lobes—bodily sensation; temporal lobes—hearing and language; frontal lobes—motor control, speech, and abstract thought. Association areas of the cortex are related to complex abilities such as language, memory, and problem solving. The left and right cerebral hemispheres have different specialized abilities.

The brain is subdivided into the forebrain, midbrain, and hindbrain. The subcortex includes important brain structures at all three levels. These are: the medulla ("vegetative" functions), the pons (a bridge between higher and lower brain areas), the cerebellum (coordination), the reticular formation (sensory and motor messages and arousal), the thalamus (sensory information), and the hypothalamus (basic motives). The limbic system is related to emotion.

The endocrine system provides chemical communication in the body through the release of hormones into the bloodstream.

Hand dominance ranges from strongly left- to strongly right-handed, with mixed handedness and ambidexterity in between. In general, the left-handed are less strongly lateralized in brain function than are right-handed persons.

The brain is capable of changing its structure and functions following damage and in response to changing environmental conditions. This capacity is called brain plasticity. The brain is also capable of neurogenesis (the production of new neurons). Neuroscientists are working on various ways to use brain plasticity and neurogenesis to repair damaged brains.

LEARNING OBJECTIVES

To demonstrate mastery of this unit you should be able to:

1. Name the basic unit that makes up the nervous system, state what it is specifically designed to do, and list and describe its four parts.
2. Define the terms *resting potential, threshold,* and *ion channels.*
3. Explain how a nerve impulse (action potential) occurs and how it is an all-or-nothing event.
4. Describe the difference between the nature of a nerve impulse and the nature of the communication between neurons.
5. Name the four structures that possess receptor sites for neurotransmitters.
6. Explain how nerve impulses are carried from one neuron to another.
7. Explain what determines whether an action potential will be triggered in a neuron.
8. Explain the functions of neuropeptides, enkephalins, and endorphins.
9. Differentiate a nerve from a neuron. Describe the effect of myelin on the speed of the nerve impulse.
10. Explain what determines whether or not a neuron or a nerve will regenerate. Explain how, in some cases, brain damage can be partially alleviated.
11. Differentiate between the two branches of the autonomic nervous system.
12. Explain the mechanism of the reflex arc.
13. Describe the following techniques for studying the brain: ablation, deep lesioning, electrical brain stimulation, micro-electrode recording, EEG, CT scan, MRI, functional MRI, and PET scan.
14. Describe the main difference between the brains of lower and higher animals. Name what appears to be the foundation of human intelligence. Describe the two main differences between the brains of people who score high on mental tests and those who score low.
15. Identify the two hemispheres of the brain. Describe the problem known as *spatial neglect.*
16. Describe the function of the corpus callosum.
17. Explain how and why a brain is "split," and describe what the resulting effects are.
18. Differentiate the abilities of the two hemispheres of the cerebral cortex. Describe what is known about how they work together as well as how they process information.
19. Describe the function(s) of each of the following:
    a. occipital lobes
    b. parietal lobes (include the somatosensory areas)
    c. temporal lobes
    d. frontal lobes (include the motor cortex)
    e. associative areas (include Broca's and Wernicke's areas)
20. Explain the relationship between the size of the various parts of the somatosensory and motor areas of the cortex and the degree of sensitivity or importance of the corresponding body parts.
21. Explain how brain injuries in the different lobes are related to different behavioral outcomes.
22. Describe the causes and effects of aphasia, agnosia, and facial agnosia. Compare sex differences in the hemispheric responsibility for language.

23. List and be able to recognize the three areas of the subcortex.

24. Explain the function of each of the following parts of the subcortex:
   a. hindbrain (brainstem)
         1. medulla   2. pons   3. cerebellum   4. reticular formation
   b. forebrain
         1. thalamus 2. hypothalamus

25. Name the structures that comprise the limbic system and explain its function (include a description of the functions of the amygdala and the hippocampus).

26. List six basic functions of the brain.

27. Briefly describe the significance of "pleasure" and "aversive" areas in the limbic system.

28. Briefly explain the purpose of the endocrine system.

29. Describe the action of hormones in the body.

30. Describe the effects that the following glands have on the body and behavior:
   a. pituitary (include a description of gigantism, dwarfism, and acromegaly)
   b. pineal
   c. thyroid (include a description of hyperthyroidism and hypothyroidism)
   d. adrenal medulla
   e. adrenal cortex (include a description of virilism, premature puberty, and the problems of
      anabolic steroids)

*The following objectives are related to the material in the "Psychology in Action" and "A Step
Beyond" sections of your text.*

31. Describe the relationship among handedness, brain dominance, and speech.

32. Explain how a person can determine which hemisphere is dominant.

33. State the incidence of left-handedness and discuss the relative advantages and/or disadvantages
of being right-handed versus left-handed.

34. Describe the element of handedness that appears to be inherited.

35. Briefly discuss the concept of plasticity in the brain, including how plasticity is accomplished,
the affect of plasticity on brain damage, and how it is influenced by age.

36. Define the term *neurogenesis*, including how neurogenesis might be used to repair damaged
brains, including the findings of Gould and Gross, 2002.

37. Briefly discuss the possibilities for future treatments of brain damage, including the work of
Bakay and Kennedy.

RECITE AND REVIEW

● *How do nerve cells operate and communicate?*

Recite and Review: Pages 57-61

1. The _____ and nervous system are made up of linked nerve cells called _____, which pass information from one to another through synapses.

2. The basic conducting fibers of neurons are _____, but dendrites (a receiving area), the soma (the cell body and also a receiving area), and _____ terminals (the branching ends of a neuron) are also involved in communication.

3. The firing of an action potential (_____ _____) is basically electrical, whereas communication between neurons is chemical.

4. An action potential occurs when the _____ potential is altered enough to reach the threshold for firing. At that point, sodium _____ flow into the axon, through _____ channels.

5. After each action potential, potassium ions flow out of the _____, restoring the resting potential.

6. The _____ potential is an all-or-nothing event.

7. Neurons release neurotransmitters at the synapse. These cross to _____ sites on the receiving cell, causing it to be excited or inhibited. For example, the transmitter chemical acetylcholine activates _____.

8. Chemicals called neuropeptides do not carry messages directly. Instead, they _____ the activity of other neurons.

9. Opiate-like neural regulators called enkephalins and endorphins are released in the brain to relieve _____ and stress.

● *What are the functions of major parts of the nervous system?*

Recite and Review: Pages 61-64

10. Nerves are made of large bundles of _____ and dendrites. Neurons and nerves in the peripheral nervous system can often regenerate; damage in the central nervous system is usually _____, unless a repair is attempted by grafting or implanting healthy tissue.

11. The nervous system can be divided into the _____ nervous system (the _____ and spinal cord) and the peripheral nervous system.

12. The CNS includes the somatic (_____) and autonomic (_____) nervous systems.

13. The autonomic system has two divisions: the sympathetic (emergency, activating) _____ and the parasympathetic (sustaining, conserving) _____.

14. Thirty-one pairs of spinal _____ leave the spinal cord. Twelve pairs of cranial _____ leave the brain directly. Together, they carry sensory and motor messages between the brain and the body.

15. The simplest _____ is a reflex arc, which involves a sensory neuron, a connector neuron, and a _____ neuron.

● *How do we know how the brain works?*

Recite and Review: Pages 64-67

16. Conventional brain research relies on dissection, staining, ablation, deep lesioning, electrical recording, _____ stimulation, micro-electrode recording, EEG recording, and _____ studies.

17. Computer-enhanced techniques are providing three-dimensional _____ of the living human brain and its _____. Examples of such techniques are CT scans, MRI scans, and PET scans.

● *How is the brain organized and what do its higher structures do?*

Recite and Review: Pages 68-73

18. The human _____ is marked by advanced corticalization, or enlargement of the cerebral _____, which covers the outside surface of the cerebrum.

19. "Split brains" have been created by _____ the corpus callosum. The split-brain individual shows a remarkable degree of independence between the right and left _____.

20. The _____ cerebral hemisphere contains speech or language "centers" in most people. It also specializes in _____, calculating, judging time and rhythm, and ordering complex movements.

21. The _____ hemisphere is largely nonverbal. It excels at spatial and perceptual skills, visualization, and recognition of _____, faces, and melodies.

22. Another way to summarize specialization in the brain is to say that the _____ hemisphere is good at analysis and processing information sequentially; the _____ hemisphere processes information simultaneously and holistically.

23. The most basic functions of the lobes of the cerebral cortex are as follows: occipital lobes—_____; parietal lobes—bodily sensation; temporal lobes—_____and language; frontal lobes—motor control, speech, and abstract thought.

● *Why are the brain's association areas important? What happens when they are injured?*

Recite and Review: Pages 73-75

24. Association areas on the cortex are neither _____ nor _____ in function. They combine information from the senses and they are related to more _____ skills such as language, memory, recognition, and problem solving.

25. Damage to either Broca's area or Wernicke's area causes _____ and language problems known as aphasias.

26. Damage to Broca's area causes problems with _____ and pronunciation. Damage to Wernicke's area causes problems with the _____ of words.

27. Damage in other association areas may cause agnosia, the inability to _____ objects by sight. This disability can sometimes impair the ability to recognize _____, a condition called facial agnosia.

● *What kinds of behaviors are controlled by the subcortex?*

Recite and Review: Pages 76-78

28. All of the brain areas below the _____ are called the subcortex.

29. The medulla contains centers essential for reflex control of _____ _____, breathing, and other "vegetative" functions.

30. The pons connects the medulla with _____ brain areas and it influences _____ and arousal.

31. The cerebellum maintains _____, posture, and muscle tone.

32. The reticular formation directs sensory and motor messages, and part of it, known as the RAS, acts as an _____ system for the cerebral cortex.

33. The thalamus carries _____ information to the cortex. The hypothalamus exerts powerful control over eating, drinking, sleep cycles, body temperature, and other basic _____ and behaviors.

34. The limbic system is strongly related to _____ and motivated behavior. It also contains distinct reward and punishment areas.

35. A part of the limbic system called the amygdala is related to _____. An area known as the hippocampus is important for forming _____.

● *Does the glandular system affect behavior?*

Recite and Review: Pages 79-81

36. The endocrine system provides _____ communication in the body through the release of _____ into the bloodstream. Endocrine glands influence moods, behavior, and even personality.

37. Many of the endocrine glands are influenced by the pituitary (the "_____ gland"), which is in turn influenced by the hypothalamus.

38. The pituitary supplies _____ hormone. Too little GH causes _____; too much causes giantism or acromegaly.

39. Body rhythms and _____ cycles are influenced by melatonin, secreted by the pineal gland.

40. The thyroid gland regulates _____. Hyperthyroidism refers to an overactive thyroid gland; hypothyroidism to an underactive thyroid.

41. The adrenal glands supply _____ and norepinephrine to activate the body. They also regulate salt balance, responses to stress, and they are a secondary source of _____ hormones.

● *How do right- and left-handed individuals differ?*

Recite and Review: PSYCHOLOGY IN ACTION

42. Hand dominance ranges from strongly left- to strongly right-handed, with _____ handedness and ambidexterity in between.

43. Ninety percent of the population is basically _____, 10 percent _____.

44. The vast majority of people are right-handed and therefore _____ brain dominant for motor skills. Ninety-seven percent of right-handed persons and 68 percent of the left-handed also produce _____ from the left hemisphere.

45. In general, the _____ are less strongly lateralized in brain function than are _____ persons.

● *Is brain damage always permanent?*

Recite and Review: A STEP BEYOND

46. Throughout life, the brain modifies its _____. New synapses form and dendrites grow longer or sprout new branches. Likewise, some _____ disappear and some dendrites are "pruned" away.

47. The brain loses cells every day, but it replaces them by growing new _____, a process called neurogenesis.

48. Injecting immature nerve cells into the brain may allow the repair of some forms of brain _____.

49. Also, the use of neurotrophic _____ that connect with brain tissue is making it possible for people to mentally control computers.

CONNECTIONS

1. _____	soma
2. _____	neurilemma
3. _____	axon collateral
4. _____	myelin
5. _____	dendrites
6. _____	axon terminals
7. _____	axon

8. _____ spinal cord
9. _____ autonomic system
10. _____ parasympathetic branch
11. _____ peripheral nervous system
12. _____ sympathetic branch
13. _____ brain
14. _____ somatic system

15. _____ Wernicke's area
16. _____ temporal lobe
17. _____ cerebellum
18. _____ Broca's area
19. _____ parietal lobe
20. _____ frontal lobe
21. _____ occipital lobe

22. _____ midbrain
23. _____ reticular formation
24. _____ cerebrum
25. _____ medulla
26. _____ hypothalamus
27. _____ corpus callosum
28. _____ pituitary
29. _____ spinal cord
30. _____ thalamus

31. _____	pituitary	a.	brain waves
32. _____	pineal gland	b.	radioactive glucose
33. _____	thyroid gland	c.	testosterone
34. _____	adrenal glands	d.	surgery
35. _____	testes	e.	metabolism
36. _____	CT scan	f.	electrode
37. _____	EEG	g.	growth hormone
38. _____	ablation	h.	epinephrine
39. _____	deep lesioning	i.	computerized X-rays
40. _____	PET scan	j.	melatonin

CHECK YOUR MEMORY

Check Your Memory: Pages 57-61

1. The dendrites receive incoming information from the neurilemma. T or F?
2. Human axons may be up to a meter long. T or F?
3. The resting potential is about plus 70 millivolts. T or F?
4. The interior of the axon becomes positive during an action potential. T or F?
5. The action potential is an all-or-nothing event. T or F?
6. The resting potential is caused by an inward flow of potassium ions. T or F?
7. Neurotransmitters activate other neurons; neuropeptides activate muscles and glands. T or F?
8. Enkephalins are neuropeptides. T or F?
9. Neuropeptides regulate the activity of other neurons. T or F?

Check Your Memory: Pages 61-64

10. Nerve impulses travel faster in axons surrounded by myelin. T or F?
11. The neurilemma helps damaged nerve cell fibers regenerate after an injury. T or F?
12. Neurons in the brain and spinal cord must last a lifetime; damage to them is usually permanent. T or F?
13. The word *autonomic* means "self-limiting." T or F?
14. Researchers have had some success in stimulating regrowth of cut nerve fibers in the spinal cord. T or F?
15. The sympathetic system generally controls voluntary behavior. T or F?
16. Thirty-one cranial nerves leave the brain directly. T or F?
17. "Fight-or-flight" emergency reactions are produced by the autonomic nervous system. T or F?
18. Activity in the parasympathetic system increases heart rate and respiration. T or F?
19. In a reflex arc, motor neurons carry messages to effector cells. T or F?

Check Your Memory: Pages 64-67

20. Deep lesioning in the brain is usually done surgically. T or F?
21. Micro-electrodes are needed in order to record from single neurons. T or F?

22. CT scans form "maps" of brain activity. T or F?
23. Electroencephalography records waves of electrical activity produced by the brain. T or F?
24. Radioactive glucose is used to make PET scans. T or F?

Check Your Memory: Pages 68-73

25. Elephants have brain-body ratios similar to those of humans. T or F?
26. The corpus callosum connects the right and left brain hemispheres. T or F?
27. The cerebellum makes up a large part of the cerebral cortex. T or F?
28. Much of the cerebral cortex is made up of gray matter. T or F?
29. Damage to the left cerebral hemisphere usually causes spatial neglect. T or F?
30. In general, smart brains tend to be the hardest working brains. T or F?
31. The right half of the brain mainly controls left body areas. T or F?
32. Roger Sperry won a Nobel prize for his work on corticalization. T or F?
33. Cutting the reticular formation produces a "split brain." T or F?
34. Information from the right side of vision is sent directly to the right cerebral hemisphere. T or F?
35. The right hemisphere tends to be good at speaking, writing, and math. T or F?
36. The left hemisphere is mainly involved with analysis. T or F?
37. The right hemisphere sees overall patterns and general connections. The left brain focuses on small details. T or F?
38. An inability to move the right side of the body is the most common neurological soft sign following an injury to the brain. T or F?
39. The motor cortex is found on the occipital lobes. T or F?
40. The somatosensory area is located on the parietal lobes. T or F?
41. Electrically stimulating the motor cortex causes movement in various parts of the body. T or F?

Check Your Memory: Pages 73-75

42. Large parts of the lobes of the brain are made up of association cortex. T or F?
43. Damage to either brain hemisphere usually causes an aphasia. T or F?
44. A person with Broca's aphasia might say "pear" when shown an apple. T or F?
45. Damage to Wernicke's area causes the condition known as mindblindness. T or F?
46. Women are much more likely than men to use both cerebral hemispheres for language processing. T or F?

Check Your Memory: Pages 76-78

47. The cerebrum makes up much of the medulla. T or F?
48. Injury to the medulla may affect breathing. T or F?
49. Injury to the cerebellum affects attention and wakefulness. T or F?
50. Smell is the only major sense that does not pass through the thalamus. T or F?
51. Stimulating various parts of the limbic system can produce rage, fear, pleasure, or arousal. T or F?
52. The hippocampus is associated with hunger and eating. T or F?

Check Your Memory: Pages 79-81

53. Androgens ("male" hormones) are related to the sex drive in both men and women. T or F?
54. "Normal short" children grow faster when given synthetic growth hormone, but their final height is not taller. T or F?
55. Activity of the pituitary is influenced by the hypothalamus. T or F?
56. A person who is slow, sleepy, and overweight could be suffering from hypothyroidism. T or F?
57. Virilism and premature puberty may be caused by problems with the adrenal glands. T or F?
58. Steroid drugs may cause sexual impotence and breast enlargement in males. T or F?

Check Your Memory: PSYCHOLOGY IN ACTION

59. Left-handers have an advantage in fencing, boxing, and baseball. T or F?
60. Most left-handed persons produce speech from their right hemispheres. T or F?
61. To a degree left or right handedness is influenced by heredity, especially by a gene on the *X* chromosome. T or F?
62. On average, left-handed persons die at younger ages than right-handed persons do. T or F?

Check Your Memory: A STEP BEYOND

63. Over the course of a lifetime, learning and experience "rewire" and "tune" the brain. T or F?
64. Neurons in the brain cannot be replaced. T or F?
65. Language processing can shift from the left to the right side of the brain if the left brain is not injured until early adulthood, when neurons have fully matured. T or F?
66. The hippocampus is capable of growing new neurons, which may help us store memories. T or F?
67. Attempts to repair the damage caused by a stroke will only work if mature brain cells are injected into the brain. T or F?
68. The "locked-in syndrome" occurs when neurotrophic electrodes damage the corpus callosum during split-brain operations. T or F?

FINAL SURVEY AND REVIEW

● *How do nerve cells operate and communicate?*

1. The brain and nervous system are made up of linked nerve cells called _____, which pass information from one to another through _____.
2. The basic conducting fibers of neurons are axons, but _____ (a receiving area), the _____ (the cell body and also a receiving area), and axon terminals (the branching ends of an axon) are also involved in communication.
3. The firing of an _____ _____ (nerve impulse) is basically electrical, whereas communication between neurons is chemical.
4. An action potential occurs when the resting potential is altered enough to reach the _____ for firing. At that point, _____ ions flow into the axon, through ion channels.

5. After each action potential, _____ ions flow out of the axon, restoring the resting potential.

6. The action potential is an _____ event.

7. In chemical synapses, neurons release _____. These cross to receptor sites on the receiving cell, causing it to be excited or inhibited. For example, the transmitter chemical _____ activates muscles.

8. Chemicals called _____ do not carry messages directly. Instead, they regulate the activity of other neurons.

9. Opiate-like neural regulators called enkephalins and _____ are released in the brain to relieve pain and stress.

● *What are the functions of major parts of the nervous system?*

10. _____ are made of axons and associated tissues. Neurons and nerves in the _____ nervous system can often regenerate; damage in the _____ nervous system is usually permanent.

11. The nervous system can be divided into the _____ nervous system (the brain and _____ _____) and the peripheral nervous system.

12. The CNS includes the _____ (bodily) and _____ (involuntary) nervous systems.

13. The autonomic system has two divisions: the _____ (emergency, activating) branch and the _____ (sustaining, conserving) branch.

14. Thirty-one pairs of _____ nerves leave the spinal cord. Twelve pairs of _____ nerves leave the brain directly. Together, these nerves carry sensory and _____ messages between the brain and the body.

15. The simplest behavior is a _____ _____, which involves a sensory neuron, an _____ neuron, and a _____ neuron.

● *How do we know how the brain works?*

16. Conventional brain research relies on _____ (separation into parts), staining, ablation, deep lesioning, electrical recording, electrical _____, micro-electrode recording, EEG recording, and clinical studies.

17. Computer-enhanced techniques are providing three-dimensional images of the living human brain and its activities. Examples of such techniques are CT scans, _____ scans, and _____ scans, which record brain activity.

● *How is the brain organized and what do its higher structures do?*

18. The human brain is marked by advanced _____, or enlargement of the cerebral cortex, which covers the outside surface of the _____.

19. "Split brains" have been created by cutting the _____ _____. The split-brain individual shows a remarkable degree of independence between the right and left _____.

20. The right cerebral _____ contains speech or language "centers" in most people. It also specializes in writing, calculating, judging time and rhythm, and ordering complex _____.
21. The left hemisphere is largely nonverbal. It excels at _____ and perceptual skills, visualization, and recognition of patterns, _____, and melodies.
22. Another way to summarize specialization in the brain is to say that the left hemisphere is good at _____ and processing information sequentially; the right hemisphere processes information _____ and holistically.
23. The most basic functions of the lobes of the cerebral _____ are as follows: occipital lobes—vision; parietal lobes—bodily _____; temporal lobes—hearing and language; frontal lobes—motor control, _____, and abstract thought.

● *Why are the brain's association areas important? What happens when they are injured?*

24. Association areas on the cortex are neither _____ nor _____ in function. They _____ information from the senses, and they are related to more complex skills such as _____, memory, recognition, and problem solving.
25. Damage to either Broca's area or Wernicke's area causes speech and language problems known as _____.
26. Damage to _____ area causes problems with speech and pronunciation. Damage to _____ area causes problems with the meaning of words.
27. Damage in other association areas may cause _____, the inability to identify objects by sight. This disability can sometimes impair the ability to recognize faces, a condition called _____ _____.

● *What kinds of behaviors are controlled by the subcortex?*

28. All of the brain areas below the cortex are called the _____.
29. The _____ contains centers essential for reflex control of heart rate, breathing, and other "vegetative" functions.
30. The _____ connects the medulla with higher brain areas and it influences sleep and arousal.
31. The _____ maintains coordination, posture, and muscle tone.
32. The _____ formation directs sensory and motor messages, and part of it, known as the RAS, acts as an activating system for the _____ _____.
33. The _____ carries sensory information to the cortex. The _____ exerts powerful control over eating, drinking, sleep cycles, body temperature, and other basic motives and behaviors.
34. The _____ system is strongly related to emotion and motivation. It also contains distinct _____ and punishment areas.
35. The part of the limbic system called the _____ is related to fear. An area known as the _____ is important for forming lasting memories.

● *Does the glandular system affect behavior?*

36. The _____ system provides chemical communication in the body through the release of hormones into the _____.

37. Many of the endocrine glands are influenced by the _____ (the "master gland"), which is in turn influenced by the _____.

38. The _____ supplies growth hormone. Too little GH causes dwarfism; too much causes giantism or _____.

39. Body rhythms and sleep cycles are influenced by _____, secreted by the _____ gland.

40. The thyroid gland regulates metabolism. Hyperthyroidism refers to an _____ thyroid gland; hypothyroidism refers to an _____ thyroid.

41. The _____ glands supply epinephrine and norepinephrine to activate the body. They also regulate salt balance, responses to _____, and they are a secondary source of sex hormones.

● *How do right- and left-handed individuals differ?*

42. _____ _____ ranges from strongly left- to strongly right-handed, with mixed handedness and _____ in between.

43. _____ percent of the population is basically right-handed, _____ percent left-handed.

44. The vast majority of people are _____ and therefore _____ brain dominant for motor skills. Ninety-seven percent of right-handed persons and 68 percent of the left-handed produce speech from the _____ hemisphere.

45. In general, the left-handed are less strongly _____ in brain function than are right-handed persons.

● *Is brain damage always permanent?*

46. Throughout life, the brain modifies its circuits. New _____ form and dendrites grow longer or sprout new branches. Likewise, some synapses disappear, and some dendrites are " _____ " away.

47. The brain loses cells every day, but it replaces them by growing new neurons, a process called _____.

48. Injecting immature _____ _____ into the brain may allow the repair of some types of brain damage.

49. Also, the use of _____ electrodes that connect with brain tissue is making it possible for people to mentally control computers.

MASTERY TEST

1. At times of emergency, anger, or fear, what part of the nervous system becomes more active?
   a. corpus callosum of the forebrain   b. sympathetic branch of the ANS
   c. parasympathetic branch of the PNS   d. Broca's area

2. The highest and largest brain area in humans is the
   a. cerebrum   b. cerebellum   c. frontal lobes   d. gray matter of the callosum

3. A tumor in which brain area would most likely cause blind spots in vision?
   a. occipital lobe   b. temporal lobe   c. somatosensory area   d. association cortex

4. Neurotransmitters are found primarily in
   a. the spinal cord   b. neurilemmas   c. synapses   d. motor neurons

5. Enkephalins are an example of
   a. acetylcholine blockers   b. neuropeptides   c. receptor sites   d. adrenal hormones

6. Electrically stimulating a portion of which brain area would produce movements in the body?
   a. occipital lobe   b. frontal lobe   c. parietal lobe   d. temporal lobe

7. When a neuron reaches its threshold, a/an _____ occurs.
   a. volume potential   b. ion potential   c. action potential   d. dendrite potential

8. A person's ability to work as a commercial artist would be most impaired by damage to the
   a. left temporal lobe   b. right cerebral hemisphere   c. left cerebral hemisphere
   d. frontal association cortex

9. Electrically stimulating the brain would most likely produce anger if it activated the
   a. association cortex   b. limbic system   c. parasympathetic branch   d. reticular activating system

10. Information in neurons usually flows in what order?
    a. soma, dendrites, axon   b. dendrites, soma, axon   c. dendrites, myelin, axon terminals
    d. axon, soma, axon terminals

11. Regulating the activity of other neurons is most characteristic of
    a. neuropeptides   b. acetylcholine   c. reflex arcs   d. resting potentials

12. Nerve impulses occur when _____ rush into the axon.
    a. sodium ions   b. potassium ions   c. negative charges   d. neurotransmitters

13. Experiments involving the grafting of nerve cells have been
    a. unsuccessful at present   b. successful in animals   c. successful only in the peripheral nervous
    system   d. successful only in the CNS

14. Attempts to link the brain with a computer (to treat the locked-in syndrome) have made use of
    a. PET scans   b. neurotrophic electrodes   c. neurotransmitters   d. sodium ions

15. A person who says "bife" for bike and "seep" for sleep probably suffers from
    a. Broca's aphasia   b. Wernicke's aphasia   c. functional agnosia
    d. the condition known as "mindblindness"

16. Damage to which part of the limbic system would most likely impair memory?
    a. thalamus   b. hypothalamus   c. amygdala   d. hippocampus

17. Involuntary changes in heart rate, blood pressure, digestion, and sweating are controlled by the
    a. thoracic nerves   b. parietal lobes   c. somatic system   d. autonomic system

18. In which of the following pairs are both structures part of the forebrain?
    a. medulla, hypothalamus   b. cerebrum, cerebellum   c. medulla, thalamus   d. cerebrum, thalamus

19. Which of the following is a specialized type of X-ray?
    a. PET scan   b. CT scan   c. MRI scan   d. EEG scan

20. Which two problems are associated with the pituitary gland?
    a. dwarfism, acromegaly   b. virilism, acromegaly   c. mental retardation, dwarfism
    d. giantism, premature puberty

21. The cerebral hemispheres are interconnected by the
    a. reticular system   b. cerebellum   c. cerebrum   d. corpus callosum

22. Damage to which of the following would most likely make it difficult for a person to play catch
    with a ball?
    a. reticular formation   b. limbic system   c. cerebellum   d. association cortex

23. Speech, language, calculation, and analysis are special skills of the
    a. right cerebral hemisphere   b. limbic system   c. left cerebral hemisphere
    d. right somatosensory area

24. The usual flow of information in a reflex arc is
    a. cranial nerve, connector neuron, spinal nerve   b. sensory neuron, connector neuron, motor neuron
    c. effector cell, interneuron, connector neuron   d. sensory neuron, connector neuron, reflex neuron

25. A person will "hear" a series of sounds when which area of the cortex is electrically stimulated?
    a. frontal lobe   b. parietal lobe   c. occipital lobe   d. temporal lobe

26. Which of the following pairs contains the "master gland" and its master?
    a. pineal—thalamus   b. thyroid—RAS   c. pituitary—hypothalamus   d. adrenal—cortex

27. Many basic motives and emotions are influenced by the
a. thalamus   b. hypothalamus   c. corpus callosum   d. cerebellum

28. Both surgical ablation and _____ remove brain tissue.
a. the MEG technique   b. tomography   c. micro-electrode sampling   d. deep lesioning

29. Which of the following techniques requires access to the interior of the brain?
a. micro-electrode recording   b. EEG recordings   c. PET scanning   d. functional MRI

30. Which of the following statements about handedness is false?
a. Like eye color, handedness is inherited from one's parents.   b. A majority of left-handers produce speech from the left hemisphere.   c. The left-handed are less lateralized than the right-handed.
d. Left-handedness is an advantage in boxing and fencing.

31. The discovery of _____ has made it clear that we are not born with all of the CNS neurons we will ever have. New ones arrive daily.
a. myelination   b. trephinnation   c. neuropeptides   d. neurogenesis

ANSWERS

Recite and Review

1. brain, neurons
2. axons, axon
3. nerve impulse
4. resting, ions, ion
5. axon
6. action
7. receptor, muscles
8. regulate
9. pain
10. axons, permanent
11. central, brain
12. bodily, involuntary
13. branch, branch
14. nerves, nerves
15. behavior, motor
16. electrical, clinical
17. images, activity
18. brain, cortex
19. cutting, hemispheres
20. left, writing

21. right, patterns
22. left, right
23. vision, hearing
24. sensory, motor, complex
25. speech
26. grammar, meaning
27. identify, faces
28. cortex
29. heart rate
30. higher, sleep
31. coordination
32. activating
33. sensory, motives
34. emotion
35. fear, memories
36. chemical, hormones
37. master
38. growth, dwarfism
39. sleep
40. metabolism
41. epinephrine, sex
42. mixed

43. right-handed, left-handed
44. left, speech
45. left-handed, right-handed
46. circuits, synapses
47. neurons
48. damage
49. electrodes

Connections

1. g
2. d
3. e
4. c
5. a
6. f
7. b
8. c or b
9. e
10. f or g
11. a

12. f or g
13. c or b
14. d
15. d
16. g
17. f
18. b
19. c
20. a
21. e
22. d
23. e
24. a
25. g
26. i
27. b
28. h
29. f
30. c
31. g
32. j
33. e
34. h
35. c
36. i
37. a
38. d
39. f
40. b

Check Your Memory

1. F
2. T
3. F
4. T
5. T
6. F
7. F
8. T
9. T
10. T
11. T
12. T
13. F
14. T
15. F
16. F

17. T
18. F
19. T
20. F
21. T
22. F
23. T
24. T
25. F
26. T
27. F
28. T
29. F
30. F
31. T
32. F
33. F
34. F
35. F
36. T
37. T
38. F
39. F
40. T
41. T
42. T
43. F
44. F
45. F
46. T
47. F
48. T
49. F
50. T
51. T
52. F
53. T
54. T
55. T
56. T
57. T
58. T
59. F
60. F
61. T
62. F
63. T
64. F
65. F

66. T
67. F
68. F

Final Survey and Review

1. neurons, synapses
2. dendrites, soma
3. action potential
4. threshold, sodium
5. potassium
6. all-or-nothing
7. neurotransmitters, acetylcholine
8. neuropeptides
9. endorphins
10. Nerves, peripheral, central
11. central, spinal cord
12. somatic, autonomic
13. sympathetic, parasympathetic
14. spinal, cranial, motor
15. reflex arc, connector, motor
16. dissection, stimulation
17. MRI, PET
18. corticalization, cerebrum
19. corpus callosum, hemispheres
20. hemisphere, movements
21. spatial, faces
22. analysis, simultaneously
23. cortex, sensation, speech
24. sensory, motor, combine, language
25. aphasias
26. Broca's, Wernicke's
27. agnosia, facial agnosia
28. subcortex
29. medulla
30. pons
31. cerebellum
32. reticular, cerebral cortex
33. thalamus, hypothalamus
34. limbic, reward
35. amygdala, hippocampus
36. endocrine, bloodstream
37. pituitary, hypothalamus

38. pituitary, acromegaly
39. melatonin, pineal
40. overactive, underactive
41. adrenal, stress
42. Hand dominance, ambidexterity
43. Ninety, 10
44. right-handed, left, left
45. lateralized
46. synapses, pruned
47. nerve cells
48. neurogenesis
49. neurotrophic

Mastery Test

1. b (p. 64)
2. a (p. 68)
3. a (p. 73)
4. c (p. 60)
5. b (p. 61)
6. b (p. 73)
7. c (p. 58)
8. b (p. 71)
9. b (p. 78)
10. b (p. 57-58)
11. a (p. 61)
12. a (p. 58)
13. b (p. 63)
14. b (p. 88)
15. a (p. 74)

16. d (p. 78)
17. d (p. 63)
18. d (p. 77)
19. b (p. 66)
20. a (p. 81)
21. d (p. 69)
22. c (p. 76)
23. c (p. 71)
24. b (p. 64)
25. d (p. 73)
26. c (p. 81)
27. b (p. 77)
28. d (p. 65)
29. a (p. 65)
30. a (p. 84)
31. d (p. 87)

Chapter 3
Child Development

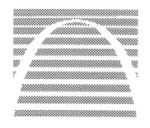

CHAPTER OVERVIEW

Heredity affects personal characteristics, including temperament, and it organizes the human growth sequence. Environmental influences can have especially lasting effects during sensitive periods in development. Prenatal development is affected by diseases, drugs, radiation, or the mother's diet and health. Early perceptual, intellectual, and emotional deprivation seriously retards development. Deliberate enrichment of the environment has a beneficial effect on early development.

Most psychologists accept that heredity and environment are inseparable and interacting forces. A child's developmental level reflects heredity, environment, and the effects of the child's own behavior.

Human newborns have adaptive reflexes, are capable of learning, and have visual preferences, especially for familiar faces. Maturation underlies the orderly sequence of motor, cognitive, language, and emotional development.

Emotional attachment of infants to their caregivers is a critical event in social development.

Caregiving styles affect social, emotional, and intellectual development. Optimal caregiving includes proactive involvement, a good fit between the temperaments of parent and child, and responsiveness to a child's needs and signals. Three major parenting styles are authoritarian, permissive, and authoritative (effective). Effective parental discipline tends to emphasize child management techniques, rather than power assertion or withdrawal of love.

Language development is based on a biological predisposition, which is augmented by learning. Language acquisition begins with prelanguage communication between parent and child.

Jean Piaget theorized that children go through a series of cognitive stages as they develop intellectually. Learning principles provide an alternate explanation which does not assume that cognitive development occurs in stages. Lev Vygotsky's sociocultural theory says that cognitive gains occur primarily in a child's zone of proximal development. Adults who engage in the scaffolding of a child's intellectual growth also impart cultural values and beliefs to the child.

Responsibility, mutual respect, consistency, love, encouragement, and clear communication are features of effective parenting.

Recent advances in genetics and reproduction raise ethical and social questions.

LEARNING OBJECTIVES

To demonstrate mastery of this chapter, you should be able to:

1. Define *developmental psychology.*
2. Explain the basic mechanisms of the transmission of heredity.
3. Define or describe each of the following terms in your own words:
    a. chromosome   d. polygenic
    b. DNA   e. dominant trait (gene)
    c. gene   f. recessive trait (gene)
4. Define the terms *senescence* and *human growth sequence.*
5. Describe the three types of children's temperament and give examples of behaviors characteristic of the different temperaments.
6. Briefly describe the impact that environment can have on development.
7. Briefly discuss the concept of critical periods.
8. Distinguish between congenital and genetic problems. Define the term *teratogen.*
9. Discuss the effects of environmental influences (including drugs and tobacco) on an unborn child. Include a description of the relationship between the blood supplies of the mother and her developing child.
10. Describe the symptoms of fetal alcohol syndrome.
11. Explain what is meant by the nature-nurture controversy. Discuss the outcome of this debate.
12. Define the term *developmental level* and list the three factors that combine to determine it.
13. Name and describe four adaptive reflexes displayed by neonates and the importance of their presence and later disappearance.
14. Describe the intellectual capabilities and the sensory preferences of a neonate.
15. Discuss the concepts of *maturation, cephalocaudal pattern, proximodistal pattern,* and *readiness.*
16. Describe (in general) the course of emotional development according to Bridges.
17. Explain the importance of self-awareness and social referencing in development.
18. Discuss the similarities and differences between imprinting and emotional attachment (including the concept of separation anxiety).
19. Differentiate between the three types of attachment identified by Mary Ainsworth.
20. Discuss the effects of day care on a child's sense of security and attachment.
21. Describe Harlow's experiment dealing with contact comfort, and state the results of the experiment. Relate his findings to Freud's psychodynamic theory.
22. Discuss the meaning and importance of infant affectional needs.
23. Describe the range of effects of maternal caregiving styles.
24. Discuss the importance of paternal influences in child development.
25. Describe Baumrind's three major styles of parenting, including characteristics of both parents and children in each style.

26. Give a brief description of each of the following child-rearing techniques and describe their effects on children and children's self-esteem:

    a. power assertion

    b. withdrawal of love

    c. management techniques

27. List and briefly describe five stages of language acquisition (including crying).

28. Briefly discuss the period known as the "terrible twos."

29. Describe the "language dance" and explain why children probably do it.

30. Define the term *psycholinguist*. Describe the role of learning in the acquisition of language.

31. Explain how parents communicate with infants before the infants can talk. Include the ideas of signals, turn-taking, and parentese.

32. Explain how a child's intelligence and thinking differ from an adult's. Explain the concept of transformation.

33. With regard to Piaget's stages of cognitive development:

    a. explain the concepts of assimilation and accommodation.

    b. list (in order) and briefly describe each stage listing the specific characteristics of each stage.

    c. evaluate the usefulness of Piaget's theory, including a review of current research on infant cognition.

34. Briefly discuss Vygotsky's sociocultural theory, including how his theory differs from Piaget's theory. Define the terms *zone of proximal development* and *scaffolding*.

35. Compare, contrast, and give examples of the effects of enrichment and deprivation on development. Include a description of the two factors or elements in early deprivation.

36. Discuss the effects of deliberate enrichment of the environment in infancy.

37. Describe the benefits of early childhood education programs (e.g., Headstart).

38. Discuss some ways in which parents can provide beneficial stimulation to infants.

The following objectives are related to the material in the "Psychology in Action" and "A Step Beyond" sections of your text.

39. Describe two key ingredients in effective parenting.

40. Describe the four basic ingredients of positive parent-child interactions.

41. Discuss the elements of effective communication, including the concepts of I-messages and you-messages. Define natural and logical consequences.

42. Define, describe and discuss the social implications of each of the following:

    a. artificial insemination   f. . chorionic villus sampling

    b. in vitro fertilization   g. eugenics

    c. sex selection   h. genetic engineering

    d. genetic counseling   i. gene therapy

    e. amniocentesis   j. gene cards

RECITE AND REVIEW

● *How do heredity and environment affect development?*

Recite and Review: Pages 92-100

1. Developmental psychology is the study of progressive changes in _____ and abilities, from _____ to _____.
2. Hereditary instructions are carried by _____ (deoxyribonucleic acid) in the form of chromosomes and _____ in each cell of the body.
3. Most characteristics are polygenic (influenced by a combination of _____) and reflect the combined effects of dominant and recessive _____.
4. Heredity organizes the general human growth sequence—the general pattern of _____ _____ from birth to death.
5. Heredity also influences differences in temperament (the physical core of _____). Most infants fall into one of three temperament categories: easy children, _____ children, and slow-to-warm-up children.
6. Environment refers to all _____ conditions that affect development.
7. A variety of sensitive periods (times of increased _____ to environmental influences) exist in development.
8. Prenatal development is subject to _____ influences in the form of diseases, drugs, radiation, or the mother's diet and health.
9. Prenatal damage to the fetus may cause congenital problems, or _____ _____. In contrast, genetic problems are inherited from one's parents.
10. Prepared childbirth tends to reduce pain and shorten _____.
11. Early perceptual, intellectual, and emotional deprivation seriously retards _____.
12. Poverty greatly increases the likelihood that children will experience various forms of

_____.
13. Deliberate enrichment of the _____ in infancy and early childhood has a beneficial effect on development.
14. The nature-nurture debate concerns the relative contributions to development of heredity (_____) and environment (_____).
15. Ultimately, most psychologists accept that _____ and environment are inseparable and interacting forces.
16. A child's developmental level (current state of development) reflects heredity, environment, and the effects of the child's _____ _____.

● *What can newborn babies do?*

Recite and Review: Pages 100-103

17. The human _____ (newborn) has a number of _____ reflexes, including the grasping, rooting, sucking, and Moro reflexes.
18. Newborns begin to _____ immediately and they imitate adults.
19. Tests in a looking chamber reveal a number of _____ preferences in the newborn. The neonate is drawn to complex, _____, curved, and brightly-lighted designs.

20. Infants prefer human face patterns, especially _____ _____. In later infancy, interest in the unfamiliar emerges.

● *What influence does maturation have on early development?*

Recite and Review: Pages 103-105

21. Maturation of the body and nervous system underlies the orderly _____ of motor, cognitive, language, and emotional development.

22. While the rate of maturation varies from child to child, the _____ is nearly universal.

23. The development of _____ control (motor development) is cephalocaudal (from head to toe) and proximodistal (from the _____ of the body to the extremities).

24. Many early _____ are subject to the principle of readiness.

25. Emotional development begins with a capacity for _____ excitement. After that the first pleasant and unpleasant emotions develop.

26. Some psychologists believe that basic emotional expressions are _____ and that some appear as early as 2.5 months of age.

27. By age 10 months, babies display a social smile when other _____ are nearby.

● *Of what significance is a child's emotional bond with parents?*

Recite and Review: Pages 105-110

28. _____ development refers to the emergence of self-awareness and forming relationships with parents and others.

29. Self-awareness (consciousness of oneself as a person) and _____ referencing (obtaining guidance from others) are elements of early _____ development.

30. Emotional attachment of human infants to their _____ is a critical early event.

31. Infant attachment is reflected by _____ anxiety (distress when infants are away from parents).

32. The quality of attachment can be classified as _____, insecure-avoidant, or insecure-ambivalent.

33. High-quality day care does not _____ children; high-quality care can, in fact, accelerate some areas of development.

34. Babies need contact comfort, a reassuring feeling they get from _____ their mother.

35. A child's _____ development is also affected by playing with other children. For example, cooperative _____ is a major step toward participation in social life outside the family.

36. An infant's affectional _____ are every bit as important as more obvious needs for physical care.

● *How important are parenting styles?*

Recite and Review: Pages 111-115

37. Caregiving styles (patterns of parental care) have a substantial impact on emotional and intellectual _____.

38. Maternal influences (the effects _____ have on their children) tend to center on caregiving.

39. Optimal caregiving includes proactive maternal _____, a good fit between the temperaments of parent and child, and responsiveness to a child's needs and _____.

40. Paternal influences differ in their impact because _____ tend to function as a playmate for the infant.

41. Authoritarian parents enforce rigid _____ and demand strict obedience to _____.

42. Overly permissive parents give little _____ and don't hold children accountable for their actions.

43. Authoritative (_____) parents supply firm and consistent guidance, combined with love and affection.

44. Effective child _____ is based on a consistent framework of guidelines for acceptable behavior.

45. Good discipline tends to emphasize child management techniques (especially communication), rather than _____ assertion or withdrawal of _____.

46. _____ techniques tend to produce the highest levels of self-esteem in children.

● *How do children acquire language?*

Recite and Review: Pages 115-118

47. Language development proceeds from control of _____, to cooing, then babbling, the use of single words, and then to telegraphic _____.

48. The patterns of early speech suggest a _____ predisposition to acquire language.

49. Psycholinguists (psychologists who study _____) believe that innate language predispositions are augmented by _____.

50. Prelanguage communication between parent and child involves shared rhythms, nonverbal _____, and turn-taking.

51. Parents help children learn language by using distinctive caretaker _____ or parentese.

● *How do children learn to think?*

Recite and Review: Pages 119-125

52. The intellects of children are _____ abstract than those of adults. Jean Piaget theorized that _____ growth occurs through a combination of assimilation and accommodation.

53. Piaget also held that children go through a fixed series of cognitive _____.

54. These are: sensorimotor (0-2), preoperational (2-7), _____ operational (7-11), and formal _____ (11-adult).

55. Learning theorists dispute the idea that cognitive development occurs in _____. Recent studies suggest infants are capable of levels of thinking beyond that observed by _____.

56. Young children don't seem to understand that the _____ of other people contain different information, beliefs, and thoughts than theirs do. In other words, they have a very simplified theory of _____.

57. A one-step-ahead strategy that takes into account the child's level of _____ development helps adapt instruction to a child's needs.

58. According to the sociocultural theory of Russian scholar Lev Vygotsky, a child's interactions with others are most likely to aid _____ development if they they take place within the child's _____ of proximal _____.

59. Adults help children learn how to think by scaffolding, or _____, their attempts to solve problems or discover principles.

60. During their collaborations with adults, children learn important cultural _____ and values.

● *How do effective parents discipline their children?*

Recite and Review: PSYCHOLOGY IN ACTION

61. Responsibility, mutual _____, consistency, love, encouragement, and clear _____ are features of effective parenting.

62. Much misbehavior can be managed by use of I-_____ and by applying _____ and logical consequences to children's behavior.

● *How has new genetic knowledge affected parenthood?*

Recite and Review: A STEP BEYOND

63. Many recent developments in _____ and reproduction raise ethical and social questions.

64. Examples of such developments are _____ insemination (medically engineered pregnancy) and in vitro fertilization (test-tube _____).

65. _____ selection techniques, amniocentesis (testing of the _____ fluid) and chorionic _____ testing also create ethical dilemmas.

66. Mapping of the human genome (entire set of human _____), eugenics (breeding for _____ characteristics), and genetic counseling pose particularly difficult questions for scientists and the general public.

CONNECTIONS

1. _____	grasping reflex	a. rapid motor learning
2. _____	rooting reflex	b. DNA area
3. _____	Moro reflex	c. old age
4. _____	readiness	d. nature
5. _____	gene	e. palm grip
6. _____	chromosome	f. nurture
7. _____	senescence	g. startled embrace
8. _____	heredity	h. conception to birth
9. _____	environment	i. colored body
10. _____	prenatal period	j. food search

11. _____	FAS	a. control of muscles and movement
12. _____	Vygotsky	b. caregiving style
13. _____	motor development	c. love and attention
14. _____	super mother	d. vowel sounds
15. _____	sensitive period	e. prenatal alcohol
16. _____	attachment	f. sociocultural theory
17. _____	affectional needs	g. vowels and consonants
18. _____	cooing	h. emotional bond
19. _____	babbling	i. caretaker speech
20. _____	parentese	j. magnified environmental impact

21. _____	assimilation	a. changing existing mental patterns
22. _____	accommodation	b. egocentricism
23. _____	sensorimotor stage	c. applying mental patterns
24. _____	preoperational stage	d. abstract principles
25. _____	concrete operations	e. social development
26. _____	formal operations	f. stage theory of cognitive development
27. _____	cooperative play	h. conservation
28. _____	Piaget	i. object permanence
29. _____	hothousing	j. skilled support for learning
30. _____	scaffolding	k. forced teaching

CHECK YOUR MEMORY

Check Your Memory: Pages 92-100

1. Developmental psychology is the study of progressive changes in behavior and abilities during childhood. T or F?

2. Each cell in the human body (except sperm cells and ova) contains 23 chromosomes. T or F?

3. The order of organic bases in DNA acts as a genetic code. T or F?

4. Two brown-eyed parents cannot have a blue-eyed child. T or F?

5. Identical twins have identical genes. T or F?

6. More children have a slow-to-warm up temperament than a difficult temperament. T or F?

7. The sensitive period during which German measles can damage the fetus occurs near the end of pregnancy. T or F?

8. Teratogens are substances capable of causing birth defects. T or F?

9. An infant damaged by exposure to X-rays during the prenatal period suffers from a genetic problem. T or F?

10. Many drugs can reach the fetus within the intrauterine environment. T or F?

11. To prevent FAS, the best advice to pregnant women is to get plenty of rest, vitamins, and good nutrition. T or F?

12. Prepared childbirth tends to reduce the need for pain medications during birth. T or F?

13. Poverty is associated with retarded emotional and intellectual development. T or F?
14. In animals, enriched environments can actually increase brain size and weight. T or F?
15. There is evidence that the "Mozart effect" might just be based on the fact that college students were more alert or in a better mood after listening to music. T or F?

Check Your Memory: Pages 100-103

16. The Moro reflex helps infants hold onto objects placed in their hands. T or F?
17. As early as 9 weeks of age, infants can imitate actions a full day after seeing them. T or F?
18. Three-day-old infants prefer to look at simple colored backgrounds, rather than more complex patterns. T or F?
19. After age 2, familiar faces begin to hold great interest for infants. T or F?

Check Your Memory: Pages 103-105

20. Most infants learn to stand alone before they begin crawling. T or F?
21. Motor development follows a top-down, center-outward pattern. T or F?
22. Toilet training should begin soon after a child is 1 year old. T or F?
23. Anger and fear are the first two emotions to emerge in infancy. T or F?
24. An infant's social smile appears within one month after birth. T or F?

Check Your Memory: Pages 105-110

25. Most infants have to be 15 weeks old before they can recognize themselves on videotape. T or F?
26. Securely attached infants turn away from mother when she returns after a period of separation. T or F?
27. *Separation anxiety disorder* is the medical term for homesickness. T or F?
28. A small number of children per caregiver is desirable in day care settings. T or F?
29. Children who spend too much time in poor quality day care tend to be insecure and aggressive. T or F?
30. The question of when secure attachment occurs is less important than the question of whether it occurs at all. T or F?
31. Children typically first begin to engage in cooperative play around age 4 or 5. T or F?

Check Your Memory: Pages 111-115

32. Early patterns of competence are well established by the time a child reaches age 3. T or F?
33. The "zoo-keeper" mother provides poor physical, emotional, and intellectual care for her child. T or F?
34. The goodness of fit between parents and children refers mainly to how compatible their temperaments are. T or F?
35. Responsive parents are sensitive to a child's feelings, need, rhythms, and signals. T or F?
36. Fathers typically spend about half their time in caregiving and half playing with the baby. T or F?
37. Paternal play tends to be more physically arousing for infants than maternal play is. T or F?
38. Authoritarian parents view children as having adult-like responsibilities. T or F?
39. Permissive parents basically give their children the message "Do it because I say so." T or F?
40. The children of authoritarian parents tend to be independent, assertive, and inquiring. T or F?
41. Asian cultures tend to be group-oriented and they emphasize interdependence among individuals. T or F?
42. As a means of child discipline, power assertion refers to rejecting a child. T or F?

43. With respect to spanking, psychological research indicates that parents should minimize spanking or avoid it entirely. T or F?
44. Severely punished children tend to be defiant and aggressive. T or F?
45. Punishment is most effective when it is given immediately after a disapproved act. T or F?

Check Your Memory: Pages 115-118

46. The single-word stage begins at about 6 months of age. T or F?
47. "That red ball mine," is an example of telegraphic speech. T or F?
48. Noam Chomsky believes that basic language patterns are innate. T or F?
49. The "terrible twos" refers to the two-word stage of language development. T or F?
50. The "I'm going to get you" game is an example of prelanguage communication. T or F?
51. Parentese is spoken in higher pitched tones with a musical inflection. T or F?

Check Your Memory: Pages 119-125

52. According to Piaget, children first learn to make transformations at about age 3. T or F?
53. Assimilation refers to modifying existing ideas to fit new situations or demands. T or F?
54. Cognitive development during the sensorimotor stage is mostly nonverbal. T or F?
55. Reversibility of thoughts and the concept of conservation both appear during the concrete operational stage. T or F?
56. Three-year-old children are surprisingly good at understanding what other people are thinking. T or F?
57. An understanding of hypothetical possibilities develops during the preoperational stage. T or F?
58. Playing peekaboo is a good way to establish the permanence of objects for children in the sensorimotor stage. T or F?
59. Contrary to what Piaget observed, infants as young as 3 months of age show signs of object permanence. T or F?
60. Vygotsky's key insight was that children's thinking develops through dialogues with more capable persons. T or F?
61. Learning experiences are most helpful when they take place outside of a child's zone of proximal development. T or F?
62. Scaffolding is like setting up temporary bridges to help children move into new mental territory. T or F?
63. Vygotsky empasized that children use adults to learn about their culture and society. T or F?

Check Your Memory: PSYCHOLOGY IN ACTION

64. Consistency of child discipline is more important than whether limits on children's behavior are strict or lenient. T or F?
65. Encouragement means giving recognition for effort and improvement. T or F?
66. Logical consequences should be stated as you-messages. T or F?

Check Your Memory: A STEP BEYOND

67. Artificial insemination is formally known as in vitro fertilization. T or F?
68. Currently, sex selection techniques are not 100 percent successful in producing children of the desired sex. T or F?
69. A majority of people who would use sex-selection methods say they would choose to have a boy. T or F?

70. Amniocentesis can be done earlier in pregnancy than chorionic villus sampling can. T or F?

71. Eugenics cannot be done until cloning has been applied to humans. T or F?

FINAL SURVEY AND REVIEW

● *How do heredity and environment affect development?*

1. _____ psychology is the study of _____ changes in behavior and abilities, from birth to death.

2. Hereditary instructions are carried by DNA (_____ acid) in the form of _____ ("colored bodies") and genes in every cell.

3. Most characteristics are _____ (influenced by a combination of genes) and reflect the combined effects of dominant and _____ genes.

4. Heredity organizes the general human _____ _____—the general pattern of physical development from birth to death.

5. Heredity also influences differences in _____ (the physical foundations of personality). Most infants fall into one of three categories: _____ children, difficult children, and _____ children.

6. _____ refers to all external conditions that affect development.

7. A variety of _____ _____ (times of increased sensitivity to environmental influences) exist in development.

8. During pregnancy, _____ development is subject to environmental influences in the form of diseases, _____, _____, or the mother's diet and health.

9. Prenatal damage to the fetus may cause _____ problems, or birth defects. In contrast, _____ problems are inherited from one's parents.

10. _____ childbirth tends to reduce _____ and shorten labor.

11. Early perceptual and intellectual _____ seriously retards development.

12. _____ greatly increases the likelihood that children will experience various forms of deprivation.

13. Deliberate _____ of the environment in infancy and early childhood has a beneficial effect on development.

14. The nature-nurture debate concerns the relative contributions to development of _____ (nature) and _____ (nurture).

15. Ultimately, most psychologists accept that heredity and environment are inseparable and _____ forces.

16. A child's _____ _____ (current state of development) reflects heredity, environment, and the effects of the child's own behavior.

● *What can newborn babies do?*

17. The human neonate (newborn) has a number of adaptive reflexes, including the _____, rooting, _____, and _____ reflexes.

18. Newborns begin to learn immediately and they _____ (mimic) adults.

19. Tests in a _____ _____ reveal a number of visual preferences in the newborn. The neonate is drawn to _____, circular, curved, and brightly-lighted designs.

20. Infants prefer _____ _____ patterns, especially familiar faces. In later infancy, interest in the _____ emerges.

● *What influence does maturation have on early development?*

21. _____ of the body and _____ _____ underlies the orderly sequence of motor, cognitive, language, and emotional development.

22. While the _____ of maturation varies from child to child, the order is nearly _____.

23. The development of muscular control (_____ development) is _____ (from head to toe) and _____ and from the center of the body to the extremities.

24. Many early skills are subject to the principle of _____.

25. Emotional development begins with a capacity for general _____. After that the first _____ and _____ emotions develop.

26. Some psychologists believe that basic _____ expressions are innate and that some appear as early as 2.5 _____ of age.

27. By age 10 months, babies display a _____ smile when other people are nearby.

● *Of what significance is a child's emotional bond with parents?*

28. Social development refers to the emergence of self-_____ and forming _____ with parents and others.

29. _____ (consciousness of oneself as a person) and social _____ (obtaining guidance from others) are elements of early social development.

30. Emotional _____ of human infants to their caregivers is a critical early event.

31. Infant attachment is reflected by separation _____ (distress when infants are away from parents).

32. The quality of attachment can be classified as secure, insecure-_____, or insecure-_____.

33. _____ day care does not harm children; excellent care can, in fact, _____ some areas of development.

34. Babies need _____ comfort, a reassuring feeling they get from touching their mother.

35. A child's social development is also affected by playing with other children. For example, _____ play is a major step toward participation in social life outside the family.

36. An infant's _____ needs are every bit as important as more obvious needs for physical care.

● *How important are parenting styles?*

37. _____ _____ (patterns of parental care) have a substantial impact on emotional and intellectual development.
38. _____ influences (the effects mothers have on their children) tend to center on _____.
39. Optimal caregiving includes _____ maternal involvement, a good fit between the _____ of parent and child, and responsiveness to a child's needs and signals.
40. _____ influences differ in their impact because fathers tend to function as a _____ for the infant.
41. _____ parents enforce rigid rules and demand strict obedience to authority.
42. Overly _____ parents give little guidance and don't hold children accountable for their actions.
43. _____ (effective) parents supply firm and consistent guidance, combined with love and affection.
44. Effective child discipline is based on consistent parental _____ concerning acceptable behavior.
45. Good discipline tends to emphasize child _____ techniques (especially communication), rather than power _____ or withdrawal of love.
46. Management techniques tend to produce the highest levels of _____ in children.

● *How do children acquire language?*

47. Language development proceeds from control of crying, to _____, then _____, the use of single words, and then to _____ speech (two-word sentences).
48. The patterns of early speech suggest a biological _____ to acquire language.
49. _____ (psychologists who study language) believe that innate language predispositions are augmented by learning.
50. _____ communication between parent and child involves shared rhythms, nonverbal signals, and _____-taking.
51. Parents help children learn language by using distinctive caretaker speech or _____.

● *How do children learn to think?*

52. The intellects of children are less _____ than those of adults. Jean Piaget theorized that cognitive growth occurs through a combination of _____ and accommodation.
53. Piaget also held that children go through a fixed series of _____ stages.
54. The stages are: _____ (0-2), _____ (2-7), concrete operational (7-11), and formal operations (11-adult).
55. _____ theorists dispute the idea that cognitive development occurs in stages. Recent studies suggest infants are capable of levels of _____ beyond that observed by Piaget.

56. Young children don't seem to understand that the _____ of other people contain different information, beliefs, and thoughts than theirs do. In other words, they have a very simplified _____ of _____.

57. A _____ strategy that takes into account the child's level of cognitive development helps adapt instruction to a child's needs.

58. According to the _____ theory of Russian scholar Lev _____, a child's interactions with others are most likely to aid cognitive development if they take place within the child's zone of _____ development.

59. Adults help children learn how to think by _____, or supporting, their attempts to solve problems or discover principles.

60. During their collaborations with others, children learn important _____ beliefs and values.

● *How do effective parents discipline their children?*

61. Responsibility, mutual respect, _____, love, _____, and clear communication are features of effective parenting.

62. Much misbehavior can be managed by use of I-messages and by applying natural and _____ _____ to children's behavior.

● *How has new genetic knowledge affected parenthood?*

63. Many recent developments in genetics and reproduction raise _____ and social questions.

64. Examples of such developments are artificial _____ (medically engineered pregnancy) and _____ _____ fertilization (test-tube fertilization).

65. Sex selection techniques, _____ (testing of the amniotic fluid) and _____ villus testing also create ethical dilemmas.

66. Mapping of the human _____ (entire set of human genes), _____ (breeding for desirable characteristics), and genetic counseling pose particularly difficult questions for scientists and the general public.

MASTERY TEST

1. The universal patterns of the human growth sequence can be attributed to
   a. recessive genes   b. environment   c. polygenic imprinting   d. heredity

2. Exaggerated or musical voice inflections are characteristic of
   a. prelanguage turn-taking   b. parentese   c. telegraphic speech   d. prompting and expansion

3. The emotion most clearly expressed by newborn infants is
   a. joy   b. fear   c. anger   d. excitement

4. Explaining things abstractly or symbolically to a child becomes most effective during which stage of cognitive development?
   a. postconventional   b. formal operations   c. preoperational   d. post-intuitive

5. An infant startled by a loud noise will typically display
   a. a Moro reflex   b. a rooting reflex   c. a Meltzoff reflex   d. an imprinting reflex

6. If one identical twin has a *Y* chromosome, the other must have a
   a. recessive chromosome   b. sex-linked trait   c. dominant chromosome   d. *Y* chromosome

7. Ideas about Piaget's stages and the cognitive abilities of infants are challenged by infants' reactions to
   a. hypothetical possibilities   b. impossible events   c. turn-taking   d. separation anxiety

8. The type of play that is observed first in most children is called
   a. selective play   b. secure play   c. solitary play   d. social play

9. The largest percentage of children display what type of temperament?
   a. easy   b. difficult   c. slow-to-warm-up   d. generic

10. Which of the following is a congenital problem?
    a. FAS   b. sickle-cell anemia   c. hemophilia   d. muscular dystrophy

11. A child might begin to question the idea that Santa Claus's sack could carry millions of toys when the child has grasped the concept of
    a. assimilation   b. egocentricism   c. conservation   d. reversibility of permanence

12. In most areas of development, heredity and environment are
    a. independent   b. interacting   c. conflicting   d. responsible for temperament

13. Children who grow up in poverty run a high risk of
    a. insecure scaffolding   b. hospitalism   c. deprivation   d. colostrum

14. By definition, a trait that is controlled by a dominant gene cannot be
    a. eugenic   b. hereditary   c. carried by DNA   d. polygenic

15. _____ development proceeds head-down and center-outward.
    a. Cognitive   b. Motor   c. Prelanguage   d. Preoperational

16. You could test for _____ by videotaping a child and then letting the child see the video on television.
    a. social referencing   b. self-awareness   c. the quality of attachment   d. the degree of readiness

17. After age 2, infants become much more interested in
    a. bonding   b. nonverbal communication   c. familiar voices   d. unfamiliar faces

18. According to Piaget, one of the major developments during the sensorimotor stage is emergence of the concept of
a. assimilation   b. accommodation   c. object permanence   d. transformation

19. Poverty is to deprivation as early childhood stimulation is to
a. imprinting   b. enrichment   c. responsiveness   d. assimilation

20. Which principle is most relevant to the timing of toilet training?
a. readiness   b. sensitive periods   c. nonverbal signals   d. assimilation

21. High self-esteem is most often a product of what style of child discipline?
a. power assertion   b. child management   c. withdrawal of love   d. the natural consequences method

22. Consonants first enter a child's language when the child begins
a. babbling   b. cooing   c. the single word stage   d. turn-taking

23. Physically arousing play is typically an element of
a. the zoo-keeper mother's caregiving style   b. paternal influences   c. proactive maternal involvement
d. secure attachment

24. Insecure attachment is revealed by
a. separation anxiety   b. seeking to be near the mother after separation
c. turning away from the mother after separation   d. social referencing

25. A healthy balance between the rights of parents and their children is characteristic of
a. authoritarian parenting   b. permissive parenting   c. authoritative parenting   d. consistent parenting

26. Studies of infant imitation
a. are conducted in a looking chamber   b. confirm that infants mimic adult facial gestures
c. show that self-awareness precedes imitation   d. are used to assess the quality of infant attachment

27. Threatening, accusing, bossing, and lecturing children is most characteristic of
a. PET   b. you-messages   c. applying natural consequences   d. management techniques

28. Three-year-old Sheila is unable to fully understand what other people think and feel, because at her age she has a very limited
a. attachment to others   b. theory of mind   c. sensorimotor capacity
d. zone of proximal development

29. According to Vygotsky, children learn important cultural beliefs and values when adults provide
_____ to help them gain new ideas and skills.
a. scaffolding   b. proactive nurturance   c. imprinting stimuli   d. parentese

30. One thing that all forms of effective child discipline have in common is that they
a. are consistent   b. make use of punishment   c. involve temporary withdrawal of love
d. emphasize you-messages

31. A *major* problem with using the "Mozart effect" as a basis for promoting intellectual development in babies is that the original research was done on
a. laboratory animals   b. mentally retarded infants   c. children in the concrete operations stage
d. college students

32. Sex selection involves
a. in vitro fertilization   b. genetic engineering   c. separating *X*- and *Y*-bearing sperm
d. all of the preceding

33. Which of the following techniques has not yet been done with humans?
a. cloning   b. amniocentesis   c. in vitro fertilization   d. artificial insemination

ANSWERS

Recite and Review

1. behavior, birth, death
2. DNA, genes
3. genes, genes
4. physical development
5. personality, difficult
6. external
7. sensitivity
8. environmental
9. birth defects
10. labor
11. development
12. deprivation
13. environment
14. nature, nurture
15. heredity
16. own behavior
17. neonate, adaptive
18. learn
19. visual, circular
20. familiar faces
21. sequence
22. order
23. muscular, center
24. skills
25. general
26. innate
27. people
28. Social
29. social, social
30. caregivers
31. separation
32. secure
33. harm
34. touching
35. social, play
36. needs
37. development
38. mothers
39. involvement, preferences
40. fathers
41. rules, authority
42. guidance
43. effective
44. discipline
45. power, love
46. Management
47. crying, speech
48. biological
49. language, learning
50. signals
51. speech
52. less, intellectual
53. stages
54. concrete, operations
55. stages, Piaget
56. minds, mind
57. cognitive
58. cognitive, zone, development
59. supporting
60. beliefs
61. respect, communication
62. messages, natural
63. genetics
64. artificial, fertilization
65. Sex, amniotic, villus

66. genes, desirable

Connections

1. e
2. j
3. g
4. a
5. b
6. i
7. c
8. d
9. f
10. h
11. e
12. f
13. a
14. b
15. j
16. h
17. c
18. d
19. g
20. i
21. c
22. a
23. j
24. b
25. h
26. d
27. e
28. f
29. k
30. j

Check Your Memory

1. F
2. F
3. T
4. F
5. T
6. T
7. F
8. T
9. F
10. T
11. F
12. T
13. T
14. T
15. T
16. F
17. F
18. F
19. F
20. F
21. T
22. F
23. F
24. F
25. F
26. F
27. F
28. T
29. T
30. T
31. T
32. T
33. F
34. T
35. T
36. F
37. T
38. T
39. F
40. F
41. T
42. F
43. T
44. T
45. T
46. F
47. F
48. T
49. F
50. T
51. T
52. F
53. F
54. T
55. T
56. F
57. F
58. T
59. T
60. T
61. F
62. T
63. T
64. T
65. T
66. F
67. F
68. T
69. T
70. F
71. F

Final Survey and Review

1. Developmental, progressive
2. deoxyribonucleic, chromosomes
3. polygenic, recessive
4. growth sequence
5. temperament, easy, slow-to-warm-up
6. Environment
7. sensitive periods
8. prenatal, drugs, radiation
9. congenital, genetic
10. Prepared, pain
11. deprivation
12. Poverty
13. enrichment
14. heredity, environment
15. interacting
16. developmental level
17. grasping, sucking, Moro
18. imitate

19. looking chamber, complex
20. human face, unfamiliar
21. Maturation, nervous system
22. rate, universal
23. motor, cephalocaudal, proximodistal
24. readiness
25. excitement, pleasant, unpleasant
26. emotional, months
27. social
28. awareness, relationships
29. Self-awareness, referencing
30. attachment
31. anxiety
32. avoidant, ambivalent
33. High-quality, accelerate
34. contact
35. cooperative
36. affectional
37. Caregiving styles
38. Maternal, caregiving
39. proactive, temperaments
40. Paternal, playmate
41. Authoritarian
42. permissive
43. Authoritative
44. guidance
45. management, assertion
46. self-esteem
47. cooing, babbling, telegraphic
48. predisposition
49. Psycholinguists
50. Prelanguage, turn
51. parentese
52. abstract, assimilation
53. cognitive
54. sensorimotor, preoperational
55. Learning, thinking
56. minds, theory, mind
57. one-step-ahead
58. sociocultural, Vygotsky, proximal
59. scaffolding
60. cultural
61. consistency, encouragement
62. logical consequences
63. ethical
64. insemination, in vitro
65. amniocentesis, chorionic
66. genome, eugenics

Mastery Test

1. d (p. 94)
2. b (p. 118)
3. d (p. 104)
4. b (p. 123)
5. a (p. 101)
6. d (p. 95)
7. b (p. 123)
8. c (p. 110)
9. a (p. 95)
10. a (p. 96)
11. c (p. 122)
12. b (p. 100)
13. c (p. 98)
14. d (p. 94)
15. b (p. 103)
16. b (p. 105)
17. d (p. 103)
18. c (p. 120)
19. b (p. 98)
20. a (p. 103)
21. b (p. 115)
22. a (p. 116)
23. b (p. 112)
24. c (p. 108)
25. c (p. 113)
26. b (p. 101)
27. b (p. 128)
28. b (p. 121)
29. a (p. 124)
30. a (p. 126)
31. d (p. 99)
32. c (p. 130)
33. a (p. 132)

Chapter 4

From Birth to Death: Life-Span Development

CHAPTER OVERVIEW

Life-span psychologists study continuity and change in behavior, as well as tasks, challenges, milestones, and problems throughout life. According to Erikson, each life stage provokes a different psychosocial dilemma.

Some major problems in childhood are toilet training, feeding disturbances, speech disturbances, learning disorders, and attention-deficit hyperactivity disorder. Childhood autism and child abuse are examples of the more severe problems that can occur.

Adolescence is culturally defined; puberty is a biological event. Early maturation is beneficial mostly for boys; its effects are mixed for girls. Adolescent identity formation is accelerated by cognitive development and influenced by parents and peer groups.

Moral development bridges childhood, adolescence, and early adulthood. Lawrence Kohlberg believed that moral development occurs in stages. Some psychologists question whether moral development is based only on a sense of justice. Caring for others also appears to be important.

Adult development is marked by events that range from escaping parental dominance in the late teens to a noticeable acceptance of one's lot in life during the 50s. Some people experience a mid-life crisis, but this is not universal. Adjustment to later middle age is sometimes complicated by menopause and the climacteric. Biological aging begins between 25 and 30, but peak performance in specific pursuits may come at any point in life. Intellectual declines due to aging are limited. Two major theories of successful aging are disengagement and activity. Activity theory appears to apply to more people. Ageism is especially damaging to older people. Impending death and bereavement both produce a series of typical emotional reactions.

Subjective well-being (happiness) is a combination of general life satisfaction and positive emotions. People with extraverted and optimistic personalities tend to be happy. Making progress toward your goals is associated with happiness, especially if the goals express your personal interests and values.

New approaches to death include the hospice movement, living wills, and cryonic suspension. The ethics of passive euthanasia and active euthanasia continue to generate controversy.

LEARNING OBJECTIVES

To demonstrate mastery of this chapter, you should be able to:

1. List the life stages experienced by all people.
2. Define the terms *developmental task* and *psychosocial dilemma.*
3. Explain, according to Erikson, how the resolution of the psychosocial dilemmas affects a person's adjustment to life.
4. Describe the psychosocial crisis and possible outcome for each of Erikson's eight life stages. Give approximate age ranges for each stage.
5. State how one can tell if a child is being subjected to too much stress.
6. Discuss the role of stress in a child's life, including the concept of overprotection.
7. Describe the role of parents in helping children cope with sibling rivalry and rebellion.
8. Tell how one can determine if a childhood problem is a normal behavior or a serious difficulty.
9. Give a brief description of the following serious childhood disorders and their possible causes:

    a. enuresis
    b. encopresis
    c. overeating
    d. anorexia nervosa
    e. pica
    f. delayed speech
    g. stuttering

10. Define the term *learning disorder*. Briefly describe dyslexia and ADHD in terms of symptoms, causes, and treatments.
11. Describe a childhood conduct disorder.
12. Describe childhood autism in terms of symptoms, causes, and treatment.
13. Describe the characteristics of abusive parents and conditions likely to foster abusive behavior.
14. Describe what can be done to prevent child abuse.
15. Define and differentiate between adolescence and puberty.
16. Discuss the advantages and disadvantages of early and late maturation for males vs. females.
17. Explain what Elkind means by children being "hurried into adulthood." Explain how social markers are related to "hurried" adolescence.
18. With regard to the adolescent's search for identity:

    a. explain what that means
    b. explain how being a member of a minority ethnic group influences the identity search
    c. describe the interactions between an adolescent and his/her parents
    d. discuss the importance of imaginary audiences
    e. describe the influence of peer groups on the search for identity

19. Regarding moral development:

    a. list (in order) and briefly describe each of Kohlberg's three levels (six stages) of moral development
    b. describe what proportions of the population function at each of Kohlberg's moral development levels

      c. explain Gilligan's argument against Kohlberg's system, and describe the current status of the argument.

      d. describe the impact of culture on morality

20. Describe the seven common patterns for adults and the dominant activities and goals for each, according to Roger Gould.

21. Suggest reasons that marriages are particularly vulnerable during the early thirties.

22. Synthesize how Erikson's stage of generativity correlates with Gould's "crisis of urgency."

23. Describe what a midlife crisis is and how it can be both a danger and an opportunity. Explain how the midlife transition is different for women than for men.

24. Compare and contrast the stages of adulthood with regard to the theories of Gould, Erikson, and Levinson (Table 4.4).

25. List Ryff's six elements of well-being in adulthood.

26. Contrast biological aging with our society's expectations of aging.

27. Differentiate the concepts maximum life span and life expectancy. List seven suggestions for increasing life expectancy.

28. Describe the differences between fluid and crystallized abilities.

29. Compare and contrast the disengagement and activity theories of aging. Include a description of Baltes' strategy of "selective optimization with compensation."

30. Describe what is meant by the term *ageism*.

31. List the four myths of aging refuted by Neugarten's research.

32. List the four main psychological characteristics of healthy aging found in Vaillant's study.

33. Regarding our emotional reactions toward death:

      a. explain what people fear about death

      b. list and briefly characterize the five emotional reactions typically experienced by people facing death, according to Kubler-Ross

      c. explain why knowledge of the reactions to impending death is important

      d. describe the general reaction of people who survive a near-death experience (NDE)

34. Discuss the general characteristics of each stage of the bereavement process. State the relationship between suppressing grief and later problems.

The following objectives are related to the material in the "Psychology in Action" and "A Step Beyond" sections of your text.

35. Briefly discuss the concept of *subjective well-being*, including the role of life satisfaction and positive/negative emotions.

36. Discuss the relationship of eight personal factors (such as wealth and personality) to happiness.

37. Briefly discuss McGregor and Little's findings regarding integrity, goals, and happiness.

38. Describe the philosophy and functions of hospices.

39. Explain the purpose of a "living will."

40. Define the terms *active euthanasia, passive euthanasia,* and *cryonics.*

RECITE AND REVIEW

● *What are the typical tasks and dilemmas through the life span?*

Recite and Review: Pages 136-140

1. Life-span psychologists study continuity and _____ over the life span.
2. They are also interested in _____ milestones, or prominent landmarks in personal development.
3. According to Erik Erikson, each life stage provokes a specific psychosocial _____.
4. During childhood these are: trust versus mistrust, autonomy versus _____ and doubt, initiative versus _____, and industry versus _____.
5. In _____, identity versus role confusion is the principal dilemma.
6. In young adulthood we face the dilemma of intimacy versus _____. Later, generativity versus _____ becomes prominent.
7. Old age is a time when the dilemma of integrity versus _____ must be faced.
8. In addition, each life stage requires successful mastery of certain _____ tasks (personal changes required for optimal development).

● *What are some of the more serious childhood problems?*

Recite and Review: Pages 141-147

9. Few children grow up without experiencing some of the normal problems of childhood, including negativism, clinging, specific fears, sleep _____, general dissatisfaction, regression, sibling _____, and rebellion.
10. Major areas of difficulty in childhood are _____ _____ (including enuresis and encopresis) and _____ disturbances, such as overeating, anorexia nervosa (self-starvation), and pica (eating nonfood substances).
11. Other problems include _____ disturbances (delayed speech, stuttering); _____ disorders, including dyslexia (an inability to read with understanding); and attention-deficit hyperactivity _____ (ADHD).
12. Children suffering from conduct _____ engage in aggressive, destructive, and antisocial behavior.
13. Childhood _____ is a severe problem involving mutism, sensory disturbances, tantrums, and a lack of responsiveness to other people.
14. Some cases of autism are being treated successfully with _____ modification.
15. Child abuse (physically or emotionally _____ a child) is a major problem. Roughly _____ percent of all abused children become abusive adults. Emotional support and therapy can help break the cycle of abuse.

● *Why is adolescent development especially challenging?*

Recite and Review: Pages 147-151

16. Adolescence is a culturally defined _____ status. Puberty is a _____ event.

17. On average, the peak growth spurt during puberty occurs earlier for _____ than for _____ .

18. Early maturation is beneficial mostly for _____ ; its effects are mixed for _____ .

19. Establishing a clear sense of personal identity is a major task of _____ . One danger of _____ maturation is premature identity formation.

20. Many adolescents become self-conscious and preoccupied with imaginary _____ (imagined viewers).

21. Adolescent identity formation is accelerated by cognitive development and influenced by _____ and peer groups (age mates).

22. For many young people in North America a period of emerging adulthood stretches from the late _____ to the _____ .

● *How do we develop morals and values?*

Recite and Review: Pages 151-153

23. Lawrence Kohlberg theorized that _____ development passes through a series of stages revealed by _____ reasoning about _____ dilemmas.

24. Kohlberg identified preconventional, conventional, and postconventional levels of moral _____ .

25. Some psychologists have questioned whether measures of moral development should be based only on a morality of _____ . Adults appear to base moral choices on either _____ or caring, depending on the situation.

● *What happens psychologically during adulthood?*

Recite and Review: Pages 153-157

26. Certain relatively consistent events mark _____ _____ in our society.

27. In order, these are: _____ from parental dominance, leaving the _____ , building a workable life, a crisis of questions, a crisis of urgency, attaining stability, and mellowing.

28. A midlife crisis affects many people in the 37-41 age range, but this is by no means _____ .

29. Adjustment to later middle age is sometimes complicated for _____ by menopause and for _____ by andropause or a climacteric.

30. When the last child leaves home, women who define themselves as traditional _____ may become _____ (the empty nest syndrome).

31. Well-being at midlife is related to self-acceptance, positive relationships, autonomy, mastery, a _____ in life, and continued personal _____ .

● *What are some of the psychological challenges of aging?*

Recite and Review: Pages 157-162

32. The elderly are the _____ growing segment of society in North America.

33. Biological _____ begins between 25 and 30, but peak performance in specific pursuits may come at various points throughout life.

34. The length of human lives is limited by the _____ life span. _____ expectancy (the average number of years people live) is much shorter.

35. Intellectual declines associated with aging are limited, at least through one's _____. This is especially true of individuals who remain mentally _____.

36. The greatest losses occur for fluid abilities (which require _____ or rapid learning); crystallized abilities (stored up _____ and skills) show much less decline and may actually improve.

37. Gerontologists (those who study _____) have proposed the disengagement theory of successful _____. It holds that withdrawal from society is necessary and desirable in old age.

38. The activity theory states that optimal adjustment to aging is tied to continuing _____ and involvement. The activity theory applies to more people than disengagement does.

39. Ageism refers to prejudice, discrimination, and stereotyping on the basis of _____. It affects people of all ages, but is especially damaging to _____ people.

● *How do people typically react to death and bereavement?*

Recite and Review: Pages 162-166

40. Older people fear the circumstances of _____ more than the fact that it will occur.

41. Typical emotional reactions to impending death are denial, _____, bargaining, _____, and acceptance.

42. Near-death _____ (NDEs) frequently result in significant changes in personality, _____, and life goals.

43. Bereavement also brings forth a typical series of _____ reactions.

44. Initial shock is followed by pangs of _____. Later, apathy, dejection, and depression may occur. Eventually, grief moves toward _____, an acceptance of the loss.

45. Grief _____ helps people adapt to their loss and integrate changes into their lives.

● *What factors contribute most to a happy and fulfilling life?*

Recite and Review: PSYCHOLOGY IN ACTION

46. Subjective well being (_____) occurs when _____ emotions outnumber _____ emotions and a person is satisfied with his or her life.

47. Happiness is only mildly related to _____, education, marriage, religion, age, sex, and work. However, people who have an extraverted, optimistic _____ do tend to be happier.

48. People who are making progress toward their long-term _____ tend to be happier. This is especially true if the _____ have integrity and personal meaning.

● *In what ways are attitudes toward death changing?*

Recite and Review: A STEP BEYOND

49. One approach to death is the hospice movement, which is devoted to providing humane care to persons who are _____.

50. A living will may help a person ensure that his or her life will not be artificially prolonged during a _____ illness.

51. Cryonic suspension has been attempted as a way of preserving people after death for possible future _____.

52. A continuing controversy concerns the ethics of passive euthanasia (allowing _____ to occur) and active euthanasia (inducing _____).

CONNECTIONS

1. _____	Erik Erikson	a.	"smother love"
2. _____	overprotection	b.	"soiling"
3. _____	regression	c.	reading disorder
4. _____	enuresis	d.	autism symptom
5. _____	encopresis	e.	psychosocial dilemmas
6. _____	pica	f.	hyperactive
7. _____	dyslexia	g.	bed wetting
8. _____	echolalia	h.	clinical death
9. _____	NDE	i.	eating disorder
10. _____	ADHD	j.	infantile behavior

11. _____	child abuse	a.	sexual maturation
12. _____	adolescence	b.	reaction to impending death
13. _____	puberty	c.	social-contract/individual principles
14. _____	social marker	d.	good boy or girl/respect for authority
15. _____	preconventional	e.	avoiding punishment or seeking pleasure
16. _____	conventional	f.	children leave
17. _____	postconventional	g.	life change
18. _____	bargaining	h.	cultural status
19. _____	"empty nest"	i.	status or role clue
20. _____	transition period	j.	shaken baby

21. _____	menopause	a. successful aging
22. _____	climacteric	b. expert on death
23. _____	Roger Gould	c. happiness and meaningful goals
24. _____	Elizabeth Kübler-Ross	d. care for dying
25. _____	ageism	e. expert on aging
26. _____	gerontologist	f. common prejudice
27. _____	thanatologist	g. end of menstruation
28. _____	compensation and optimization	h. reactions to dying
29. _____	good life	i. significant physical change
30. _____	hospice	j. adult development

CHECK YOUR MEMORY

Check Your Memory: Pages 136-140

1. Learning to read in childhood and establishing a vocation as an adult are typical life stages. T or F?
2. Psychosocial dilemmas occur when a person is in conflict with his or her social world. T or F?
3. Initiative versus guilt is the first psychosocial dilemma a child faces. T or F?
4. Answering the question "Who am I?" is a primary task during adolescence. T or F?
5. Generativity is expressed through taking an interest in the next generation. T or F?

Check Your Memory: Pages 141-147

6. It is best for parents to protect children from all stressful stimulation, as much as possible. T or F?
7. Clinging is one of the more serious problems of childhood. T or F?
8. Supportive and affectionate fathers tend to minimize sibling rivalry. T or F?
9. Toilet training is typically completed by age 3 or earlier. T or F?
10. A child who eats mud, buttons, or rubber bands suffers from enuresis nervosa. T or F?
11. Stuttering is more common among girls than boys. T or F?
12. Autism can be described as "word blindness." T or F?
13. ADHD affects 5 times as many boys as girls and may be partly hereditary. T or F?
14. Eating too much sugar is one of the main causes of hyperactivity in children. T or F?
15. The first signs of autism often appear in infancy, when autistic children may be extremely aloof and withdrawn. T or F?
16. Ritalin is used primarily to treat delayed speech. T or F?
17. The risk of committing child abuse is highest for young parents. T or F?
18. Abusive mothers tend to believe that their children are intentionally annoying them. T or F?
19. One third of abused children become abusive adults. T or F?
20. Children who have been physically abused are extremely good at detecting the slightest hints of anger in the facial expressions of adults. T or F?
21. Parents Anonymous is an organization for parents who have autistic children. T or F?

Check Your Memory: Pages 147-151

22. The length of adolescence varies in different cultures. T or F?
23. The average onset of puberty is age 12 for boys and age 14 for girls. T or F?
24. Early maturation tends to enhance self-image for boys. T or F?
25. Early-maturing girls tend to date sooner and are more likely to get into trouble. T or F?
26. David Elkind believes that today's adolescents should be "hurried into adulthood" to maximize their potentials. T or F?
27. The term *imaginary audience* refers to adolescent peer groups and the influence they have on personal identity. T or F?
28. Being able to think about hypothetical possibilities helps adolescents in their search for identity. T or F?
29. Increased conflict with parents tends to occur early in adolescence. T or F?
30. Early maturation can contribute to adopting a foreclosed identity. T or F?

Check Your Memory: Pages 151-153

31. Lawrence Kohlberg used moral dilemmas to assess children's levels of moral development. T or F?
32. At the preconventional level, moral decisions are guided by the consequences of actions, such as punishment or pleasure. T or F?
33. The traditional morality of authority defines moral behavior in the preconventional stage. T or F?
34. Most adults function at the conventional level of moral reasoning. T or F?
35. Both men and women may use justice or caring as a basis for making moral judgments. T or F?

Check Your Memory: Pages 153-157

36. According to Gould, building a workable life is the predominant activity between ages 16 to 18. T or F?
37. A crisis of urgency tends to hit people around the age of 30. T or F?
38. Maintaining good health is a prominent goal among the elderly. T or F?
39. Levinson places the midlife transition in the 40-55 age range. T or F?
40. Only a small minority of the men studied by Levinson experienced any instability or urgency at midlife. T or F?
41. During the mid-life transition, women are less likely than men to define success in terms of a key event. T or F?
42. Wealth is one of the primary sources of happiness in adulthood. T or F?
43. Over half of all women have serious emotional problems during menopause. T or F?
44. After the climacteric has occurred, men become infertile. T or F?
45. Having a sense of purpose in life is one element of well-being during adulthood. T or F

Check Your Memory: Pages 157-162

46. By the year 2020, 1 of every 5 North Americans will be over age 65. T or F?
47. Peak functioning in most physical capacities occurs between ages 25 and 30. T or F?
48. The maximum human life span is around 120 years. T or F?
49. Life expectancy has increased dramatically in the last 200 years. T or F?
50. Crystallized abilities are the first to decline as a person ages. T or F?

51. Perceptual speed declines steadily after age 25. T or F?
52. People older than 50 who have a positive attitude toward aging live an average of 17 years longer than people with negative attitudes toward aging. T or F?
53. For many people, successful aging requires a combination of activity and disengagement. T or F?
54. Ageism refers to prejudice and discrimination toward the elderly. T or F?
55. Few elderly persons become senile or suffer from mental decay. T or F?

Check Your Memory: Pages 162-166

56. Most of the deaths portrayed on television are homicides. T or F?
57. A living will is not legally binding in most states in the U.S. T or F?
58. The "Why me" reaction to impending death is an expression of anger. T or F?
59. Trying to be "good" in order to live longer is characteristic of the denial reaction to impending death. T or F?
60. It is best to go through all the stages of dying described by Kübler-Ross in the correct order. T or F?
61. Medical explanations of NDEs attribute them to brain activities caused by oxygen starvation. T or F?
62. Bereaved persons should work through their grief as quickly as possible. T or F?

Check Your Memory: PSYCHOLOGY IN ACTION

63. Subjective well being is primarily a matter of having relatively few negative emotions. T or F?
64. A person who agrees that "The conditions of my life are excellent," would probably score high in life satisfaction. T or F?
65. Wealthier people are generally happier people. T or F?
66. Life satisfaction and happiness generally decline with increasing age. T or F?
67. You are likely to be happy if you are making progress on smaller goals that relate to long-term, life goals. T or F?
68. Usually, a good life is one that is happy and meaningful. T or F?

Check Your Memory: A STEP BEYOND

69. Hospice care can be provided at home, as well as in medical centers. T or F?
70. Hospice programs are designed to avoid the use of painkilling drugs. T or F?
71. A living will is not legally binding in most states in the U.S. T or F?
72. There is currently no way to freeze human bodies so their organs will resume functioning when thawed. T or F?

FINAL SURVEY AND REVIEW

● *What are the typical tasks and dilemmas through the life span?*

1. _____ psychologists study _____ and change from birth to death.

2. They are also interested in developmental _____, or prominent landmarks in personal development.

3. According to Erik _____, each life stage provokes a specific _____ dilemma.

4. During childhood these are: _____ versus mistrust, _____ versus shame and doubt, initiative versus guilt, and _____ versus inferiority.

5. In adolescence, _____ versus _____ confusion is the principal dilemma.

6. In young adulthood we face the dilemma of _____ versus isolation. Later, _____ versus stagnation becomes prominent.

7. Old age is a time when the dilemma of _____ versus despair must be faced.

8. In addition, each life stage requires successful mastery of certain developmental _____ (personal changes required for optimal development).

● *What are some of the more serious childhood problems?*

9. Few children grow up without experiencing some of the normal problems of childhood, including _____, _____, specific _____, sleep disturbances, general dissatisfaction, regression, sibling rivalry, and rebellion.

10. Major areas of difficulty in childhood are toilet training (including _____ and _____) and feeding disturbances, such as overeating, anorexia nervosa (self-starvation), and _____ (eating nonfood substances).

11. Other problems include speech disturbances (delayed speech, _____); learning disorders, including _____ (an inability to read with understanding); and attention-deficit _____ disorder (ADHD).

12. Children suffering from _____ disorder engage in aggressive, destructive, and antisocial behavior.

13. Childhood autism is a severe problem involving _____ (failure to speak), sensory disturbances, tantrums, and a lack of responsiveness to _____ _____.

14. Some cases of autism are being treated successfully with behavior _____.

15. _____ _____ (physically or emotionally harming a child) is a major problem. Roughly 30 percent of all abused children become abusive _____. Emotional support and therapy can help break the cycle of abuse.

● *Why is adolescent development especially challenging?*

16. _____ is a culturally defined social status. _____ is a biological event.

17. On average, the peak _____ spurt during _____ occurs earlier for girls than for boys.

18. Early _____ is beneficial mostly for boys; its effects are mixed for girls.

19. Establishing a clear sense of personal _____ is a major task of adolescence. One danger of early maturation is premature _____ formation.
20. Many adolescents become self-conscious and preoccupied with _____ audiences.
21. Adolescent identity formation is accelerated by _____ development and influenced by parents and _____ groups (age mates).
22. For many young people in North America a period of _____ _____ stretches from the late teens to the mid-twenties.

● *How do we develop morals and values?*

23. Lawrence Kohlberg theorized that moral development passes through a series of stages revealed by moral _____ about moral _____.
24. Kohlberg identified _____, conventional, and postconventional levels of moral reasoning.
25. Some psychologists have questioned whether measures of moral development should be based only on a morality of justice. Adults appear to base moral choices on either justice or _____, depending on the _____.

● *What happens psychologically during adulthood?*

26. Certain relatively _____ events mark adult development in our society.
27. In order these are: escape from parental _____, leaving the family, building a workable life, a crisis of _____, a crisis of _____, attaining stability, and mellowing.
28. A _____ _____ affects many people in the 37-41 age range, but this is by no means universal.
29. Adjustment to later middle age is sometimes complicated for women by menopause and for men by _____ or a climacteric.
30. When the last child leaves home, women who define themselves as traditional mothers may become depressed (the _____ _____ _____).
31. Well-being at midlife is related to self-_____, positive relationships, _____, mastery, a purpose in life, and continued personal growth.

● *What are some of the psychological challenges of aging?*

32. The _____ are the fastest growing segment of society in North America.
33. Biological aging begins between 25 and 30, but _____ _____ in specific pursuits may come at various points throughout life.
34. The length of human lives is limited by the maximum _____ _____. Life _____ (the average number of years people live) is much shorter.
35. _____ declines associated with aging are limited, at least through one's 70s. This is especially true of individuals who remain mentally active.

36. The greatest losses occur for _____ abilities (which require speed or rapid learning); _____ abilities (stored up knowledge and skills) show much less decline and may actually improve.

37. _____ (those who study aging) have proposed the _____ theory of successful aging. It holds that withdrawal from society is necessary and desirable in old age.

38. The _____ theory states that optimal adjustment to aging is tied to continuing action and involvement. This theory applies to more people than withdrawal from society does.

39. _____ refers to prejudice, discrimination, and stereotyping on the basis of age. It affects people of all ages, but is especially damaging to older people.

● *How do people typically react to death and bereavement?*

40. Older people fear the _____ of death more than the fact that it will occur.

41. Typical emotional reactions to impending death are _____, anger, _____, depression, and acceptance.

42. _____ experiences (NDEs) frequently result in significant changes in personality, values, and life goals.

43. _____ also brings forth a typical series of grief reactions.

44. Initial _____ is followed by _____ of grief. Later, apathy, dejection, and _____ may occur. Eventually, grief moves toward resolution, an acceptance of the loss.

45. _____ work helps people adapt to their loss and _____ changes into their lives.

● *What factors contribute most to a happy and fulfilling life?*

46. _____ _____ _____ (happiness) occurs when positive emotions outnumber negative emotions and a person is satisfied with his or her life.

47. Happiness is only mildly related to wealth, education, marriage, religion, age, sex, and work. However, people with _____, optimistic personalities do tend to be happier.

48. People who are making progress toward their long-term goals tend to be happier. This is especially true if the goals have _____ and personal _____.

● *In what ways are attitudes toward death changing?*

49. One approach to death is the _____ movement, which is devoted to providing humane care to persons who are dying.

50. A _____ _____ may help a person ensure that his or her life will not be artificially prolonged during a terminal illness.

51. _____ suspension has been attempted as a way of preserving people after death for possible future revival; however, both suspension and revival are presently impossible.

52. A continuing controversy concerns the ethics of passive _____ (allowing death to occur) and active _____ (inducing death).

MASTERY TEST

1. According to Erikson, a conflict between trust and mistrust is characteristic of
   a. infancy b. adolescence c. marriage d. old age

2. Identity formation during adolescence is aided by
   a. cognitive development b. attaining the preoperational stage c. emotional bargaining
   d. you-messages from parents

3. Which of the following is not a normal, relatively mild childhood problem?
   a. negativism b. clinging c. sibling rivalry d. delayed speech

4. Infancy, childhood, adolescence, and young adulthood are
   a. developmental tasks b. life stages c. psychosocial dilemmas
   d. biologically defined social statuses

5. Premature identity formation is one of the risks of early
   a. generativity b. preoccupation with imaginary audiences c. trust-mistrust resolution d. puberty

6. The thought, "It's all a mistake" would most likely occur as part of which reaction to impending death?
   a. anger b. freezing up c. denial d. bargaining

7. The choice of whether to use justice or caring to make moral decisions depends on the
   _____ a person faces.
   a. situation b. punishment c. level of authority d. exchange

8. Which of the following is a correct match?
   a. enuresis—eating disorder b. anorexia—speech disturbance c. dyslexia—learning disorder
   d. pica—autism

9. According to Erikson, the first dilemma a newborn infant must resolve is
   a. independence versus dependence b. initiative versus guilt c. trust versus mistrust
   d. attachment versus confusion

10. Seeking approval and upholding law, order, and authority are characteristics of what stage of moral development?
    a. preconventional b. conventional c. postconventional d. postformal

11. An inability to read with understanding defines the problem formally known as
    a. ADHD b. dyslexia c. NDE d. echolalia

12. For both boys and girls, a growth spurt corresponds with _____.
    a. adolescence b. puberty c. cognitive maturation d. less prestige with peers

13. Autonomy, environmental mastery, a purpose in life, and continued personal growth help maintain
    well-being in old age. This observation supports the _____ theory of successful
    aging.
    a. disengagement b. re-engagement c. activity d. re-activation

14. Research on well being suggests that a good life is one that combines happiness and
    a. financial success b. educational achievement c. an introverted personality
    d. achieving meaningful goals

15. According to Erikson, developing a sense of integrity is a special challenge in
    a. adolescence b. young adulthood c. middle adulthood d. late adulthood

16. The event for males that is most comparable to menopause in women is the
    a. andropause b. midlife crisis c. generativity transition d. genophase

17. Grief following bereavement typically begins with _____ and ends with _____.
    a. anger, disengagement b. dejection, disengagement c. isolation, depression d. shock, resolution

18. Physicians typically use the stimulant drug Ritalin to control
    a. encopresis b. ADHD c. echolalia d. anorexia nervosa

19. The smallest number of Levinson's subjects experienced midlife as a(an)
    a. last chance b. period of serious decline c. time to start over d. escape from dominance

20. According to Erikson, a dilemma concerning _____ usually follows one that focuses on
    identity.
    a. trust b. industry c. initiative d. intimacy

21. Which combination would lead to the highest risk of child abuse?
    a. young parent, high income, child over 3 years b. stressed parent, abused as a child c. older parent,
    highly religious, child over 3 years d. older parent, uses verbal punishment, median income

22. Foreclosed identity formation is a special risk for
    a. late maturing boys b. adolescents c. the elementary school years
    d. the preoperational stage

23. Oxygen deprivation in the brain best accounts for which element of a NDE?
    a. the tunnel of light b. the pangs of grief c. the period of depression d. the life review and
    personality changes

24. People who have many positive emotional experiences and relatively few negative experiences usually rate high in
    a. generativity b. moral reasoning c. subjective well-being d. crystallized abilities

25. Overprotective parenting ignores the fact that _____ is a normal part of life.
    a. rebellion b. punishment c. rejection d. stress

26. Ivar Lovaas has successfully used _____ to treat _____.
    a. Ritalin, echolalia b. operant shaping, dyslexia c. restricted sugar diets, ADHD
    d. behavior modification, autism

27. Skills that rely on fluid abilities could be expected to show declines beginning in
    a. adolescence b. young adulthood c. middle adulthood d. late adulthood

28. Which of the following is a common myth about old age?
    a. Most elderly persons are isolated and neglected.
    b. A large percentage of the elderly suffer from senility.
    c. A majority of the elderly are dissastified with their lives.
    d. All of the preceding are myths.

29. Gould's study of adult development found that a crisis of _____ is common between the ages of 35 and 43.
    a. urgency b. questions c. dominance d. stability

30. With respect to aging, it is least possible to modify which of the following?
    a. life expectancy b. crystallized abilities c. mental abilities d. maximum life span

ANSWERS

Recite and Review

1. change
2. developmental
3. dilemma
4. shame, guilt, inferiority
5. adolescence
6. isolation, stagnation
7. despair
8. developmental
9. disturbances, rivalry
10. toilet training, feeding
11. speech, learning, disorder
12. disorder
13. autism
14. behavior
15. harming, 30
16. social, biological
17. girls, boys
18. boys, girls
19. adolescence, early
20. audiences
21. parents
22. teens, mid-twenties
23. moral, moral, moral
24. reasoning
25. justice, justice
26. adult development
27. escape, family
28. universal
29. women, men
30. mothers, depressed
31. purpose, growth
32. fastest
33. aging
34. maximum, Life
35. 70s, active
36. speed, knowledge
37. aging, aging

38. activity
39. age, older
40. death
41. anger, depression
42. experiences, values
43. grief
44. grief, resolution
45. work
46. happiness, positive, negative
47. wealth, personality
48. goals, goals
49. dying
50. terminal
51. revival
52. death, death

Connections

1. e
2. a
3. j
4. g
5. b
6. i
7. c
8. d
9. h
10. f
11. j
12. h
13. a
14. i
15. e
16. d
17. c
18. b
19. f
20. g
21. g
22. i
23. j
24. h
25. f
26. e
27. b

28. a
29. c
30. d

Check Your Memory

1. F
2. T
3. F
4. T
5. T
6 F
7. F
8. T
9. T
10. F
11. F
12. F
13. T
14. F
15. T
16. F
17. T
18. T
19. T
20. T
21. F
22. T
23. F
24. T
25. T
26. F
27. F
28. T
29. T
30. T
31. T
32. T
33. F
34. T
35. T
36. F
37. F
38. T
39. F
40. F
41. T
42. F

43. F
44. F
45. T
46. T
47. T
48. T
49. T
50. F
51. T
52. F
53. T
54. F
55. T
56. T
57. T
58. T
59. F
60. F
61. T
62. F
63. F
64. T
65. F
66. F
67. T
68. T
69. T
70. F
71. T
72. T

Final Survey and Review

1. Life-span, continuity
2. milestones
3. Erikson, psychosocial
4. trust, autonomy, industry
5. identity, role
6. intimacy, generativity
7. integrity
8. tasks
9. negativism, clinging, fears
10. enuresis, encopresis, pica
11. stuttering, dyslexia, hyperactivity
12. conduct
13. mutism, other people
14. modification

15. Child abuse, adults
16. Adolescence, Puberty
17. growth, puberty
18. maturation
19. identity, identity
20. imaginary
21. cognitive, peer
22. emerging adulthood
23. reasoning, dilemmas
24. preconventional
25. caring, situation
26. consistent
27. dominance, questions, urgency
28. midlife crisis
29. andropause
30. empty nest syndrome
31. acceptance, autonomy
32. elderly
33. peak performance

34. life span, expectancy
35. Intellectual
36. fluid, crystallized
37. Gerontologists, disengagement
38. activity
39. Ageism
40. circumstances
41. denial, bargaining
42. Near-death
43. Bereavement
44. shock, pangs, depression
45. Grief, integrate
46. Subjective, well, being
47. extraverted
48. integrity, meaning
49. hospice
50. living will
51. Cryonic
52. euthanasia, euthanasia

Mastery Test

1. a (p. 137)
2. a (p. 149)
3. d (p. 143)
4. b (p. 137)
5. d (p. 149)
6. c (p. 163)
7. a (p. 153)
8. c (p. 143)
9. c (p. 137)
10. b (p. 152)
11. b (p. 143)
12. b (p. 148)
13. c (p. 160)
14. d (p. 168)
15. d (p. 140)
16. a (p. 156)
17. d (p. 165)
18. b (p. 144)
19. c (p. 155)
20. d (p. 138)
21. b (p. 145)
22. b (p. 151)
23. a (p. 164)
24. c (p. 167)
25. d (p. 141)
26. d (p. 145)
27. b (p. 159)
28. d (p. 161)
29. a (p. 154)
30. d (p. 158)

Chapter 5
Sensation and Reality

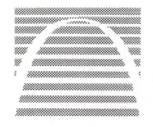

CHAPTER OVERVIEW

Sensory systems collect, select, transduce, analyze, and code information from the environment and send it to the brain. Psychophysics is the study of the relationship between physical stimuli and psychological sensations. Both absolute and difference thresholds have been identified for various senses. Subliminal perception occurs, but its impact tends to be weak.

Vision and visual problems can be partly understood by viewing the eyes as optical systems. However, the visual system also analyzes light stimuli to identify patterns and basic visual features. Color sensations are explained by the trichromatic theory (in the retina) and the opponent-process theory (for the rest of the visual system).

The inner ear is a sensory mechanism for transducing sound waves in the air into nerve impulses. The frequency and place theories of hearing explain how sound information is coded.

Olfaction is based on receptors that respond to gaseous molecules in the air. The lock-and-key theory and the locations of olfactory receptors activated by different scents explain how various odors are coded. Taste is another chemical sense. A lock-and-key match between dissolved molecules and taste receptors also explains many taste sensations.

The somesthetic, or bodily, senses include the skin senses, the kinesthetic senses, and the vestibular senses. Various forms of motion sickness are related to mismatches between sensory information from the vestibular system, kinesthesis, and vision.

Our awareness of sensory information is altered by sensory adaptation, selective attention, and sensory gating. Pain sensations in particular are affected by anxiety, feelings of control, attention, and the interpretation given to aversive stimuli.

In synesthesia, stimulation of one sense also arouses sensations in another. Color-hearing is the most common form of sensory blending. Synesthesia shows that the senses obey similar laws of intensity, size, and quality and that they normally assist one another.

LEARNING OBJECTIVES

To demonstrate mastery of this chapter you should be able to:

1. Explain how our senses act as a data reduction system by selecting, analyzing, and coding incoming information. Include the concepts of *perceptual features* and *feature detectors*.
2. Explain how sensory receptors act as biological transducers.
3. Explain the concept of localization of function.
4. Explain the idea behind the statement: "Seeing does not take place in the eyes."
5. Define *sensation*.
6. Define the term *absolute threshold*.
7. Explain Weber's law and the concept of the difference threshold (JND).
8. Explain the process of perceptual defense.
9 Define *limen* and describe subliminal perception, including its effectiveness.
10. Describe hue, saturation, and brightness in terms of their representation in the visual spectrum of electromagnetic radiation.
11. Briefly describe the functions of the lens, the photoreceptors, and the retina. Explain how the eye focuses and describe the process of accommodation.
12. Describe the following four conditions:
    - a. hyperopia
    - b. myopia
    - c. astigmatism
    - d. presbyopia.
13. Explain how the eye controls light.
14. Describe the functions of the rods and cones.
15. Explain how the visual area of the brain detects features.
16. Explain the relationship between the fovea and visual acuity.
17. Discuss peripheral vision. Include the structures responsible for it and how this type of vision affects night vision.
18. Compare and contrast the *trichromatic* and *opponent-process* theories of color vision, including a description of afterimages and the concept of simultaneous color contrast.
19. Describe color blindness and color weakness.
20. Briefly describe the process of dark adaptation, including the function of rhodopsin in night vision and night blindness.
21. Explain the stimulus for hearing.
22. Describe the location and function(s) of the following parts of the ear:
    - a. pinna
    - b. eardrum (tympanic membrane)
    - c. auditory ossicles
    - d. oval window
    - e. cochlea
    - f. hair cells
    - g. stereocilia
    - h. organ of Corti
23. Describe the frequency theory and the place theory of hearing.
24. List and describe the three general types of deafness. Include a description of cochlear implants.

25. Describe the factors that determine whether hearing loss will occur from stimulation deafness. Discuss the relationship of stimulation deafness to temporary threshold shift and tinnitus.
26. Describe the sense of smell including:
    a. its nature and how it works
    b. a description of the condition called *anosmia*
    c. a description of the lock and key theory
    d. how pheromones work and what they do
27. Describe the sense of taste including:
    a. its nature and how it works
    b. the five basic taste sensations
    c. the tastes to which humans are most and least sensitive
    d. how the vast number of flavors is explained
    e. the location and function of the taste buds
    f. how taste is affected by smell, genetics, and age
28. List the three somesthetic senses and be able to describe the function of each.
29. List and be able to recognize the five different sensations produced by the skin receptors.
30. Explain why certain areas of the body are more sensitive to touch than other areas.
31. Describe the concepts *visceral pain* and *referred pain*. Name and describe the two different pain systems in the body.
32. Define the term *dynamic touch*.
33. Describe motion sickness and explain how the otolith organs and the semicircular canals of the vestibular system are related to it.
34. Describe how the sensory conflict theory explains motion sickness.
35. Discuss the three reasons why many sensory events never reach conscious awareness.
36. Discuss how endorphins explain some of the feelings associated with running and acupuncture.

The following objectives are related to the material in the "Psychology in Action" and "A Step Beyond" sections of your text.

37. Discuss four techniques that can be used to reduce the amount of pain perceived.
38. Define *synesthesia* and give an example of the most common type of synesthetic experience.
39. Explain what is meant by the phrase, *the unity of the senses.*

RECITE AND REVIEW

● *In general, how do sensory systems function?*

Recite and Review: Pages 174-177

1. Sensory organs transduce physical energies into _____ impulses.

2. The senses act as _____ reduction systems that select, _____, and code sensory information.

3. A good example of sensory analysis is the identification of basic _____ features in a stimulus pattern.

4. In fact, many sensory systems act as feature _____.

5. Phosphenes and visual pop-out are examples of feature detection and _____ coding in action.

6. Sensory response can be partially understood in terms of _____ localization in the brain. That is, the area of the brain _____ ultimately determines which type of sensory experience we have.

● *What are the limits of our sensory sensitivity?*

Recite and Review: Pages 177-179

7. Psychophysics is the study of _____ stimuli and the _____ they evoke.

8. The _____ amount of physical energy necessary to produce a _____ defines the absolute threshold.

9. The amount of _____ necessary to produce a just noticeable difference (or JND) in a stimulus defines a _____ threshold.

10. In general, the amount of change needed to produce a JND is a constant proportion of the original stimulus _____. This relationship is known as Weber's _____.

11. Threatening or anxiety-provoking stimuli may _____ the threshold for recognition, an effect called perceptual _____.

12. Any stimulus _____ the level of conscious awareness is said to be subliminal.

13. There is evidence that subliminal perception occurs, but subliminal advertising is largely

_____.

● *How is vision accomplished?*

Recite and Review: Pages 180-184

14. The _____ spectrum consists of electromagnetic radiation in a narrow range.

15. The electromagnetic spectrum ranges from violet, with a _____ of 400 nanometers, to red, with a _____ of 700 nanometers.

16. Hue refers to a color's name, which corresponds to its _____. Saturated or "pure" colors come from a _____ band of wavelengths. Brightness corresponds to the amplitude of light waves.

17. The eye is in some ways like a camera. At its back lies an array of photoreceptors, called _____ and _____, that make up a light-sensitive layer called the retina.

18. Vision is focused by the _____ of the cornea and lens and by changes in the _____ of the lens, called accommodation.

19. Four common visual defects, correctable with glasses, are myopia (_____),
hyperopia (farsightedness), presbyopia (loss of _____), and astigmatism (in which
portions of vision are out of focus).

20. The amount of light entering the eye is controlled by movements of the iris, which dilates
(_____) and constricts (_____) the pupil.

21. In the retina, the _____ specialize in night vision, black and white reception, and motion
detection.

22. The _____, found exclusively in the fovea and otherwise toward the middle of the eye,
specialize in _____ vision, acuity (perception of fine detail), and daylight vision.

23. Individual cells in the visual cortex of the brain act as feature _____ to analyze visual
information.

24. The _____ supply much of our peripheral vision. Loss of peripheral vision is called tunnel
vision.

● *How do we perceive colors?*

Recite and Review: Pages 184-189

25. The rods and cones differ in color _____. Yellow-green is brightest for cones; blue-
green for the rods (although they will see it as colorless).

26. In the _____, color vision is explained by the trichromatic theory. The theory says that three
types of _____ exist, each most sensitive to either red, green, or blue.

27. Three types of light-sensitive visual pigments are found in the _____, each pigment is most
sensitive to either red, green, or blue light.

28. Beyond the retina, the visual system analyzes colors into _____ messages. According
to the opponent-process theory, color information can be coded as either red or green, yellow or blue, and
_____ _____ _____ messages.

29. Ultimately, color experiences are constructed in the _____. This is apparent when you look at
a stimulus that produces simultaneous contrast.

30. _____ color blindness is rare, but 8 percent of males and 1 percent of females are red-green
color blind or color weak.

31. Color blindness is a sex-linked trait carried on the X (_____) chromosome and passed from
mother to son.

32. The Ishihara test is used to detect _____ _____.

33. Dark adaptation, an _____ in sensitivity to light, is caused by increased concentrations
of visual pigments in the _____ and the _____.

34. Most dark adaptation is the result of increased rhodopsin concentrations in the _____. Vitamin
A deficiencies may cause _____ blindness by impairing the production of rhodopsin.

● *What are the mechanisms of hearing?*

Recite and Review: Pages 189-193

35. Sound waves are the stimulus for hearing. Sound travels as waves of compression (_____) and
rarefaction (_____) in the air.

36. The _____ of a sound corresponds to the frequency of sound waves. Loudness corresponds to the amplitude (_____) of sound waves.

37. Sound waves are transduced by the _____, auditory ossicles, oval window, cochlea, and ultimately, the _____ cells in the organ of Corti.

38. The frequency theory says that the _____ of nerve impulses in the auditory nerves matches the _____ of incoming sounds (up to 4000 hertz).

39. Place theory says that _____ tones register near the base of the cochlea and _____ tones near its tip.

40. Three basic types of deafness are _____ deafness, conduction deafness, and stimulation deafness.

41. Conduction deafness can often be overcome with a hearing aid. _____ deafness can sometimes be alleviated by cochlear implants.

42. Stimulation deafness can be prevented by avoiding excessive exposure to _____ sounds. Sounds above 120 decibels pose an immediate danger to hearing. Two warning signs of stimulation deafness are temporary threshold _____ and tinnitus.

● *How do the chemical senses operate?*

Recite and Review: Pages 193-197

43. Olfaction (_____) and gustation (_____) are chemical senses responsive to airborne or liquefied molecules.

44. It is suspected that humans are also sensitive to _____ signals called pheromones, although the evidence remains preliminary. Pheromones may be sensed by the vomeronasal _____.

45. The lock and key theory partially explains smell. In addition, the _____ of the olfactory receptors in the nose helps identify various scents.

46. The top outside edges of the tongue are responsive to sweet, salty, sour, and _____ tastes. It is suspected that a fifth taste quality called *umami* also exists.

47. Taste also appears to be based in part on lock-and-key _____ of molecule shapes.

● *What are the somesthetic senses and why are they important?*

Recite and Review: Pages 197-202

48. The somesthetic senses include the _____ senses, vestibular senses, and kinesthetic senses (receptors that detect muscle and joint positioning).

49. The skin senses include touch, _____, pain, cold, and warmth. Sensitivity to each is related to the _____ of receptors found in an area of skin.

50. Distinctions can be made among various types of pain, including visceral pain, somatic pain, referred pain, warning system pain, and _____ system pain.

51. Most amputees have phantom _____ sensations long after losing a limb.

52. Various forms of motion sickness are related to messages received from the vestibular system, which senses gravity and _____ movement.

53. The otolith organs detect the pull of _____ and rapid head movements.

54. The movement of _____ within the semicircular canals, and the movement of the _____ within each ampulla, detects head movement and positioning.

55. According to sensory conflict theory, motion sickness is caused by a _____ of visual, kinesthetic, and vestibular sensations. Motion sickness can be avoided by minimizing sensory conflict.

● *Why are we more aware of some sensations than others?*

Recite and Review: Pages 202-204

56. Incoming sensations are affected by sensory adaptation (a _____ in the number of nerve impulses sent).

57. Selective attention (selection and diversion of messages in the brain) and sensory _____ (blocking or alteration of messages flowing toward the brain) also alter sensations.

58. Selective gating of pain messages apparently takes place in the _____ _____ . Gate control theory proposes an explanation for many pain phenomena.

59. "Runner's high," the painkilling effects of the Chinese medical art of acupuncture, and other pain phenomena appear to be explained by the release of a _____-like chemical in the brain, called beta-endorphin.

● *How can pain be reduced in everyday situations?*

Recite and Review: PSYCHOLOGY IN ACTION

60. Pain can be reduced by _____ anxiety and redirecting attention to stimuli other than the pain stimulus.

61. Feeling that you have control over a stimulus tends to _____ the amount of pain you experience.

62. The interpretation placed on a _____ affects how painful it is perceived to be.

63. Sending _____ pain messages to the spinal cord can close the gates to more severe pain. This effect is called counterirritation.

● *What is synesthesia? What does it reveal about sensory systems?*

Recite and Review: A STEP BEYOND

64. In synesthesia, stimulation of one sense also arouses _____ in another.

65. For true synesthetes, cross-sense experiences are _____.

66. Synesthesia occurs when stimulating one sense activates brain areas for _____ _____, too.

CONNECTIONS

1. _____ ciliary muscle
2. _____ iris
3. _____ cornea
4. _____ blind spot
5. _____ lens
6. _____ fovea
7. _____ retinal veins
8. _____ optic nerve
9. _____ aqueous humor
10. _____ pupil
11. _____ retina

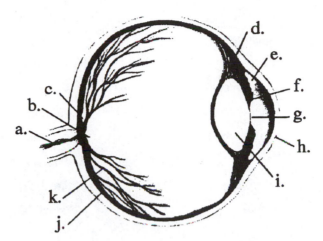

12. _____ vestibular system
13. _____ cochlea
14. _____ round window
15. _____ auditory canal
16. _____ stapes
17. _____ auditory nerve
18. _____ incus
19. _____ oval window
20. _____ tympanic membrane
21. _____ malleus

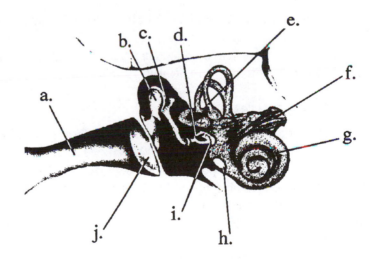

22. _____	limen	a. physiological nystagmus
23. _____	Landolt rings	b. visual acuity
24. _____	anosmia	c. perceptual features
25. _____	pressure	d. localization of function
26. _____	eye tremors	e. vibrations per second
27. _____	"bug detector"	f. vitamin A
28. _____	artificial vision	g. opponent process theory
29. _____	hertz	h. Pacinian corpuscle
30. _____	afterimages	i. threshold
31. _____	retinal	j. "smell blindness"

CHECK YOUR MEMORY

Check Your Memory: Pages 174-177

1. The electromagnetic spectrum includes ultraviolet light and radio waves. T or F?
2. Each sensory organ is sensitive to a select range of physical energies. T or F?
3. The artificial vision system described in the text is based on electrodes implanted in the retina. T or F?
4. The retina responds to pressure, as well as light. T or F?

Check Your Memory: Pages 177-179

5. It takes only one photon striking the retina to produce a sensation of light. T or F?
6. Humans can hear sounds from 2 to 2,000 hertz. T or F?
7. It is possible to taste 1 teaspoon of sugar dissolved in 2 gallons of water. T or F?
8. Some music fans have been harmed by subliminal backmasking. T or F?
9. The JND for loudness is 1/10. T or F?
10. Weber's law applies mainly to stimuli in the mid-range. T or F?

Check Your Memory: Pages 180-184

11. A nanometer is one-millionth of a meter. T or F?
12. The lens of the eye is about the size and thickness of a postage stamp. T or F?
13. Farsightedness is corrected with a convex lens. T or F?
14. The myopic eye is longer than normal. T or F?
15. There are more rods than cones in the eyes. T or F?
16. Hubel and Wiesel directly recorded activity in single cells in the visual cortex. T or F?
17. The blind spot is the point where the optic nerve leaves the eye. T or F?
18. The fovea contains only retinal arteries and veins. T or F?
19. Vision rated at 20/200 is better than average. T or F?

20. Visual acuity decreases near the edges of the retina. T or F?

Check Your Memory: Pages 184-189

21. Blue emergency lights and taxiway lights are used because at night they are more visible to the cones. T or F?
22. The trichromatic theory of color vision assumes that black and white sensations are produced by the rods. T or F?
23. According to the opponent-process theory it is impossible to have a reddish green or yellowish blue. T or F?
24. The afterimage produced by staring at a red object is green. T or F?
25. Visual pigments bleach, or breakdown chemically, when struck by light. T or F?
26. Yellow-blue color weakness is very rare. T or F?
27. In the U.S. and Canada, stoplights are always on the bottom of traffic signals. T or F?
28. Complete dark adaptation takes about 12 minutes. T or F?
29. Dark adaptation can be preserved by working in an area lit with red light. T or F?

Check Your Memory: Pages 189-193

30. Sound cannot travel in a vacuum. T or F?
31. The visible, external portion of the ear is the malleus. T or F?
32. The hair cells are part of the organ of Corti. T or F?
33. Hunter's notch occurs when the auditory ossicles are damaged by the sound of gunfire. T or F?
34. Cochlear implants stimulate the auditory nerve directly. T or F?
35. A 40 decibel sound could be described as quiet. T or F?
36. A 100 decibel sound can damage hearing in less than 8 hours. T or F?
37. Every 20 decibels increases sound energy by a factor of 10. T or F?

Check Your Memory: Pages 193-197

38. At least 1000 different types of olfactory receptors exist. T or F?
39. Etherish odors smell like garlic. T or F?
40. Ansomia can be caused by exposure to chemical odors. T or F?
41. Human pheromones (if they exist) are sensed as a subtle, perfume-like odor. T or F?
42. Flavors are greatly influenced by odor, as well as taste. T or F?
43. Taste buds are found throughout the mouth, not just on the tongue. T or F?
44. *Umami* is a pleasant "brothy" taste. T or F?
45. Women are more likely to be supertasters. T or F?
46. PTC tastes bitter to about 70 percent of those tested. T or F?
47. The sense of taste tends to be weaker in early childhood than it is later as the body matures. T or F?

Check Your Memory: Pages 197-202

48. Free nerve endings can produce any of the basic skin sensations. T or F?
49. Vibration is one of the five basic skin sensations. T or F?
50. Areas of the skin that have high concentrations of pain receptors are no more sensitive to pain than other areas of the body. T or F?

51. Visceral pain is often felt at a location on the surface of the body. T or F?

52. Small nerve fibers generally carry warning-system pain messages. T or F?

53. Pain originating in the heart may be felt all the way down the left arm. T or F?

54. Most physical skills rely on dynamic touch, which combines touch sensations with kinesthetic information. T or F?

55. The semicircular canals are especially sensitive to the pull of gravity. T or F?

56. Motion sickness is believed to be related to the body's reactions to being poisoned. T or F?

57. A horizontal body position tends to intensify motion sickness. T or F?

Check Your Memory: Pages 202-204

58. Unlike other receptor cells, the rods and cones do not undergo sensory adaptation. T or F?

59. If you wear a ring, you are rarely aware of it because of sensory gating. T or F?

60. The "seat-of-your pants" phenomenon is related to selective attention. T or F?

61. Stabilized visual images appear brighter and more intense than normal. T or F?

62. Mild electrical stimulation of the skin can block reminding system pain. T or F?

63. Mild electrical stimulation of the skin causes a release of endorphins in free nerve endings. T or F?

Check Your Memory: PSYCHOLOGY IN ACTION

64. High levels of anxiety tend to amplify the amount of pain a person experiences. T or F?

65. Prepared childbirth training helps women feel in control of the birth process. T or F?

66. Physical relaxation exercises can be used to lower anxiety in situations involving pain. T or F?

67. As a means of reducing pain, hot-water bottles are an example of counterirritation. T or F?

Check Your Memory: A STEP BEYOND

68. Visual images produced by taste are the most common form of synesthesia. T or F?

69. When color-hearing synesthetes hear words or tones, their brains become more active in areas involved in the perception of colors. T or F?

70. The unity of the senses is reflected by the fact that all the senses obey similar laws of intensity, size, and quality. T or F?

FINAL SURVEY AND REVIEW

● *In general, how do sensory systems function?*

1. Sensory organs _____ physical energies into nerve impulses.

2. The senses act as data _____ systems that select, analyze, and _____ sensory information.

3. A good example of _____ _____ is the identification of basic perceptual features in a stimulus pattern.

4. In fact, many sensory systems act as _____ detectors.

5. _____ and visual pop-out are examples of feature detection and sensory _____ in action.

6. Sensory response can be partially understood in terms of sensory _____ in the brain. That is, the _____ of the brain activated ultimately determines which type of sensory experience we have.

● *What are the limits of our sensory sensitivity?*

7. _____ is the study of physical stimuli and the sensations they evoke.

8. The minimum amount of physical energy necessary to produce a sensation defines the _____ threshold.

9. The amount of change necessary to produce a _____ _____ difference (or JND) in a stimulus defines a _____ threshold.

10. In general, the amount of change needed to produce a JND is a _____ _____ of the original stimulus intensity. This relationship is known as _____ law.

11. Threatening or anxiety-provoking stimuli may raise the _____ for recognition, an effect called _____ defense.

12. Any stimulus below the level of conscious awareness is said to be _____.

13. There is evidence that subliminal perception occurs, but subliminal _____ is largely ineffective.

● *How is vision accomplished?*

14. The visible spectrum consists of _____ radiation in a narrow range.

15. The visible spectrum ranges from violet, with a wavelength of _____ _____, to red with a wavelength of _____ _____.

16. _____ refers to a color's name, which corresponds to its wavelength. Saturated or "pure" colors come from a narrow band of wavelengths. Brightness corresponds to the _____ of light waves.

17. The eye is in some ways like a camera. At its back lies an array of _____, called rods and cones, that make up a light-sensitive layer called the _____.

18. Vision is focused by the shape of the _____ and lens and by changes in the shape of the lens, called _____.

19. Four common visual defects, correctable with glasses, are _____ (nearsightedness), hyperopia (farsightedness), presbyopia (loss of accommodation), and _____ (in which portions of vision are out of focus).

20. The amount of light entering the eye is controlled by movements of the _____, which _____ (enlarges) and _____ (narrows) the pupil.

21. In the retina, the rods specialize in night vision, black and white reception, and _____ detection.

22. The cones, found exclusively in the _____ and otherwise toward the middle of the eye, specialize in color vision, _____ (perception of fine detail), and daylight vision.

23. Individual cells in the visual _____ of the brain act as feature detectors to analyze visual information.

24. The rods supply much of our _____ vision. Loss of _____ vision is called tunnel vision.

● *How do we perceive colors?*

25. The rods and cones differ in color sensitivity. _____-green is brightest for cones; _____-green for the rods (although they will see it as colorless).

26. In the retina, color vision is explained by the _____ theory. The theory says that three types of cones exist, each most sensitive to either red, green, or blue.

27. Three types of light-sensitive visual _____ are found in the cones, each is most sensitive to either red, green, or blue light.

28. Beyond the retina, the visual system analyzes colors into either-or messages. According to the _____ theory, color information can be coded as either _____ ____ _____, yellow or blue, and black or white messages.

29. Ultimately, _____ experiences are constructed in the brain. This is apparent when you look at a stimulus that produces simultaneous _____.

30. Total color blindness is rare, but 8 percent of males and 1 percent of females are _____ color blind or color weak.

31. Color blindness is a _____ trait carried on the *X* (female) chromosome and passed from _____ to son.

32. The _____ test is used to detect color blindness.

33. Dark adaptation, an increase in sensitivity to light, is caused by increased concentrations of _____ _____ in the rods and the cones.

34. Most dark adaptation is the result of increased _____ concentrations in the rods. Vitamin ____ deficiencies may cause night blindness.

● *What are the mechanisms of hearing?*

35. Sound waves are the stimulus for hearing. Sound travels as waves of _____ (peaks) and _____ (valleys) in the air.

36. The pitch of a sound corresponds to the _____ of sound waves. Loudness corresponds to the _____ (height) of sound waves.

37. Sound waves are transduced by the eardrum, auditory _____, oval window, cochlea, and ultimately, the hair cells in the organ of _____.

38. The frequency theory says that the frequency of nerve impulses in the _____ _____ matches the frequency of incoming sounds (up to 4000 hertz).

39. Place theory says that high tones register near the _____ of the cochlea and low tones near its _____.

40. Three basic types of deafness are nerve deafness, conduction deafness, and _____ deafness.

41. Conduction deafness can often be overcome with a hearing aid. Nerve deafness can sometimes be alleviated by _____ implants.

42. Stimulation deafness can be prevented by avoiding excessive exposure to loud sounds. Sounds above _____ _____ pose an immediate danger to hearing. Two warning signs of stimulation deafness are temporary threshold shift and a ringing in the ears, called _____.

● *How do the chemical senses operate?*

43. _____ (smell) and _____ (taste) are chemical senses responsive to airborne or liquefied molecules.
44. It is suspected that humans are also sensitive to chemical signals called _____, which may be sensed by the _____ organ.
45. The _____ _____ _____ theory partially explains smell. In addition, the location of the olfactory receptors in the nose helps identify various scents.
46. The top outside edges of the tongue are responsive to _____, _____, _____, and bitter tastes. It is suspected that a fifth taste quality called _____ also exists.
47. Taste also appears to be based in part on lock-and-key coding of _____ shapes.

● *What are the somesthetic senses and why are they important?*

48. The somesthetic senses include the skin senses, vestibular senses, and _____ senses (receptors that detect muscle and joint positioning).
49. The skin senses include touch, pressure, _____, cold, and warmth. Sensitivity to each is related to the number of _____ found in an area of skin.
50. Distinctions can be made among various types of pain, including visceral pain, somatic pain, _____ pain, _____ system pain, and reminding system pain.
51. Most amputees have _____ limb sensations long after losing a limb.
52. Various forms of motion sickness are related to messages received from the _____ system, which senses gravity and head movement.
53. The _____ organs detect the pull of gravity and rapid head movements.
54. The movement of fluid within the _____ canals, and the movement of the crista within each _____, detects head movement and positioning.
55. According to _____ _____ theory, motion sickness is caused by a mismatch of visual, kinesthetic, and vestibular sensations. Motion sickness can be avoided by minimizing sensory conflict.

● *Why are we more aware of some sensations than others?*

56. Incoming sensations are affected by sensory _____ (a decrease in the number of nerve impulses sent).
57. Selective _____ (selection and diversion of messages in the brain) and sensory gating (blocking or alteration of messages flowing toward the brain) also alter sensations.
58. Selective gating of pain messages apparently takes place in the spinal cord. _____ _____ theory proposes an explanation for many pain phenomena.

59. "Runner's high," the painkilling effects of the Chinese medical art of _____, and other pain phenomena appear to be explained by the release of a morphine-like chemical in the brain, called beta-_____.

● *How can pain be reduced in everyday situations?*

60. Pain can be reduced by lowering anxiety and redirecting _____ to stimuli other than the pain stimulus.

61. Feeling that you have _____ over a stimulus tends to reduce the amount of pain you experience.

62. The _____ or meaning placed on a stimulus affects how painful it is perceived to be.

63. Sending mild pain messages to the spinal cord can close the gates to more severe pain. This effect is called _____.

● *What is synesthesia? What does it reveal about sensory systems?*

64. In _____, stimulation of one sense also arouses sensations in another.

65. For true _____ (people who have synesthesia), cross-sense experiences are involuntary.

66. Synesthesia occurs when stimulating one sense activates _____ _____ for other senses, too.

MASTERY TEST

1. A person with tunnel vision has mainly lost the ability to use the _____ and _____ vision.
   a. cones, foveal   b. photoreceptors, color   c. iris, retinal   d. rods, peripheral

2. Sensory conflict theory attributes motion sickness to mismatches between what three systems?
   a. olfaction, kinesthesis, and audition   b. vision, kinesthesis, and the vestibular system
   c. kinesthesis, audition, and the somesthetic system   d. vision, gustation, and the skin senses

3. Which of the following types of color blindness is most common?
   a. yellow-blue, male   b. yellow-blue, female   c. red-green, female   d. red-green, male

4. A reasonable conclusion about subliminal perception is that
   a. subliminal stimuli have weak effects
   b. backmasking poses a serious threat to listeners
   c. subliminal tapes are more effective than subliminal advertising
   d. subliminal perception applies to hearing, but not to vision

5. Which of the following does not belong with the others?
   a. Pacinian corpuscle   b. Merkle's disk   c. vomeronasal organ   d. free nerve endings

6. The fact that the eyes are only sensitive to a narrow band of electromagnetic energies shows that vision acts as a (an) _____ system.
   a. opponent-process   b. gate-control   c. central biasing   d. data reduction

7. Which theory of color vision best explains the fact that we do not see yellowish blue?
   a. trichromatic   b. chromatic gating   c. Ishihara hypothesis   d. opponent process

8. A person with inflamed kidneys feels pain in her hips. This is an example of
   a. warning system pain   b. referred pain   c. somatic pain   d. vestibular pain

9. Hubel and Wiesel found that nerve cells in the visual cortex of the brain respond most to specific
   a. phosphenes   b. perceptual features   c. areas of the visible spectrum   d. numbers of photons

10. Which of the following pain control strategies makes use of gate control theory?
    a. counterirritation   b. distraction and reinterpretation   c. anxiety reduction
    d. gaining control over pain stimuli

11. New mothers who are depressed take longer than usual to recognize pictures of babies. This is an example of
    a. backmasking   b. visual accommodation   c. difference thresholds   d. perceptual defense

12. According to Weber's law, the _____ is a constant proportion of the original intensity of a stimulus.
    a. absolute threshold   b. JND   c. phosphene   d. sensory limen

13. Dark adaptation is closely related to concentrations of _____ in the _____.
    a. retinal, aqueous humor   b. photopsin, cones   c. rhodopsin, rods   d. photons, optic nerve

14. Sensory analysis tends to extract perceptual _____ from stimulus patterns.
    a. thresholds   b. features   c. transducers   d. amplitudes

15. Which pair of terms is most closely related?
    a. hyperopia—color blindness   b. astigmatism—presbyopia   c. myopia—astigmatism
    d. hyperopia—presbyopia

16. The painkilling effects of acupuncture are partly explained by _____ theory and the release of _____.
    a. lock-and-key, pheromones   b. gate control, pheromones   c. gate control, endorphins
    d. lock-and-key, endorphins

17. Three photons of light striking the _____ defines the _____ for vision.
    a. retina, absolute threshold   b. cornea, difference threshold   c. iris, upper limen   d. cornea, JND

18. According to the _____ theory of hearing, low tones cause the greatest movement near the _____ of the cochlea.
    a. place, outer tip   b. frequency, outer tip   c. place, base   d. frequency, base

19. Where vision is concerned, physiological nystagmus helps prevent
    a. sensory gating   b. tunnel vision   c. sensory adaptation   d. night blindness

20. Which of the following best represents the concept of a transducer?
    a. Translating English into Spanish.   b. Copying a computer file from one floppy disk to another.
    c. Speaking into a telephone receiver.   d. Turning water into ice.

21. Visual pop-out is closely related to which sensory process?
    a. transduction   b. feature detection   c. difference thresholds   d. perception below the limen

22. Rods and cones are to vision as _____ are to hearing.
    a. auditory ossicles   b. vibrations   c. pinnas   d. hair cells

23. You lose the ability to smell floral odors. This is called _____ and it is compatible with the _____ theory of olfaction.
    a. anosmia, lock-and-key   b. anhedonia, place   c. tinnitus, gate-control
    d. sensory adaptation, molecular

24. The main problem with current artificial vision systems is
    a. the retina's lack of an absolute threshold   b. the danger of damaging the eyes while producing phosphenes   c. their inability to transduce letters   d. the rejection of implanted electrodes

25. Which two dimensions of color are related to the wavelength of electromagnetic energy?
    a. hue and saturation   b. saturation and brightness   c. brightness and hue
    d. brightness and amplitude

26. Temporary threshold shifts are related to
    a. conduction deafness   b. nerve deafness   c. stimulation deafness   d. damage to the ossicles

27. The existence of the blind spot is explained by a lack of
    a. rhodopsin   b. peripheral vision   c. photoreceptors   d. activity in the fovea

28. Which of the following normally has the most effect on the amount of light entering the eye?
    a. fovea   b. iris   c. aqueous humor   d. cornea

29. In vision, a loss of accommodation is most associated with aging of the
    a. iris   b. fovea   c. lens   d. cornea

30. Visual acuity and color vision are provided by the _____ found in large numbers in the _____ of the eye.
    a. cones, fovea b. cones, periphery c. rods, fovea d. rods, periphery

ANSWERS

Recite and Review

1. nerve
2. data, analyze
3. perceptual
4. detectors
5. sensory
6. sensory, activated
7. physical, sensations
8. minimum, sensation
9. change, difference
10. intensity, law
11. raise, defense
12. below
13. ineffective
14. visible
15. wavelength, wavelength
16. wavelength, narrow
17. rods, cones
18. shape, shape
19. nearsightedness, accommodation
20. enlarges, narrows
21. rods
22. cones, color
23. detectors
24. rods
25. sensitivity
26. retina, cones
27. cones
28. either-or, black or white
29. brain
30. Total
31. female
32. color blindness
33. increase, rods, cones
34. rods, night
35. peaks, valleys
36. pitch, height

37. eardrum, hair
38. frequency, frequency
39. high, low
40. nerve
41. Nerve
42. loud, shifts
43. smell, taste
44. chemical, organ
45. location
46. bitter
47. coding
48. skin
49. pressure, number
50. reminding
51. limb
52. head
53. gravity
54. fluid, crista
55. mismatch
56. reduction (or decrease)
57. gating
58. spinal cord
59. morphine (or opiate)
60. lowering
61. reduce
62. stimulus
63. mild
64. sensations
65. involuntary
66. other senses

Connections

1. d
2. f
3. h
4. b
5. i

6. c
7. k
8. a
9. e
10. g
11. j
12. e
13. g
14. h
15. a
16. d
17. f
18. c
19. i
20. j
21. b
22. i
23. b
24. j
25. h
26. a
27. c
28. d
29. e
30. g
31. f

Check Your Memory

1. T
2. T
3. F
4. T
5. F
6. F
7. T
8. F
9. T

10. T
11. F
12. F
13. T
14. T
15. T
16. T
17. T
18. F
19. F
20. T
21. F
22. T
23. T
24. T
25. T
26. T
27. F
28. F
29. T
30. T
31. F
32. T
33. F
34. T
35. T
36. T
37. T
38. T
39. F
40. T
41. F
42. T
43. T
44. T
45. T
46. T
47. F
48. T
49. F
50. F
51. T
52. F
53. T
54. T
55. F
56. T
57. F
58. F

59. F
60. T
61. F
62. T
63. F
64. T
65. T
66. T
67. T
68. F
69. T
70. T

Final Survey and Review

1. transduce
2. reduction, code
3. sensory analysis
4. feature
5. Phosphenes, coding
6. localization, area
7. Psychophysics
8. absolute
9. just noticeable, difference
10. constant proportion, Weber's
11. threshold, perceptual
12. subliminal
13. advertising
14. electromagnetic
15. 400 nanometers, 700 nanometers
16. Hue, amplitude
17. photoreceptors, retina
18. cornea, accommodation
19. myopia, astigmatism
20. iris, dilates, constricts
21. motion
22. fovea, acuity
23. cortex
24. peripheral, peripheral
25. Yellow, blue
26. trichromatic
27. pigments
28. opponent-process, red or green
29. color, contrast
30. red-green

31. sex-linked, mother
32. Ishihara
33. visual pigments
34. rhodopsin, A
35. compression, rarefaction
36. frequency, amplitude
37. ossicles, Corti
38. auditory nerves
39. base, tip
40. stimulation
41. cochlear
42. 120 decibels, tinnitus
43. Olfaction, gustation
44. pheromones, vomeronasal
45. lock and key
46. sweet, salty, sour, umami
47. molecule
48. kinesthetic
49. pain, receptors
50. referred, warning
51. phantom
52. vestibular
53. otolith
54. semicircular, ampulla
55. sensory conflict
56. adaptation
57. attention
58. Gate control
59. acupuncture, endorphin
60. attention
61. control
62. interpretation
63. counterirritation
64. synesthesia
65. synesthetes
66. brain areas

Mastery Test

1. d (p. 184)
2. b (p. 201)
3. d (p. 186)
4. a (p. 178)
5. c (p. 195, 198)
6. d (p. 175)
7. d (p. 185)
8. b (p. 199)
9. b (p. 183)

10. a (p. 207)
11. d (p. 178)
12. b (p. 178)
13. c (p. 187)
14. b (p. 175)
15. d (p. 181)
16. c (p. 203)

17. a (p. 177)
18. a (p. 191)
19. c (p. 202)
20. c (p. 175)
21. b (p. 176)
22. d (p. 183, 191)
23. a (p. 193-194)

24. d (p. 177)
25. a (p. 180)
26. c (p. 192)
27. c (p. 183)
28. b (p. 181)
29. c (p. 181)
30. a (p. 183)

Chapter 6
Perceiving the World

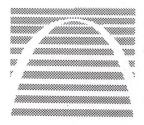

CHAPTER OVERVIEW

Perception involves organizing sensations into meaningful patterns. Perceptions are hypotheses about sensory events or models of the world. Visual perceptions are stabilized by size, shape, and brightness constancies. The most basic perceptual pattern (in vision) is figure-ground organization. Sensations tend to be organized on the basis of nearness, similarity, continuity, closure, contiguity, and common region.

Depth perception depends on accommodation, convergence, retinal disparity, and various pictorial cues. The pictorial cues include linear perspective, relative size, light and shadow, overlap, texture gradients, aerial haze, and relative motion.

Learning, in the form of perceptual habits, influences perceptions. Perceptual judgments are related to stimulus context and to internal frames of reference, such as one's adaptation level. Perceptions are also greatly affected by attention, motives, values, and expectations. Selective attention and divided attention influence what information we are aware of at any moment. So do habituation, motives and values, and perceptual sets.

Because perceptions are reconstructions of events, eyewitness testimony can be unreliable. Perceptual accuracy can be improved by reality testing, dishabituation, actively paying attention, breaking perceptual habits, using broad frames of reference, and being aware of perceptual sets.

Parapsychology is the study of purported psi phenomena, including clairvoyance, telepathy, precognition, and psychokinesis. The bulk of the evidence to date is against the existence of extrasensory perception. Stage ESP is based on deception and tricks.

LEARNING OBJECTIVES

To demonstrate mastery of this chapter you should be able to:

1. Define *perception*.
2. Describe the following constancies:
   a. size   b. shape   c. brightness
3. Give examples of the following as they relate to the organization of perception:
   a. figure-ground (include the concept of reversible figures)
   b. nearness
   c. similarity
   d. continuity

e. closure (include the concept of illusory figures)

f. contiguity

g. common region

4. Describe the activities of an engineering psychologist. Include a discussion of the two components of effective design.

5. Explain what a perceptual hypothesis is.

6. Define and give an example of an ambiguous stimulus.

7. Define *depth perception* and discuss the nativistic and empirical view of it. Describe the visual cliff research.

8. Describe the following cues for depth perception and indicate in each case whether the cue is monocular or binocular:

a. accommodation

b. convergence

c. retinal disparity (include the term stereoscopic vision)

9. Describe the visual adaptations found among birds.

10. Describe the following two-dimensional, monocular, pictorial depth cues and give examples of how artists use them to give the appearance of three-dimensional space:

a. linear perspective

b. relative size

c. height in the picture plane

d. light and shadow

e. overlap

f. texture gradients

g. aerial perspective

h. relative motion (motion parallax)

11. Describe the phenomenon of the moon illusion. Include in your explanation the apparent distance hypothesis and a description of the work of the Kaufmans..

12. Define the terms *perceptual learning* and *perceptual habit,* and explain how the latter allows learning to affect perception.

13. Explain how the Ames room poses problems for organization and for a person's perceptual habits.

14. Describe the research which demonstrates the brain's sensitivity to perceptual features in the environment.

15. Explain how the results of inverted vision experiments support the concept of perceptual habits. Explain why active movement is so important in adapting to inverted vision.

16. Give an example of context and frames of reference.

17. Describe and give an example of the concept of adaptation level.

18. Differentiate between an illusion and a hallucination.

19. Describe at least one practical use of the stroboscopic movement illusion.

20. Describe the Müller-Lyer illusion and explain how and explain how size-distance invariance may account for this illusion.

21. Define *attention* and list the factors that affect it. Distinguish between selective attention and divided attention.

22. Differentiate habituation from sensory adaptation. Include the concept of the orientation response.

23. Explain the boiled frog syndrome and how it may affect the ultimate survival of humans.

24. Explain what inattentional blindness is and how it can affect what we perceive.

25. Explain and give experimental evidence of how motives may alter attention and perception.

26. Explain what bottom-up and top-down processing are.

27. Explain how perceptual expectancies may influence perception. Include the concepts of perceptual sets and perceptual categories.

28. Briefly describe the research of Cohen and Bennett concerning the influence of prior perception on drawing ability.

The following objectives are related to the material in the "Psychology in Action" and "A Step Beyond" sections of your text.

29. Explain the phrase "We see what we believe."

30. Explain why most eyewitness testimony is inaccurate, (regardless of one's confidence). Include the concept of weapon focus.

31. Explain what the term *reality testing* means.

32. Explain Maslow's theory of perceptual awareness.

33. Discuss how attention affects perception.

34. List seven ways to become a better "eyewitness" to life.

35. Define *extrasensory perception.*

36. Define the term *parapsychology.*

37. Describe the following purported psychic abilities:

    a. clairvoyance   c. precognition

    b. telepathy   d. psychokinesis

38. Describe the research with Zener cards, and explain why most psychologists remain skeptical about psi abilities. Include a discussion of Honorton's ganzfeld research and stage ESP.

39. Describe the best conclusion to make about psi events.

RECITE AND REVIEW

● *What are perceptual constancies, and what is their role in perception?*

Recite and Review: Pages 212-215

1. Perception is the process of assembling sensations into _____ that provide a usable mental _____ of the world.

2. In vision, the retinal _____ changes from moment to moment, but the external world appears stable and undistorted because of _____ constancies.

3. In size and shape _____, the perceived sizes and shapes of objects remain the same even though their retinal images change size and shape. The apparent brightness of objects remains stable (a property called brightness constancy) because each reflects a _____ proportion of light.

4. Perceptual constancies are partly native (_____) and partly empirical (_____).

● *What basic principles do we use to group sensations into meaningful patterns?*

Recite and Review: Pages 215-219

5. The most basic organization of sensations is a division into figure and ground (_____ and _____). Reversible figures, however, allow figure-ground organization to be reversed.

6. A number of factors, identified by the Gestalt psychologists, contribute to the _____ of sensations. These are nearness, _____, continuity, closure, contiguity, _____ region, and combinations of the preceding.

7. Stimuli near one another tend to be perceptually _____ together. So, too, do stimuli that are similar in _____. Continuity refers to the fact that perceptions tend to be organized as simple, uninterrupted patterns.

8. Closure is the tendency to _____ a broken or incomplete pattern. Contiguity refers to nearness in _____ and space. Stimuli that fall in a defined area, or common region, also tend to be grouped together.

9. _____ psychologists are also known as human factors _____.

10. These specialists make machine _____ and controls compatible with human _____ and motor capacities.

11. The most effective _____ _____ engineering follows the principles of natural design.

12. Basic elements of line drawings, especially the edges of _____ and parallel edges, appear to be universally recognized.

13. A perceptual organization may be thought of as an _____ held until evidence contradicts it. Camouflage patterns disrupt perceptual _____, especially figure-ground perceptions.

14. Perceptual organization shifts for ambiguous _____, which may have more than one interpretation. An example is Necker's _____. Impossible figures resist stable organization altogether.

● *How is it possible to see depth and judge distance?*

Recite and Review: Pages 219-227

15. _____ perception is the ability to perceive three-dimensional space and judge distances.

16. Depth perception is present in basic form soon after, _____ as shown by testing with the visual cliff and other methods. As soon as infants become active _____, they refuse to cross the visual cliff.

17. Depth perception depends on the muscular cues of accommodation (bending of the _____) and convergence (inward movement of the _____).

18. The area of binocular vision is _____ in some birds than in humans. However, birds and other animals may have extremely _____ field of view.

19. A number of pictorial _____, which will work in _____ paintings, drawings, and photographs, also underlie normal depth perception.

20. Some pictorial cues are: linear perspective (the apparent convergence of _____ _____), relative size (more distant objects appear _____), height in the _____ plane, light and shadow (shadings of light), and overlap or interposition (one object overlaps another).

21. Additional pictorial cues include: texture gradients (textures become _____ in the distance), aerial haze (loss of color and detail at large distances), and relative _____ or _____ parallax (differences in the apparent movement of objects when a viewer is moving).

22. All the pictorial cues are monocular depth cues (only _____ _____ is needed to make use of them).

23. The moon illusion refers to the fact that the moon appears _____ near the horizon than it does when overhead.

24. The moon illusion appears to be explained by the apparent _____ hypothesis, which emphasizes the greater number of depth cues present when the moon is on the _____.

● *What effect does learning have on perception?*

Recite and Review: Pages 227-233

25. Organizing and interpreting sensations is greatly influenced by learned perceptual _____. An example is the Ames room, which looks rectangular but is actually distorted so that objects in the room appear to change _____.

26. Sensitivity to perceptual _____ is also partly learned. Studies of inverted vision show that even the most basic organization is subject to a degree of change. Active _____ speeds adaptation to new perceptual environments.

27. Perceptual judgments are almost always related to the _____ surrounding a stimulus, or to an internal frame of reference called the adaptation _____, which is a personal _____ point for making judgments.

28. Perceptual _____ (misleading perceptions) differ from hallucinations (perceptions of nonexistent stimuli).

29. Illusions are often related to perceptual _____. One of the most familiar of all illusions, the Müller-Lyer illusion, seems to be related to perceptual learning based on experience with box-shaped _____ and rooms.

30. Linear perspective, _____ invariance relationships, and mislocating the end-points of the _____ also contribute to the Müller-Lyer illusion.

● *How is perception altered by attention, motives, values, and expectations?*

Recite and Review: Pages 234-238

31. _____ attention refers to giving priority to some sensory messages while excluding others.

32. Attention acts like a _____ or narrowing of the information channel linking the senses to perception.

33. Attention may also be divided among various activities. Divided attention suggests that our _____ for storing and thinking about information is limited.

34. Attention is aroused by _____ stimuli, by repetition (with variation), by stimulus contrast, _____, or incongruity.

35. Attention is accompanied by an orientation response (OR). When a stimulus is repeated without _____, the orientation response _____, an effect known as habituation.

36. Personal motives and _____ often alter perceptions by changing the evaluation of what is seen or by altering attention to specific details.

37. Perceptions may be based on _____ or bottom-up processing of information.

38. Bottom-up processing, perceptions begin with the organization of low-level _____. In top-down processing, previous knowledge is used to rapidly _____ sensory information.

39. Attention, prior experience, suggestion, and motives combine in various ways to create perceptual sets, or _____. A perceptual set is a readiness to perceive in a particular way, induced by strong expectations.

● *How reliable are eyewitness reports?*

Recite and Review: PSYCHOLOGY IN ACTION

40. Perception is an _____ reconstruction of events. This is one reason why eyewitness testimony is surprisingly _____.

41. In many crimes, eyewitness accuracy is further damaged by weapon _____. Similar factors, such as observer stress, brief exposure times, cross-racial inaccuracies, and the wording of questions can _____ eyewitness accuracy.

42. Perceptual accuracy is enhanced by reality _____, dishabituation, and conscious efforts to pay _____.

43. It is also valuable to break perceptual habits, to _____ frames of reference, to beware of perceptual sets, and to be aware of the ways in which motives and emotions influence perceptions.

● *Is extrasensory perception possible?*

Recite and Review: A STEP BEYOND

44. Parapsychology is the study of purported _____ phenomena, including clairvoyance (perceiving events at a distance), _____ ("mind reading"), precognition (perceiving future events), and psychokinesis (mentally influencing inanimate objects).

45. Clairvoyance, telepathy, and precognition are purported types of extrasensory _____.

46. Research in parapsychology remains controversial owing to a variety of problems. _____ and after-the-fact reinterpretation are problems with "natural" ESP episodes.

47. Many studies of ESP overlook the impact of statistically unusual outcomes that are no more than runs of _____.

48. The bulk of the evidence to date is _____ the existence of ESP. Very few positive results in ESP research have been replicated (_____) by independent scientists.

49. Stage ESP is based on _____ and tricks.

CONNECTIONS

1. _____   texture gradients
2. _____   stereoscopic vision
3. _____   convergence
4. _____   continuity
5. _____   light and shadow
6. _____   common region
7. _____   relative size
8. _____   closure
9. _____   overlap
10. _____   retinal disparity
11. _____   linear perspective
12. _____   nearness
13. _____   similarity

14. _____	reversible figure	a.	convergence
15. _____	visual cliff	b.	stereogram
16. _____	binocular cue	c.	360 degree view
17. _____	mismatch	d.	moon illusion
18. _____	woodcock	e.	Müller-Lyer illusion
19. _____	Ponzo illusion	f.	infant depth perception
20. _____	motion pictures	g.	figure-ground
21. _____	OR	h.	stroboscopic movement
22. _____	Zulus	i.	double take

23. _____	advertising	a.	perceptual expectancy
24. _____	top-down	b.	Zen and attention
25. _____	perceptual awareness	c.	run of luck
26. _____	dishabituation	d.	sex and anxiety
27. _____	psi events	f.	J. B. Rhine
28. _____	decline effect	g.	Uri Geller
29. _____	stage ESP	h.	clairvoyance test
30. _____	Zener cards	i.	surrender to experience

CHECK YOUR MEMORY

Check Your Memory: Pages 212-215

1. Perception involves selecting, organizing, and integrating sensory information. T or F?
2. Some perceptual abilities must be learned after sight is restored to the previously blind. T or F?
3. Newborn babies show some evidence of size constancy. T or F?
4. Houses and cars look like toys from a low-flying airplane because of shape constancy. T or F?
5. Drunkenness impairs brightness constancy, but size and shape constancy are not usually affected. T or F?
6. Brightness constancy does not apply to objects illuminated by different amounts of light. T or F?

Check Your Memory: Pages 215-219

7. Basic figure-ground organization is learned at about age 2. T or F?
8. Illusory figures are related to the principle of closure. T or F?
9. Contiguity refers to our tendency to see lines as continuous. T or F?
10. A user-friendly camera must have displays and controls that are compatible with human sensory and motor capacities. T or F?
11. Natural design minimizes feedback so that people are not distracted by unnecessary information. T or F?
12. Pre-existing ideas actively guide our interpretation of sensations in many cases. T or F?

13. Necker's cube and the "three-pronged widget" are impossible figures. T or F?
14. Color boundaries on objects in drawings are intuitively understood by just about everyone. T or F?

Check Your Memory: Pages 219-227

15. Depth perception is partly learned and partly innate. T or F?
16. Human depth perception typically emerges at about 4 months of age. T or F?
17. All depth cues are basically binocular. T or F?
18. Accommodation and convergence are muscular depth cues. T or F?
19. Accommodation acts as a depth cue primarily for distances greater than 4 feet from the eyes. T or F?
20. Convergence acts as a depth cue primarily for distances less than 4 feet from the eyes. T or F?
21. The brain is sensitive to mismatches in information received from the right and left eyes. T or F?
22. Depth perception is actually as good when using just one eye as it is when both eyes are open. T or F?
23. Pigeons, ducks, and hummingbirds can see ultraviolet light. T or F?
24. With one eye closed, the pictorial depth cues no longer provide information about depth and distance. T or F?
25. Changing the image size of an object implies that its distance from the viewer has changed, too. T or F?
26. In a drawing, the closer an object is to the horizon line, the nearer it appears to be to the viewer. T or F?
27. Aerial perspective is most powerful when the air is exceptionally clear. T or F?
28. When an observer is moving forward, objects beyond the observer's point of fixation appear to move forward too. T or F?
29. Accommodation is a binocular depth cue. T or F?
30. Some familiarity with drawings is required to use overlap as a depth cue. T or F?
31. The moon's image is magnified by the dense atmosphere near the horizon. T or F?
32. More depth cues are present when the moon is viewed near the horizon. T or F?

Check Your Memory: Pages 227-233

33. A lack of relevant perceptual experience makes it difficult to judge upside-down faces. T or F?
34. Stimuli that lie above the horizon line in a scene are more likely to been perceived as "figure" than as "ground." T or F?
35. The Ames room is primarily used to test the effects of inverted vision. T or F?
36. Cats who grow up surrounded by horizontal stripes are unusually sensitive to vertical stripes when they reach maturity. T or F?
37. People who wear inverting goggles say that eventually the visual world turns right side up again. T or F?
38. Divers must learn to compensate for visual distortions while underwater. T or F?
39. Perception is most accurate during active interactions with one's surroundings. T or F?
40. If your adaptation level for judging weight is 30 pounds, you would judge a 30-pound object as "heavy." T or F?
41. Hearing voices when no one is speaking is an example of a perceptual illusion. T or F?
42. Perceptual illusions are usually not noticeable until measurements reveal that our perceptions are inaccurate or distorted. T or F?

43. According to Richard Gregory, the arrowhead-tipped line in the Müller-Lyer illusion looks like the outside corner of a building. T or F?

44. Zulus rarely see round shapes and therefore fail to experience the Müller-Lyer illusion. T or F?

Check Your Memory: Pages 234-238

45. Messages passing through the "bottleneck" of selective attention appear to prevent other messages from passing through. T or F?

46. As skills become automated, they free mental capacity for other activities. T or F?

47. Repetitious stimuli must vary a little to gain attention, otherwise repetition leads to habituation. T or F?

48. Enlarged pupils and brain-wave changes typically accompany the OR. T or F?

49. Humans are especially sensitive to slow, gradual changes that occur over very long time periods. T or F?

50. Inattenional blindness refers to the fact that paying close attention to one stimulus can pervent a person from seeing other stimuli that are nearby. T or F?

51. Emotional stimuli can shift attention away from other information. T or F?

52. Analyzing information into small features and then building a recognizable pattern is called top-up processing. T or F?

53. Perceptual sets are frequently created by suggestion. T or F?

54. You could use a tachistoscope to flash stimuli on a screen for very brief periods. T or F?

55. Labels and categories have been shown to have little real effect on perceptions. T or F?

Check Your Memory: PSYCHOLOGY IN ACTION

56. In many ways we see what we believe, as well as believe what we see. T or F?

57. The more confident an eyewitness is about the accuracy of his or her testimony, the more likely it is to be accurate. T or F?

58. The testimony of crime victims is generally more accurate than the testimony of bystanders. T or F?

59. Police officers and other trained observers are more accurate eyewitnesses than the average person. T or F?

60. Reality testing is the process Abraham Maslow described as a "surrender" to experience. T or F?

61. Perceptually, Zen masters have been shown to habituate more rapidly than the average person. T or F?

Check Your Memory: A STEP BEYOND

62. Uri Geller was one of the first researchers in parapsychology to use the Zener cards. T or F?

63. Psychokinesis is classified as a psi event, but not a form of ESP. T or F?

64. Prophetic dreams are regarded as a form of precognition. T or F?

65. Strange coincidences are strong evidence for the existence of ESP. T or F?

66. The Zener cards eliminated the possibility of fraud and "leakage" of information in ESP experiments. T or F?

67. "Psi missing" is perhaps the best current evidence for ESP. T or F?

68. Belief in psi events has declined among parapsychologists in recent years. T or F?

FINAL SURVEY AND REVIEW

● *What are perceptual constancies, and what is their role in perception?*

1. Perception is the process of assembling _____ into patterns that provide a usable _____ _____ of the world.

2. In vision, the _____ image changes from moment to moment, but the external world appears stable and undistorted because of perceptual _____.

3. In size and shape constancy, the perceived sizes and shapes of objects remain the same even though their retinal images change size and shape. The apparent _____ of objects remains stable (a property called brightness constancy) because each reflects a constant _____ of _____.

4. Perceptual constancies are partly _____ (inborn) and partly _____ (learned).

● *What basic principles do we use to group sensations into meaningful patterns?*

5. The most basic organization of sensations is a division into _____ and _____ (object and background).

6. A number of factors, identified by the _____ psychologists, contribute to the organization of sensations. These are _____, similarity, continuity, _____, contiguity, common region, and combinations of the preceding.

7. Stimuli near one another tend to be perceptually grouped together. So, too, do stimuli that are similar in appearance. _____ refers to the fact that perceptions tend to be organized as simple, uninterrupted patterns.

8. _____ refers to nearness in time and space. Stimuli that fall in a defined area, or common region, also tend to be grouped together.

9. Engineering psychologists are also known as _____ _____ engineers.

10. These specialists make machine displays and _____ compatible with human sensory and _____ capacities.

11. The most effective human factors engineering follows the principles of _____ _____.

12. Basic elements of line drawings, especially the edges of surfaces and _____ _____, appear to be universally recognized.

13. A perceptual organization may be thought of as an hypothesis held until evidence contradicts it. _____ patterns disrupt perceptual organization, especially figure-ground perceptions.

14. Perceptual organization shifts for _____ stimuli, which may have more than one interpretation. An example is _____ cube. Impossible _____ resist stable organization altogether.

● *How is it possible to see depth and judge distance?*

15. Depth perception is the ability to perceive _____ space and judge distances.

16. Depth perception is present in basic form soon after birth, as shown by testing with the _____ _____ and other methods. As soon as infants become active crawlers they refuse to cross the deep side of the _____ _____.

17. Depth perception depends on the muscular cues of _____ (bending of the lens) and _____ (inward movement of the eyes).

18. The area of _____ vision is smaller in some birds than in humans. However, birds and other animals may have extremely wide _____ _____ _____.

19. A number of _____ cues, which will work in flat paintings, drawings, and photographs, also underlie normal depth perception.

20. Some of these cues are: _____ _____ (the apparent convergence of parallel lines), relative size (more distant objects appear smaller), height in the picture plane, light and shadow (shadings of light), and overlap or _____ (one object overlaps another).

21. Additional pictorial cues include: texture _____ (textures become finer in the distance), aerial haze (loss of color and detail at large distances), and relative motion or motion _____ (differences in the apparent movement of objects when a viewer is moving).

22. All the pictorial cues are _____ depth cues (only one eye is needed to make use of them).

23. The moon illusion refers to the fact that the moon appears larger near the _____.

24. The moon illusion appears to be explained by the _____ _____ hypothesis, which emphasizes the greater number of _____ _____ present when the moon is on the horizon.

● *What effect does learning have on perception?*

25. Organizing and interpreting sensations is greatly influenced by learned _____ _____. An example is the _____ room, which looks rectangular but is actually distorted so that objects in the room appear to change size.

26. Sensitivity to perceptual features is also partly learned. Studies of _____ vision show that even the most basic organization is subject to a degree of change. Active movement speeds _____ to new perceptual environments.

27. Perceptual judgments are almost always related to the context surrounding a stimulus, or to an internal _____ _____ _____ called the _____ level, which is a personal medium point for making judgments.

28. Perceptual _____ (misleading perceptions) differ from _____ (perceptions of nonexistent stimuli).

29. Illusions are often related to perceptual habits. One of the most familiar of all illusions, the _____ illusion, involves two equal-length lines tipped with arrowheads and V's. This illusion seems to be related to perceptual learning based on experience with box-shaped buildings and rooms.

30. Linear perspective, size-distance _____ relationships, and mislocating the _____ of the lines also contribute to the Müller-Lyer illusion.

● *How is perception altered by attention, motives, values, and expectations?*

31. _____ _____ refers to giving priority to some sensory messages while excluding others.

32. Attention acts like a bottleneck or narrowing of the information _____ linking the senses to perception.

33. Attention may also be split among various activities. _____ attention suggests that our capacity for storing and thinking about information is limited.

34. Attention is aroused by intense stimuli, by repetition (with variation), by stimulus _____, change, or _____.

35. Attention is accompanied by an _____ _____ (OR). When a stimulus is repeated without change, the OR decreases, an effect known as _____.

36. Personal _____ and values often alter perceptions by changing the evaluation of what is seen or by altering attention to specific details.

37. Perceptions may be based on top-down or bottom-up _____ of information.

38. _____ perceptions begin with the organization of low-level features. In _____ processing, previous knowledge is used to rapidly organize sensory information.

39. Attention, prior experience, suggestion, and motives combine in various ways to create _____ _____, or expectancies. A _____ _____ is a readiness to perceive in a particular way, induced by strong expectations.

● *How reliable are eyewitness reports?*

40. Perception is an active _____ of events. This is one reason why eyewitness testimony is surprisingly inaccurate.

41. In many crimes, eyewitness accuracy is further damaged by _____ focus. Similar factors, such as observer _____, brief exposure times, cross-racial inaccuracies, and the wording of questions can lower eyewitness accuracy.

42. Perceptual accuracy is enhanced by reality testing, _____, and conscious efforts to pay attention.

43. It is also valuable to break _____ _____, to broaden frames of reference, to beware of perceptual sets, and to be aware of the ways in which motives and emotions influence perceptions.

● *Is extrasensory perception possible?*

44. _____ is the study of purported psi phenomena, including clairvoyance (perceiving events at a distance), telepathy ("mind reading"), _____ (perceiving future events), and psychokinesis (mentally influencing inanimate objects).

45. Clairvoyance, telepathy, and precognition are purported types of _____ perception.

46. Research in parapsychology remains controversial owing to a variety of problems. Coincidence and after-the-fact _____ are problems with "natural" ESP episodes.

47. Many studies of ESP overlook the impact of _____ unusual outcomes that are no more than runs of luck.

48. The bulk of the evidence to date is against the existence of ESP. Very few positive results in ESP research have been _____ (repeated) by independent scientists.

49. _____ ESP is based on deception and tricks.

MASTERY TEST

1. The Ames room creates a conflict between
   a. horizontal features and vertical features b. attention and habituation c. top-down and bottom-up processing d. shape constancy and size constancy

2. Weapon focus tends to lower eyewitness accuracy because it affects
   a. selective attention b. the adaptation level c. perceptions of contiguity d. dishabituation

3. Stereograms create an illusion of depth by mimicking the effects of
   a. accommodation b. convergence c. retinal disparity d. stroboscopic motion

4. Which perceptual constancy is most affected by sitting in the front row at a movie theater?
   a. size constancy b. shape constancy c. brightness constancy d. depth constancy

5. The fact that American tourists in London tend to look in the wrong direction before stepping into crosswalks is based on
   a. habituation b. perceptual habits c. adaptation levels d. unconscious transference

6. When they look at drawings and photographs, people are more likely to notice unexpected objects. This is explained by the effects of _____ on perception.
   a. pictorial depth cues b. selective attention c. habituation d. figure-ground organization

7. Size constancy
   a. is strongest when objects are above the horizon line b. is affected by experience with seeing objects of various sizes c. requires that objects be illuminated by light of the same intensity d. all of the preceding

8. Adaptation to visual distortions is most rapid if people are allowed to
   a. remain immobile b. move actively c. move their eye muscles d. habituate their adaptation levels

9. Perceptual categories and perceptual expectancies tend to promote
   a. top-down processing b. bottom-up processing c. divided attention d. reality testing

10. Both internal frames of reference and external _____ alter the interpretation given to a stimulus.
    a. reconstructions b. bottlenecks c. accommodations d. contexts

11. Which of the following cues would be of greatest help to a person trying to thread a needle?
    a. light and shadow b. texture gradients c. linear perspective d. overlap

12. The American woodcock has a narrow band of _____ but an unusually wide _____.
    a. monocular vision, spectral sensitivity b. accommodation, field of view c. binocular vision, field of view d. spectral sensitivity, binocular range

13. Which of the following purported paranormal phenomena is not a form of ESP?
    a. clairvoyance b. telepathy c. precognition d. psychokinesis

14. Size-distance invariances contribute to which of the following?
    a. Müller-Lyer illusion b. the stroboscopic illusion c. perceptual hallucinations
    d. changes in a person's adaptation level

15. The visual cliff is used primarily to test infant
    a. size constancy b. figure-ground perception c. depth perception
    d. adaptation to spatial distortions

16. Which of the following organizational principles is based on nearness in time and space?
    a. continuity b. closure c. contiguity d. size constancy

17. Which of the following is both a muscular and a monocular depth cue?
    a. convergence b. relative motion c. aerial perspective d. accommodation

18. The problem with "natural" ESP occurrences is that it is usually impossible to rule out
    a. the fact that they are replicated b. the possibility that they are caused by habituation
    c. the ganzfeld effect d. coincidences

19. Which of the following is not part of the explanation of the Müller-Lyer illusion?
    a. aerial perspective b. accommodation c. living in a "square" culture d. mislocating the ends of the lines

20. The term _____ refers to our limited capacity for storing and thinking about information.
    a. selective attention b. habituated attention c. divided attention d. selective expectancy

21. A previously blind person has just had her sight restored. Which of the following perceptual experiences is she most likely to have?
    a. perceptual set b. size constancy c. linear perspective d. figure-ground

22. An artist manages to portray a face with just a few unconnected lines. Apparently the artist has capitalized on
    a. closure b. contiguity c. the reversible figure effect d. the principle of camouflage

23. The "boiled frog syndrome" is related to the idea that _____ elicit attention.
    a. repetition, habituation, and categories b. expectancies, constancies, and ambiguities
    c. change, contrast, and incongruity d. continuity, camouflage, and similarity

24. The most basic source of stereoscopic vision is
    a. accommodation b. retinal disparity c. convergence d. stroboscopic motion

25. Necker's cube is a good example of
    a. an ambiguous stimulus b. an impossible figure c. camouflage d. a binocular depth cue

26. Enlarged pupils, a pause in breathing, and increased blood flow to the head are associated with
    a. brightness constancy b. the onset of habituation c. reality testing d. an orientation response

27. Skeptics regard the decline effect as evidence that _____ occurred in an ESP test.
    a. replication b. cheating c. a run of luck d. leakage

28. Which of the following is a binocular depth cue?
    a. accommodation b. convergence c. linear perspective d. motion parallax

29. Ambiguous stimuli allow us to hold more than one perceptual
    a. gradient b. parallax c. constancy d. hypothesis

30. Increased perceptual awareness is especially associated with
    a. dishabituation b. unconscious transference c. high levels of stress d. stimulus repetition without variation

31. Effective, natural design provides
    a. clear feedback b. behavioral settings c. participative displays d. lifelike models

ANSWERS

Recite and Review

1. patterns, model
2. image, perceptual
3. constancy, constant
4. inborn, learned
5. object, background
6. organization, similarity, common
7. grouped, appearance
8. complete, time
9. Engineering, engineers
10. displays, sensory
11. human factors
12. surfaces
13. hypothesis, organization
14. stimuli, cube
15. Depth

16. birth, crawlers
17. lens, eyes
18. smaller, wide
19. cues, flat
20. parallel lines, smaller, picture
21. finer, motion, motion
22. one eye
23. larger
24. distance, horizon
25. habits, size
26. features, movement
27. context, level, medium
28. illusions
29. habits, buildings
30. size-distance, lines
31. Selective
32 bottleneck
33. capacity
34. intense, change
35. change, decreases
36. values
37. top-down
38. features, organize
39. expectancies
40. active, inaccurate
41. focus, lower
42. testing, attention
43. broaden
44. psi, telepathy
45. perception
46. Coincidence
47. luck
48. against, repeated
49. deception

Connections

1. m
2. g
3. f
4. c
5. l
6. e
7. j
8. d
9. k
10. h

11. i
12. a
13. b
14. g
15. f
16. a
17. b
18. c
19. d
20. h
21. i
22. e
23. d
24. a
25. i
26. b
27. f
28. c
29. g
30. h

Check Your Memory

1. T
2. T
3. T
4. F
5. F
6. T
7. F
8. T
9. F
10. T
11. F
12. T
13. F
14. F
15. T
16. T
17. F
18. T
19. F
20. F
21. T
22. F
23. T
24. F
25. T

26. F
27. F
28. T
29. F
30. F
31. F
32. T
33. T
34. F
35. F
36. F
37. F
38. T
39. T
40. F
41. F
42. T
43. T
44. F
45. T
46. T
47. T
48. T
49. F
50. T
51. T
52. F
53. T
54. T
55. F
56. T
57. F
58. F
59. F
60. F
61. F
62. F
63. T
64. T
65. F
66. F
67. F
68. T

Final Survey and Review

1. sensations, mental model
2. retinal, constancies

3. brightness, proportion, light
4. native, empirical
5. figure, ground
6. Gestalt, nearness, closure
7. Closure
8. Contiguity,
9. human factors
10. controls, motor
11. natural design
12. parallel edges
13. Camouflage
14. ambiguous, Necker's, figures
15. three-dimensional
16. visual cliff, visual cliff
17. accommodation, convergence
18. binocular, field of view
19. pictorial
20. linear perspective, interposition
21. gradients, parallax
22. monocular
23. horizon
24. apparent distance, depth cues
25. perceptual habits, Ames
26. inverted, adaptation
27. frame of reference, adaptation
28. illusions, hallucinations
29. Müller-Lyer
30. invariance, end-points
31. Selective attention
32. channel
33. Divided
34. contrast, incongruity
35. orientation response, habituation
36. motives
37. processing
38. Bottom-up, top-down
39. perceptual sets, perceptual set
40. reconstruction
41. weapon, stress
42. dishabituation
43. perceptual habits
44. Parapsychology, precognition
45. extrasensory
46. reinterpretation
47. statistically
48. replicated
49. Stage

Mastery Test

1. d (229)
2. a (240)
3. c (222)
4. b (214)
5. b (227)
6. b (235)
7. b (214)
8. b (230)
9. a (237)
10. d (230-231)
11. d (220)
12. c (222)
13. d (243)
14. a (232)
15. c (219)
16. c (216)
17. d (220)
18. d (243)
19. a (232-233)
20. c (234)
21. d (215)
22. a (215)
23. c (235)
24. b (221)
25. a (218)
26. d (236)
27. c (244)
28. b (220)
29. d (218)
30. a (242)
31. a (217)

Chapter 7
States of Consciousness

CHAPTER OVERVIEW

Consciousness consists of everything you are aware of at a given instant. Altered states of consciousness (ASCs) differ significantly from normal waking consciousness. Many conditions produce ASCs, which frequently have culturally defined meanings.

Sleep is an innate biological rhythm characterized by changes in consciousness and brain activity. Brain-wave patterns and sleep behaviors define four stages of sleep. The two most basic forms of sleep are rapid eye movement (REM) sleep and non-rapid eye movement (NREM) sleep. Dreams and nightmares occur primarily in REM sleep. Sleepwalking, sleeptalking, and night terrors are NREM events. Insomnia and other sleep disturbances are common, but generally treatable. Dreaming is emotionally restorative and it may help form adaptive memories. The psychodynamic view portrays dreams as a form of wish fulfillment; the activation-synthesis hypothesis says that dreaming is a physiological process with little meaning.

Hypnosis is characterized by narrowed attention and increased openness to suggestion. People vary in hypnotic susceptibility. Most hypnotic phenomena are related to the basic suggestion effect. Hypnosis can relieve pain and it has other useful effects, but it is not magic. Stage hypnotists simulate hypnosis in order to entertain.

Sensory deprivation refers to any major reduction in external stimulation. Sensory deprivation also produces deep relaxation and a variety of perceptual effects. It can be used to help people enhance creative thinking and to change bad habits.

Psychoactive drugs are substances that alter consciousness. Most can be placed on a scale ranging from stimulation to depression, although some drugs are better classified as hallucinogens. The potential for abuse is high for drugs that lead to physical dependence, but psychological dependence can also be a serious problem. Drug abuse is often a symptom, rather than a cause, of personal maladjustment. It is supported by the immediate pleasure but delayed consequences associated with many psychoactive drugs, and by cultural values that encourage drug abuse.

Various strategies, ranging from literal to highly symbolic, can be used to reveal the meanings of dreams. Dreaming—especially lucid dreaming—can be a source of creativity and it may be used for problem solving and personal growth.

LEARNING OBJECTIVES

To demonstrate mastery of this chapter, you should be able to:

1. Define *consciousness* and *waking consciousness*.
2. Define *altered state of consciousness*, and list several causes of an ASC.
3. Explain how Webb defines sleep.
4. Define the term *microsleep*.
5. Describe the effects of two or three days of sleep deprivation.
6. Describe the symptoms of sleep-deprivation psychosis.
7. Discuss the concept of sleep patterns. Describe the characteristics of long and short sleepers.
8. Explain the relationship between age and sleep needs.
9. Discuss the brain's involvement in controlling sleep.
10. Explain the four stages of sleep, briefly describing the events in each stage.
11. Differentiate between the two basic states of sleep, REM and NREM.
12. Explain the relationship between REM sleep and dreaming, and tell how many times per night most people dream and how long dreams usually last.
13. Describe the effects of REM behavior disorder.
14. Define *insomnia*. Describe the effects of nonprescription and prescription drugs on insomnia.
15. List and describe the characteristics and treatments of the three types of insomnia.
16. Describe six behavioral interventions for insomnia.
17. Describe and differentiate between sleepwalking and sleeptalking and nightmares *vs.* night terrors. State three steps that can be used to eliminate nightmares.
18. Describe narcolepsy and cataplexy.
19. Describe the sleep disorder known as sleep apnea, including its nature, cause, treatments, and relationship to SIDS. Describe some possible causes of SIDS and the sleep position that seems to minimize SIDS in infants.
20. Discuss the cause and symptoms of REM rebound and possible functions of REM sleep, including its relationship to memory.
21. Explain how Freud viewed dreams and present the evidence against his view.
22. Describe the activation-synthesis hypothesis of dreaming.
23. Define *hypnosis*. Describe the history of hypnosis from Mesmer through its use today.
24. Explain how a person's hypnotic susceptibility can be determined.
25. List four factors common to all hypnotic techniques.
26. Explain how hypnosis may affect a person's willingness to act in a way that he or she would not normally act.
27. Explain what the basic suggestion effect is.
28. Describe the dissociation in awareness caused by hypnosis. Include the concept of the hidden observer.
29. Explain six conclusions concerning what can and cannot be achieved with hypnosis. Describe five features of the stage that are used by stage hypnotists to perform their acts.
30. Explain what sensory deprivation is and describe its positive and negative effects.
31. Define the term *psychoactive drug*.
32. Differentiate physical dependence from psychological dependence.
33. Describe five different patterns of drug use.

34. Describe the following frequently abused drugs in terms of their effects, possible medical uses, side effects or long term symptoms, organic damage potential, and potential for physical and/or psychological dependence.
    a. amphetamines (include the term amphetamine psychosis)
    b. cocaine (include the three signs of abuse)
    c. MDMA ("Ecstasy")
    d. caffeine (include the term *caffeinism*)
    e. nicotine
    f. barbiturates
    g. GHB
    h. tranquilizers (including the concept of drug interaction)
    i. alcohol (include the concept of binge drinking)
    j. hallucinogens (including marijuana)
35. Explain the three phases in the development of a drinking problem. Describe moderated drinking.
36. Describe the usual treatment process for alcoholism. Name the form of therapy that has probably been the most successful.

The following objectives are related to the material in the "Psychology in Action" and "A Step Beyond" sections of your text.

37. Describe the four dream processes identified by Freud that disguise the hidden meaning of dreams.
38. Describe the dream theories of Freud, Hall, and Cartwright.
39. Outline procedures for using dreams to improve creativity.
40. Define *lucid dreams* and describe methods for increasing their frequency.
41. List the predictors of adolescent drug abuse.
42. Discuss social and psychological factors involved in drug abuse.
43. Describe both traditional and contemporary approaches to the prevention of drug abuse.

RECITE AND REVIEW

● *What is an altered state of consciousness?*

Recite and Review: Page 250-252

1. States of _____ that differ from normal, alert, _____ consciousness are called altered states of consciousness (ASCs).
2. ASCs involve distinct shifts in the quality and _____ of mental activity.
3. Altered states are especially associated with _____ and _____, hypnosis, meditation, _____ deprivation, and psychoactive drugs.
4. Cultural conditioning greatly affects what altered states a person recognizes, seeks, considers _____, and attains.

● *What are the effects of sleep loss or changes in sleep patterns?*

Recite and Review: Pages 252-255

5. Sleep is an innate biological _____ essential for _____.
6. Higher animals and people deprived of sleep experience _____ microsleeps.
7. Moderate sleep loss mainly affects alertness and self-motivated performance on _____ or boring tasks.
8. Extended sleep _____ can (somewhat rarely) produce a _____ sleep-deprivation psychosis, marked by confusion, delusions, and possibly hallucinations.
9. Sleep patterns show some flexibility, but 7 to 8 hours remains average. The unscheduled human sleep-waking cycle averages _____ hours and _____ minutes, but cycles of _____ and _____ tailor it to 24-hour days.
10. The amount of daily sleep _____ steadily from birth to old age and switches from multiple sleep-wake cycles to once-a-day sleep periods.
11. Adapting to _____ or _____ sleep cycles is difficult and inefficient for most people.

● *Are there different stages of sleep?*

Recite and Review: Pages 255-256

12. Sleepiness is associated with the accumulation of a sleep hormone in the _____ and spinal cord.
13. Sleep depends on which of _____ opposed sleep and waking systems in the _____ is dominant at any given moment.
14. Sleep occurs in _____ stages defined by changes in behavior and brain _____ recorded with an electroencephalograph (EEG).
15. Stage 1, _____ sleep, has small irregular brain waves. In stage 2, _____ spindles appear. _____ waves appear in stage 3. Stage 4, or deep sleep, is marked by almost pure delta waves.
16. Sleepers _____ between stages 1 and 4 (passing through stages 2 and 3) several times each night.

● *How does dream sleep differ from dreamless sleep?*

Recite and Review: Pages 256-258

17. There are two basic sleep states, rapid eye _____ (REM) sleep and non-REM (NREM) sleep.
18. REM sleep is much more strongly associated with _____ than non-REM sleep is.
19. _____ and REMs occur mainly during stage 1 sleep, but usually not during the first stage 1 period.
20. Dreaming is accompanied by sexual and _____ arousal but relaxation of the skeletal _____. People who move about violently while asleep may suffer from _____ behavior disorder.
21. People deprived of REM sleep showed an urgent need to _____ and mental disturbances the next day. However, total sleep loss seems to be more important than loss of a single sleep _____.

22. One of the more important functions of REM sleep appears to be the processing of adaptive _____.

● *What are the causes of sleep disorders and unusual sleep events?*

Recite and Review: Pages 258-261

23. Insomnia, which is difficulty in getting to sleep or staying asleep, may be _____ or chronic.

24. When insomnia is treated with drugs, sleep quality is often _____ and drug-dependency _____ may develop.

25. The amino acid tryptophan, found in bread, pasta, and other foods, helps promote _____.

26. Behavioral approaches to managing insomnia, such as relaxation, sleep restriction, _____ control, and paradoxical _____ are quite effective.

27. _____ (somnambulism) and sleeptalking occur during NREM sleep in stages 3 and 4.

28. Night terrors occur in _____ sleep, whereas nightmares occur in _____ sleep.

29. Nightmares can be eliminated by the method called imagery _____.

30. During sleep apnea, people repeatedly stop _____. Apnea is suspected as one cause of _____ infant death syndrome (SIDS).

● *Do dreams have meaning?*

Recite and Review: Pages 261-263

31. Calvin Hall found that most dream content is about _____ settings, people, and actions. Dreams more often involve negative _____ than positive _____.

32. The Freudian, or psychodynamic, view is that dreams express unconscious _____, frequently hidden by dream symbols.

33. Allan Hobson and Robert McCarley's _____-synthesis model portrays dreaming as a physiological process. The brain, they say, creates dreams to explain _____ and motor messages that occur during REM sleep.

● *How is hypnosis done, and what are its limitations?*

Recite and Review: Pages 263-266

34. Hypnosis is an altered state characterized by narrowed attention and _____ suggestibility.

35. In the 1700s, Franz Mesmer (whose name is the basis for the term mesmerize) practiced "_____ magnetism," which was actually a demonstration of the power of _____.

36. The term _____ was first used by James Braid, an English doctor.

37. People vary in hypnotic susceptibility; _____ out of 10 can be hypnotized, as revealed by scores on the Stanford Hypnotic Susceptibility _____.

38. The core of hypnosis is the _____ suggestion effect—a tendency to carry out suggested actions as if they were involuntary.

39. Hypnosis appears capable of producing relaxation, controlling _____, and altering perceptions.

40. Stage hypnotism takes advantage of typical stage behavior, _____ suggestibility, responsive subjects, disinhibition, and _____ to simulate hypnosis.

● *How does sensory deprivation affect consciousness?*

Recite and Review: Pages 266-267

41. Sensory deprivation takes place when there is a major reduction in the amount or variety of sensory _____ available to a person.

42. Prolonged sensory deprivation is stressful and disruptive, leading to _____ distortions.

43. Brief or mild sensory deprivation can enhance sensory sensitivity and induce deep

_____ .

44. Sensory deprivation also appears to aid the breaking of long-standing _____ and promotes creative thinking. This effect is the basis for Restricted Environmental Stimulation Therapy (REST).

● *What are the effects of the more commonly used psychoactive drugs?*

Recite and Review: Pages 267-282

45. A psychoactive drug is a substance that affects the brain in ways that _____ consciousness.

46. Most psychoactive drugs can be placed on a scale ranging from stimulation to

_____ . Some, however, are best described as hallucinogens (drugs that alter

_____ impressions).

47. Drugs may cause a physical dependence (_____) or a psychological dependence, or both.

48. Drug use can be classified as experimental, recreational, situational, intensive, and

_____ . Drug abuse is most often associated with the last three.

49. The physically addicting drugs are alcohol, amphetamines, barbiturates, cocaine, codeine, GHB, heroin, methadone, morphine, tobacco, and tranquilizers. All psychoactive drugs can lead to

_____ dependence.

50. Stimulant drugs are readily abused because of the period of _____ that often follows stimulation. The greatest risks are associated with amphetamines, cocaine, MDMA, and nicotine, but even _____ can be a problem.

51. MDMA or "_____," which is similar to amphetamine, has been linked with numerous deaths and with mental impairment.

52. _____ includes the added risk of lung cancer, heart disease, and other health problems.

53. Barbiturates are _____ drugs whose overdose level is close to the intoxication dosage, making them dangerous drugs. Mixing barbiturates and alcohol may result in a fatal _____

interaction (in which the joint effect of two drugs exceeds the effects of adding one drug's effects to the other's).

54. The depressant drug _____ (gamma-hydroxybuyrate) can cause coma, breathing failure, and death in relatively low doses.

55. Benzodiazepine tranquilizers, such as _____, are used to lower anxiety. When abused, they have a strong _____ potential.

56. Alcohol is the most heavily abused drug in common use today. The development of a drinking problem is usually marked by an _____ phase of increasing consumption, a crucial phase, in which a _____ drink can set off a chain reaction, and a chronic phase, in which a person lives to drink and drinks to live.

57. Marijuana is a hallucinogen subject to an _____ pattern similar to alcohol. Studies have linked chronic marijuana use with memory impairment, lung cancer, reproductive problems, immune system disorders, and other health problems.

● *How are dreams used to promote personal understanding?*

Recite and Review: PSYCHOLOGY IN ACTION

58. Freud held that the meaning of dreams is _____ by four dream _____ he called condensation, displacement, symbolization, and secondary elaboration.

59. Calvin Hall emphasizes the setting, cast, _____, and emotions of a dream.

60. Rosalind Cartwright's view of dreams as feeling statements and Fritz Perls's technique of _____ for dream elements are also helpful.

61. Dreams may be used for _____ problem solving, especially when dream control is achieved through lucid dreaming (a dream in which the dreamer feels capable of normal thought and action).

● *Why is drug abuse so widespread?*

Recite and Review: A STEP BEYOND

62. Drug abuse is related to personal and social maladjustment, attempts to cope, and the _____ reinforcing qualities of psychoactive drugs.

63. Peer group influences, false expectations about the effects of drugs, and cultural _____ also encourage drug abuse.

64. Proposed remedies for drug abuse range from severe punishment to _____. The search for a solution continues.

CONNECTIONS

1. _____	REST	a. over 9 hours
2. _____	Randy Gardner	b. infancy
3. _____	long sleepers	c. reflex muscle contraction
4. _____	sleep patterns	d. awake, alert
5. _____	short sleep cycles	e. sensory deprivation
6. _____	beta waves	f. interrupted breathing
7. _____	alpha waves	g. relaxed
8. _____	hypnic jerk	h. sleep deprivation
9. _____	apnea	i. sexual arousal
10. _____	REM sleep	j. 2 to 1 ratio

11. _____	sleep drunkenness	a. violent actions
12. _____	hypersomnia	b. fatal to infants
13. _____	REM behavior disorder	c. unconscious meanings
14. _____	narcolepsy	d. slow awakening
15. _____	SIDS	e. dangerous stimulant
16. _____	tryptophan	f. sudden daytime REM sleep
17. _____	dream symbols	g. sensory deprivation
18. _____	autosuggestion	h. self-hypnosis
19. _____	MDMA	i. sleep inducing foods
20. _____	flotation tank	j. excessive sleepiness

21. _____	drug tolerance	a. cocaine rush
22. _____	amphetamine	b. cancer agent
23. _____	dopamine	c. addiction
24. _____	nicotine	d. sedative
25. _____	carcinogen	e. hallucinogen
26. _____	barbiturate	f. detoxification
27. _____	AAA	g. loss of pleasure
28. _____	alcohol treatment	h. stimulant
29. _____	THC	i. self-help group
30. _____	anhedonia	j. insecticide

CHECK YOUR MEMORY

Check Your Memory: Page 250-252

1. The quality and pattern of mental activity changes during an ASC. T or F?
2. All people experience at least some ASCs. T or F?
3. Both sensory overload and monotonous stimulation can produce ASCs. T or F?
4. Almost every known religion has accepted some ASCs as desirable. T or F?

Check Your Memory: Pages 252-255

5. Through sleep learning it is possible to master a foreign language. T or F?
6. A total inability to sleep results in death. T or F?
7. Even after extended sleep loss, most symptoms are removed by a single night's sleep. T or F?
8. Hallucinations and delusions are the most common reaction to extended sleep deprivation. T or F?
9. Without scheduled light and dark periods, human sleep rhythms would drift into unusual patterns. T or F?
10. The average human sleep-wake cycle lasts 23 hours and 10 minutes. T or F?
11. Short sleepers are defined as those who average less than 5 hours of sleep per night. T or F?
12. Shortened sleep cycles, such as 3 hours of sleep to 6 hours awake, are more efficient that sleeping once a day. T or F?

Check Your Memory: Pages 255-256

13. Sleep is promoted by a chemical that accumulates in the bloodstream. T or F?
14. Body temperature drops as a person falls asleep. T or F?
15. A hypnic jerk is a sign of serious problems. T or F?
16. Delta waves typically first appear in stage 2 sleep. T or F?

Check Your Memory: Pages 256-258

17. About 45 percent of awakenings during REM periods produce reports of dreams. T or F?
18. REM sleep occurs mainly in stages 3 and 4. T or F?
19. REM sleep increases when a person is subjected to daytime stress. T or F?
20. The average dream only lasts 3 to 4 minutes. T or F?
21. Most people change positions in bed during REM sleep. T or F?
22. REM behavior disorder causes people to briefly fall asleep and become paralyzed during the day. T or F?

Check Your Memory: Pages 258-261

23. Bread, pasta, pretzels, cookies, and cereals all contain melatonin. T or F?
24. Caffeine, alcohol, and tobacco can all contribute to insomnia. T or F?
25. The two most effective behavioral treatments for insomnia are sleep restriction and stimulus control. T or F?
26. Sleepwalking occurs during NREM periods, sleeptalking during REM periods. T or F?
27. People who have NREM night terrors usually can remember very little afterward. T or F?

28. Imagery rehearsal is an effective way to treat recurrent nightmares. T or F?
29. REM sleep appears to help the brain process memories formed during the day. T or F?
30. People who take barbiturate sleeping pills may develop drug-dependency insomnia. T or F?
31. Newborn babies spend 8 or 9 hours a day in REM sleep. T or F?

Check Your Memory: Pages 261-263

32. The favorite dream setting is outdoors. T or F?
33. Pleasant emotions are more common in dreams than unpleasant emotions. T or F?
34. According to Freud, dreams represent thoughts and wishes expressed as images. T or F?
35. The activation-synthesis hypothesis emphasizes the unconscious meanings of dream symbols. T or F?

Check Your Memory: Pages 263-266

36. The Greek word hypnos means "magnetism." T or F?
37. Only about 4 people out of 10 can be hypnotized. T or F?
38. The "finger-lock" is an example of animal magnetism. T or F?
39. Physical strength cannot be increased with hypnosis. T or F?
40. Hypnosis is better at changing subjective experiences than behaviors. T or F?
41. Stage hypnotists look for responsive volunteers who will cooperate and not spoil the show. T or F?

Check Your Memory: Pages 266-267

42. Sensory deprivation is almost always unpleasant, and it usually causes distorted perceptions. T or F?
43. Sensory sensitivity temporarily increases after a period of sensory deprivation. T or F?
44. Prolonged sensory deprivation produces deep relaxation. T or F?
45. REST is a form of brainwashing used during the Vietnam war. T or F?

Check Your Memory: Pages 267-282

46. Abuse of any psychoactive drug can produce physical dependence. T or F?
47. Amphetamines are used to treat narcolepsy and hyperactivity. T or F?
48. Amphetamine is more rapidly metabolized by the body than cocaine is. T or F?
49. MDMA is chemically similar to amphetamine. T or F?
50. Disregarding consequences is a sign of cocaine abuse. T or F?
51. Caffeine can increase the risk of miscarriage during pregnancy. T or F?
52. Twenty-five cigarettes could be fatal for a nonsmoker. T or F?
53. Regular use of nicotine leads to drug tolerance, and often to physical addiction. T or F?
54. Every cigarette reduces a smoker's life expectancy by 7 minutes. T or F?
55. In order to stop smoking, tapering off is generally more successful than quitting abruptly. T or F?
56. One of the most effective ways to stop smoking is to schedule the number of cigarettes smoked each day. T or F?
57. There have been no known deaths caused by barbiturate overdoses. T or F?
58. It is legal and safe to drive as long as blood alcohol level does not exceed .8. T or F?
59. Drinking alone is a serious sign of alcohol abuse. T or F?
60. To pace alcohol intake, you should limit drinking primarily to the first hour of a social event or party. T or F?

61. Over 80 percent of fraternity and sorority members in the U.S. have engaged in binge drinking. T or F?
62. Hallucinogens generally affect brain transmitter systems. T or F?
63. THC receptors are found in large numbers in the cerebellum of the brain. T or F?
64. Drug abuse is frequently part of general pattern of personal maladjustment. T or F?
65. The negative consequences of drug use typically follow long after the drug has been taken. T or F?

Check Your Memory: PSYCHOLOGY IN ACTION

66. Displacement refers to representing two or more people with a single dream image. T or F?
67. Secondary elaboration is the tendency to make a dream more logical when remembering it. T or F?
68. According to Calvin Hall, the overall emotional tone of a dream is the key to its meaning. T or F?
69. Alcohol decreases REM sleep. T or F?
70. It is basically impossible to solve daytime problems in dreams. T or F?
71. Lucid dreams either occur or they don't; there is no way to increase their frequency. T or F?

Check Your Memory: A STEP BEYOND

72. Drug abuse is frequently a symptom, rather than a cause, of personal maladjustment. T or F?
73. Heavy drinkers expect positive effects from drinking, but realize that severe negative consequences will follow. T or F?
74. Abuse of legally prescribed drugs is widespread. T or F?
75. Thomas Szasz believes that, where drug abuse is concerned, we should "legislate morality." T or F?

FINAL SURVEY AND REVIEW

● *What is an altered state of consciousness?*

1. States of awareness that differ from normal, alert, waking _____ are called altered states of _____ (ASCs).
2. ASCs involve distinct shifts in the quality and pattern of _____ _____.

3. Altered states are especially associated with sleep and dreaming, _____, meditation, sensory _____, and psychoactive drugs.
4. _____ conditioning greatly affects what altered states a person recognizes, seeks, considers normal, and attains.

● *What are the effects of sleep loss or changes in sleep patterns?*

5. Sleep is an _____ _____ rhythm essential for survival.
6. Higher animals and people deprived of sleep experience involuntary _____ (a brief shift to sleep patterns in the brain).
7. Moderate sleep loss mainly affects _____ and self-motivated performance on routine or boring tasks.

8. Extended sleep loss can (somewhat rarely) produce a temporary sleep-deprivation _____, marked by confusion, _____, and possibly hallucinations.

9. Sleep patterns show some flexibility, but 7 to 8 hours remains average. The unscheduled human _____ _____ averages 24 hours and 10 minutes, but cycles of light and dark tailor it to 24-hour days.

10. The amount of daily sleep decreases steadily from birth to _____ _____ and switches from _____ sleep-wake cycles to once-a-day sleep periods.

11. Adapting to shorter or longer _____ _____ is difficult and inefficient for most people.

● *Are there different stages of sleep?*

12. Sleepiness is associated with the accumulation of a sleep _____ in the brain and _____ _____.

13. Sleep depends on which of two _____ sleep and waking _____ in the brain is dominant at any given moment.

14. Sleep occurs in 4 stages defined by changes in behavior and brain waves recorded with an _____ (EEG).

15. Stage 1, light sleep, has small irregular brain waves. In stage 2, sleep _____ appear. Delta waves appear in stage 3. Stage 4, or deep sleep, is marked by almost pure _____ _____.

16. Sleepers alternate between stages _____ and _____ (passing through stages _____ and _____) several times each night.

● *How does dream sleep differ from dreamless sleep?*

17. There are two basic sleep states, _____ _____ movement (REM) sleep and non-REM (NREM) sleep.

18. _____ sleep is much more strongly associated with dreaming than _____ sleep is.

19. Dreams and REMs occur mainly during _____ _____ sleep, but usually not during the first _____ _____ period.

20. Dreaming is accompanied by sexual and emotional _____ but _____ of the skeletal muscles. People who move about violently while asleep may suffer from REM behavior _____.

21. People deprived of _____ sleep showed an urgent need to dream and _____ disturbances the next day. However, the _____ amount of sleep loss seems to be more important than loss of a single sleep stage.

22. One of the more important functions of _____ _____ appears to be the processing of adaptive memories.

● What are the causes of sleep disorders and unusual sleep events?

23. Insomnia, which is difficulty in getting to sleep or staying asleep, may be temporary or _____.

24. When insomnia is treated with drugs, sleep quality is often lowered and drug-_____ insomnia may develop.

25. The amino acid _____, found in bread, pasta, and other foods, helps promote sleep.

26. Behavioral approaches to managing insomnia, such as relaxation, sleep _____, stimulus control, and _____ intention are quite effective.

27. Sleepwalking (_____) and sleeptalking occur during _____ sleep in stages 3 and 4.

28. Night terrors occur in _____ sleep, whereas nightmares occur in _____ sleep.

29. Nightmares can be eliminated by the method called _____ _____.

30. During sleep _____, people repeatedly stop breathing. _____ is suspected as one cause of sudden _____ _____ syndrome.

● Do dreams have meaning?

31. Calvin _____ found that most dream content is about familiar settings, people, and actions. Dreams more often involve _____ emotions than _____ emotions.

32. The Freudian, or _____, view is that dreams express unconscious wishes, frequently hidden by dream _____.

33. Allan Hobson and Robert McCarley's activation-_____ model portrays dreaming as a physiological process. The brain, they say, creates dreams to explain sensory and _____ messages that occur during REM sleep.

● How is hypnosis done, and what are its limitations?

34. Hypnosis is an altered state characterized by narrowed attention and increased _____.

35. In the 1700s, Franz _____ (whose name is the basis for the term _____) practiced "animal magnetism," which was actually a demonstration of the power of suggestion.

36. The term hypnosis was first used by James _____, an English doctor.

37. People vary in hypnotic susceptibility; 8 out of 10 can be hypnotized, as revealed by scores on the _____ Hypnotic Susceptibility Scale.

38. The core of hypnosis is the basic _____ effect—a tendency to carry out suggested actions as if they were _____.

39. Hypnosis appears capable of producing _____, controlling pain, and altering perceptions.

40. _____ _____ takes advantage of typical stage behavior, waking suggestibility, responsive subjects, disinhibition, and deception to _____ hypnosis.

● *How does sensory deprivation affect consciousness?*

41. Sensory deprivation takes place when there is a major reduction in the amount or variety of _____ _____ available to a person.

42. _____ sensory deprivation is stressful and disruptive, leading to perceptual distortions.

43. Brief or mild sensory _____ can induce deep _____.

44. Sensory deprivation also appears to aid the breaking of long-standing habits and promotes creative thinking. This effect is the basis for _____ _____ Stimulation Therapy (REST).

● *What are the effects of the more commonly used psychoactive drugs?*

45. A psychoactive drug is a substance that affects the brain in ways that alter _____.

46. Most psychoactive drugs can be placed on a scale ranging from _____ to _____. Some, however, are best described as _____ (drugs that alter sensory impressions).

47. Drugs may cause a physical _____ (addiction) or a psychological _____, or both.

48. Drug use can be classified as experimental, _____, situational, intensive, and compulsive. Drug abuse is most often associated with the last three.

49. The _____ _____ drugs are alcohol, amphetamines, barbiturates, cocaine, codeine, GHB, heroin, methadone, morphine, tobacco, and tranquilizers. All psychoactive drugs can lead to psychological dependence.

50. Stimulant drugs are readily abused because of the period of depression that often follows stimulation. The greatest risks are associated with amphetamines, _____, MDMA, and nicotine, but even caffeine can be a problem.

51. MDMA or "Ecstasy," which is similar to _____, has been linked with numerous deaths and with _____ impairment.

52. Nicotine (smoking) includes the added risk of _____ _____, heart disease, and other health problems.

53. Barbiturates are depressant drugs whose overdose level is close to the intoxication dosage, making them dangerous drugs. Mixing barbiturates and _____ may result in a fatal drug _____ (in which the joint effect of two drugs exceeds the effects of adding one drug's effects to the other's).

54. The _____ drug GHB (_____) can cause coma, breathing failure, and death in relatively low doses.

55. _____ tranquilizers, such as Valium, are used to lower anxiety. When abused, they have a strong addictive potential.

56. _____ is the most heavily abused drug in common use today. The development of a drinking problem is usually marked by an initial phase of increasing consumption, a _____ phase, in which a single drink can set off a chain reaction, and a chronic phase, in which a person lives to drink and drinks to live.

57. Marijuana is a _____ subject to an abuse pattern similar to alcohol. Studies have linked chronic marijuana use with memory impairment, _____ cancer, reproductive problems, immune system disorders, and other health problems.

● *How are dreams used to promote personal understanding?*

58. Freud held that the meaning of dreams is hidden by the dream processes he called _____, displacement, symbolization, and _____ elaboration.

59. Calvin Hall emphasizes the _____, _____, plot, and emotions of a dream.

60. Rosalind Cartwright's view of dreams as _____ statements and Fritz _____ technique of speaking for dream elements are also helpful.

61. Dreams may be used for creative problem solving, especially when dream control is achieved through _____ dreaming (a dream in which the dreamer feels capable of normal thought and action).

● *Why is drug abuse so widespread?*

62. Drug abuse is related to personal and social _____, attempts to cope, and the immediate reinforcing qualities of psychoactive drugs.

63. Peer group influences, false _____ about the effects of drugs, and cultural values also encourage drug abuse.

64. Proposed remedies for drug abuse range from severe _____ to legalization. The search for a solution continues.

MASTERY TEST

1. Delirium, ecstasy, and daydreaming all have in common the fact that they are
   a. forms of normal waking consciousness   b. caused by sensory deprivation
   c. perceived as subjectively real   d. ASCs

2. The street drug GHB is
   a. chemically similar to morphine   b. a depressant   c. capable of raising body temperature to dangerous levels   d. a common cause of sleep-deprivation psychosis

3. Which of the following does not belong with the others?
   a. nicotine   b. caffeine   c. cocaine   d. codeine

4. Sleep spindles usually first appear in stage _____, whereas delta waves first appear in stage _____.
   a. 1, 2   b. 2, 3   c. 3, 4   d. 1, 4

5. Which of the following is NOT one of the dream processes described by Freud?
   a. condensation   b. illumination   c. displacement   d. symbolization

6. Which of the following most clearly occurs under hypnosis?
   a. unusual strength b. memory enhancement c. pain relief d. age regression

7. Alcohol, amphetamines, cocaine, and marijuana have in common the fact that they are all
   a. physically addicting b. psychoactive c. stimulants d. hallucinogens

8. Emotional arousal, blood pressure changes, and sexual arousal all primarily occur during
   a. REM sleep b. NREM sleep c. Delta sleep d. stage 4 sleep

9. The REST technique makes use of
   a. sensory deprivation b. hypodynamic imagery c. hallucinogens d. a CPAP mask

10. Mesmerism, hypnosis, hypnotic susceptibility scales, and stage hypnotism all rely in part on
    a. disinhibition b. rapid eye movements c. suggestibility d. imagery rehearsal

11. Shortened sleep-waking cycles overlook the fact that sleep
    a. must match a 3 to 1 ratio of time awake and time asleep b. is an innate biological rhythm
    c. is caused by a sleep-promoting substance in the blood d. cycles cannot be altered by external factors

12. Morning drinking appears during the _____ phase in the development of a drinking problem.
    a. initial b. crucial c. chronic d. rebound

13. Which of the following statements about sleep is true?
    a. Learning math or a foreign language can be accomplished during sleep. b. Some people can learn to do without sleep. c. Calvin Hall had hallucinations during a sleep deprivation experiment. d. Randy Gardner slept for 14 hours after ending his sleep deprivation.

14. Amphetamine is very similar in effects to
    a. narcotics and tranquilizers b. methaqualone c. codeine d. cocaine

15. Microsleeps would most likely occur
    a. in stage 4 sleep b. in a 3 to 1 ratio to microawakenings c. in conjunction with delusions and hallucinations d. during sleep deprivation

16. Adolescents who abuse drugs tend to be
    a. suffering from brain dysfunctions b. high in self-esteem but unrealistic about consequences
    c. maladjusted and impulsive d. similar in most respects to nonabusers

17. Sleepwalking, sleeptalking, and severe nightmares all have in common the fact that they
    a. are REM events b. are NREM events c. are sleep disorders d. can be controlled with imagery rehearsal

18. In its milder forms, sensory deprivation sometimes produces
    a. cataplectic images b. deep relaxation c. tryptophanic images d. REM symbolizations

19. The basic suggestion effect is closely related to
    a. hypnosis b. sensory enhancement after sensory deprivation c. hypersomnia d. the frequency of dreaming during REM sleep

20. A person who feels awake and capable of normal action while sleeping has experienced
   a. lucid dreaming   b. the basic suggestion effect   c. sleep drunkeness   d. REM rebound

21. Which of the following is a hallucinogen?
   a. LSD   b. THC   c. hashish   d. all of the preceding

22. The two most basic states of sleep are
   a. stage 1 sleep and stage 4 sleep   b. REM sleep and NREM sleep   c. Alpha sleep and Delta sleep
   d. Alpha sleep and hypnic sleep

23. Thinking and perception become dulled in the condition known as
   a. alcohol rebound   b. alcohol apnea   c. alcohol anhedonia   d. alcohol myopia

24. Learning to use a computer would most likely be slowed if you were _____ each night.
   a. deprived of a half hour of NREM sleep   b. allowed to engage in extra REM sleep
   c. prevented from dreaming   d. awakened three times at random

25. By definition, compulsive drug use involves
   a. dependence   b. experimentation   c. repeated overdoses   d. anhedonia

26. A particularly dangerous drug interaction occurs when _____ and _____ are combined.
   a. alcohol, amphetamine   b. barbiturates, nicotine   c. alcohol, barbiturates   d. amphetamine, codeine

27. Narcolepsy is an example of
   a. a night terror   b. a sleep disorder   c. a tranquilizer   d. an addictive drug

28. Sleep restriction and stimulus control techniques would most likely be used to treat
   a. insomnia   b. narcolepsy   c. sleepwalking   d. REM behavior disorder

29. In addition to the nicotine they contain, cigarettes release
   a. dopamine   b. tryptophan   c. noradrenaline   d. carcinogens

30. Disguised dream symbols are to psychodynamic dream theory as sensory and motor messages are to
   a. the Freudian theory of dreams   b. the activation-synthesis hypothesis   c. Fritz Perls' methods of
   dream interpretation   d. paradoxical intention

ANSWERS

Recite and Review

1. awareness, waking
2. pattern
3. sleep, dreaming, sensory
4. normal

5. rhythm, survival
6. involuntary
7. routine
8. loss, temporary
9. 24, 10, light, dark
10. decreases

11. shorter, longer
12. brain
13. two, brain
14. 4, waves
15. light, sleep, Delta
16. alternate

17. movement
18. dreaming
19. Dreaming
20. emotional, muscles, REM
21. dream, stage
22. memories
23. temporary
24. lowered, insomnia
25. sleep
26. stimulus, intention
27. Sleepwalking
28. NREM, REM
29. rehearsal
30. breathing, sudden
31. familiar, emotions, emotions
32. wishes
33. activation, sensory
34. increased
35. animal, suggestion
36. hypnosis
37. 8, Scale
38. basic
39. pain
40. waking, deception
41. stimulation
42. perceptual
43. relaxation
44. habits
45. alter (affect or change)
46. depression, sensory
47. addiction
48. compulsive
49. psychological
50. depression, caffeine
51. Ecstasy
52. Nicotine (or Smoking)
53. depressant, drug
54. GHB
55. Valium, addictive
56. initial, single
57. abuse
58. hidden, processes
59. plot
60. speaking
61. creative
62. immediate
63. values
64. legalization

Connections

1. e
2. h
3. a
4. j
5. b
6. d
7. g
8. c
9. f
10. i
11. d
12. j
13. a
14. f
15. b
16. i
17. c
18. h
19. e
20. g
21. c
22. h
23. a
24. j
25. b
26. d
27. i
28. f
29. e
30. g

Check Your Memory

1. T
2. T
3. T
4. T
5. F
6. T
7. T
8. F
9. T
10. F
11. T
12. F
13. F
14. T

15. F
16. F
17. F
18. F
19. T
20. F
21. F
22. F
23. F
24. T
25. T
26. F
27. T
28. T
29. T
30. T
31. T
32. F
33. F
34. T
35. F
36. F
37. F
38. F
39. T
40. T
41. T
42. F
43. T
44. F
45. F
46. F
47. T
48. F
49. T
50. T
51. T
52. T
53. T
54. T
55. T
56. T
57. F
58. F
59. T
60. T
61. T
62. T
63. F
64. T

65. T
66. F
67. T
68. F
69. T
70. F
71. F
72. T
73. F
74. T
75. F

Final Survey and Review

1. consciousness, consciousness
2. mental activity
3. hypnosis, deprivation
4. Cultural
5. innate biological
6. microsleeps
7. alertness
8. psychosis, delusions
9. sleep-waking cycle
10. old age, multiple
11. sleep cycles
12. hormone, spinal cord
13. opposed, systems
14. electroencephalograph
15. spindles, delta waves
16. 1, 4, 2, 3
17. rapid eye
18. REM, non-REM
19. stage 1, stage 1
20. arousal, relaxation, disorder
21. chronic
22. dependency
23. tryptophan

24. restriction, paradoxical
25. somnambulism, NREM
26. NREM, REM
27. imagery rehearsal
28. apnea, Apnea, infant death
29. REM, mental, total
30. REM sleep
31. Hall, negative, positive
32. psychodynamic, symbols
33. synthesis, motor
34. suggestibility
35. Mesmer, mesmerize
36. Braid
37. Stanford
38. suggestion, involuntary
39. relaxation
40. Stage hypnotism, simulate
41. sensory stimulation
42. Prolonged
43. deprivation, relaxation
44. Restricted Environmental
45. consciousness
46. stimulation, depression, hallucinogens
47. dependence, dependence
48. recreational
49. physically addicting
50. cocaine
51. amphetamine, mental
52. lung cancer
53. alcohol, interaction
54. depressant, gamma-hydroxybuyrate
55. Benzodiazepine
56. Alcohol, crucial
57. hallucinogen, lung
58. condensation, secondary
59. setting, cast
60. feeling, Perls's
61. lucid

62. maladjustment
63. expectations
64. punishment

Mastery Test

1. d (p. 2518)
2. b (p. 276)
3. d (p. 271-274)
4. b (p. 256)
5. b (p. 283-284)
6. c (p. 265)
7. b (p. 268)
8. a (p. 257)
9. a (p. 267)
10. c (p. 265)
11. b (p. 252)
12. a (p. 279)
13. d (p. 253)
14. d (p. 271)
15. d (p. 253)
16. c (p. 287)
17. c (p. 259)
18. b (p. 267)
19. a (p. 265)
20. a (p. 285)
21. d (p. 280)
22. b (p. 257)
23. d (p. 277)
24. c (p. 257)
25. a (p. 269)
26. c (p. 277)
27. b (p. 259, 260)
28. a (p. 260)
29. d (p. 274)
30. b (p. 262-263)

Chapter 8
Conditioning and Learning

CHAPTER OVERVIEW

Learning is a relatively permanent change in behavior due to experience. Two basic forms of learning are classical conditioning and operant conditioning.

Classical conditioning is also called respondent or Pavlovian conditioning. Classical conditioning occurs when a neutral stimulus is associated with an unconditioned stimulus (which reliably elicits an unconditioned response). After many pairings of the NS and the US, the NS becomes a conditioned stimulus that elicits a conditioned response. Learning is reinforced during acquisition of a response. Withdrawing reinforcement leads to extinction (although some spontaneous recovery of conditioning may occur). It is apparent that stimulus generalization has occurred when a stimulus similar to the CS also elicits a learned response. In stimulus discrimination, people or animals learn to respond differently to two similar stimuli. Conditioning often involves simple reflex responses, but emotional conditioning is also possible.

In operant conditioning (or instrumental learning), the consequences that follow a response alter the probability that it will be made again. Positive and negative reinforcers increase responding; punishment suppresses responding; nonreinforcement leads to extinction. Various types of reinforcers and different patterns of giving reinforcers greatly affect operant learning. Informational feedback (knowledge of results) also facilitates learning and performance. Antecedent stimuli (those that precede a response) influence operant learning, through stimulus generalization, discrimination, and stimulus control.

Learning, even simple conditioning, is based on acquiring information. Higher level cognitive learning involves memory, thinking, problem solving, and language. At a simpler level, cognitive maps, latent learning, and discovery learning show that learning is based on acquiring information. Learning also occurs through observation and imitating models. Observational learning imparts large amounts of information that would be hard to acquire in other ways.

Operant principles can be applied to manage one's own behavior and to break bad habits. A mixture of operant principles and cognitive learning underlies self-regulated learning—a collection of techniques to improve learning in school.

Learning in animals is limited at times by various biological constraints and species-typical behaviors.

LEARNING OBJECTIVES

To demonstrate mastery of this chapter, you should be able to:

1. Define *learning*.
2. Define *reinforcement* and explain its role in conditioning.
3. Differentiate between antecedents and consequences and explain how they are related to classical and operant conditioning.
4. Give a brief history of classical conditioning.
5. Describe the following terms as they apply to classical conditioning:
   - a. neutral stimulus (NS)
   - b. conditioned stimulus (CS)
   - c. unconditioned stimulus (US)
   - d. unconditioned response (UR)
   - e. conditioned response (CR)
6. Describe and give an example of classical conditioning using the abbreviations US, UR, CS, and CR.
7. Explain how reinforcement occurs during the acquisition of a classically conditioned response. Explain higher order conditioning.
8. Explain classical conditioning in terms of the informational view.
9. Describe and give examples of the following concepts as they relate to classical conditioning:
   - a. extinction
   - b. spontaneous recovery
   - c. stimulus generalization
   - d. stimulus discrimination
10. Describe the relationship between classical conditioning and reflex responses.
11. Explain what a conditioned emotional response (CER) is and how it is acquired. Describe the process of desensitization.
12. Explain the concept and the importance of vicarious classical conditioning.
13. State the basic principle of operant conditioning.
14. Contrast operant conditioning with classical conditioning. Briefly compare the differences between what is meant by the terms *reward* and *reinforcement*
15. Explain operant conditioning in terms of the informational view. Explain what response-contingent reinforcement is.
16. Describe how the delay of reinforcement can influence the effectiveness of the reinforcement.
17. Describe response chaining and explain how it can counteract the effects of delaying reinforcement.
18. Explain why superstitious behavior develops and why it persists.
19. Explain how shaping occurs.
20. Explain how extinction and spontaneous recovery occur in operant conditioning.
21. Describe how negative attention seeking demonstrates reinforcement and extinction in operant conditioning.
22. Compare and contrast positive reinforcement, negative reinforcement, and punishment, and give an example of each (including two types of punishment).

23. Differentiate primary reinforcers from secondary reinforcers and list several examples of each kind.

24. Discuss the way in which a secondary reinforcer becomes reinforcing.

25. Discuss the major advantages and disadvantages of primary reinforcers and secondary reinforcers (tokens, for example), and describe how tokens have been used to help "special" groups of people. Describe what a social reinforcer is.

26. Define *feedback*, explain its importance in learning, and indicate three factors that increase its effectiveness.

27. Briefly describe some ways in which conditioning techniques can be used to help people learn to conserve energy resources.

28. Describe the following kinds of instruction and discuss their application in learning and teaching: programmed, computer-assisted, and interactive videodisc.

29. Compare and contrast the effects of continuous and partial reinforcement.

30. Describe, give an example of, and explain the effects of the following schedules of partial reinforcement:

    a. fixed ratio (FR)   b. variable ratio (VR)   c. fixed interval (FI)

    d. variable interval (VI)

31. Explain the concept of stimulus control.

32. Describe the processes of generalization and discrimination as they relate to operant conditioning.

33. Explain how punishers can be defined by their effects on behavior.

34. Discuss three factors that influence the effectiveness of punishment.

35. Differentiate the effects of severe punishment from mild punishment.

36. List the three basic tools available to control simple learning.

37. Discuss how and why reinforcement should be used with punishment in order to change an undesirable behavior.

38. List six guidelines that should be followed when using punishment.

39. Discuss three problems associated with punishment.

40. Explain how using punishment can be habit forming and describe the behavior of children who are frequently punished.

41. Name two key elements that underlie learning and explain how they function together in learning situations.

42. Define *cognitive learning*.

43. Describe the concepts of a cognitive map and latent learning.

44. Explain the difference between discovery learning and rote learning and describe the behavior of students who use each approach.

45. Discuss the factors that determine whether observational learning (modeling) will occur.

46. Describe the experiment with children and the Bo-Bo doll that demonstrates the powerful effect of modeling on behavior.

47. Explain why what a parent does may be more important than what a parent says.

48. Describe the procedures and results of Williams' natural experiment with TV.

49. Briefly describe the general conclusion that can be drawn from studies on the effects of TV violence on children. Explain whether this means that TV violence causes aggression or not and why.

The following objectives are related to the material in the "Psychology in Action" and "A Step Beyond" sections of your text.

50. Briefly describe the seven steps in a behavioral self-management program.
51. Describe how self-recording can aid a self-management program.
52. List four strategies for changing bad habits.
53. Describe and give an example of a fixed action pattern.
54. Define instinct and explain why most psychologists reject the idea that humans have any.
55. Discuss the concept of biological constraints.
56. Explain why some fears are easier to acquire than others and name the explanatory theory.
57. Discuss the concept of instinctive drift.

RECITE AND REVIEW

● *What is learning?*

Recite and Review: Pages 292-294

1. Learning is a relatively permanent change in _____ due to experience. To understand learning we must study antecedents (events that _____ responses) and consequences (events that _____ responses).

2. Classical, or respondent, _____ and instrumental, or operant, _____ are two basic types of learning.

3. In classical conditioning, a previously neutral _____ is associated with a stimulus that elicits a response. In operant conditioning, the pattern of voluntary _____ is altered by consequences.

4. Both types of conditioning depend on reinforcement. In classical conditioning, learning is _____ when a US follows the NS or CS. _____ reinforcement is based on the consequences that follow a response.

● *How does classical conditioning occur?*

Recite and Review: Pages 294-298

5. Classical conditioning, studied by Ivan Pavlov, occurs when a _____ stimulus (NS) is associated with an unconditioned stimulus (US). The US triggers a reflex called the unconditioned _____ (UR).

6. If the NS is consistently paired with the US, it becomes a conditioned _____ (CS) capable of producing a response by itself. This response is a conditioned (_____) response (CR).

7. During acquisition of classical conditioning, the conditioned stimulus must be consistently followed by the unconditioned _____.

8. Higher-order conditioning occurs when a well-learned conditioned stimulus is used as if it were an unconditioned _____, bringing about further learning.

9. When the CS is repeatedly presented alone, extinction takes place. That is, _____ is weakened or inhibited.

10. After extinction seems to be complete, a rest period may lead to the temporary reappearance of a conditioned _____. This is called spontaneous recovery.

11. Through stimulus generalization, stimuli _____ to the conditioned stimulus will also produce a response.

12. Generalization gives way to _____ discrimination when an organism learns to respond to one stimulus, but not to similar stimuli.

13. From an informational view, conditioning creates expectancies (or expectations about events), which alter _____ patterns.

14. In classical conditioning, the CS creates an expectancy that the US will _____ it.

● *Does conditioning affect emotions?*

Recite and Review: Pages 298-299

15. Conditioning applies to visceral or emotional responses as well as simple _____. As a result, _____ emotional responses (CERs) also occur.

16. Irrational fears called phobias may be CERs that are extended to a variety of situations by _____ generalization.

17. The conditioning of emotional responses can occur vicariously (_____) as well as directly. Vicarious classical conditioning occurs when we _____ another person's emotional responses to a stimulus.

● *How does operant conditioning occur?*

Recite and Review: Pages 300-304

18. Operant conditioning (or instrumental _____) occurs when a voluntary action is followed by a reinforcer.

19. Reinforcement in operant conditioning _____ the frequency or probability of a response. This result is based on what Edward L. Thorndike called the law of _____.

20. An operant reinforcer is any event that follows a _____ and _____ its probability.

21. Learning in operant conditioning is based on the expectation that a response will have a specific _____.

22. To be effective, operant _____ must be _____ contingent.

23. Delay of reinforcement reduces its effectiveness, but long _____ of responses may be built up so that a _____ reinforcer maintains many responses.

24. Superstitious behaviors (unnecessary responses) often become part of _____ chains because they appear to be associated with reinforcement.

25. In a process called shaping, complex _____ responses can be taught by reinforcing successive approximations (ever closer matches) to a final desired response.

26. If an operant response is not reinforced, it may extinguish (disappear). But after extinction seems complete, it may temporarily reappear (spontaneous _____).

27. In positive reinforcement, _____ or a pleasant event follows a response. In negative reinforcement, a response that _____ discomfort becomes more likely to occur again.

28. Punishment _____ responding. Punishment occurs when a response is followed by the onset of an aversive event or by the removal of a positive event (response _____).

● *Are there different kinds of operant reinforcement?*

Recite and Review: Pages 304-308

29. Primary reinforcers are "natural," physiologically-based rewards. Intra-cranial stimulation of "_____ centers" in the _____ can also serve as a primary reinforcer.

30. Secondary reinforcers are _____. They typically gain their reinforcing value by association with primary reinforcers or because they can be _____ for primary reinforcers. Tokens and money gain their reinforcing value in this way.

31. Human behavior is often influenced by social reinforcers, which are based on learned desires for attention and _____ from others.

32. Feedback, or knowledge of _____, aids learning and improves performance.

33. Programmed instruction breaks learning into a series of small steps and provides immediate

_____.

34. Computer-assisted _____ (CAI) does the same, but has the added advantage of providing alternate exercises and information when needed.

35. Four variations of CAI are drill and _____, instructional games, educational simulations, and interactive videodisc instruction.

● *How are we influenced by patterns of reward?*

Recite and Review: Pages 309-312

36. Reward or reinforcement may be given continuously (after every _____), or on a schedule of _____ reinforcement. The study of schedules of reinforcement was begun by B. F. Skinner.

37. Partial reinforcement produces greater resistance to extinction. This is the partial reinforcement

_____.

38. The four most basic schedules of reinforcement are _____ ratio (FR), variable ratio (VR), _____ interval (FI), and variable interval (VI).

39. FR and VR schedules produce _____ rates of responding. An FI schedule produces moderate rates of responding with alternating periods of activity and inactivity. VI schedules produce _____, steady rates of responding and strong resistance to extinction.

40. Stimuli that _____ a reinforced response tend to control the response on future occasions (stimulus control).

41. Two aspects of stimulus control are generalization and _____.

42. In generalization, an operant response tends to occur when stimuli _____ to those preceding reinforcement are present.

43. In discrimination, responses are given in the presence of discriminative stimuli associated with reinforcement (____) and withheld in the presence of stimuli associated with nonreinforcement (____).

● *What does punishment do to behavior?*

Recite and Review: Pages 313-316

44. A punisher is any consequence that _____ the frequency of a target behavior.

45. Punishment is most effective when it is _____, consistent, and intense.

46. Mild punishment tends only to temporarily _____ responses that are also reinforced or were acquired by reinforcement.

47. The undesirable side effects of punishment include the conditioning of fear; the learning of _____ and avoidance responses; and the encouragement of aggression.

48. Reinforcement and nonreinforcement are better ways to change behavior than punishment. When punishment is used, it should be _____ and combined with reinforcement of alternate

_____.

● *What is cognitive learning?*

Recite and Review: Pages 316-318

49. Cognitive learning involves higher mental processes, such as understanding, knowing, or anticipating. Evidence of cognitive learning is provided by cognitive _____ (internal representations of spatial relationships) and latent (hidden) _____.

50. Discovery learning emphasizes insight and _____, in contrast to rote learning.

● *Does learning occur by imitation?*

Recite and Review: Pages 319-322

51. Much human learning is achieved through _____, or modeling. Observational learning is influenced by the personal characteristics of the _____ and the success or failure of the _____ behavior.

52. Television characters can act as powerful _____ for observational learning. Televised violence increases the likelihood of aggression by viewers.

● *How does conditioning apply to practical problems?*

Recite and Review: PSYCHOLOGY IN ACTION

53. Operant principles can be readily applied to manage behavior in everyday settings. Self-management of behavior is based on self-reinforcement, self-recording, _____, and behavioral contracting.

54. Prepotent, or frequent, high-probability _____, can be used to reinforce low-frequency responses. This is known as the Premack _____.

55. Attempts to break bad habits are aided by reinforcing alternate _____, by extinction, breaking _____ chains, and _____ cues or antecedents.

56. In school, self-regulated _____ typically involves all of the following: setting learning _____, planning learning strategies, using self-instruction, monitoring progress, evaluating yourself, reinforcing _____, and taking corrective action when required.

● *How does biology influence learning?*

Recite and Review: A STEP BEYOND

57. Many animals are born with _____ behavior patterns far more complex than reflexes. These are organized into fixed _____ patterns (FAPs), which are stereotyped, species-specific behaviors.

58. Learning in animals is limited at times by various _____ constraints and species-typical behaviors.

59. According to prepared _____ theory, some stimuli are especially effective conditioned stimuli.

60. Many operant responses are subject to instinctive drift—the tendency for learned responses to shift toward _____ response patterns.

CONNECTIONS

1. _____	respondent conditioning	a. before responses
2. _____	instrumental learning	b. Pavlov's CS
3. _____	antecedents	c. after responses
4. _____	meat powder	d. higher-order conditioning
5. _____	bell	e. Pavlovian conditioning
6. _____	salivation	f. US missing
7. _____	consequences	g. reinforcement period
8. _____	CS used as US	h. UR
9. _____	extinction	i. Pavlov's US
10. _____	acquisition	j. operant conditioning

11. _____	phobia	a. CER
12. _____	desensitization	b. conditioning chamber
13. _____	Skinner	c. increased responding
14. _____	shaping	d. decreased responding
15. _____	negative reinforcement	e. social reinforcer
16. _____	punishment	f. Chimp-O-Mat
17. _____	tokens	g. approximations
18. _____	approval	h. resistance to extinction
19. _____	partial reinforcement	i. antecedent stimuli
20. _____	stimulus control	j. extinction of fear

21. _____	punishment	a. number of responses per reinforcer
22. _____	expectancies	b. reinforcement schedule
23. _____	KR	c. incomplete extinction
24. _____	CAI	d. escape and avoidance
25. _____	discovery learning	e. informational view
26. _____	modeling	f. educational simulations
27. _____	self-instruction	g. feedback
28. _____	fixed ratio	h. insight
29. _____	spontaneous recovery	i. self-regulated learning
30. _____	fixed interval	j. imitation

CHECK YOUR MEMORY

Check Your Memory: Pages 292-294

1. Learning to press the buttons on a vending machine is based on operant conditioning. T or F?
2. In classical conditioning, the consequences that follow responses become associated with one another. T or F?
3. Getting compliments from friends could serve as reinforcement for operant learning. T or F?

Check Your Memory: Pages 294-298

4. Ivan Pavlov studied digestion and operant conditioning in dogs. T or F?
5. Pavlov used meat powder to reinforce conditioned salivation to the sound of a bell. T or F?
6. During successful conditioning, the NS becomes a CS. T or F?
7. During acquisition, the CS is presented repeatedly without the US. T or F?

8. The optimal delay between the CS and the US is 5 to 15 seconds. T or F?

9. Spontaneous recovery occurs when a CS becomes strong enough to be used like a US. T or F?

10. Discriminations are learned when generalized responses to stimuli similar to the CS are extinguished. T or F?

Check Your Memory: Pages 298-299

11. Narrowing of the pupils in response to bright lights is learned in early infancy. T or F?

12. Emotional conditioning involves autonomic nervous system responses. T or F?

13. Stimulus generalization helps convert some CERs into phobias. T or F?

14. Pleasant music can be used as a UR to create a CER. T or F?

15. To learn a CER vicariously, you would observe the actions of another person and try to imitate them. T or F?

16. Eye blink conditioning tends to occur faster than normal in people who are in the early stages of dementia. T or F?

Check Your Memory: Pages 300-304

17. In operant conditioning, learners actively emit responses. T or F?

18. Rewards are the same as reinforcers. T or F?

19. The Skinner box is primarily used to study classical conditioning. T or F?

20. Reinforcement in operant conditioning alters how frequently involuntary responses are elicited. T or F?

21. Operant reinforcers are most effective when they are response-contingent. T or F?

22. Operant learning is most effective if you wait a minute or two after the response is over before reinforcing it. T or F?

23. Response chains allow delayed reinforcers to support learning. T or F?

24. Superstitious responses appear to be associated with reinforcement, but they are not. T or F?

25. Teaching a pigeon to play Ping-Pong would most likely make use of the principle of response cost. T or F?

26. Children who misbehave may be reinforced by attention from parents. T or F?

27. Negative reinforcement is a type of punishment that is used to strengthen learning. T or F?

28. Both response cost and negative reinforcement decrease responding. T or F?

Check Your Memory: Pages 304-308

29. Food, water, grades, and sex are primary reinforcers. T or F?

30. ICS is a good example of a secondary reinforcer. T or F?

31. Social reinforcers are secondary reinforcers. T or F?

32. Attention and approval can be used to shape another person's behavior. T or F?

33. The effects of primary reinforcers may quickly decline as the person becomes satiated. T or F?

34. The Chimp-O-Mat accepted primary reinforcers and dispensed secondary reinforcers. T or F?

35. People are more likely to recycle used materials if they receive weekly feedback about how much they have recycled. T or F?

36. CAI is another term for informational feedback. T or F?

37. In sports, feedback is most effective when a skilled coach directs attention to important details. T or F?

38. The final level of skill and knowledge is almost always higher following CAI than it is with conventional methods. T or F?

Check Your Memory: Pages 309-312

39. Continuous reinforcement means that reinforcers are given continuously, regardless of whether or not responses are made. T or F?

40. An FR-3 schedule means that each correct response produces 3 reinforcers. T or F?

41. The time interval in FI schedules is measured from the last reinforced response. T or F?

42. In business, commissions and profit sharing are examples of FI reinforcement. T or F?

43. Antecedent stimuli tend to control when and where previously rewarded responses will occur. T or F?

44. Stimulus generalization is the primary method used to train dogs to detect contraband. T or F?

Check Your Memory: 313-316

45. Like reinforcement, punishment should be response-contingent. T or F?

46. Punishment is most effective if it is unpredictable. T or F?

47. Speeding tickets are an example of response cost. T or F?

48. Mild punishment causes reinforced responses to extinguish more rapidly. T or F?

49. Generally, punishment should be the last resort for altering behavior. T or F?

50. An apparatus known as a shuttle box is used to study escape and avoidance learning. T or F?

51. For humans, avoidance learning is reinforced by a sense of relief. T or F?

52. Punishment frequently leads to increases in aggression by the person who is punished. T or F?

Check Your Memory: Pages 316-318

53. Cognitive learning involves thinking, memory, and problem solving. T or F?

54. Animals learning their way through a maze memorize the correct order of right and left turns to make. T or F?

55. Typically, reinforcement must be provided in order to make latent learning visible. T or F?

56. In many situations, discovery learning produces better understanding of problems. T or F?

Check Your Memory: Pages 319-322

57. Modeling is another term for discovery learning. T or F?

58. After a new response is acquired through modeling, normal reinforcement determines if it will be repeated. T or F?

59. Children imitate aggressive acts performed by other people, but they are not likely to imitate cartoon characters. T or F?

60. Violence on television causes children to be more violent. T or F?

61. Playing violent video games tends to increase aggressive behavior in children and young adults. T or F?

Check Your Memory: PSYCHOLOGY IN ACTION

62. Choosing reinforcers is the first step in behavioral self-management. T or F?

63. Self-recording can be an effective way to change behavior, even without using specific reinforcers. T or F?

64. A prepotent response is one that occurs frequently. T or F?

65. To use extinction to break a bad habit, you should remove, avoid, or delay the reinforcement that is supporting the habit. T or F?

66. In a behavioral contract, you spell out what response chains you are going to extinguish. T or F?

67. Self-regulated learners actively seek feedback in both formal and informal ways. T or F?

Check Your Memory: A STEP BEYOND

68. A cat's face-washing routine is an example of an FAP. T or F?

69. Other than reflexes, humans generally lack rigidly programmed species-specific behaviors. T or F?

70. Biological constraints influence human learning, but animals are rarely affected by them. T or F?

71. Biological constraints affect both classical and operant conditioning. T or F?

FINAL SURVEY AND REVIEW

● *What is learning?*

   1. Learning is a relatively permanent change in behavior due to experience. To understand learning we must study _____ (events that precede responses) and _____ (events that follow responses).

   2. Classical, or _____, conditioning and instrumental, or _____, conditioning are two basic types of learning.

   3. In classical conditioning, a previously _____ stimulus is associated with another stimulus that elicits a response. In operant conditioning, the pattern of voluntary responses is altered by _____.

   4. Both types of conditioning depend on _____. In classical conditioning, learning is reinforced when a _____ follows the NS or CS. Operant reinforcement is based on the consequences that follow a response.

● *How does classical conditioning occur?*

   5. Classical conditioning, studied by _____ _____, occurs when a neutral stimulus (NS) is associated with an _____ stimulus (US). The US triggers a _____ called the unconditioned response (UR).

6. If the NS is consistently paired with the US, it becomes a _____ stimulus (CS) capable of producing a response by itself. This response is a _____ (learned) response (CR).

7. During acquisition of classical conditioning, the conditioned stimulus must be consistently followed by the _____ _____.

8. _____ conditioning occurs when a well-learned conditioned stimulus is used as if it were an unconditioned stimulus, bringing about further learning.

9. When the CS is repeatedly presented alone, _____ takes place (learning is weakened or inhibited).

10. After extinction seems to be complete, a rest period may lead to the temporary reappearance of a conditioned response. This is called _____ _____.

11. Through stimulus _____, stimuli similar to the conditioned stimulus will also produce a response.

12. Generalization gives way to stimulus _____ when an organism learns to respond to one stimulus, but not to similar stimuli.

13. From an _____ view, conditioning creates expectancies (or expectations about events), that alter response patterns.

14. In classical conditioning, the _____ creates an expectancy that the ____ will follow it.

● *Does conditioning affect emotions?*

15. Conditioning applies to visceral or emotional responses as well as simple reflexes. As a result, conditioned _____ _____ (CERs) also occur.

16. Irrational fears called _____ may be CERs that are extended to a variety of situations by stimulus _____.

17. The conditioning of emotional responses can occur secondhand as well as directly. _____ classical conditioning occurs when we observe another person's emotional responses to a stimulus.

● *How does operant conditioning occur?*

18. Operant conditioning (or _____ learning) occurs when a voluntary action is followed by a reinforcer.

19. Reinforcement in operant conditioning increases the frequency or _____ of a response. This result is based on what Edward L. _____ called the law of effect.

20. An operant reinforcer is any event that follows a _____ and _____ its probability.

21. Learning in operant conditioning is based on the _____ that a response will have a specific effect.

22. To be effective, operant reinforcers must be response _____.

23. Delay of reinforcement _____ its effectiveness, but long chains of responses may be built up so that a single _____ maintains many responses.

24. _____ behaviors (unnecessary responses) often become part of response chains because they appear to be associated with reinforcement.

25. In a process called _____, complex operant responses can be taught by reinforcing successive _____ (ever closer matches) to a final desired response.

26. If an operant response is not reinforced, it may _____ (disappear). But after extinction seems complete, it may temporarily reappear (_____ recovery).

27. In _____ reinforcement, reward or a pleasant event follows a response. In _____ reinforcement, a response that ends discomfort becomes more likely to occur again.

28. Punishment decreases responding. Punishment occurs when a response is followed by the onset of an _____ event or by the removal of a _____ event (response cost).

● *Are there different kinds of operant reinforcement?*

29. _____ reinforcers are "natural," physiologically-based rewards. Intra-cranial _____ of "pleasure centers" in the brain can also serve as reinforcers of this type.

30. _____ reinforcers are learned. They typically gain their reinforcing value by association with _____ reinforcers or because they can be exchanged for _____ reinforcers. Tokens and money gain their reinforcing value in this way.

31. Human behavior is often influenced by _____ reinforcers, which are based on learned desires for attention and approval from others.

32. Feedback, or _____ of results, aids learning and improves performance.

33. Programmed _____ breaks learning into a series of small steps and provides immediate feedback.

34. _____ _____ (CAI) does the same, but has the added advantage of providing alternate exercises and information when needed.

35. Four variations of _____ are drill and practice, instructional games, educational simulations, and interactive videodisc instruction.

● *How are we influenced by patterns of reward?*

36. Reward or reinforcement may be given continuously (after every response), or on a _____ of partial reinforcement like those studied by B. F. _____.

37. Partial reinforcement produces greater resistance to _____. This is the _____ reinforcement effect.

38. The four most basic schedules of reinforcement are fixed and variable _____ (FR and VR) and fixed and variable _____ (FI and VI).

39. _____ and _____ schedules produce high rates of responding. An _____ schedule produces moderate rates of responding with alternating periods of activity and inactivity. VI schedules produce slow, steady rates of responding and strong resistance to _____.

40. Stimuli that precede a reinforced response tend to control the response on future occasions. This is called _____ _____.

41. Two aspects of stimulus control are _____ and discrimination.

42. In _____, an operant response tends to occur when stimuli similar to those preceding reinforcement are present.

43. In _____, responses are given in the presence of stimuli associated with reinforcement (S+) and withheld in the presence of stimuli associated with nonreinforcement (S⁻).

● *What does punishment do to behavior?*

44. A _____ is any consequence that lowers the frequency of a target behavior.

45. Punishment is most effective when it is immediate, _____, and intense.

46. Mild punishment tends only to temporarily suppress responses that are also _____ in some way.

47. The undesirable side effects of punishment include the conditioning of fear; the learning of escape and _____ responses; and the encouragement of _____ against others.

48. _____ and _____ are better ways to change behavior than punishment.

● *What is cognitive learning?*

49. Cognitive learning involves higher mental processes, such as understanding, knowing, or anticipating. Evidence of cognitive learning is provided by _____ _____ (internal representations of spatial relationships) and _____ (hidden) learning.

50. Discovery learning emphasizes insight and understanding, in contrast to _____ learning.

● *Does learning occur by imitation?*

51. Much human learning is achieved through observation, or _____. _____ learning is influenced by the personal characteristics of the model and the success or failure of the model's behavior.

52. Television characters can act as powerful models for _____ learning. Televised violence increases the likelihood of aggression by viewers.

● *How does conditioning apply to practical problems?*

53. Operant principles can be readily applied to manage behavior in everyday settings. Self-management of behavior is based on self-reinforcement, self-recording, feedback, and behavioral _____.

54. Prepotent, or frequent, high-probability responses, can be used to _____ low-frequency responses. This is known as the _____ principle.

55. Attempts to break bad habits are aided by reinforcing _____ responses, by extinction, breaking response _____, and removing cues or _____.

56. In school, self-regulated learning typically involves all of the following: setting learning goals, planning learning _____, using self-instruction, monitoring progress, evaluating yourself, _____ successes, and taking corrective action when required.

● *How does biology influence learning?*

57. Many animals are born with innate behavior patterns far more complex than _____. These are organized into fixed action patterns (FAPs), which are stereotyped, _____-specific behaviors.

58. Learning in animals is limited at times by various biological _____ and species-typical behaviors.

59. According to _____ fear theory, some stimuli are especially effective conditioned stimuli.

60. Many operant responses are subject to instinctive _____—the tendency for learned responses to shift toward innate response patterns.

MASTERY TEST

1. Tokens are a good example of
   a. secondary reinforcers b. the effects of ICS on behavior c. noncontingent reinforcers
   d. generalized reinforcers

2. The principle of feedback is of particular importance to
   a. CERs b. ICS c. CAI d. higher-order conditioning

3. As a coffee lover, you have become very efficient at carrying out the steps necessary to make a cup of espresso. Your learning is an example of
   a. response chaining b. spontaneous recovery c. vicarious reinforcement
   d. secondary reinforcement

4. To teach a pet dog to use a new dog door, it would be helpful to use
   a. the Premack principle b. shaping c. respondent conditioning d. delayed reinforcement

5. To test for the presence of classical conditioning you would omit the
   a. CS b. US c. CR d. S+

6. Which of the following does not belong with the others?
   a. Thorndike b. Skinner c. Pavlov d. instrumental learning

7. To teach a child to say "Please" when she asks for things, you should make getting the requested item
   a. the CS b. a token c. a negative reinforcer d. response-contingent

8. Money is to secondary reinforcer as food is to
   a. ICS b. prepotent responses c. primary reinforcer d. negative reinforcer

9. Whether a model is reinforced has a great impact on
   a. discovery learning   b. latent learning   c. observational learning   d. self-regulated learning

10. One thing that classical and operant conditioning have in common is that both
    a. were discovered by Pavlov   b. depend on reinforcement   c. are affected by the consequences of making a response   d. permanently change behavior

11. To shape the behavior of a teacher in one of your classes you would probably have to rely on
    a. tokens   b. primary reinforcers   c. negative attention seeking   d. social reinforcers

12. The concept that best explains persistence at gambling is
    a. partial reinforcement   b. continuous reinforcement   c. fixed interval reinforcement
    d. fixed ratio reinforcement

13. Which of the following is NOT a common side effect of mild punishment?
    a. escape learning   b. avoidance learning   c. aggression   d. accelerated extinction

14. With respect to televised violence it can be said that TV violence
    a. causes viewers to be more aggressive   b. makes aggression more likely   c. has no effect on the majority of viewers   d. vicariously lowers aggressive urges

15. Which of the following types of learning is most related to the consequences of making a response?
    a. Pavlovian conditioning   b. classical conditioning   c. operant conditioning
    d. respondent conditioning

16. Which combination would most likely make a CER into a phobia?
    a. CER-discrimination   b. CER-desensitization   c. CER-response cost   d. CER-generalization

17. Slower than normal eye blink conditioning is an early sign of
    a. two-factor avoidance learning   b. escape learning   c. vicarious extinction   d. dementia

18. A loud, unexpected sound causes a startle reflex; thus, a loud sound could be used as a _____ in conditioning.
    a. NS   b. CR   c. UR   d. US

19. Antecedents are to _____ as consequences are to _____.
    a. discriminative stimuli, reinforcers   b. shaping, response chaining   c. conditioned stimuli, cognitive maps   d. punishment, negative reinforcement

20. The use of self-recording to change personal behavior is closely related to the principle of
    a. response chaining   b. feedback   c. two-factor reinforcement   d. stimulus control

21. _____ typically only temporarily suppresses reinforced responses.
    a. Negative reinforcement   b. Extinction   c. Mild punishment   d. Stimulus generalization

22. In general, the highest rates of responding are associated with
    a. delayed reinforcement b. variable reinforcement c. interval reinforcement
    d. fixed ratio reinforcement

23. A child who has learned, through classical conditioning, to fear sitting in a dentist's chair becomes frightened when he is placed in a barber's chair. This illustrates the concept of
    a. stimulus generalization b. spontaneous recovery c. higher-order discrimination
    d. vicarious conditioning

24. The informational view of learning places emphasis on the creation of mental
    a. expectancies b. reinforcement schedules c. contracts d. antecedents

25. For some adults, blushing when embarrassed or ashamed is probably a _____ first formed in childhood.
    a. conditioned stimulus b. CAI c. discriminative stimulus d. CER

26. Learning to obey traffic signals is related to the phenomenon called
    a. stimulus control b. spontaneous recovery c. avoidance learning d. modeling

27. To be most effective, punishment should be combined with
    a. response costs b. aversive stimuli c. delayed feedback d. reinforcement

28. Involuntary responses are to _____ conditioning as voluntary responses are to _____ conditioning.
    a. classical, respondent b. classical, operant c. operant, classical d. operant, instrumental

29. Negative attention seeking by children demonstrates the impact of _____ on behavior.
    a. operant extinction b. social reinforcers c. response costs d. prepotent responses

30. Which consequence increases the probability that a response will be repeated?
    a. punishment b. response cost c. nonreinforcement d. negative reinforcement

ANSWERS

Recite and Review

1. behavior, precede, follow
2. conditioning, conditioning
3. stimulus, responses
4. reinforced, Operant
5. neutral, response
6. stimulus, learned
7. stimulus
8. stimulus
9. conditioning
10. response
11. similar
12. stimulus
13. response
14. follow
15. reflexes, conditioned
16. stimulus
17. secondhand, observe
18. learning
19. increases, effect
20. response, increases
21. effect
22. reinforcement, response

23. chains, single
24. response
25. operant
26. recovery
27. reward, ends
28. decreases, cost
29. pleasure, brain
30. learned, exchanged
31. approval
32. results
33. feedback
34. instruction
35. practice
36. response, partial
37. effect
38. fixed, fixed
39. high, slow
40. precede
41. discrimination
42. similar
43. S+, S−
44. decreases
45. immediate
46. suppress
47. escape
48. mild, responses
49. maps, learning
50. understanding
51. imitation, model, model's
52. models
53. feedback
54. responses, principle
55. responses, response, removing
56. learning, goals, successes
57. innate, action
58. biological
59. fear
60. innate

Connections

1. e
2. j
3. a
4. i
5. b
6. h
7. c
8. d
9. f
10. g
11. a
12. j
13. b
14. g
15. c
16. d
17. f
18. e
19. h
20. i
21. d
22. e
23. g
24. f
25. h
26. j
27. i
28. a
29. c
30. b

Check Your Memory

1. T
2. F
3. T
4. F
5. T
6. T
7. F
8. F
9. F
10. T
11. F
12. T
13. T
14. F
15. F
16. T
17. T
18. F
19. F
20. F
21. T

22. F
23. T
24. T
25. F
26. T
27. F
28. F
29. F
30. F
31. T
32. T
33. T
34. F
35. T
36. F
37. T
38. F
39. F
40. F
41. T
42. F
43. T
44. F
45. T
46. F
47. T
48. F
49. T
50. T
51. T
52. T
53. T
54. F
55. T
56. T
57. F
58. T
59. F
60. F
61. T
62. F
63. T
64. T
65. T
66. F
67. T
68. T
69. T
70. F

71. T

Final Survey and Review

1. antecedents, consequences
2. respondent, operant
3. neutral, consequences
4. reinforcement, US
5. Ivan Pavlov, unconditioned, reflex
6. conditioned, conditioned
7. unconditioned stimulus
8. Higher-order
9. extinction
10. spontaneous recovery
11. generalization
12. discrimination
13. informational
14. CS, US
15. emotional responses
16. phobias, generalization
17. Vicarious
18. instrumental
19. probability, Thorndike
20. response, increases
21. expectation
22. contingent
23. decreases, reinforcer
24. Superstitious
25. shaping, approximations
26. extinguish, spontaneous
27. positive, negative
28. aversive, positive
29. Primary, stimulation
30. Secondary, primary, primary
31. social
32. knowledge
33. instruction
34. Computer-assisted
35. CAI
36. schedule, Skinner
37. extinction, partial
38. ratio, interval
39. FR, VR, FI, extinction
40. stimulus control
41. generalization
42. generalization
43. discrimination
44. punisher
45. consistent
46. reinforced
47. avoidance, aggression
48. Reinforcement, nonreinforcement
49. cognitive maps, latent
50. rote
51. modeling, Observational
52. observational
53. contracting
54. reinforce, Premack
55. alternate, chains, antecedents
56. strategies, reinforcing
57. reflexes, species
58. constraints
59. prepared
60. drift

Mastery Test

1. a (p. 305)
2. c (p. 307)
3. a (p. 302)
4. b (p. 303)
5. b (p. 295)
6. c (p. 300)
7. d (p. 302)
8. c (p. 304-305)
9. c (p. 319)
10. b (p. 293)
11. d (p. 306)
12. a (p. 309)
13. d (p. 314)
14. b (p. 321)
15. c (p. 294)
16. d (p. 298)
17. d (p. 298)
18. d (p. 298)
19. a (p. 293-294)
20. b (p. 323)
21. c (p. 314)
22. d (p. 310)
23. a (p. 297)
24. a (p. 296, 301)
25. d (p. 298)
26. a (p. 312)
27. d (p. 314-315)
28. b (p. 300)
29. b (p. 304)
30. d (p. 304)

Chapter 9
Memory

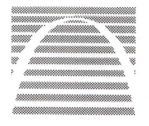

CHAPTER OVERVIEW

Memory systems encode and store information for later retrieval. A popular model divides memory into three systems: sensory memory, short-term memory (STM), and long-term memory (LTM). Sensory memory stores exact copies of sensory information for very brief periods. STM is limited to about 7 bits of information, but chunking and recoding allow more information to be stored. LTM has nearly unlimited storage. Short-term memories last only a short time; long-term memories are relatively permanent. Long-term memories can be further divided into declarative memories (which may be semantic or episodic) and procedural memories.

Explicit memories are revealed by recall, recognition, and relearning tasks. Implicit memories are revealed by priming. Eidetic imagery (photographic memory) is fairly common in children, but rare among adults. Many people have internal memory images and some have exceptional memory based on internal imagery. Exceptional memory capacity is based on both learned strategies and natural abilities.

Forgetting is most rapid immediately after learning. Some "forgetting" is based on a failure to encode information. Short-term forgetting is partly explained by the decay (weakening) of memory traces. Some long-term forgetting may also occur this way. Some forgetting is related to a lack of memory cues. Much forgetting is related to interference among memories. Clinical psychologists believe that memories are sometimes repressed (unconsciously held out of awareness). Some also believe that repressed childhood memories of abuse can be "recovered." However, there is often no way to separate true memories from fantasies.

In the brain, memory traces (engrams) must be consolidated before they become relatively permanent. The hippocampus is a structure involved in memory consolidation. Information appears to be stored in the brain through changes in nerve cells.

Memory can be improved by the use of mnemonic systems and by attention to factors that affect memory, such as overlearning, serial position, organization, and the like.

Memory frustrates us in seven basic ways. These are transience, absent-mindedness, blocking, misattribution, suggestibility, bias, and persistence. These "sins" of memory are usually virtues, except under certain circumstances when they become problems.

LEARNING OBJECTIVES

To demonstrate mastery of this chapter, you should be able to:

1. Define *memory*.
2. Explain the three processes of memory.
3. Explain sensory memory. Include an explanation of how icons and echoes function in this memory system.
4. Explain how information is transferred from sensory memory to short-term memory.
5. Describe short-term memory in terms of capacity, how information is encoded, permanence, and susceptibility to interference.
6. Describe long-term memory in terms of permanence, capacity, and the basis on which information is stored. Include a brief description of dual memory.
7. Explain the "magic number" seven. Describe chunking and the two types of rehearsal and explain how they help memory.
8. Discuss the permanence of memory, including the work of Penfield and the Loftuses.
9. Explain how memories are constructed. Include the concepts of constructive processing and pseudo-memories.
10. Discuss the effects of hypnosis on memory.
11. Briefly describe how long-term memories are organized including the network model and redintegrative memories.
12. Differentiate procedural (skill) memory from declarative (fact) memory.
13. Differentiate the two kinds of declarative memory—semantic memory and episodic memory.
14. Explain the tip-of-the-tongue phenomenon (including the feeling of knowing).
15. Describe and give an example of each of the following ways of measuring memory:
    a. recall (include the serial position effect)
    b. recognition (compare to recall and include the idea of distractors)
    c. relearning (include the concept of savings)
16. Distinguish between explicit and implicit memories. Include a discussion of priming.
17. Describe the concept of internal imagery and explain how it differs from eidetic imagery and exceptional memory.
18. Describe eidetic imagery and its effects on long-term memory.
19. Describe exceptional memory, including the concepts of learned strategies, the characteristics of exceptional memorizers, and mnemonics.
20. Explain Ebbinghaus's curve of forgetting.
21. Discuss the following explanations of forgetting:
    a. encoding failure
    b. decay of memory traces
    c. disuse (give three reasons to question this explanation)
    d. cue-dependent forgetting
    e. state-dependent learning

      f. interference (list and explain the two types of interference and how they are investigated in the laboratory)

      g. positive and negative transfer

      h. repression (and differentiate it from suppression)

22. Describe the false memory syndrome.

23. Define *flashbulb memories,* and *retrograde* and *anterograde amnesia.*

24. Describe the effects of stimulants and alcohol on memory.

25. Describe the role of consolidation in memory, including the effects of (ECS).

26. Name the structure in the brain that is responsible for switching information from STM to LTM. Include a discussion of the engram and the relationship between learning and transmitter chemicals.

27. Describe each of the following in terms of how it can improve memory:

      a. knowledge of results

      b. recitation

      c. rehearsal

      d. selection

      e. organization

      f. whole versus part learning

      g. serial position effect

      h. cues

      i. overlearning

      j. spaced practice

      k. sleep

      l. hunger

      m. extension of memory intervals

      n. review

      o. strategies to aid recall

28. Briefly discuss the four steps in a cognitive interview.

The following objectives are related to the material in the "Psychology in Action" and "A Step Beyond" sections of your text.

29. Define *mnemonics* and explain the four basic principles of using mnemonics.

30. List and describe three techniques for using mnemonics to remember things in order.

31. Suggest why evolution-shaped memory mainly stores information we might need today.

32. Describe the "seven sins of memory" discussed by Daniel Schacter and explain their adaptive value.

RECITE AND REVIEW

Recite and Review: Pages 330-333

1. Memory is an active _____. _____ is first encoded (changed into the form in which it will be retained).

2. Next it is _____ in memory. Later it must be retrieved to be put to use.

3. Humans appear to have _____ interrelated memory systems. These are sensory memory, _____ memory (STM), and _____ memory (LTM).

4. Sensory memory holds an _____ copy of what is seen or heard, in the form of an icon (_____) or echo (sound sensation).

5. Short-term memories tend to be stored as _____. Long-term memories are stored on the basis of _____, or importance.

6. STM acts as a _____ storehouse for small amounts of information. It provides a working memory where thinking, mental arithmetic, and the like take place. LTM acts as a _____ storehouse for meaningful information.

Recite and Review: Pages 333-338

7. Sensory memory is exact, but very brief, lasting only a few _____ or less. Through selective attention, some information is transferred to _____.

8. The digit-span test reveals that STM has an average upper limit of about 7 _____ of information. However, this can be extended by chunking, or recoding information into _____ units or groups.

9. Short-term memories are brief and very sensitive to _____, or interference; however, they can be prolonged by maintenance rehearsal (silent _____).

10. Elaborative rehearsal, which emphasizes meaning, helps transfer information from _____ to LTM. Elaborative rehearsal links new information with existing _____.

11. LTM seems to have an almost unlimited storage capacity. However, LTM is subject to constructive processing, or ongoing revision and _____. As a result, people often have pseudo-memories (_____ memories) that they believe are true.

12. LTM is highly _____ to allow retrieval of needed information. The pattern, or structure, of memory networks is the subject of current memory research. Network _____ portray LTM as a system of linked ideas.

13. Redintegrative memories unfold as each added memory provides a cue for retrieving the next _____. Seemingly forgotten memories may be reconstructed in this way.

Recite and Review: Pages 338-339

14. Within long-term memory, declarative memories for _____ seem to differ from procedural memories for _____.

15. _____ memories may be further categorized as semantic memories or episodic memories.

16. Semantic memories consist of basic factual knowledge that is almost immune to _____.

17. Episodic memories record _____ experiences that are associated with specific times and places.

● *How is memory measured?*

Recite and Review: Pages 340-342

18. The tip-of-the-tongue _____ shows that memory is not an all-or-nothing event. Memories may be revealed by _____, recognition, or relearning.

19. In recall, memory proceeds without specific cues, as in an _____ exam. Recall of listed information often reveals a serial position effect (_____ items on the list are most subject to errors).

20. A common test of _____ is the multiple-choice question. _____ is very sensitive to the kinds of distractors (wrong choices) used.

21. In relearning, "forgotten" material is learned again, and memory is indicated by a _____ score.

22. Recall, recognition, and relearning mainly measure explicit _____ that we are aware of having. Other techniques, such as priming, are necessary to reveal implicit _____, which are unconscious.

● *What are "photographic" memories?*

Recite and Review: Pages 342-345

23. Eidetic imagery (photographic memory) occurs when a person is able to project an _____ onto an external surface. Such images allow brief, nearly complete recall by some children.

24. Eidetic imagery is rarely found in _____. However, many adults have internal images, which can be very vivid and a basis for remembering.

25. Exceptional memory can be learned by finding ways to directly store information in _____. Learning has no effect on the limits of _____. Some people may have naturally superior memory abilities that exceed what can be achieved through learning.

● *What causes forgetting?*

Recite and Review: Pages 345-350

26. Forgetting and memory were extensively studied by Herman Ebbinghaus, whose _____ of forgetting shows that forgetting is typically most rapid immediately _____ learning.

27. Ebbinghaus used nonsense syllables to study memory. The forgetting of _____ material is much _____ than shown by his curve of forgetting.

28. Failure to encode _____ is a common cause of "forgetting."

29. Forgetting in sensory memory and STM probably reflects decay of memory _____ in the nervous system. Decay or _____ of memories may also account for some LTM loss, but most forgetting cannot be explained this way.

30. Often, forgetting is cue dependent. The power of cues to trigger memories is revealed by state-dependent _____, in which bodily _____ at the time of learning and of retrieval affect memory.

31. Much _____ in both STM and LTM can be attributed to interference of memories with one another.

32. When recent learning _____ with retrieval of prior learning, retroactive interference has occurred. If old memories _____ with new memories, proactive interference has occurred.

● *How accurate are everyday memories?*

Recite and Review: Pages 350-352

33. Repression is the _____ of painful, embarrassing, or traumatic memories.

34. Repression is thought to be unconscious, in contrast to suppression, which is a _____ attempt to avoid thinking about something.

35. Experts are currently debating the validity of childhood memories of _____ that reappear after apparently being repressed for decades.

36. Independent evidence has verified that some recovered memories are _____. However, others have been shown to be _____.

37. In the absence of confirming or disconfirming _____, there is currently no way to separate true memories from fantasies. Caution is advised for all concerned with attempts to retrieve supposedly hidden memories.

38. Flashbulb memories, which seem especially vivid, are created at emotionally significant times. While such memories may not be accurate, we tend to place great _____ in them.

● *What happens in the brain when memories are formed?*

Recite and Review: Pages 353-354

39. Retrograde _____ and the effects of electroconvulsive _____ (ECS) may be explained by the concept of consolidation.

40. Consolidation theory holds that engrams (permanent _____ _____) are formed during a critical period after learning. Until they are consolidated, long-term memories are easily destroyed.

41. The hippocampus is a _____ structure associated with the consolidation of memories.

42. The search within the brain for engrams has now settled on changes in individual _____ cells.

43. The best-documented changes are alterations in the amounts of transmitter _____ released by nerve cells.

● *How can memory be improved?*

Recite and Review: Pages 355-358 & PSYCHOLOGY IN ACTION

44. Memory can be improved by using feedback, recitation, and rehearsal, by selecting and _____ information, and by using the progressive _____ method, spaced practice, overlearning, and active search strategies.

45. The effects of serial _____, sleep, review, cues, and elaboration should also be kept in mind when studying or memorizing.

46. Mnemonic systems, such as the _____ method, use mental images and unusual associations to link new information with familiar memories already stored in _____. Such strategies give information personal meaning and make it easier to recall.

● *How has evolution shaped human memory?*

Recite and Review: A STEP BEYOND

47. Evolution shaped memory to mainly store information about recent _____ and repeated information or _____.

48. Transience refers to the fact that information stored in memory tends to _____ with the passage of time.

49. Absent-mindedness tends to occur when we form weak memories because we fail to pay _____ while creating the memory.

50. Blocking is the frustrating experience of not being able to recall a word or a name that you _____ _____.

51. Misattribution refers to linking a memory with the wrong source, _____, or _____.

52. Suggestions and misleading questions can implant information that leads people to alter or revise their _____.

53. Memories of traumatic events may persist for many years even though we wish we could _____.

CONNECTIONS

1. _____   echos and icons   a. STM
2. _____   working memory   b. constructive processing
3. _____   7 information bits   c. network model
4. _____   chunking   d. sensory memory
5. _____   revised memories   e. procedures
6. _____   memory structure   f. recoding
7. _____   skill memory   g. memory test
8. _____   relearning   h. magic number

9. _____ selective attention
10. _____ long-term memory
11. _____ incoming information
12. _____ encoding for LTM
13. _____ sensory memory
14. _____ short-term memory
15. _____ rehearsal buffer

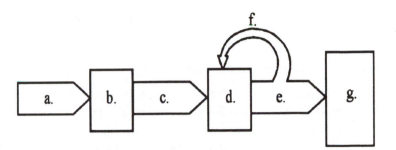

16. _____ semantic memory
17. _____ long-term memory
18. _____ procedural memory
19. _____ sensory memory
20. _____ episodic memory
21. _____ short-term memory
22. _____ declarative memory

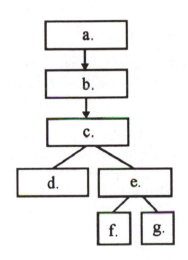

23. _____ memory prediction
24. _____ false positive
25. _____ implicit memories
26. _____ memory expert
27. _____ repression
28. _____ nonsense syllable
29. _____ erases memory
30. _____ spaced practice

a. unconscious forgetting
b. ECS
c. WOL
d. study and rest
e. mnemonist
f. mistaken recognition
g. priming
h. feeling of knowing

CHECK YOUR MEMORY

Check Your Memory: **Pages 330-333**

1. Incoming information must be encoded before it is stored in memory. T or F?
2. Sensory memories last for a few minutes or less. T or F?
3. A memory that cannot be retrieved has little value. T or F?
4. Selective attention influences what information enters STM. T or F?
5. Working memory is another name for sensory memory. T or F?
6. Errors in long-term memory tend to focus on the sounds of words. T or F?
7. Generally, the more you know, the more new information you can store in long-term memory. T or F?

Check Your Memory: Pages 333-338

8. For many kinds of information, STM can store an average of 5 bits of information. T or F?
9. Chunking recodes information into smaller units that are easier to fit into STM. T or F?
10. The more times a short-term memory is rehearsed, the better its chance of being stored in LTM. T or F?
11. On average, short-term memories last only about 18 minutes, unless they are rehearsed. T or F?
12. Maintenance rehearsal keeps memories active in sensory memory. T or F?
13. The surface of the brain records the past like a movie, complete with sound track. T or F?
14. Being confident about a memory tells little about the true accuracy of the memory. T or F?
15. Hypnosis increases false memories more than it does true ones. T or F?
16. Long-term memories appear to be organized alphabetically for speedy access. T or F?

Check Your Memory: Pages 338-339

17. Knowing how to swing a golf club is a type of declarative memory. T or F?
18. A person lacking declarative memory might still remember how to solve a mechanical puzzle. T or F?
19. Semantic memories are almost immune to forgetting. T or F?
20. Semantic memories are a type of declarative memory. T or F?
21. Episodic memories have no connection to particular times and places. T or F?

Check Your Memory: Pages 340-342

22. Remembering the first sound of a name you are trying to recall is an example of the tip-of-the-tongue state. T or F?
23. Tests of recognition require verbatim memory. T or F?
24. The serial position effect measures the strength of the feeling of knowing. T or F?
25. Recognition tends to be a more sensitive test of memory than recall. T or F?
26. False positives and distractors greatly affect the accuracy of relearning tests. T or F?
27. Recall, recognition, and relearning are used to measure explicit memories. T or F?
28. Priming is used to activate explicit (hidden) memories. T or F?

Check Your Memory: Pages 342-345

29. Eidetic images last for 30 seconds or more. T or F?
30. About 8 percent of all children have eidetic images. T or F?

31. Eidetic imagery becomes rare by adulthood. T or F?

32. Mr. S (the mnemonist) had virtually unlimited eidetic imagery. T or F?

33. Practice in remembering one type of information increases the capacity of STM to store other types of information, too. T or F?

34. All contestants in the World Memory Championship performed poorly on tasks that prevented the use of learned strategies. T or F?

Check Your Memory: Pages 345-350

35. Ebbinghaus chose to learn nonsense syllables so that they would all be the same length. T or F?

36. Ebbinghaus's curve of forgetting levels off after 2 days, showing little further memory loss after that. T or F?

37. Decay of memory traces clearly applies to information in STM. T or F?

38. Disuse theories of forgetting answer the question: Have I been storing the information in the first place? T or F?

39. The presence of memory cues almost always improves memory. T or F?

40. Information learned under the influence of a drug may be best remembered when the drugged state occurs again. T or F?

41. If you are in a bad mood, you are more likely to remember unpleasant events. T or F?

42. Categorizing a person as a member of a group tends to limit the accuracy of memories about the person's appearance. T or F?

43. Sleeping tends to interfere with retaining new memories. T or F?

44. You learn information A and then information B. If your memory of B is lowered by having first learned A, you have experienced retroactive interference. T or F?

Check Your Memory: Pages 350-352

45. Unconsciously forgetting painful memories is called negative transfer. T or F?

46. A conscious attempt to put a memory out of mind is called repression. T or F?

47. Suggestion and fantasy are elements of many techniques used in attempts to recover repressed memories. T or F?

48. Unless a memory can be independently confirmed, there is no way to tell if it is real or not. T or F?

49. Flashbulb memories tend to be formed when an event is surprising or emotional. T or F?

50. The confidence we have in flashbulb memories is well placed—they are much more accurate than most other memories. T or F?

Check Your Memory: 353-354

51. Retrograde amnesia is a gap in memories of events preceding a head injury. T or F?

52. Stimulant drugs may speed up consolidation, but at high doses they disrupt memory. T or F?

53. People with damage to the hippocampus typically cannot remember events that occurred before the damage. T or F?

54. In the early 1920s, Karl Lashley found the location of engrams in the brain. T or F?

55. Storing memories alters the activity, structure, and chemistry of the brain. T or F?

Check Your Memory: Pages 355-358 & PSYCHOLOGY IN ACTION

56. Recitation is a good way to generate feedback while studying. T or F?

57. Elaborative rehearsal involving "why" questions improves memory. T or F?

58. Overlearning is inefficient; you should stop studying at the point of initial mastery of new information. T or F?

59. Massed practice is almost always superior to spaced practice. T or F?

60. When learning, it helps to gradually extend how long you remember new information before reviewing it again. T or F?

61. Recalling events from different viewpoints is part of doing a cognitive interview. T or F?

62. *Roy G. Biv* is a mnemonic for the notes on a musical staff. T or F?

63. Many mnemonics make use of mental images or pictures. T or F?

64. Mnemonics often link new information to familiar memories. T or F?

65. The keyword method is superior to rote learning for memorizing vocabulary words in another language. T or F?

Check Your Memory: A STEP BEYOND

66. It is accurate to say that total recall would paralyze us mentally. T or F?

67. Transience ensures that our most recent and useful memories are given priority. T or F?

68. Blocking tends to be the result of failing to pay attention when forming a memory. T or F?

69. The fact that misattribution is common suggests that we should be skeptical of our memories. T or F?

70. Many people find they need the assistance of a therapist to deal with persistent traumatic memories. T or F?

FINAL SURVEY AND REVIEW

● *Is there more than one type of memory?*

1. Memory is an active system. Information is first _____ (changed into the form in which it will be retained).

2. Next it is stored in memory. Later it must be _____ to be put to use.

3. Humans appear to have 3 interrelated memory systems. These are _____ memory, _____ memory (STM), and long-term memory (LTM).

4. Sensory memory holds an exact copy of what is seen or heard, in the form of an _____ (image) or _____ (sound sensation).

5. _____ memories tend to be stored as sounds. _____ memories are stored on the basis of meaning, or importance.

6. _____ acts as a temporary storehouse for small amounts of information. It provides a _____ memory where thinking, mental arithmetic, and the like take place. LTM acts as a permanent storehouse for _____ information.

● *What are the features of each type of memory?*

7. _____ memory is exact but very brief, lasting only a few seconds or less. Through
_____ _____, some information is transferred to STM.

8. The _____ test reveals that STM has an average upper limit of about 7 bits of
information. However, this can be extended by chunking, or _____ information into larger
units or groups.

9. Short-term memories are brief and very sensitive to interruption , or _____;
however, they can be prolonged by _____ rehearsal (silent repetition).

10. _____ rehearsal, which emphasizes meaning, helps transfer information from
STM to LTM.

11. LTM seems to have an almost unlimited storage capacity. However, LTM is subject to
_____ processing, or ongoing revision and updating. As a result, people often have
_____ (false memories) that they believe are true.

12. LTM is highly organized to allow retrieval of needed information. The pattern, or structure, of memory
_____ is the subject of current memory research. _____ models portray
LTM as a system of linked ideas.

13. _____ memories unfold as each added memory provides a cue for retrieving
the next memory. Seemingly forgotten memories may be reconstructed in this way.

● *Is there more than one type of long-term memory?*

14. Within long-term memory, _____ memories for facts seem to differ from
_____ memories for skills.

15. Declarative memories may be further categorized as _____ memories or
_____ memories.

16. _____ memories consist of basic factual knowledge that is almost immune to
forgetting.

17. _____ memories record personal experiences that are associated with specific times
and places.

● *How is memory measured?*

18. The _____-of-the-_____ state shows that memory is not an all-or-nothing event.
Memories may be revealed by recall, _____, or relearning.

19. In _____, memory proceeds without specific cues, as in an essay exam. Remembering a
list of information often reveals a _____ _____ effect (middle items on the
list are most subject to errors).

20. A common test of recognition is the _____-choice question. Recognition is very
sensitive to the kinds of _____ (wrong choices) used.

21. In _____, "forgotten" material is learned again, and memory is indicated by a savings
score.

22. Recall, recognition, and relearning mainly measure _____ memories that we are aware of having. Other techniques, such as priming, are necessary to reveal _____ memories, which are unconscious.

● *What are "photographic" memories?*

23. _____ _____ (photographic memory) occurs when a person is able to project an image onto an external surface. Such images allow brief, nearly complete recall by some children.
24. _____ _____ is rarely found in adults. However, many adults have internal images, which can be very vivid and a basis for remembering.
25. _____ memory can be learned by finding ways to directly store information in LTM. Learning has no effect on the _____ of STM. Some people may have naturally superior memory abilities that exceed what can be achieved through learning.

● *What causes forgetting?*

26. Forgetting and memory were extensively studied by Herman _____, whose curve of forgetting shows that forgetting is typically most rapid immediately after learning.
27. He used _____ syllables to study memory. The forgetting of meaningful material is much slower than shown by his curve of forgetting.
28. Failure to _____ information is a common cause of "forgetting."
29. Forgetting in _____ memory and _____ probably reflects decay of memory traces in the nervous system. Decay or disuse of memories may also account for some _____ loss, but most forgetting cannot be explained this way.
30. Often, forgetting is _____ dependent. The power of _____ to trigger memories is revealed by _____ learning, in which bodily states at the time of learning and of retrieval affect memory.
31. Much forgetting in both STM and LTM can be attributed to _____ of memories with one another.
32. When recent learning interferes with retrieval of prior learning, _____ interference has occurred. If old memories interfere with new memories, _____ interference has occurred.

● *How accurate are everyday memories?*

33. _____ is the motivated forgetting of painful, embarrassing, or traumatic memories.
34. _____ is thought to be unconscious, in contrast to _____, which is a conscious attempt to avoid thinking about something.
35. Experts are currently debating the validity of childhood memories of abuse that reappear after apparently being _____ for decades.
36. Independent evidence has verified that some _____ memories are true. However, others have been shown to be false.

37. In the absence of confirming or disconfirming evidence, there is currently no way to separate true memories from _____. Caution is advised for all concerned with attempts to retrieve supposedly hidden memories.

38. _____ memories, which seem especially vivid, are created at emotionally significant times. While such memories may not be _____, we tend to place great confidence in them.

● *What happens in the brain when memories are formed?*

39. _____ amnesia and the effects of _____ shock (ECS) may be explained by the concept of consolidation.

40. Consolidation theory holds that _____ (permanent memory traces) are formed during a critical period after learning. Until they are _____, long-term memories are easily destroyed.

41. The _____ is a brain structure associated with the consolidation of memories.

42. The search within the brain for engrams has now settled on changes in individual _____.

43. The best-documented changes are alterations in the amounts of _____ chemicals released by nerve cells.

● *How can memory be improved?*

44. Memory can be improved by using _____ (knowledge of results), recitation, and rehearsal, by _____ and organizing information, and by using the progressive part method, spaced practice, overlearning, and active _____ strategies.

45. The effects of _____ position, sleep, review, cues, and _____ (connecting new information to existing knowledge) should also be kept in mind when studying or memorizing.

46. _____ systems, such as the keyword method, use mental images and unusual associations to link new information with familiar memories already stored in LTM. Such strategies give information personal meaning and make it easier to recall.

● *How has evolution shaped human memory?*

Recite and Review: A STEP BEYOND

47. _____ shaped memory to mainly store information about recent events and repeated information or events.

48. _____ refers to the fact that information stored in memory tends to fade with the passage of time.

49. _____ tends to occur when we form weak memories because we fail to pay attention while creating the memory.

50. _____ is the frustrating experience of not being able to recall a word or a name that you know well.

51. _____ refers to linking a memory with the wrong source, time, or place.
52. Suggestions and misleading questions can implant information that leads people to _____ or _____ their memories.
53. Memories of _____ events may persist for many years even though we wish we could forget.

MASTERY TEST

1. The meaning and importance of information has a strong impact on
    a. sensory memory   b. eidetic memory   c. long-term memory   d. procedural memory

2. Pseudo-memories are closely related to the effects of
    a. repression   b. suppression   c. semantic forgetting   d. constructive processing

3. The occurrence of _____ implies that consolidation has been prevented.
    a. retrograde amnesia   b. hippocampal transfer   c. suppression   d. changes in the activities of individual nerve cells

4. Most of the techniques used to recover supposedly repressed memories involve
    a. redintegration and hypnosis   b. suggestion and fantasy   c. reconstruction and priming
    d. coercion and fabrication

5. Most daily memory chores are handled by
    a. sensory memory and LTM   b. STM and working memory   c. STM and LTM
    d. STM and declarative memory

6. Three key processes in memory systems are
    a. storage, organization, recovery   b. encoding, attention, reprocessing   c. storage, retrieval, encoding
    d. retrieval, reprocessing, reorganization

7. Procedural memories are to skills as _____ memories are to facts.
    a. declarative   b. short-term   c. redintegrative   d. eidetic

8. An ability to answer questions about distances on a map you have seen only once implies that some memories are based on
    a. constructive processing   b. redintegration   c. internal images   d. episodic processing

9. The first potential cause of forgetting that may occur is
    a. engram decay   b. disuse   c. cue-dependent forgetting   d. encoding failure

10. The persistence of icons and echoes is the basis for
    a. sensory memory   b. short-term memory   c. long-term memory   d. working memory

11. Priming is most often used to reveal
    a. semantic memories   b. episodic memories   c. implicit memories   d. eidetic memories

12. "Projection" onto an external surface is most characteristic of
    a. sensory memories   b. eidetic images   c. flashbulb memories   d. mnemonic images

13. Chunking helps especially to extend the capacity of
    a. sensory memory   b. STM   c. LTM   d. declarative memory

14. There is presently no way to tell if a "recovered" memory is true or false unless independent
    _____ exists.
    a. evidence   b. amnesia   c. elaboration   d. consolidation

15. Taking an essay test inevitably requires a person to use
    a. recall   b. recognition   c. relearning   d. priming

16. A savings score is used in what memory task?
    a. recall   b. recognition   c. relearning   d. priming

17. _____ rehearsal helps link new information to existing memories by concentrating on meaning.
    a. Redintegrative   b. Constructive   c. Maintenance   d. Elaborative

18. Middle items are neither held in STM nor moved to LTM. This statement explains the
    a. feeling of knowing   b. serial position effect   c. tip-of-the-tongue state   d. semantic forgetting curve

19. According to the curve of forgetting, the greatest decline in the amount recalled occurs during the
    _____ after learning.
    a. first hour   b. second day   c. third to sixth days   d. retroactive period

20. Work with brain stimulation, truth serums, and hypnosis suggests that long-term memories are
    a. stored in the hippocampus   b. relatively permanent   c. unaffected by later input
    d. always redintegrative

21. Which of the following is most likely to improve the accuracy of memory?
    a. hypnosis   b. constructive processing   c. the serial position effect   d. memory cues

22. To qualify as repression, forgetting must be
    a. retroactive   b. proactive   c. unconscious   d. explicit

23. Which of the following typically is NOT a good way to improve memory?
    a. massed practice   b. overlearning   c. rehearsal   d. recall strategies

24. A witness to a crime is questioned in ways that re-create the context of the crime and that provide many memory cues. It appears that she is undergoing
    a. retroactive priming   b. the progressive part method   c. retroactive consolidation
    d. a cognitive interview

25. One thing that is clearly true about flashbulb memories is that
    a. they are unusually accurate   b. we place great confidence in them   c. they apply primarily to public tragedies   d. they are recovered by using visualization and hypnosis

26. One common mnemonic strategy is the
    a. serial position technique   b. feeling of knowing tactic   c. network procedure   d. keyword method

27. A perspective that helps explain redintegrative memories is
    a. the feeling of knowing model   b. recoding and chunking   c. the network model
    d. mnemonic models

28. Which of the following is NOT considered a part of long-term memory?
    a. echoic memory   b. semantic memory   c. episodic memory   d. declarative memory

29. You are very thirsty. Suddenly you remember a time years ago when you became very thirsty while hiking. This suggests that your memory is
    a. proactive   b. state dependent   c. still not consolidated   d. eidetic

30. After memorizing 5 lists of words you recall less of the last list than a person who only memorized list number five. This observation is explained by
    a. reactive processing   b. reconstructive processing   c. proactive interference
    d. retroactive interference

31. If you are temporarily unable to recall information that you know well, it could be said that _____ has occurred.
    a. transience   b. blocking   c. misattribution   d. state-dependent forgetting

32. On a TV game show, you are asked which way Lincoln's head faces on a penny. You are unable to answer correctly and you lose a large prize. Your memory failure is most likely a result of
    a. the serial position effect   b. repression   c. encoding failure   d. priming

ANSWERS

Recite and Review

1. system, Information
2. stored
3. 3, short-term, long-term
4. exact, image
5. sounds, meaning
6. temporary, permanent
7. seconds, STM
8. bits, larger
9. interruption, repetition
10. STM, memories
11. updating, false
12. organized, models
13. memory
14. facts, skills
15. Declarative
16. forgetting
17. personal
18. state, recall
19. essay, middle
20. recognition, Recognition
21. savings
22. memories, memories
23. image
24. adults
25. LTM, STM
26. curve, after
27. meaningful, slower
28. information
29. traces, disuse
30. learning, states
31. forgetting
32. interferes, interfere
33. forgetting
34. conscious
35. abuse
36. true, false
37. evidence
38. confidence
39. amnesia, shock
40. memory traces
41. brain
42. nerve
43. chemicals
44. organizing, part
45. position
46. keyword, LTM
47. events, events
48. fade
49. attention
50. know well
51. time, place
52. memories
53. forget

Connections

1. d
2. a
3. h
4. f
5. b
6. c
7. e
8. g
9. c
10. g
11. a
12. e
13. b
14. d
15. f
16. f or g
17. c
18. d
19. a
20. f or g
21. b
22. e
23. h
24. f
25. g
26. e
27. a
28. c
29. b
30. d

Check Your Memory

1. T
2. F
3. T
4. T
5. F
6. F
7. T
8. T
9. F
10. T
11. F
12. F
13. F
14. T
15. T
16. F
17. F
18. T
19. T
20. T
21. F
22. T
23. F
24. F
25. T
26. F
27. T
28. F
29. T
30. T
31. T
32. F
33. F
34. F
35. F
36. T
37. T
38. F
39. T
40. T
41. T
42. T
43. F

44. F
45. F
46. F
47. T
48. T
49. T
50. F
51. T
52. T
53. F
54. F
55. T
56. T
57. T
58. F
59. F
60. T
61. T
62. F
63. T
64. T
65. T
66. T
67. T
68. F
69. T
70. T

Final Survey and Review

1. encoded
2. retrieved
3. sensory, short-term
4. icon, echo
5. Short-term, Long-term
6. STM, working, meaningful
7. Sensory, selective attention
8. digit-span, recoding
9. interference, maintenance
10. Elaborative
11. constructive, pseudo-memories
12. networks, Network
13. Redintegrative
14. declarative, procedural
15. semantic, episodic
16. Semantic
17. Episodic
18. tip, tongue, recognition
19. recall, serial position
20. multiple, distractors
21. relearning
22. explicit, implicit
23. Eidetic imagery
24. Eidetic imagery
25. Exceptional, limits
26. Ebbinghaus
27. nonsense
28. encode
29. sensory, STM, LTM
30. cue, cues, state-dependent
31. interference
32. retroactive, proactive
33. Repression
34. Repression, suppression
35. repressed
36. recovered
37. fantasies
38. Flashbulb, accurate
39. Retrograde, electroconvulsive
40. engrams, consolidated
41. hippocampus
42. nerve cells
43. transmitter
44. feedback, selecting, search
45. serial, elaboration
46. Mnemonic
47. Evolution
48. Transience
49. Absent-mindedness
50. Blocking
51. Misattribution
52. alter, revise
53. traumatic

Mastery Test

1. c (p. 333)
2. d (p. 336)
3. a (p. 353)
4. b (p. 351)
5. c (p. 333)
6. c (p. 331)
7. a (p. 338)
8. c (p. 342)
9. d (p. 346)
10. a (p. 332)
11. c (p. 342)
12. b (p. 342)
13. b (p. 334)
14. a (p. 351)
15. a (p. 340)
16. c (p. 431)
17. d (p. 334)
18. b (p. 340)
19. a (p. 345)
20. b (p. 335)
21. d (p. 356)
22. c (p. 350)
23. a (p. 356)
24. d (p. 358)
25. b (p. 352)
26. d (p. 360)
27. c (p. 337-338)
28. a (p. 339)
29. b (p. 348)
30. c (p. 349)
31. b (p. 362)
32. c (p. 346)

Chapter 10
Cognition, Language, and Creativity

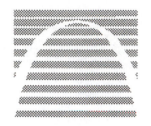

CHAPTER OVERVIEW

Thinking is the mental manipulation of images, concepts, and language (or symbols). Most people use internal images for thinking. Kinesthetic images come from remembered actions and implicit actions. A concept is a generalized idea of a class of objects or events. We learn concepts from positive and negative instances and from rules. Prototypes are often used to identify concepts. Language translates events into symbols, which are combined using the rules of grammar and syntax. True languages are productive. Studies suggest that primates are capable of some language use.

The solution to a problem may be arrived at mechanically (by trial and error or by rote). Solutions by understanding usually begin with discovering the general properties of an answer. Next, functional solutions are proposed. Problem solving is frequently aided by heuristics, which narrow the search for solutions. When understanding leads to a rapid solution, it is said that insight has occurred. Insight can be blocked by fixations. Work on artificial intelligence has focused on computer simulations and expert systems. Computer simulations of human problem solving are usually based on a means-ends analysis. Human expertise is based on organized knowledge and acquired strategies.

Creative solutions are practical, sensible, and original. Creative thinking requires divergent thought, characterized by fluency, flexibility, and originality. Tests of creativity measure these qualities. Five stages often seen in creative problem solving are orientation, preparation, incubation, illumination, and verification. However, much creative work is simply based on incremental problem solving. Studies suggest that there is little correlation between IQ and creativity.

Intuitive thinking often leads to errors. Wrong conclusions may be drawn when an answer seems highly representative of what we already believe is true. A second problem is ignoring the base rate of an event. Clear thinking is usually aided by stating or framing a problem in broad terms. Major sources of thinking errors include rigid mental sets, faulty logic, and over-simplifications. Various strategies, including brainstorming, tend to enhance creative problem solving.

Animals reveal a rudimentary capacity for thought when they solve delayed response problems and, in some cases, problems that appear to require understanding or insight. There is also evidence that higher animals, such as chimpanzees, can learn to use basic symbolic thought.

LEARNING OBJECTIVES

To demonstrate mastery of this chapter you should be able to:

1. Define *cognition* and *cognitive psychology*.
2. List the three basic units of thought.
3. Describe mental imagery, synesthesia, and the properties of mental images. Explain how both stored and created images may be used to solve problems (including how the size of a mental image may be important).
4. Explain how kinesthetic imagery aids thinking.
5. Define the terms *concept* and *concept formation*, explain how they aid thought processes, and describe how they are learned.
6. Define the terms *conjunctive concept, relational concept, disjunctive concept,* and *prototype.*
7. Explain the difference between the denotative and connotative meaning of a word or concept, and describe how the connotative meaning of a word is measured.
8. Briefly describe the problems associated with social stereotypes and all-or-nothing thinking.
9. Explain how language aids thought, and define *semantics.*
10. Discuss bilingual education, including the concepts of additive and subtractive bilingualism, and two-way bilingual education.
11. Briefly describe the following three requirements of a language and their related concepts:
    - a. symbols
        1. phonemes
        2. morphemes
    - b. grammar
        1. syntax
        2. transformational rules
    - c. productivity
12. Explain why forms of language other than speech are believed to be possible.
13. Explain the extent to which primates have been taught to use language.
14. Describe both the criticisms and the practical value of attempts to teach language to primates.
15. Differentiate between mechanical problem-solving and problem-solving through understanding.
16. Define *heuristics* and explain how they aid problem-solving.
17. Tell how each of the following contributes to insight:
    - a. selective encoding　　b. selective combination　　c. selective comparison
18. Explain how fixation and functional fixedness block problem solving, and give an example of each.
19. List and explain four common barriers to creative thinking.
20. Define the term *artificial intelligence* (including a description of what it is based on).
21. Describe both the potential uses and limitations of artificial intelligence.
22. Describe the following four kinds of thought:
    - a. inductive　　b. deductive　　c. logical　　　d. illogical

23. Describe the following characteristics of creative thinking:
    a. fluency   b. flexibility   c. originality
24. Explain the relationship of creativity to divergent and convergent thinking.
25. List the two most common daydream themes and discuss how fantasy (daydreaming) relates to creativity.
26. List three characteristics of creativity other than divergent thinking.
27. Describe how the ability to think divergently can be measured.
28. List and describe the five stages of creative thinking.
29. Discuss the five qualities that characterize creative persons.
30. Briefly discuss the use of syllogisms in logical thinking.
31. Explain the following three common intuitive thinking errors:
    a. representativeness (including representativeness heuristic)
    b. underlying odds (base rate)
    c. framing

The following objectives are related to the material in the "Psychology in Action" and "A Step Beyond" sections of your text.

32. Describe nine practical steps to encourage creativity.
33. Describe the process of brainstorming, and explain how it can be used to solve problems.
34. Describe thinking in animals as exemplified by delayed response problems and insight.
35. Give several examples of apparently intelligent thought by an animal.

RECITE AND REVIEW

● *What is the nature of thought?*

Recite and Review: Pages 366-368

1. Cognitive psychology is the study of _____, language, problem solving, and _____ processing.
2. Thinking is the manipulation of _____ representations of external problems or situations.
3. Three basic units of thought are images, concepts, and _____ or symbols.

● *In what ways are images related to thinking?*

Recite and Review: Pages 368-371

4. Most people have internal images of one kind or another. Images may be based on information stored in memory or they may be _____.

5. Sometimes images cross normal _____ boundaries in a type of imagery called synesthesia.

6. The size of images used in problem solving may _____. Images may be three-dimensional and they may be rotated in _____ to answer questions.

7. Many of the systems in the brain that are involved in processing _____ images work in reverse to create mental images.

8. Kinesthetic images are created by memories of _____ or by implicit (unexpressed) _____. Kinesthetic sensations and micromovements seem to help structure thinking for many people.

● How are concepts learned? Are there different kinds of concepts?

Recite and Review: Pages 371-373

9. A concept is a generalized idea of a _____ of objects or events.

10. Forming concepts may be based on experiences with _____ and negative instances.

11. Concepts may also be acquired by learning rules that define the _____.

12. In practice, we frequently use prototypes (general _____ of the concept class) to identify concepts.

13. Concepts may be classified as conjunctive ("_____" concepts), disjunctive ("_____" concepts), or relational concepts.

14. The denotative meaning of a word or concept is its dictionary _____. Connotative meaning is _____ or emotional.

15. Connotative meaning can be measured with the semantic differential. Most connotative meaning involves the dimensions _____, strong-weak, and active-passive.

16. Two common thinking errors are _____ thinking (thinking in black and white terms) and use of social stereotypes (inaccurate and oversimplified images of _____ _____).

● What is the role of language in thinking?

Recite and Review: Pages 373-376

17. Language allows events to be encoded into _____ for easy mental manipulation.

18. Language is built out of phonemes (basic speech _____) and morphemes (speech sounds collected into _____ units).

19. Thinking in language is influenced by meaning. The study of _____ is called semantics.

20. Learning a second _____ (bilingualism) during the elementary school years is most likely to benefit students who participate in _____ bilingual education.

21. Language carries meaning by combining a set of symbols or signs according to a set of _____ (grammar), which includes rules about word _____ (syntax).

22. Various sentences are created by applying transformation _____ to simple statements.

23. A true language is productive, and can be used to generate new ideas or possibilities. American Sign Language (ASL) and other _____ languages used by the deaf are true languages.

● *Can animals be taught to use language?*

Recite and Review: Pages 376-378

24. Animal communication is relatively limited because it lacks symbols that can be
_____ easily.

25. Attempts to teach chimpanzees ASL and other nonverbal systems suggest to some that primates are capable of language use. However, others believe that the chimps are merely using
_____ responses to get food and other reinforcers.

26. Studies that make use of lexigrams (_____ word-symbols) provide the best evidence yet of animal language use.

● *What do we know about problem solving?*

Recite and Review: Pages 379-383

27. The solution to a problem may be found mechanically (by trial and error or by _____ application of rules). However, mechanical solutions are frequently inefficient or ineffective, except where aided by _____.

28. Solutions by understanding usually begin with discovery of the _____ properties of an answer. Next comes proposal of a number of functional _____.

29. Problem solving is frequently aided by heuristics. These are strategies that typically
_____ the search for solutions. The _____ strategy (identify, define, explore, act, look and learn) is a general heuristic.

30. When understanding leads to a rapid _____, insight has occurred. Three elements of insight are _____ encoding, selective combination, and selective comparison.

31. Insights and other problem solving attempts can be blocked by fixation (a tendency to repeat
_____ solutions).

32. Functional fixedness is a common _____, but emotional blocks, cultural values, learned conventions, and perceptual _____ are also problems.

● *What is artificial intelligence?*

Recite and Review: Pages 383-384

33. Artificial intelligence refers to any artificial _____ that can perform tasks that require _____ when done by people.

34. Two principal areas of artificial intelligence research are _____ simulations and expert systems.

35. Computer simulations of human problem solving are usually based on a means-ends
_____ (finding ways to reduce the difference between the present state and the desired goal).

36. Expert human problem solving is based on organized _____ and acquired strategies, rather than some general improvement in thinking ability. Expertise also allows more automatic _____ of problems.

● *What is the nature of creative thinking?*

Recite and Review: Pages 384-390

37. To be creative, a solution must be _____ and sensible as well as original.
38. _____ may be deductive or inductive, logical or illogical.
39. Creative thinking requires divergent thought, characterized by fluency, flexibility, and _____. Creativity is also marked by problem _____, the active discovery of problems to be solved.
40. Daydreaming and _____ are a source of much divergent thinking. Two very common daydream plots are the conquering _____ and the suffering martyr.
41. Tests of _____, such as the *Unusual Uses Test,* the *Consequences Test,* and the *Anagrams Test,* measure the capacity for divergent thinking.
42. Five stages often seen in creative problem solving are orientation, _____, incubation, illumination, and verification.
43. Not all creative thinking fits this pattern. Much creative activity is based on incremental problem solving (many small _____).
44. Studies suggest that creative persons share a number of identifiable general traits, _____ abilities, thinking _____, and personality characteristics. There is little or no correlation between IQ and creativity.
45. Many of history's most _____ creative artists, writers, poets, and composers suffered from mood disorders.

● *How accurate is intuition?*

Recite and Review: Pages 390-393

46. Syllogisms can be evaluated for the _____ of their premises, the validity of the reasoning, and the truth of the _____.
47. Intuitive thinking often leads to _____. Wrong conclusions may be drawn when an answer seems highly representative of what we already believe is _____. (That is, when people apply the representativeness heuristic.)
48. A second problem is ignoring the base rate (or underlying _____) of an event.
49. Clear thinking is usually aided by stating or framing a problem in _____ terms.

● *What can be done to promote creativity?*

Recite and Review: PSYCHOLOGY IN ACTION

50. Rigid mental sets are a major barrier to _____ thinking.
51. Creativity can be enhanced by defining problems _____, by establishing a creative atmosphere, by allowing _____ for incubation, by seeking _____ input, and by looking for analogies.
52. Brainstorming, in which the production and criticism of ideas is kept _____, also tends to enhance creative problem solving.

● *Do animals think?*

Recite and Review: A STEP BEYOND

53. Animals reveal a rudimentary capacity for thought when they solve _____ response problems.

54. Köhler's chimp solved multiple-stick problems that appeared to require understanding or _____. Some natural "problem solving" by animals appears to be versatile and appropriate enough to qualify as _____.

55. In a recent study, three kinds of apes showed evidence of understanding in a problem that involved using _____ to obtain food hidden in a transparent plastic tube.

56. There is also evidence that higher animals, such as chimpanzees, can learn to use rudimentary symbolic _____. For the moment, however, some psychologists remain unconvinced about such abilities.

CONNECTIONS

1. _____	cognition	a. 3-D images
2. _____	language	b. remembered perceptions
3. _____	synesthesia	c. brain imaging
4. _____	mental rotation	d. mental class
5. _____	reverse vision	e. implicit actions
6. _____	stored images	f. thinking
7. _____	kinesthetic imagery	g. ideal or model
8. _____	concept	h. semantic differential
9. _____	prototype	i. crossed senses
10. _____	connotative meaning	j. symbols and rules

11. _____	word meanings	a. meaningful unit
12. _____	morpheme	b. ASL
13. _____	phoneme	c. semantics
14. _____	"hidden" grammar	d. lexigrams
15. _____	Washoe	e. language sound
16. _____	if-then statement	f. mechanical solution
17. _____	Kanzi	g. thinking strategy
18. _____	trial-and-error	h. element of insight
19. _____	heuristic	i. conditional relationship
20. _____	selective comparison	j. transformation rules

21. _____	fixation	a. knowledge plus rules
22. _____	expert system	b. many types of solutions
23. _____	fluency	c. one correct answer
24. _____	flexibility	d. moment of insight
25. _____	originality	e. underlying odds
26. _____	convergent thinking	f. analysis of logic
27. _____	Anagrams Test	g. many solutions
28. _____	illumination	h. blind to alternatives
29. _____	base rate	i. measures divergent thinking
30. _____	syllogism	j. novelty of solutions

CHECK YOUR MEMORY

Check Your Memory: Pages 366-368

1. Cognitive psychology is the study of sensation, memory, and learning. T or F?
2. Images, concepts, and language may be used to mentally represent problems. T or F?
3. Images are generalized ideas of a class of related objects or events. T or F?
4. Blindfolded chess players mainly use concepts to represent chess problems and solutions. T or F?

Check Your Memory: Pages 368-371

5. Experiencing color sensations while listening to music is an example of mental rotation. T or F?
6. Mental images may be used to improve memory and skilled actions. T or F?
7. In an imagined space, it is easiest to locate objects placed above and below yourself. T or F?
8. The visual cortex is activated when a person has a mental image. T or F?
9. The more the image of a shape has to be rotated in space, the longer it takes to tell if it matches another view of the same shape. T or F?
10. People who have good imaging abilities tend to score high on tests of creativity. T or F?
11. The smaller a mental image is, the harder it is to identify its details. T or F?
12. People with good synesthetic imagery tend to learn sports skills faster than average. T or F?

Check Your Memory: Pages 371-373

13. Concept formation is typically based on examples and rules. T or F?
14. Prototypes are very strong negative instances of a concept. T or F?
15. "Greater than" and "lopsided" are relational concepts. T or F?
16. Classifying things as absolutely right or wrong may lead to all-or-nothing thinking. T or F?
17. The semantic differential is used to rate the objective meanings of words and concepts. T or F?

Check Your Memory: Pages 373-376

18. Encoding is the study of the meanings of language. T or F?
19. The Stroop interference test shows that thought is greatly influenced by language. T or F?

20. Morphemes are the basic speech sounds of a language. T or F?
21. Syntax is a part of grammar. T or F?
22. Noam Chomsky believes that a child who says, "I drinked my juice," has applied the semantic differential to a simple, core sentence. T or F?
23. Similar universal language patterns are found in both speech and gestural languages, such as ASL. T or F?
24. ASL has 600,000 root signs. T or F?
25. True languages are productive, thus ASL is not a true language. T or F?

Check Your Memory: Pages 376-378

26. Animal communication can be described as productive. T or F?
27. Chimpanzees have never learned to speak even a single word. T or F?
28. One of Sarah chimpanzee's outstanding achievements was mastery of sentences involving transformational rules. T or F?
29. Some "language" use by chimpanzees appears to be no more than simple operant responses. T or F?
30. Only a minority of the things that language-trained chimps "say" have anything to do with food. T or F?
31. Language-trained chimps have been known to hold conversations when no humans were present. T or F?
32. Kanzi's use of grammar is on a par with that of a 2-year-old child. T or F?

Check Your Memory: Pages 379-383

33. Except for the simplest problems, mechanical solutions are typically best left to computers. T or F?
34. Karl Dunker's famous tumor problem could only be solved by trial-and-error. T or F?
35. In solutions by understanding, functional solutions are usually discovered by use of a random search strategy. T or F?
36. Working backward from the desired goal to the starting point can be a useful heuristic. T or F?
37. In problem solving, rapid insights are more likely to be correct than those that develop slowly. T or F?
38. Selective encoding refers to bringing together seemingly unrelated bits of useful information. T or F?
39. Functional fixedness is an inability to see new uses for familiar objects. T or F?

Check Your Memory: Pages 383-384

40. In general, artificial intelligence lacks the creativity and common sense of human intelligence. T or F?
41. AI is frequently based on a set of rules applied to a body of information. T or F?
42. Computer simulations are used to test models of human cognition. T or F?
43. Most computer-based models of human problem solving rely on the principle of automatic processing. T or F?
44. Much human expertise is based on acquired strategies for solving problems. T or F?
45. Chess experts have an exceptional ability to remember the positions of chess pieces placed at random on a chessboard. T or F?

Check Your Memory: Pages 384-390

46. In inductive thinking, a general rule is inferred from specific examples. T or F?
47. Fluency and flexibility are measures of convergent thinking. T or F?
48. About half of our waking thoughts are occupied by daydreams. T or F?

49. Fantasy contributes to divergent thinking and creativity. T or F?

50. Creative thinkers typically apply reasoning and critical thinking to novel ideas after they produce them. T or F?

51. Creative ideas combine originality with feasibility. T or F?

52. Creative problem solving temporarily stops during the incubation period. T or F?

53. Much creative problem solving is incremental, rather than being based on sudden insights or breakthroughs. T or F?

54. Creative people have an openness to experience and they have a wide range of knowledge and interests. T or F?

55. Most people who are mentally ill are not especially creative. In fact, the more severely disturbed a person is, the *less* creative she or he is likely to be. T or F?

56. The connection between mood swings and creativity may be mainly a matter of productivity. T or F?

Check Your Memory: Pages 390-393

57. It is possible to draw true conclusions using faulty logic. T or F?

58. It is possible to draw false conclusions using valid logic. T or F?

59. Intuition is a quick, impulsive insight into the true nature of a problem and its solution. T or F?

60. The probability of two events occurring together is lower than the probability of either one occurring alone. T or F?

61. The representativeness heuristic is the strategy of stating problems in broad terms. T or F?

62. Framing refers to the way in which a problem is stated or structured. T or F?

Check Your Memory: PSYCHOLOGY IN ACTION

63. Exposure to creative models tends to increase creativity among observers. T or F?

64. Delaying evaluation during the early stages of creative problem solving tends to lead to poor thinking. T or F?

65. Asking yourself, "If the problem were edible, how would it taste?" is an example of restating a problem in a different way. T or F?

66. People who think creatively are typically unwilling to take risks. T or F?

67. The cross-stimulation effect is an important part of brainstorming in groups. T or F?

Check Your Memory: A STEP BEYOND

68. Wolfgang Köhler believed that solving multiple-stick problems revealed insight in chimpanzees. T or F?

69. Animal thinking is implied by actions that appear to be planned with an awareness of likely results. T or F?

70. Apes attempting to use tools to obtain food from a plastic tube made more errors with "practice," suggesting that their successes reflect random trial and error. T or F?

71. Learning to use symbols appeared to free Sheba chimpanzee so that she could ignore the powerful allure of visible food. T or F?

FINAL SURVEY AND REVIEW

● *What is the nature of thought?*

1. _____ psychology is the study of thinking, language, _____ _____, and information processing.

2. Thinking is the manipulation of internal _____ of external problems or situations.

3. Three basic units of thought are _____, _____, and language or _____.

● *In what ways are images related to thinking?*

4. Most people have internal images of one kind or another. Images may be based on _____ _____ in memory or they may be created.

5. Sometimes images cross normal sense boundaries in a type of imagery called _____.

6. The _____ of images used in problem solving may change. Images may be three-dimensional and they may be _____ in space to answer questions.

7. Many of the systems in the _____ that are involved in processing _____ images work in reverse to create _____ images.

8. Kinesthetic images are created by memories of actions or by _____ (unexpressed) actions. Kinesthetic sensations and _____ seem to help structure thinking for many people.

● *How are concepts learned? Are there different kinds of concepts?*

9. A concept is a _____ idea of a class of objects or events.

10. Forming concepts may be based on experiences with positive and _____ _____.

11. Concepts may also be acquired by learning _____ that define the concept.

12. In practice, we frequently use _____ (general models of the concept class) to identify concepts.

13. Concepts may be classified as _____ ("and" concepts), _____ ("either-or" concepts), or relational concepts.

14. The _____ meaning of a word or concept is its dictionary definition. _____ meaning is personal or emotional.

15. Connotative meaning can be measured with the _____ differential. Most connotative meaning involves the dimensions good-bad, _____, and _____.

16. Two common thinking errors are _____ thinking (thinking in black and white terms) and use of _____ _____ (inaccurate and oversimplified images of social groups).

● *What is the role of language in thinking?*

17. Language allows events to be _____ into symbols for easy mental manipulation.
18. Language is built out of _____ (basic speech sounds) and
_____ (speech sounds collected into meaningful units).
19. Thinking in language is influenced by meaning. The study of meaning is called
_____.
20. Learning a second language (_____) during the elementary school years is most
likely to benefit students who participate in _____ _____ education.
21. Language carries meaning by combining a set of symbols or signs according to a set of rules
(_____), which includes rules about word order (_____).
22. Various sentences are created by applying _____ rules to simple
statements.
23. A true language is _____, and can be used to generate new ideas or possibilities.
_____ _____ Language (ASL) and other gestural languages used by the deaf
are true languages.

● *Can animals be taught to use language?*

24. Animal communication is relatively limited because it lacks _____ that can be rearranged
easily.
25. Attempts to teach chimpanzees ASL and other nonverbal systems suggest to some that
_____ are capable of language use. However, others believe that the chimps are merely
using operant responses to get food and other _____.
26. Studies that make use of _____ (geometric word-symbols) provide the best
evidence yet of animal language use.

● *What do we know about problem solving?*

27. The solution to a problem may be found _____ (by trial and error or by rote
application of rules). However, _____ solutions are frequently inefficient or ineffective,
except when aided by computer.
28. Solutions by _____ usually begin with discovery of the general properties of
an answer. Next comes proposal of a number of _____ (workable) solutions.
29. Problem solving is frequently aided by _____. These are strategies that typically
narrow the search for solutions. An example is the ideal strategy (_____, define,
_____, act, look and learn).
30. When understanding leads to a rapid solution, _____ has occurred. Three elements of
_____ are selective _____, selective combination and selective comparison.
31. Insights and other problem solving attempts can be blocked by _____ (a tendency to
repeat wrong solutions).
32. _____ fixedness is a common fixation, but emotional _____,
cultural _____, learned conventions, and perceptual habits are also problems.

● *What is artificial intelligence?*

33. Artificial intelligence refers to any _____ _____ that can perform tasks that require intelligence when done by _____.

34. Two principal areas of artificial intelligence research are computer simulations and _____ _____.

35. Computer simulations of human problem solving are usually based on a _____ analysis (finding ways to reduce the difference between the present state and the desired goal).

36. Expert human problem solving is based on _____ knowledge and acquired _____, rather than some general improvement in thinking ability. Expertise also allows more _____ processing of problems.

● *What is the nature of creative thinking?*

37. To be creative, a solution must be practical and sensible as well as _____.

38. Thinking may be deductive or _____, _____ or illogical.

39. Creative thinking requires _____ thought, characterized by _____, flexibility, and originality. Creativity is also marked by _____ _____, the active discovery of problems to be solved.

40. Daydreaming and fantasy are a source of much divergent thinking. Two very common daydream plots are the _____ hero and the suffering _____.

41. Tests of creativity, such as the *Unusual* _____ *Test*, the *Consequences Test*, and the *Anagrams Test*, measure the capacity for _____ thinking.

42. Five stages often seen in creative problem solving are orientation, preparation, _____, _____, and verification.

43. Not all creative thinking fits this pattern. Much creative activity is based on _____ problem solving (many small steps).

44. Studies suggest that creative persons share a number of identifiable general traits, thinking abilities, thinking styles, and _____ characteristics. There is little or no _____ between IQ and creativity.

45. Many of history's most creative artists, writers, poets, and composers suffered from _____ disorders.

● *How accurate is intuition?*

46. Syllogisms can be evaluated for the truth of their _____, the validity of the _____, and the truth of the conclusions.

47. Intuitive thinking often leads to errors. Wrong conclusions may be drawn when an answer seems highly _____ of what we already believe is true. (That is, when people apply the representativeness _____.)

48. A second problem is ignoring the _____ _____ (or underlying probability) of an event.

49. Clear thinking is usually aided by stating or _____ a problem in broad terms.

● *What can be done to promote creativity?*

50. Rigid _____ _____ are a major barrier to creative thinking.

51. Creativity can be enhanced by defining problems broadly, by establishing a creative atmosphere, by allowing time for _____, by seeking varied _____, and by looking for analogies.

52. _____, in which the production and criticism of ideas is kept separate, also tends to enhance creative problem solving.

● *Do animals think?*

53. Animals reveal a rudimentary capacity for thought when they solve delayed _____ problems.

54. Köhler's chimp solved _____ problems that appeared to require understanding or insight. Some natural "problem solving" by animals appears to be _____ and appropriate enough to qualify as thinking.

55. In a recent study, three kinds of apes showed evidence of _____ in a problem that involved using tools to obtain food hidden in a transparent plastic tube.

56. There is also evidence that higher animals, such as chimpanzees, can learn to use rudimentary _____ thought. For the moment, however, some psychologists remain unconvinced about such abilities.

MASTERY TEST

1. The mark of a true language is that it must be
   a. spoken b. productive c. based on spatial grammar and syntax d. capable of encoding conditional relationships

2. Computer simulations and expert systems are two major applications of
   a. AI b. ASL c. brainstorming d. problem framing

3. Failure to wear automobile seat belts is an example of which intuitive thinking error?
   a. allowing too much time for incubation b. framing a problem broadly c. ignoring base rates
   d. recognition that two events occurring together are more likely than either one alone

4. One thing that images, concepts, and symbols all have in common is that they are
   a. morphemes b. internal representations c. based on reverse vision d. translated into micromovements

5. To decide if a container is a cup, bowl, or vase, most people compare it to
   a. a prototype b. its connotative meaning c. a series of negative instances d. a series of relevant phonemes

6. During problem solving, being "cold," "warm," or "very warm" is closely associated with
   a. insight   b. fixation   c. automatic processing   d. rote problem solving

7. The *Anagrams Test* measures
   a. mental sets   b. inductive thinking   c. logical reasoning   d. divergent thinking

8. "Either-or" concepts are
   a. conjunctive   b. disjunctive   c. relational   d. prototypical

9. Which term does not belong with the others?
   a. selective comparison   b. functional fixedness   c. learned conventions   d. emotional blocks

10. The IDEAL thinking strategy is basically a
    a. prototype   b. heuristic   c. functional solution   d. form of intuitive thought

11. An incremental view of creative problem solving CONTRASTS most directly with which stage of creative thought?
    a. orientation   b. preparation   c. illumination   d. verification

12. Daydreaming and fantasy are two principal sources of
    a. intuition   b. divergent thinking   c. feasible solutions   d. selective comparison

13. The difference between prime beef and dead cow is primarily a matter of
    a. syntax   b. conjunctive meaning   c. semantics   d. the productive nature of language

14. Synesthesia is an unusual form of
    a. imagery   b. heuristic   c. insight   d. daydreaming

15. Which of the listed terms does NOT correctly complete this sentence: Insight involves selective
    _____.
    a. encoding   b. combination   c. comparison   d. fixation

16. Which of the following is LEAST likely to predict that a person is creative?
    a. high IQ   b. a preference for complexity   c. fluency in combining ideas   d. use of mental images

17. A major premise, minor premise, and conclusion are elements of
    a. brainstorming   b. a syllogism   c. selective comparison   d. the representativeness heuristic

18. Language allows events to be _____ into _____.
    a. translated, concepts   b. fixated, codes   c. rearranged, lexigrams   d. encoded, symbols

19. "A triangle must be a closed shape with three sides made of straight lines." This statement is an example of a
    a. prototype   b. positive instance   c. concept rule   d. disjunctive concept

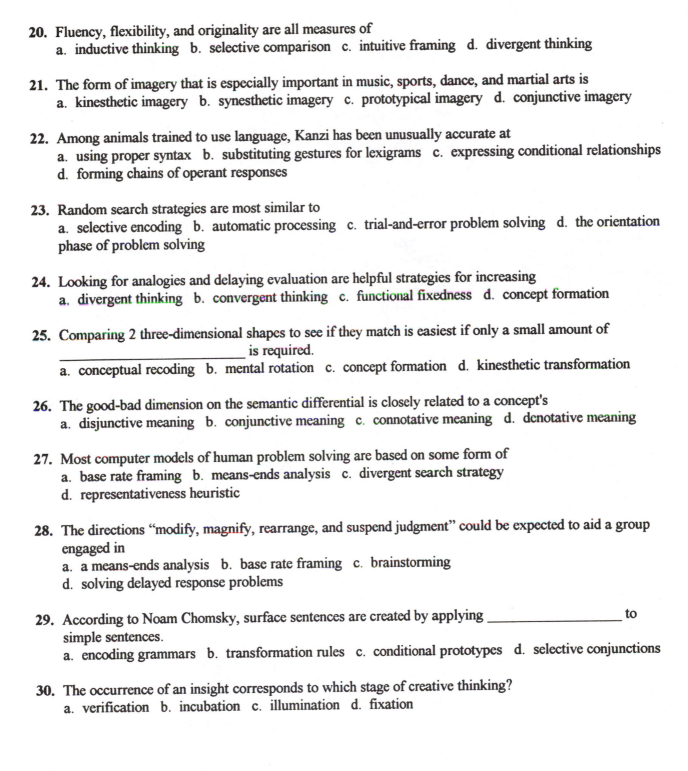

20. Fluency, flexibility, and originality are all measures of
    a. inductive thinking   b. selective comparison   c. intuitive framing   d. divergent thinking

21. The form of imagery that is especially important in music, sports, dance, and martial arts is
    a. kinesthetic imagery   b. synesthetic imagery   c. prototypical imagery   d. conjunctive imagery

22. Among animals trained to use language, Kanzi has been unusually accurate at
    a. using proper syntax   b. substituting gestures for lexigrams   c. expressing conditional relationships
    d. forming chains of operant responses

23. Random search strategies are most similar to
    a. selective encoding   b. automatic processing   c. trial-and-error problem solving   d. the orientation
    phase of problem solving

24. Looking for analogies and delaying evaluation are helpful strategies for increasing
    a. divergent thinking   b. convergent thinking   c. functional fixedness   d. concept formation

25. Comparing 2 three-dimensional shapes to see if they match is easiest if only a small amount of
    _____ is required.
    a. conceptual recoding   b. mental rotation   c. concept formation   d. kinesthetic transformation

26. The good-bad dimension on the semantic differential is closely related to a concept's
    a. disjunctive meaning   b. conjunctive meaning   c. connotative meaning   d. denotative meaning

27. Most computer models of human problem solving are based on some form of
    a. base rate framing   b. means-ends analysis   c. divergent search strategy
    d. representativeness heuristic

28. The directions "modify, magnify, rearrange, and suspend judgment" could be expected to aid a group
    engaged in
    a. a means-ends analysis   b. base rate framing   c. brainstorming
    d. solving delayed response problems

29. According to Noam Chomsky, surface sentences are created by applying _____ to
    simple sentences.
    a. encoding grammars   b. transformation rules   c. conditional prototypes   d. selective conjunctions

30. The occurrence of an insight corresponds to which stage of creative thinking?
    a. verification   b. incubation   c. illumination   d. fixation

ANSWERS

Recite and Review

1. thinking, information
2. internal
3. language
4. created
5. sense
6. change, space
7. visual
8. actions, actions
9. class
10. positive
11. concept
12. models
13. and, either-or
14. definition, personal
15. good-bad
16. all-or-nothing, social groups
17. symbols
18. sounds, meaningful
19. meaning
20. language, two-way
21. rules, order
22. rules
23. gestural
24. rearranged
25. operant
26. geometric
27. rote, computer
28. general, solutions
29. narrow, ideal
30. solution, selective
31. wrong
32. fixation, habits
33. system, intelligence
34. computer
35. analysis
36. knowledge, processing
37. practical
38. Thinking
39. originality, finding
40. fantasy, hero
41. creativity
42. preparation
43. steps
44. thinking, styles
45. creative
46. truth, conclusion
47. errors, true
48. probability
49. broad
50. creative
51. broadly, time, varied
52. separate
53. delayed
54. insight, thinking
55. tools
56. thought

Connections

1. f
2. j
3. i
4. a
5. c
6. b
7. e
8. d
9. g
10. h
11. c
12. a
13. e
14. j
15. b
16. i
17. d
18. f
19. g
20. h
21. h
22. a
23. g
24. b
25. j
26. c
27. i
28. d
29. e
30. f

Check Your Memory

1. F
2. T
3. F
4. F
5. F
6. T
7. T
8. T
9. T
10. T
11. T
12. F
13. T
14. F
15. T
16. T
17. F
18. F
19. T
20. F
21. T
22. F
23. T
24. F
25. F
26. F
27. F
28. F
29. T
30. T
31. T
32. T
33. T
34. F
35. F
36. T
37. T
38. F

39. T
40. T
41. T
42. T
43. F
44. T
45. F
46. T
47. F
48. T
49. T
50. T
51. T
52. F
53. T
54. T
55. T
56. T
57. T
58. T
59. F
60. T
61. F
62. T
63. T
64. F
65. T
66. F
67. T
68. T
69. T
70. F
71. T

Final Survey and Review

1. Cognitive, problem solving
2. representations
3. images, concepts, symbols
4. information stored
5. synesthesia
6. size, rotated
7. brain, visual, mental

8. implicit, micromovements
9. generalized
10. negative instances
11. rules
12. prototypes
13. conjunctive, disjunctive
14. denotative, Connotative
15. semantic, strong-weak, active-passive
16. all-or-nothing, social stereotypes
17. encoded
18. phonemes, morphemes
19. semantics
20. bilingualism, two-way bilingual
21. grammar, syntax
22. transformation
23. productive, American Sign
24. symbols
25. primates, reinforcers
26. lexigrams
27. mechanically, mechanical
28. understanding, functional
29. heuristics, identify, explore
30. insight, insight, encoding
31. fixation
32. Functional, blocks, values
33. artificial system, people
34. expert systems
35. means-ends
36. organized, strategies, automatic
37. original
38. inductive, logical
39. divergent, fluency, problem finding
40. conquering, martyr
41. *Uses*, divergent
42. incubation, illumination
43. incremental
44. personality, correlation
45. mood
46. premises, reasoning
47. representative, heuristic
48. base rate

49. framing
50. mental sets
51. incubation, input
52. Brainstorming
53. response
54. multiple-stick, versatile
55. understanding
56. symbolic

Mastery Test

1. b (p. 376)
2. a (p. 383)
3. c (p. 392)
4. b (p. 368)
5. a (p. 372)
6. a (p. 380)
7. d (p. 387)
8. b (p. 371)
9. a (p. 380, 382)
10. b (p. 380)
11. c (p. 388)
12. b (p. 387)
13. c (p. 374)
14. a (p. 368)
15. d (p. 381)
16. a (p. 389-390)
17. b (p. 390-391)
18. d (p. 373)
19. c (p. 371)
20. d (p. 385)
21. a (p. 370)
22. a (p. 378)
23. c (p. 380)
24. a (p. 395)
25. b (p. 368)
26. c (p. 372)
27. b (p. 383)
28. c (p. 396)
29. b (p. 375)
30. c (p. 388)

Chapter 11
Intelligence

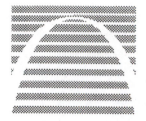

CHAPTER OVERVIEW

Intelligence refers to a general capacity to act purposefully, think rationally, and deal effectively with the environment. In practice, intelligence is operationally defined by creating tests. Aptitude tests measure a narrower range of abilities than general intelligence tests do. To be of value, an intelligence test must be reliable, valid, objective, and standardized.

The first practical individual intelligence test was assembled by Alfred Binet. A modern version is the *Stanford-Binet Intelligence Scales*. A second major intelligence test is the *Wechsler Adult Intelligence Scale*. Group intelligence tests are also available. Intelligence is expressed as an intelligence quotient (IQ) or as a deviation IQ. The distribution of IQ scores approximates a normal curve. There are no overall differences between males and females in tested intelligence.

People with IQs in the gifted or "genius" range tend to be superior in many respects. By criteria other than IQ, a large proportion of children might be considered gifted or talented in one way or another. The terms mentally retarded and developmentally disabled apply to persons with an IQ below 70 or who lack various adaptive behaviors. About 50 percent of the cases of mental retardation are organic; the remaining cases are of undetermined cause (many are thought to be familial).

Newer approaches relate intelligence to the speed with which information is processed in the nervous system. In addition, people who possess metacognitive skills tend to be superior at thinking and problem solving. As a result, they also tend to be more intelligent. Many psychologists now believe that several distinct types of intelligence exist.

Studies of animals and family relationships in humans demonstrate that intelligence reflects the combined effects of heredity and environment. Traditional IQ tests often suffer from a degree of cultural bias. For this and other reasons, it is wise to remember that IQ is merely an index of intelligence and that intelligence is narrowly defined by most tests.

LEARNING OBJECTIVES

To demonstrate mastery of this chapter you should be able to:

1. Describe the savant syndrome.
2. Describe Binet's role in intelligence testing.

3. State Wechsler's definition of intelligence.

4. Explain what an operational definition of intelligence is.

5. Define the term *aptitude*. List and briefly describe the three levels of aptitude testing.

6. Define the terms *reliability, validity, objective test,* and *test standardization,* as they relate to testing.

7. Describe the five cognitive factors measured by the *Stanford-Binet Intelligence Scales, Fifth Edition* (SB5).

8. Define the components of the Stanford-Binet intelligence quotient (IQ) and use an example to show how it was computed.

9. Differentiate between the Stanford-Binet IQ and deviation IQs.

10. Explain how age affects the stability of intelligence scores and how aging affects intelligence. Define the term *terminal decline*.

11. Regarding the types of intelligence tests:
    a. distinguish the Wechsler tests from the Stanford-Binet tests; and
    b. distinguish between group and individual intelligence tests.

12. Describe the pattern of distribution of IQ scores observed in the general population.

13. Describe sex differences in intelligence.

14. Describe the relationship between grades, occupations, and intelligence.

15. Regarding Terman's study of gifted children,
    a. list five popular misconceptions concerning genius and their corrections; and
    b. explain how successful subjects differed from the less successful ones.

16. Explain why basing judgments of giftedness on IQ scores may be misguided.

17. Briefly describe GATE programs.

18. List two possible explanations for the exceptional abilities of autistic savants.

19. State the dividing line between normal intelligence and retardation (or developmental disability) and list the degrees of retardation.

20. Differentiate between familial and organic retardation.

21. List and describe the four types of organic causes of retardation.

22. Briefly describe the causes and effects of the following conditions:
    a. PKU   b. microcephaly   c. hydrocephaly
    d. cretinism   e. Down syndrome   f. fragile-*X* syndrome

23. Briefly describe the maze-bright, maze-dull rat study as evidence for the hereditary view of intelligence, and discuss the problem with this study as support for that view.

24. Explain how the twin (fraternal and identical) studies can be used to support either side of the heredity/environment controversy.

25. Describe the evidence that most strongly supports the environmental view of intelligence.

26. Describe the studies that indicate how much the environment can alter intelligence.

27. Discuss the benefits of Instrumental Enrichment and training in thinking skills.

28. Discuss how the heredity/environment debate is resolved.

29. Explain the concept of the neural basis for intelligence and how speed of processing and inspection time are related to it.

30. Describe the three factors identified by Perkins that determine how smart you are. Explain what a metacognitive skill is.

31. Describe Gardner's broader view of multiple intelligences and list the eight different kinds of intelligence he discusses. Include the term *g-factor*.

The following objectives are related to the material in the "Psychology in Action" and "A Step Beyond" sections of your text.

32. Explain how IQ tests may be unfair to certain groups, and define the term *culture-fair test*.

33. State the arguments against Hernstein's and Murray's claim that the IQ difference between blacks and whites can be attributed to genetic inheritance.

34. Discuss the general validity of IQ testing and the advantages and disadvantages of standardized testing in public schools.

35. Describe the overall controversy in the Larry P. case.

36. Explain what SOMPA is and how it helps solve many of the problems of using standardized IQ tests to assess the abilities of minority children.

RECITE AND REVIEW

● *How do psychologists define intelligence?*

Recite and Review: Pages 402-404

1. Intelligence refers to one's general capacity to act purposefully, think _____, and deal effectively with the _____.

2. In practice, writing an intelligence test provides an operational _____ of intelligence.

3. General _____ is distinguished from specific talents called aptitudes.

4. Special _____ tests and multiple _____ tests (such as the *Scholastic Assessment Test*) are used to assess a person's capacities for learning various abilities.

5. Aptitude tests measure a _____ range of abilities than general intelligence tests do.

● *What are the qualities of a good psychological test?*

Recite and Review: Page 404-405

6. To be of any value, a psychological test must be reliable (give _____ results).

7. Three types of reliability are test-retest, _____-half, and equivalent-_____.

8. A worthwhile test must also have validity, meaning that it _____ what it claims to _____. Validity is often measured by comparing test scores to actual performance at work or in school.

9. Widely used intelligence tests are objective (they give the same result when scored by _____ _____).

10. Intelligence tests are also standardized (the same procedures are always used in giving the test, and _____, or average scores, have been established so that scores can be interpreted).

● *What are typical IQ tests like?*

Recite and Review: Pages 405-409

11. The first practical _____ _____ was assembled in 1904, in Paris, by Alfred Binet.

12. A modern version of Binet's test is the *Stanford-Binet* _____ _____, Fifth Edition.

13. The Stanford-Binet measures _____ reasoning, general knowledge, quantitative reasoning, visual-spatial processing, and working _____.

14. A second major intelligence test is the *Wechsler* _____ *Intelligence Scale, Third Edition* (WAIS-III). The WAIS-III measures both verbal and performance (_____) intelligence.

15. Intelligence tests have also been produced for use with _____ of people. A _____ test of historical interest is the *Army Alpha*.

16. The *Scholastic Assessment Test* (SAT), the *American College Test* (ACT), and the *College Qualifications Test* (CQT) are _____ scholastic aptitude tests. Although narrower in scope than IQ tests, they bear some similarities to them.

● *How do IQ scores relate to gender, age, and occupation?*

Recite and Review: Pages 410-411

17. Intelligence is expressed in terms of an intelligence _____ (IQ). IQ is defined as mental age (MA) divided by chronological age (CA) and then multiplied by _____.

18. An "average" IQ of _____ occurs when mental age _____ chronological age.

19. Modern IQ tests no longer calculate _____ directly. Instead, the final score reported by the test is a deviation IQ, which gives a person's _____ intellectual standing in his or her age group.

20. IQ scores become fairly _____ at about age 6, and they become increasingly reliable thereafter.

21. On the average, IQ scores continue to gradually _____ until middle age. Later intellectual declines are moderate for most people until their _____.

22. Shortly before _____, a more significant terminal decline (sudden drop) in intelligence is often observed.

23. When graphed, the distribution (percentage of people receiving each score) of IQ scores approximates a normal (_____-shaped) _____.

24. There are no overall differences between males and females in tested _____.

25. However, very small _____ differences may result from the intellectual skills our culture encourages males and females to develop.

26. IQ is related to school _____ and job status. The second association may be somewhat artificial because educational credentials are required for entry into many _____.

● *What does IQ tell us about genius?*

Recite and Review: Pages 411-412

27. People with IQs above 140 are considered to be in the _____ or "genius" range.
28. Studies done by Lewis Terman showed that the gifted tend to be _____ in many respects, such as achievement, physical appearance, and mental health.
29. The most successful gifted persons tend to be those who are persistent and _____ to learn and succeed.
30. By criteria other than _____, a large proportion of children might be considered gifted or talented in one way or another.
31. Intellectually gifted children often have difficulties in average classrooms and benefit from special _____ and Talented Education (GATE) programs.
32. Autistic savants have exceptional abilities in music, mechanics, _____, and remembering names or _____.

● *What causes mental retardation?*

Recite and Review: Pages 412-415

33. The terms mentally _____ and developmentally disabled are applied to those whose IQ falls below _____ or who lack various adaptive behaviors.
34. Further classifications of retardation are: _____ (50-55 to 70), moderate (35-40 to 50-55), _____ (20-25 to 35-40), and profound (below 20-25).
35. About _____ percent of the cases of mental retardation are organic, being caused by _____ injuries, fetal damage, metabolic disorders, or genetic abnormalities. The remaining cases are of undetermined cause.
36. Many cases of subnormal intelligence are thought to be the result of familial retardation (a low level of _____ stimulation in the home, poverty, and poor nutrition).
37. Three specialized forms of _____ retardation are phenylketonuria (PKU), microcephaly (small headedness), and hydrocephaly (excess cerebrospinal fluid).
38. Two additional sources of retardation are cretinism (insufficient thyroid _____), and Down syndrome (presence of an extra _____).
39. The second most common form of genetic mental retardation is fragile-X _____, a problem related to an abnormal area on the _____ chromosome.

● *How do heredity and environment affect intelligence?*

Recite and Review: Pages 416-418

40. Studies of eugenics (selective _____ for desirable characteristics) in animals suggest that intelligence is influenced by _____.
41. Studies of family relationships in humans, especially comparisons between fraternal twins and identical twins (who have identical _____), also suggest that intelligence is partly _____.
42. However, environment is also important, as revealed by changes in tested intelligence induced by _____ environments and improved education.
43. _____ therefore reflects the combined effects of heredity and environment.

● *How have views of intelligence changed in recent years?*

Recite and Review: Pages 418-420

44. To an extent, intelligence may represent the brain's _____ and efficiency, which is revealed by tasks that measure the _____ of processing.

45. How smart a person is probably depends on his or her neural intelligence, experiential intelligence (specialized _____ and skills), and reflective intelligence (the ability to become aware of one's own _____ patterns).

46. Metacognitive skills involve an ability to manage one's own _____ and problem solving efforts.

47. Howard Gardner believes that _____ IQ tests define intelligence too narrowly. According to Gardner, intelligence consists of abilities in language, logic and _____, _____ and spatial thinking, music, kinesthetic skills, intrapersonal skills, interpersonal skills, and naturalist skills.

● *Are IQ tests fair to all racial and cultural groups?*

Recite and Review: PSYCHOLOGY IN ACTION and A STEP BEYOND

48. Traditional IQ tests often suffer from a degree of cultural _____ that makes them easier for some groups and harder for others.

49. Culture-fair tests try to measure intelligence in ways that are not strongly affected by _____ background, but no test is entirely _____-free.

50. Differences in the average IQ scores for various racial groups are based on environmental differences, not _____.

51. _____ is merely an index of intelligence based tests that offer a narrow definition of intelligence.

52. The Larry P. case raised questions about the use of IQ tests to place students into special education, or educable _____ _____ (EMR) classes.

53. Tests such as SOMPA (*System of Multicultural Pluralistic Assessment*) have been created to more accurately measure the intelligence of people from _____ cultural backgrounds.

54. However, the use of standard IQ tests, or even SOMPA, for educational placement of students has been prohibited by the _____ in some states.

CONNECTIONS

1. _____   savant syndrome   a. legitimate measure
2. _____   Binet   b. average score
3. _____   reliable   c. relative standing
4. _____   valid   d. calendar calculator
5. _____   norm   e. absurdities
6. _____   IQ   f. Wechsler test
7. _____   deviation IQ   g. first intelligence test
8. _____   verbal reasoning   h. block design
9. _____   memory test   i. *Army Alpha*
10. _____   WAIS   j. bell shape
11. _____   performance test   k. digit span
12. _____   group test   l. MA/CA * 100
13. _____   normal curve   m. consistent measure

14. _____   average IQ   a. phenylalanine
15. _____   mentally retarded   b. old parents
16. _____   Termites   c. small head
17. _____   general ability   d. smart rat
18. _____   PKU   e. 70
19. _____   hydrocephaly   f. deficient thyroid
20. _____   microcephaly   g. one egg
21. _____   cretinism   h. two eggs
22. _____   Down syndrome   i. gifted children
23. _____   maze-bright   j. 100
24. _____   fraternal twins   k. *g*-factor
25. _____   identical twins   l. education controversy
26. _____   Larry P.   m. fluid in brain

CHECK YOUR MEMORY

Check Your Memory: Pages 402-404

1. The savant syndrome refers to a person of normal intelligence who has a highly developed, but specific, mental ability. T or F?
2. Alfred Binet's first test was designed to measure mechanical aptitude. T or F?
3. Most psychologists list abstract reasoning ability as an important element of intelligence. T or F?
4. A test of clerical aptitude would measure your capacity for learning to do office work. T or F?
5. The SAT is a special aptitude test. T or F?

Check Your Memory: Page 404-405

6. A test is valid if it gives the same score, or close to the same score, when given to the same person on two separate occasions. T or F?
7. To check for split-half reliability you would compare scores on two different versions of a test. T or F?
8. Criterion validity is shown by comparing scores on a test to actual performance in the "real world." T or F?
9. If a test is objective, then by definition it is fair. T or F?
10. Standardizing a test helps ensure that it is the same for everyone who takes it. T or F?

Check Your Memory: Pages 405-409

11. Lewis Terman helped write the original Stanford-Binet intelligence test. T or F?
12. Mental age refers to average mental ability for a person of a given age. T or F?
13. Mental age can't be higher than chronological age. T or F?
14. IQ is equal to MA times CA divided by 100. T or F?
15. An IQ will be greater than 100 when CA is larger than MA. T or F?
16. Average intelligence is defined as an IQ from 90 to 109. T or F?
17. Modern IQ tests give scores as deviation IQs. T or F?
18. The correlation between IQ scores obtained at ages 2 and 18 is 3.1. T or F?
19. On the average, changes in IQ are small after middle childhood. T or F?
20. The WISC is designed to test adult performance intelligence. T or F?
21. The digit symbol task is considered a performance subtest of the WAIS. T or F?
22. The Stanford-Binet, Wechsler's, and *Army Alpha* are all group intelligence tests. T or F?

Check Your Memory: Pages 410-411

23. In a normal curve, a majority of scores are found near the average. T or F?
24. An IQ above 130 is described as "bright normal." T or F?
25. The correlation between IQ scores and school grades is .5. T or F?
26. High IQ scores are strongly correlated with creativity. T or F?

Check Your Memory: Pages 411-412

27. Only 12 people out of 100 score above 130 on IQ tests. T or F?

28. Gifted children tend to get average IQ scores by the time they reach adulthood. T or F?

29. Gifted persons are more susceptible to mental illness. T or F?

30. Gifted persons are more likely to succeed in adulthood if they have a high degree of intellectual determination. T or F?

31. Talking in complete sentences at age 2 is regarded as a sign of giftedness. T or F?

32. Gifted children tend to become bored in classes designed for children of average abilities. T or F?

33. The performances of many autistic savants appear to result from intense practice. T or F?

34. Autistic savants who have unusual drawing abilities usually are also very advanced in the use of language. T or F?

Check Your Memory: Pages 412-415

35. A person must have an IQ of 80 or below to be classified as mentally retarded. T or F?

36. The moderately retarded can usually learn routine self-help skills. T or F?

37. The borderline retarded are capable of living alone. T or F?

38. Familial retardation is a genetic condition that runs in families. T or F?

39. Mental retardation caused by birth injuries is categorized as an organic problem. T or F?

40. Phenylalanine is found in the artificial sweetener Aspartame. T or F?

41. Hydrocephaly cannot be treated. T or F?

42. Iodized salt has helped prevent cretinism. T or F?

43. The risk of having a Down syndrome child increases as the mother gets older, but is unaffected by the father's age. T or F?

44. Fragile-*X* males tend to be severely retarded as children but only mildly retarded during adulthood. T or F?

Check Your Memory: Pages 416-418

45. The correlation between the IQs of unrelated people reared apart is 0.0. T or F?

46. The IQs of fraternal twins reared together are more similar than those of other siblings. T or F?

47. The IQs of identical twins are more alike than those of fraternal twins. T or F?

48. Adult intelligence is approximately 50 percent hereditary. T or F?

49. Children adopted into higher status homes tend, on average, to have higher adult IQs. T or F?

50. IQ scores tend to rise the longer people stay in school. T or F?

Check Your Memory: Pages 418-420

51. The speed with which information is processed has been used as a measure of the speed and efficiency of the brain. T or F?

52. Longer inspection times have been shown to correspond with higher intelligence. T or F?

53. Experiential intelligence is a relatively fixed element of overall intelligence. T or F?

54. Metacognitive skills are a major part of what is meant by reflective intelligence. T or F?

55. Howard Gardner's theory of multiple intelligences states that traditional measures of language, logic, and math skills have little to do with intelligence. T or F?

56. Gardner is currently gathering evidence concerning a ninth intellectual capacity he calls existential intelligence. T or F?

57. The g-factor is regarded by some psychologists as a sign that "general intelligence" underlies many different measures of intelligence. T or F?

Check Your Memory: Psychology in Action

58. The Dove Test was designed to be culturally biased. T or F?
59. A book titled *The Bell Curve* states that, as a group, African Americans score below average on IQ tests because they are more likely to attend poor-quality schools. T or F?
60. The small difference in average IQ scores for African Americans and Anglo Americans is explained by cultural and environmental differences. T or F?
61. IQ scores predict later career success. T or F?
62. Standardized testing is used primarily to select people for school and employment. T or F?
63. Changing intelligence tests would result in a change in the IQ scores of people taking the tests. T or F?

Check Your Memory: A Step Beyond

64. Larry P. was a Latino child who was mistakenly placed in an EMR class on the basis of an IQ score. T or F?
65. SOMPA assumes that a child's true potential can be hidden by his or her cultural background. T or F?
66. IQ tests are legally banned from use in California for the purposes of screening children for placement in EMR classes. T or F?
67. IQ tests continue to predict school performance quite well. T or F?

FINAL SURVEY AND REVIEW

● *How do psychologists define intelligence?*

  1. Intelligence refers to one's general capacity to act _____, _____ rationally, and deal effectively with the environment.
  2. In practice, writing an intelligence test provides an _____ definition of intelligence.
  3. General intelligence is distinguished from specific talents called _____.
  4. _____ aptitude tests and _____ aptitude tests (such as the *Scholastic Assessment Test*) are used to assess a person's capacities for _____ various abilities.
  5. _____ tests measure a narrower range of abilities than general _____ tests do.

● *What are the qualities of a good psychological test?*

  6. To be of any value, a psychological test must be _____ (give consistent results).
  7. Three types of reliability are _____, split-half, and _____- forms.

8. A worthwhile test must also have _____, meaning that it measures what it claims to measure. _____ is often measured by comparing test scores to actual _____ at work or in school.

9. Widely used intelligence tests are _____ (they give the same result when scored by different people).

10. Intelligence tests are also _____ (the same procedures are always used in giving the test, and norms have been established for _____).

● *What are typical IQ tests like?*

11. The first practical intelligence test was assembled in 1904, in Paris, by _____ _____.

12. A modern version of that test is the _____ *Intelligence Scales,* Fifth Edition.

13. The scales measure fluid reasoning, general knowledge, _____ reasoning, _____-spatial processing, and working memory.

14. A second major intelligence test is the _____ *Adult Intelligence Scale-III* (WAIS-III). The WAIS-III measures both _____ and _____ (nonverbal) intelligence.

15. Intelligence tests have also been produced for use with groups of people. A group test of historical interest is the _____ _____.

16. The *Scholastic Assessment Test* (SAT), the *American College Test* (ACT), and the *College Qualifications Test* (CQT) are group _____ _____ tests. Although narrower in scope than IQ tests, they bear some similarities to them.

● *How do IQ scores relate to gender, age, and occupation?*

17. Intelligence is expressed in terms of an intelligence quotient (IQ). IQ is defined as _____ _____ (MA) divided by _____ _____ (CA) and then multiplied by 100.

18. An "average" IQ of 100 occurs when _____ age equals _____ age.

19. Modern IQ tests no longer calculate IQ directly. Instead, the final score reported by the test is a _____ _____, which gives a person's relative intellectual standing in his or her age group.

20. IQ scores become fairly stable at about age ___, and they become increasingly _____ thereafter.

21. On the average, IQ scores continue to gradually increase until middle age. Later intellectual _____ are moderate for most people until their 70s.

22. Shortly before death, a more significant _____ _____ (sudden drop) in intelligence is often observed.

23. When graphed, the _____ (percentage of people receiving each score) of IQ scores approximates a _____ (bell-shaped) curve.

24. There are no overall _____ between males and females in tested intelligence.

25. However, very small gender differences may result from the intellectual skills our _____ encourages males and females to develop.
26. IQ is related to school grades and _____ _____. The second association may be somewhat artificial because _____ credentials are required for entry into many vocations.

● *What does IQ tell us about genius?*

27. People with IQs above _____ are considered to be in the gifted or "genius" range.
28. Studies done by Lewis _____ showed that the _____ tend to be superior in many respects, such as achievement, physical appearance, and mental health.
29. The most _____ gifted persons tend to be those who are _____ and motivated to learn and succeed.
30. By criteria other than IQ, a large proportion of children might be considered _____ or _____ in one way or another.
31. Intellectually gifted children often have difficulties in average classrooms and benefit from special Gifted and Talented _____ (GATE) programs.
32. Autistic _____ have exceptional abilities in music, mechanics, math, and remembering names or numbers.

● *What causes mental retardation?*

33. The terms mentally retarded and _____ disabled are applied to those whose IQ falls below 70 or who lack various _____ behaviors.
34. Further classifications of retardation are: mild (50-55 to 70), _____ (35-40 to 50-55), severe (20-25 to 35-40), and _____ (below 20-25).
35. About 50 percent of the cases of mental retardation are _____, being caused by birth injuries, fetal damage, metabolic disorders, or _____ abnormalities. The remaining cases are of undetermined cause.
36. Many cases of subnormal intelligence are thought to be the result of _____ retardation (a low level of intellectual stimulation in the home, poverty, and poor nutrition).
37. Three specialized forms of organic retardation are _____ (PKU), _____ (small headedness), and hydrocephaly (excess cerebrospinal fluid).
38. Two additional sources of retardation are _____ (insufficient thyroid hormone), and _____ syndrome (presence of an extra chromosome).
39. The second most common form of genetic mental retardation is _____ syndrome, a problem related to an abnormal area on the male _____.

● *How do heredity and environment affect intelligence?*

40. Studies of _____ (selective breeding for desirable characteristics) in animals suggest that intelligence is influenced by heredity.

41. Studies of family relationships in humans, especially comparisons between _____
twins and _____ twins, also suggest that intelligence is partly hereditary.
42. However, _____ is also important, as revealed by changes in tested
intelligence induced by stimulating _____ and improved education.
43. Intelligence therefore reflects the combined effects of _____ and

_____.

● *How have views of intelligence changed in recent years*

44. To an extent, intelligence may represent the _____ speed and efficiency, which is revealed by tasks
that measure the speed of_____.
45. How smart a person is probably depends on his or her_____ _____ intelligence,
experiential intelligence (specialized knowledge and skills), and intelligence (the ability to become aware of
one's own thinking patterns).
46. _____ skills involve an ability to manage one's own thinking and problem solving efforts.
47. Howard _____ believes that traditional IQ tests define intelligence too narrowly.
According to Gardner, intelligence consists of abilities in _____, logic and math, visual and
spatial thinking, _____, kinesthetic skills, intrapersonal skills, interpersonal skills, and naturalist
skills.

● *Are IQ tests fair to all racial and cultural groups?*

48. Traditional IQ tests often suffer from a degree of _____ bias that makes them easier for
some groups and harder for others.
49. _____ tests try to measure intelligence in ways that are not strongly affected
by cultural background, but no test is entirely culture-free.
50. Differences in the average IQ scores for various racial groups are based on
_____ differences, not heredity.
51. IQ is merely an _____ of intelligence based tests that offer a narrow definition of intelligence.
52. The _____ ____ case raised questions about the use of IQ tests to place students into special
education, or _____ mentally retarded (EMR) classes.
53. Tests such as SOMPA (*System of* _____ _____
Assessment) have been created to more accurately measure the intelligence of people from different cultural
backgrounds.
54. However, the use of standard _____ _____, or even _____, for educational
placement of students has been prohibited by the law in some states.

MASTERY TEST

1. The largest number of people are found in which IQ range?
   a. 80-89   b. 90-109   c. 110-119   d. below 70

2. Questions that involve copying geometric shapes would be found in which ability area of the SB5?
   a. fluid reasoning   b. quantitative reasoning   c. visual-spatial processing   d. working memory

3. The *Scholastic Assessment Test* is really a
   a. special aptitude test   b. multiple aptitude test   c. general intelligence test
   d. test of performance intelligence

4. It is unlikely that a developmentally disabled person would benefit from
   a. a sheltered workshop   b. supervised education   c. a GATE program   d. learning self-help skills

5. The term "six-hour retardates" refers to children who appear to be intelligent
   a. when given EMR training   b. when they are not at home   c. after Instrumental Enrichment
   d. outside of school

6. Which of the following is NOT a group test?
   a. SAT   b. ACT   c. WAIS   d. *Army Alpha*

7. On the average, the smallest changes in IQ would be expected between the ages of
   a. 2 and 10   b. 10 and 15   c. 2 and 18   d. 30 and 40

8. A combination of high ability and general retardation is found in
   a. autistic savants   b. Down syndrome   c. the adapted developmentally disabled
   d. maze-bright retardation

9. The distribution of IQ scores closely matches
   a. an inverted U curve   b. a normal curve   c. a g-factor curve   d. Bell's percentiles

10. Which of the following is fixed at birth?
    a. IQ   b. genes   c. giftedness   d. MA

11. Speed of neural processing has been measured by using an _____ task.
    a. inspection time   b. reflective   c. metacognitive   d. g-factor

12. Separate collections of verbal and performance subtests are a feature of the
    a. WAIS   b. *Dove Test*   c. CQT   d. SAT

13. Fourteen nations have shown large average IQ gains in a single generation. These findings support the idea that intelligence is influenced by
    a. eugenics   b. environment   c. genetics   d. the hereditary *g*-factor

14. Use of a test like _____ might have avoided the problem that led to the Larry P. case.
    a. the WAIS-C   b. SOMPA   c. the WAIS-R   d. the SB5

15. Mental retardation is formally defined by deficiencies in
    a. aptitudes and self-help skills   b. intelligence and scholastic aptitudes
    c. language and spatial thinking   d. IQ and adaptive behaviors

16. A 12-year-old child, with an IQ of 100, must have an MA of
    a. 100   b. 12   c. 10   d. 15

17. The *Stanford-Binet Intelligence Scale* was based on the work of Binet and
    a. Terman   b. Wechsler   c. Gardner   d. Feuerstein

18. A test deliberately written to be culturally biased is the
    a. WAIS   b. SB5   c. Dove Test   d. SOMPA test battery

19. A person's relative intellectual standing in his or her age group is revealed by
    a. the age quotient   b. the digit symbol index   c. chronological age   d. deviation IQ

20. The age of parents may affect the risks of having a child suffering from
    a. familial retardation   b. phenylketonuria   c. Down syndrome   d. the savant syndrome

21. Traditional intelligence tests are especially good at predicting
    a. career success   b. performance in school   c. creative achievement
    d. which children will benefit   from eugenic programs

22. The validity of a test could be assessed by comparing
    a. scores earned on one occasion to scores earned on another
    b. scores based on the first half of the test to scores based on the second half
    c. scores on two equivalent forms of the test
    d. scores on the test to an external criterion of performance

23. Creating an intelligence test provides a/an _____ definition of intelligence.
    a. valid   b. reliable   c. operational   d. chronological

24. For large groups, the greatest similarity in IQs would be expected between
    a. identical twins   b. fraternal twins   c. siblings reared together   d. parents and their children

25. Both the *Scholastic Assessment Test* and the *Law School Admissions Test* are
    a. tests of general intelligence   b. standardized aptitude tests
    c. culture-fair tests of verbal comprehension   d. objective performance tests

26. An intelligence test specifically designed for use with children is the
    a. WAIS-C   b. Dove Test   c. WISC-III   d. *Savant Developmental Scale*

27. Which statement about gifted persons is TRUE?
    a. They tend to be shy and socially withdrawn. b. They tend to be smaller and weaker than average.
    c. They have above average mental health records.
    d. They must score above 160 on IQ tests to be considered gifted.

28. Instrumental Enrichment is to _____ as eugenics is to _____.
    a. environment, genetics b. genetics, selective breeding c. culture fairness, genetics
    d. intelligence, culture

29. A type of retardation that appears to be based largely on the effects of poor environment is
    a. Down syndrome b. microcephaly c. PKU d. familial retardation

30. The idea that children can be gifted in ways other than having a high IQ is in agreement with
    a. Feuerstein's Instrumental Enrichment program b. Dove's Counterbalance model of intelligence
    c. Hernstein and Murray's bell curve model d. Gardner's eight intelligences

ANSWERS

Recite and Review

1. rationally, environment
2. definition
3. intelligence
4. aptitude, aptitude
5. narrower
6. consistent
7. split, forms
8. measures, measure
9. different people
10. norms
11. intelligence test
12. *Intelligence Scales*
13. fluid, memory
14. *Adult,* nonverbal
15. groups, group
16. group
17. quotient, 100
18. 100, equals
19. IQs, relative
20. stable
21. increase, 70s
22. death
23. bell, curve
24. intelligence
25. gender
26. grades, occupations
27. gifted
28. superior
29. motivated
30. IQ
31. Gifted
32. math, numbers
33. retarded, 70
34. mild, severe
35. 50, birth
36. intellectual
37. organic
38. hormone, chromosome
39. syndrome, *X* or female
40. breeding, heredity
41. genes, hereditary
42. stimulating
43. Intelligence
44. speed, speed
45. knowledge, thinking
46. thinking
47. traditional, math, visual
48. bias
49. cultural, culture
50. genetics (or heredity)
51. IQ
52. mentally retarded
53. different
54. law

Connections

1. d
2. g
3. m
4. a
5. b
6. l
7. c
8. e
9. k

10. f
11. h
12. i
13. j
14. j
15. e
16. i
17. k
18. a
19. m
20. c
21. f
22. b
23. d
24. h
25. g
26. l

Check Your Memory

1. F
2. F
3. T
4. T
5. F
6. F
7. F
8. T
9. F
10. T
11. T
12. T
13. F
14. F
15. F
16. T
17. T
18. F
19. T
20. F
21. T
22. F
23. T
24. F
25. T
26. F
27. F
28. F
29. F
30. T
31. T
32. T
33. T
34. F
35. F
36. T
37. T
38. F
39. T
40. T
41. F
42. T
43. F
44. F
45. T
46. T
47. T
48. T
49. T
50. T
51. T
52. F
53. F
54. T
55. F
56. T
57. T
58. T
59. F
60. T
61. F
62. T
63. T
64. F
65. T
66. T
67. T

Final Survey and Review

1. purposefully, think
2. operational
3. aptitudes
4. Special, multiple, learning
5. Aptitude, intelligence
6. reliable
7. test-retest, equivalent
8. validity, Validity, performance
9. objective
10. standardized, scores
11. Alfred Binet
12. *Stanford-Binet*
13. quantitative, visual
14. *Wechsler*, verbal, performance
15. *Army Alpha*
16. scholastic aptitude
17. mental age, chronological age
18. mental, chronological
19. deviation IQ
20. 6, reliable
21. declines
22. terminal decline
23. distribution, normal
24. differences
25. culture
26. job status, educational
27. 140
28. Terman, gifted
29. successful, persistent
30. gifted, talented
31. Education
32. savants
33. developmentally, adaptive
34. moderate, profound
35. organic, genetic
36. familial
37. phenylketonuria, microcephaly
38. cretinism, Down

39. fragile-*X*, chromosome
40. eugenics
41. fraternal, identical
42. environment, environments
43. heredity, environment
44. brain's, processing
45. neural, reflective
46. Metacognitive
47. Gardner, language, music
48. cultural
49. Culture-fair
50. environmental
51. index
52. Larry P., educable
53. *Multicultural Pluralistic*
54. IQ tests, SOMPA

Mastery Test

1. b (p. 410)
2. c (p. 406)
3. b (p. 404)
4. c (p. 412)
5. d (p. 425)
6. c (p. 408)
7. d (p. 407)
8. a (p. 413)
9. b (p. 410)
10. b (p. 418)
11. a (p. 419)
12. a (p. 408)
13. b (p. 417)
14. b (p. 425)
15. d (p. 412)
16. b (p. 407)

17. a (p. 405)
18. c (p. 422)
19. d (p. 407)
20. c (p. 415)
21. b (p. 410, 424)
22. d (p. 405)
23. c (p. 404)
24. a (p. 416)
25. b (p. 424)
26. c (p. 408)
27. c (p. 411)
28. a (p. 416, 418)
29. d (p. 414)
30. d (p. 420)

Chapter 12
Motivation and Emotion

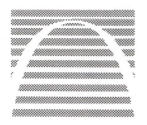

CHAPTER OVERVIEW

Motivation typically involves needs, drives, goals, and goal attainment. Three types of motives are primary motives, stimulus motives, and secondary motives. Most primary motives maintain homeostasis.

Hunger is influenced by the stomach, blood sugar levels, metabolism in the liver, fat stores in the body, activity in the hypothalamus, diet, and other factors. Eating disorders are serious and sometimes fatal problems. Behavioral dieting uses self-control techniques to change basic eating patterns and habits.

Thirst and other basic motives are affected by many factors, but they are primarily controlled by the hypothalamus. Pain avoidance is episodic and partially learned. The sex drive is non-homeostatic. To some extent, it is influenced by hormone levels in the body.

The stimulus motives include drives for information, exploration, manipulation, and sensory input. Drives for stimulation are partially explained by arousal theory. Optimal performance on a task usually occurs at moderate levels of arousal. Circadian rhythms are closely tied to sleep, activity, and energy cycles.

Social motives, which are learned, account for much of the diversity of human motivation. The need for achievement is a social motive correlated with success in many situations.

Maslow's hierarchy of motives categorizes needs as basic or growth oriented. Self-actualization, the highest and most fragile need, is reflected in meta-needs. In many situations, extrinsic motivation can lower intrinsic motivation, enjoyment, and creativity.

Emotions are linked to basic adaptive behaviors. Other major elements of emotion are bodily changes, emotional expressions, and emotional feelings. Physiological changes during emotion are caused by adrenaline and the autonomic nervous system (ANS). The sympathetic branch of the ANS arouses the body and the parasympathetic branch quiets it. Basic emotional expressions are unlearned. Facial expressions are central to emotion. Body gestures and movements (body language) also express feelings. A variety of theories have been proposed to explain emotion.

Emotional intelligence involves a combination of skills, such as self-awareness, empathy, self-control, and an understanding of how to use emotions. For success in many situations, emotional intelligence is as important as IQ.

Sternberg's triangular theory describes love as a combination of passion, intimacy, and commitment.

Learning Objectives

To demonstrate mastery of this chapter, you should be able to:

1. Define *motivation*.
2. Describe a motivational sequence using the need reduction model.
3. Explain how the incentive value of a goal can affect motivation, and describe how incentive value is related to internal need.
4. List and describe the three types of motives and give an example of each.
5. Define *homeostasis*.
6. Discuss why hunger cannot be fully explained by the contractions of an empty stomach.
7. Describe the relationship of each of the following to hunger:
    a. blood sugar
    b. liver
    c. hypothalamus
        1. feeding system (lateral hypothalamus)
        2. satiety system (ventromedial hypothalamus)
        3. blood sugar regulator (paraventricular nucleus)
    d. GLP-1
8. Explain how a person's set point is related to obesity in childhood and adulthood.
9. Describe the impact of external eating cues and dietary content on obesity.
10. Describe the relationship between emotionality and overeating.
11. Explain the paradox of "yo-yo" dieting.
12. Explain what is meant by behavioral dieting, and describe the techniques that can enable you to control your weight.
13. Describe the impact of cultural factors and taste on hunger.
14. Explain how a taste aversion is acquired, give a practical example of the process, and briefly explain why psychologists believe these aversions exist.
15. Describe the essential features of the eating disorders anorexia nervosa and bulimia nervosa. Explain what causes them and what treatment is available for them.
16. Briefly discuss the relationship of culture and ethnicity to dieting and preferred body size.
17. Name the brain structure that appears to control thirst (as well as hunger). Differentiate extracellular and intracellular thirst.
18. Explain how the drive to avoid pain and the sex drive differ from other primary drives. Include a brief explanation of the non-homeostatic nature of the sex drive.
19. Describe the evidence for the existence of stimulus drives for exploration, and manipulation, curiosity, and stimulation.
20. Explain the arousal theory of motivation and the characteristics of sensation-seekers. Describe the inverted U function. Relate arousal to the Yerkes-Dodson law and give an example of it.
21. Describe the two major components of test anxiety and describe four ways to reduce it.

22. Explain how circadian rhythms affect energy levels, motivation, and performance. Include an explanation of how and why shift work and jet lag may adversely affect a person and how to minimize the effects of shifting one's rhythms, including the use of melatonin.

23. Use the ideas of Solomon's opponent-process theory to explain how a person might learn to like hazardous, painful, or frightening pursuits.

24. Define *need for achievement* (nAch) and differentiate it from the need for power.

25. Describe people who are achievers, and relate nAch to risk taking.

26. Briefly describe the results of the subliminal tape experiment.

27. Explain the influences of drive and determination in the development of success for high achievers.

28. List seven steps to enhancing self-confidence.

29. List (in order) the needs found in Maslow's hierarchy of motives, and distinguish between basic needs and growth needs.

30. Explain why Maslow's lower (physiological) needs are considered prepotent.

31. Define *meta-need* and give an example of one.

32. Distinguish between intrinsic and extrinsic motivation, and explain how each type of motivation may affect a person's interest in work, leisure activities, and creativity.

33. Explain what is meant by the phrase, "emotions aid survival."

34. List and describe the three major elements of emotions.

35. List the eight primary emotions proposed by Plutchik and explain his concept of mixing them.

36. Explain how a person may experience two opposite emotions simultaneously.

37. State which side of the brain processes positive versus negative emotion. Describe the effect of the amygdala on emotion.

38. Describe, in general, the effects of the sympathetic and the parasympathetic branches of the ANS during and after emotion. Describe the relationship between pupil dilation and emotion.

39. Define *parasympathetic rebound* and discuss its possible involvement in cases of sudden death.

40. Explain how the polygraph detects "lies."

41. Discuss the limitations and/or accuracy of lie detector devices.

42. Discuss Darwin's view of human emotion.

43. Briefly describe cultural and gender differences in emotion.

44. Describe the evidence that supports the conclusion that most emotional expressions are universal. Include a brief description of cultural and gender differences in emotion.

45. Define *kinesics*. List and describe the emotional messages conveyed by facial expressions (include the three basic dimensions) and body language. Explain how overall posture can indicate one's emotional state.

46. Discuss the behavioral cues to lying, including a differentiation of illustrators from emblems. Explain how they and the ANS reveal lying.

47. Briefly describe the James-Lange theory of emotion.

48. Briefly describe the Cannon-Bard theory of emotion.

49. Briefly describe Schachter's cognitive theory of emotion and give experimental evidence to support his theory.

50. Describe and give an example of the effects of attribution on emotion.
51. Briefly describe the facial feedback hypothesis.
52. Discuss the role of appraisal in the contemporary model of emotion.

The following objectives are related to the material in the "Psychology in Action" and "A Step Beyond" sections of your text.

53. Describe the concept of emotional intelligence and how it may enhance one's life.
54. List five emotional intelligence skills.
55. Briefly describe the benefits of positive emotion.
56. Explain Sternberg's triangular theory of love (including the three "ingredients").
57. Describe the emotional states resulting from the various combinations of Sternberg's factors.

RECITE AND REVIEW

● *What is motivation? Are there different types of motives?*

Recite and Review: Pages 430-433

1. Motives _____ (begin), sustain (perpetuate), and direct _____.
2. Motivation typically involves the sequence _____, drive, _____, and goal attainment (need reduction).
3. Behavior can be activated either by needs (_____) or by goals (_____).
4. The attractiveness of a _____ and its ability to initiate action are related to its incentive value (its value above and beyond its capacity to fill a _____).
5. Three principal types of motives are primary motives, stimulus motives, and _____ motives.
6. Most _____ motives operate to maintain a _____ state of bodily equilibrium called homeostasis.

● *What causes hunger? Overeating? Eating disorders?*

Recite and Review: Pages 433-440

7. Hunger is influenced by a complex interplay between distention (fullness) of the _____, hypoglycemia (low _____ sugar), metabolism in the _____, and fat stores in the body.
8. The most direct control of eating is exerted by the hypothalamus, which has areas that act like feeding (_____) and satiety (_____) systems for hunger and eating.
9. The lateral hypothalamus acts as a _____ system; the ventromedial hypothalamus is part of a _____ system; the paraventricular nucleus influences both hunger and satiety.

10. Other factors influencing hunger are the set point for the proportion of _____ in the body, external eating cues, the attractiveness and variety of _____.

11. Hunger is also influenced by emotions, learned _____ preferences and _____ aversions (such as bait shyness in animals), and cultural values.

12. Anorexia nervosa (self-inflicted _____) and bulimia nervosa (_____ and purging) are two prominent eating disorders.

13. Both eating disorders tend to involve conflicts about self-image, self-control, and _____.

14. Because of the limitations of traditional dieting, changing basic eating patterns and _____ is usually more effective.

15. Behavioral _____ brings about such changes by use of self-control techniques.

● *Is there more than one type of thirst? In what ways are pain avoidance and the sex drive unusual?*

Recite and Review: Pages 440-442

16. Like hunger, thirst and other basic motives are affected by a number of _____ factors, but are primarily under the central control of the hypothalamus in the _____.

17. Thirst may be either intracellular (when _____ is lost from inside _____) or extracellular (when _____ is lost from the spaces between _____).

18. Pain avoidance is unusual because it is episodic (associated with particular conditions) as opposed to cyclic (occurring in regular _____).

19. Pain avoidance and pain tolerance are partially _____ (influenced by training).

20. The sex drive in many lower animals is related to estrus (or "heat") in _____. The sex drive is unusual in that it is non-homeostatic (both its _____ and its reduction are sought).

21. Sex _____ in both males and females may be related to bodily levels of androgens.

● *How does arousal relate to motivation?*

Recite and Review: Pages 442-447

22. The stimulus drives reflect needs for information, exploration, manipulation, and _____ input.

23. Drives for stimulation are partially explained by arousal theory, which states that an ideal level of _____ _____ will be maintained if possible.

24. The desired level of _____ or stimulation varies from person to person, as measured by the *Sensation-Seeking Scale*.

25. Optimal performance on a task usually occurs at _____ levels of arousal. This relationship is described by an inverted U function.

26. The Yerkes-Dodson law further states that for _____ tasks the ideal arousal level is higher, and for _____ tasks it is lower.

27. Circadian _____ within the body are closely tied to sleep, activity levels, and energy cycles. Time zone travel and shift work can seriously disrupt _____ and bodily rhythms.

28. If you anticipate a _____ in body rhythms, you can gradually preadapt to your new _____ over a period of days.

29. Body rhythms and _____ cycles are strongly influenced by the release of melatonin, a _____ produced at night by the pineal gland.

● *What are social motives? Why are they important?*

Recite and Review: Pages 447-450

30. _____ motives are learned through socialization and cultural conditioning.
31. Opponent-process theory, which states that strong _____ tend to be followed by an opposite _____, explains some acquired motives.
32. One of the most prominent social motives is the _____ for achievement (nAch).
33. High nAch is correlated with _____ in many situations, with occupational choice, and with moderate _____ taking.
34. Self-confidence affects _____ because it influences the challenges you will undertake, the _____ you will make, and how long you will _____ when things don't go well.

● *Are some motives more basic than others?*

Recite and Review: Pages 450-452

35. Maslow's hierarchy (rank ordering) of motives categorizes needs as _____ and growth oriented.
36. _____ needs in the hierarchy are assumed to be prepotent (dominant) over _____ needs.
37. _____-actualization, the highest and most fragile need, is reflected in meta-_____.
38. In many situations, extrinsic motivation (that which is induced by obvious _____ rewards) can reduce intrinsic motivation, enjoyment, and creativity.

● *What happens during emotion? Can "lie detectors" really detect lies?*

Recite and Review: Pages 453-458

39. Emotions are linked to many basic adaptive _____, such as attacking, retreating, feeding, and reproducing.
40. Other major elements of emotion are physiological changes in the body, emotional expressions, and emotional _____.
41. The following are considered to be primary emotions: fear, surprise, _____, disgust, _____, anticipation, joy, and trust (acceptance). Other emotions seem to represent mixtures of the primaries.
42. Physical changes associated with emotion are caused by the action of adrenaline, a _____ released into the bloodstream, and by activity in the autonomic _____ _____ (ANS).
43. The sympathetic _____ of the ANS is primarily responsible for arousing the body, the parasympathetic _____ for quieting it.

44. Sudden death due to prolonged and intense emotion is probably related to parasympathetic _____ (excess activity). Heart attacks caused by sudden intense emotion are more likely due to sympathetic _____.
45. The polygraph, or "lie detector," measures _____ _____ by monitoring heart rate, blood pressure, breathing rate, and the galvanic skin response (GSR).
46. Asking a series of _____ and irrelevant questions may allow the detection of _____, but overall, the accuracy of the lie detector has been challenged by many researchers.

● *How accurately are emotions expressed by "body language" and the face?*

Recite and Review: Pages 458-462

47. Basic emotional expressions, such as smiling or baring one's teeth when angry, appear to be _____.
48. Facial expressions of _____, anger, disgust, _____, and happiness are recognized by people of all cultures.
49. Body gestures and movements (body language) also express _____, mainly by communicating emotional _____.
50. Three dimensions of _____ expressions are pleasantness-unpleasantness, attention-rejection, and activation.
51. The study of _____ _____ is known as kinesics.

● *How do psychologists explain emotions?*

Recite and Review: Pages 462-466

52. The James-Lange theory of emotion says that emotional experience _____ an awareness of the bodily reactions of emotion.
53. In contrast, the Cannon-Bard theory says that bodily reactions and emotional experience occur _____ _____ _____ _____ and that emotions are organized in the brain.
54. Schachter's cognitive theory of emotion emphasizes the importance of _____, or interpretations, applied to feelings of bodily arousal.
55. Also important is the process of attribution, in which bodily _____ is attributed to a particular person, object, or situation.
56. The facial feedback hypothesis holds that sensations and information from emotional _____ help define what emotion a person is feeling.
57. Contemporary views of emotion place greater emphasis on how _____ are appraised. Also, all of the elements of emotion are seen as interrelated and interacting.

● *What does it mean to have "emotional intelligence"?*

Recite and Review: PSYCHOLOGY IN ACTION

58. Emotional intelligence involves the following skills: _____-awareness, empathy, _____-control, and an understanding of how to use _____.

59. Emotionally intelligent people are good at reading facial expressions, tone of voice, and other signs of _____.

60. They also use their _____ to enhance thinking and decision making.

61. _____ emotions are not just a luxury. They tend to encourage personal growth and social connection

● *What is the nature of love?*

Recite and Review: A STEP BEYOND

62. Sternberg's triangular theory describes love as a combination of _____, intimacy, and commitment.

63. Combinations of these three factors produce nonlove, _____, infatuation, romantic love, fatuous love, companionate love, _____ love, and consummate love.

CONNECTIONS

1. _____ physiological needs

2. _____ safety and security

3. _____ self-actualization

4. _____ lateral hypothalamus

5. _____ basic needs

6. _____ esteem and self-esteem

7. _____ paraventricular nucleus

8. _____ growth needs

9. _____ love and belonging

10. _____ ventromedial hypothalamus

11. _____	need	a. steady state
12. _____	incentive value	b. lateral hypothalamus
13. _____	secondary motives	c. internal deficiency
14. _____	homeostasis	d. learned goals
15. _____	satiety system	e. estrogen levels
16. _____	feeding system	f. yo-yo dieting
17. _____	hunger and satiety	g. about a day
18. _____	weight cycling	h. paraventricular nucleus
19. _____	estrus	i. ventromedial hypothalamus
20. _____	circadian	j. goal desirability

21. _____	changes eating habits	a. standards of excellence
22. _____	nAch	b. prolonged mild emotion
23. _____	meta-needs	c. lie detection
24. _____	mood	d. behavioral dieting
25. _____	sympathetic branch	e. sensation seekers
26. _____	control questions	f. appraisal of loss
27. _____	body language	g. appraisal of threat
28. _____	sadness	h. self-actualization
29. _____	anxiety	i. kinesics
30. _____	SSS	j. fight or flight

CHECK YOUR MEMORY

Check Your Memory: Pages 430-433

1. The terms need and drive are used interchangeably to describe motivation. T or F?
2. Incentive value refers to the "pull" of valued goals. T or F?
3. Primary motives are based on needs that must be met for survival. T or F?
4. Much of the time, homeostasis is maintained by automatic reactions within the body. T or F?

Check Your Memory: Pages 433-440

5. Cutting the sensory nerves from the stomach abolishes hunger. T or F?
6. Lowered levels of glucose in the blood can cause hunger. T or F?
7. The body's hunger center is found in the thalamus. T or F?
8. The paraventricular nucleus is sensitive to neuropeptide Y. T or F?
9. Both glucagon-like peptide 1 (GLP-1) and leptin act as stop signals that inhibit eating. T or F?
10. Dieting speeds up the body's metabolic rate. T or F?
11. People who diet intensely every other day lose as much weight as those who diet moderately every day. T or F?
12. Exercise makes people hungry and tends to disrupt dieting and weight loss. T or F?

13. Behavioral dieting changes habits without reducing the number of calories consumed. T or F?
14. Charting daily progress is a basic behavioral dieting technique. T or F?
15. Taste aversions may be learned after longer time delays than in other forms of classical conditioning. T or F?
16. Many victims of anorexia nervosa overestimate their body size. T or F?

Check Your Memory: Pages 440-442

17. Bleeding, vomiting, or sweating can cause extracellular thirst. T or F?
18. Intracellular thirst is best satisfied by a slightly salty liquid. T or F?
19. Tolerance for pain is largely unaffected by learning. T or F?
20. Castration of a male animal typically abolishes the sex drive. T or F?
21. Getting drunk *decreases* sexual desire, arousal, pleasure, and performance. T or F?

Check Your Memory: Pages 442-447

22. It is uncomfortable to experience both very high and very low levels of arousal. T or F?
23. Disinhibition and boredom susceptibility are characteristics of sensation-seeking persons. T or F?
24. For nearly all activities, the best performance occurs at high levels of arousal. T or F?
25. Test anxiety is a combination of arousal and excessive worry. T or F?
26. Being overprepared is a common cause of test anxiety. T or F?
27. Changes in body temperature are closely related to circadian rhythms. T or F?
28. Adapting to rapid time zone changes is easiest when a person travels east, rather than west. T or F?

Check Your Memory: Pages 447-450

29. Opponent-process theory assumes that emotional responses habituate when activities are repeated. T or F?
30. The need for achievement refers to a desire to have impact on other people. T or F?
31. People high in nAch generally prefer "long shots" or "sure things." T or F?
32. Subliminal motivational tapes are no more effective than placebo tapes that lack any "hidden messages." T or F?
33. Benjamin Bloom found that high achievement is based as much on hard work as it is on talent. T or F?
34. For many activities, self-confidence is one of the most important sources of motivation. T or F?

Check Your Memory: Pages 450-452

35. Maslow's hierarchy of needs places self-esteem at the top of the pyramid. T or F?
36. Maslow believed that needs for safety and security are more potent than needs for love and belonging. T or F?
37. Meta-needs are the most basic needs in Maslow's hierarchy. T or F?
38. Intrinsic motivation occurs when obvious external rewards are provided for engaging in an activity. T or F?
39. People are more likely to be creative when they are intrinsically motivated. T or F?

Check Your Memory: Pages 453-458

40. Most physiological changes during emotion are related to the release of adrenaline into the brain. T or F?

41. Robert Plutchik's theory lists contempt as a primary emotion. T or F?
42. For most students, elevated moods tend to occur on Saturdays and Tuesdays. T or F?
43. Positive emotions are processed mainly in the left hemisphere of the brain. T or F?
44. The brain area called the amygdala specializes in producing fear. T or F?
45. The sympathetic branch of the ANS is under voluntary control and the parasympathetic branch is involuntary. T or F?
46. The parasympathetic branch of the ANS slows the heart and lowers blood pressure. T or F?
47. Most sudden deaths due to strong emotion are associated with the traumatic disruption of a close relationship. T or F?

Check Your Memory: Pages 458-462

48. The polygraph measures the body's unique physical responses to lying. T or F?
49. Only a guilty person should react emotionally to irrelevant questions. T or F?
50. Control questions used in polygraph exams are designed to make almost everyone anxious. T or F?
51. The lie detector's most common error is to label innocent persons guilty. T or F?
52. Children born deaf and blind express emotions with their faces in about the same way as other people do. T or F?
53. An authentic, or Duchenne, smile involves the muscles near the corners of a person's eyes, not just the mouth. T of F?
54. The "A-okay" hand gesture means "everything is fine" around the world. T or F?
55. Facial blends mix two or more basic expressions. T or F?
56. Liking is expressed in body language by leaning back and relaxing the extremities. T or F?
57. Gestures such as rubbing hands, twisting hair, and biting lips are consistently related to lying. T or F?
58. People from Asian cultures are more likely to express anger in public than people from Western cultures. T or F?
59. In Western cultures, men tend to be more emotionally expressive than women. T or F?

Check Your Memory: Pages 462-466

60. The James-Lange theory of emotion says that we see a bear, feel fear, are aroused, and then run. T or F?
61. According to Schachter's cognitive theory, arousal must be labeled in order to become an emotion. T or F?
62. Making facial expressions can actually cause emotions to occur and alter physiological activities in the body. T or F?
63. Emotional appraisal refers to deciding if your own facial expressions are appropriate for the situation you are in. T or F?
64. Suppressing emotions can impair thinking and memory because a lot of energy must be devoted to self-control. T or F?
65. Moving toward a desired goal is associated with the emotion of happiness. T or F?
66. Emotional intelligence refers to the ability to use primarily the right cerebral hemisphere to process emotional events. T of F?

Check Your Memory: PSYCHOLOGY IN ACTION

67. People who excel in life tend to be emotionally intelligent. T or F?

68. People who are empathetic are keenly tuned in to their own feelings. T or F?
69. People who are emotionally intelligent know what causes them to feel various emotions. T or F?
70. Negative emotions can be valuable because they impart useful information to us. T or F?
71. Positive emotions produce urges to be creative, to explore, and to seek new experiences. T or F?
72. A first step toward becoming emotionally intelligent is to pay attention to and value your feelings and emotional reactions. T or F?

Check Your Memory: A STEP BEYOND

73. Robert Sternberg's triangular theory states that love consists of intimacy, passion, and contentment. T or F?
74. Passion refers mainly to physiological arousal. T or F?
75. Liking mainly emphasizes intimacy. T or F?
76. Romantic love combines intimacy and passion. T or F?
77. The passionate stage of love typically lasts about 6 to 30 months. T or F?

FINAL SURVEY AND REVIEW

● *What is motivation? Are there different types of motives?*

1. Motives initiate (begin), _____ (perpetuate), and _____ activities.
2. Motivation typically involves the sequence need, _____, goal, and goal _____ (need reduction).
3. Behavior can be activated either by _____ (push) or by _____ (pull).
4. The attractiveness of a goal and its ability to initiate action are related to its _____

   _____.
5. Three principal types of motives are _____ motives, _____ motives, and _____ motives.
6. Most primary motives operate to maintain a steady state of bodily equilibrium called

   _____.

● *What causes hunger? Overeating? Eating disorders?*

7. Hunger is influenced by a complex interplay between _____ (fullness) of the stomach, _____ (low blood sugar), metabolism in the liver, and fat stores in the body.
8. The most direct control of eating is exerted by the _____, which has areas that act like feeding (start) and _____ (stop) systems for hunger and eating.
9. The _____ hypothalamus acts as a feeding system; the _____ hypothalamus is part of a satiety system; the paraventricular _____ influences both hunger and satiety.
10. Other factors influencing hunger are the _____ _____ for the proportion of fat in the body, external eating _____, the attractiveness and variety of diet.

11. Hunger is also influenced by emotions, learned taste preferences and taste _____ (such as _____ _____ in animals), and cultural values.

12. _____ nervosa (self-inflicted starvation) and _____ nervosa (gorging and purging) are two prominent eating disorders.

13. Both eating disorders tend to involve conflicts about _____, self-control, and anxiety.

14. Because of the limitations of traditional dieting, changing basic _____ patterns and habits is usually more effective.

15. _____ dieting brings about such changes by use of _____-control techniques.

● *Is there more than one type of thirst? In what ways are pain avoidance and the sex drive unusual?*

16. Like hunger, thirst and other basic motives are affected by a number of bodily factors, but are primarily under the central control of the _____ in the brain.

17. Thirst may be either _____ (when fluid is lost from inside cells) or _____ (when fluid is lost from the spaces between cells).

18. Pain avoidance is unusual because it is _____ (associated with particular conditions) as opposed to _____ (occurring in regular cycles).

19. Pain _____ and pain _____ are partially learned.

20. The sex drive in many lower animals is related to _____ (or "heat") in females. The sex drive is unusual in that it is non-_____ (both its arousal and its reduction are sought).

21. Sex drive in both males and females may be related to bodily levels of _____.

● *How does arousal relate to motivation?*

22. The _____ drives reflect needs for information, _____, manipulation, and sensory input.

23. Drives for stimulation are partially explained by _____ _____, which states that an ideal level of bodily arousal will be maintained if possible.

24. The desired level of arousal or stimulation varies from person to person, as measured by the _____ *Scale*.

25. Optimal performance on a task usually occurs at moderate levels of arousal. This relationship is described by an _____ _____ function.

26. The _____ law further states that for simple tasks the ideal arousal level is higher, and for complex tasks it is lower.

27. _____ rhythms within the body are closely tied to sleep, activity levels, and energy cycles. Travel across _____ _____ and shift work can seriously disrupt sleep and bodily rhythms.

28. If you anticipate a change in body rhythms, you can gradually _____ to your new schedule over a period of days.

29. Body rhythms and sleep cycles are strongly influenced by the release of _____, a hormone produced at night by the _____ gland.

● *What are social motives? Why are they important?*

30. Social motives are learned through _____ and cultural conditioning.
31. _____ theory, which states that strong emotions tend to be followed by an opposite emotion, explains some acquired motives.
32. One of the most prominent social motives is the need for _____ (nAch).
33. _____ nAch is correlated with success in many situations, with occupational choice, and with _____ risk taking.
34. _____ affects motivation because it influences the challenges you will undertake, the effort you will make, and how long you will persist when things don't go well.

● *Are some motives more basic than others?*

35. Maslow's _____ (rank ordering) of motives categorizes needs as basic and _____ oriented.
36. Lower needs in the hierarchy are assumed to be _____ (dominant) over higher needs.
37. Self-_____, the highest and most fragile need, is reflected in _____-needs.
38. In many situations, _____ motivation (that which is induced by obvious external rewards) can reduce _____ motivation, enjoyment, and creativity.

● *What happens during emotion? Can "lie detectors" really detect lies?*

39. Emotions are linked to many basic _____ behaviors, such as attacking, retreating, feeding, and reproducing.
40. Other major elements of emotion are physiological changes in the body, emotional _____, and emotional feelings.
41. The following are considered to be _____ emotions: fear, surprise, sadness, disgust, anger, anticipation, joy, and trust (acceptance).
42. Physical changes associated with emotion are caused by the action of _____, a hormone released into the bloodstream, and by activity in the _____ nervous system (ANS).
43. The _____ branch of the ANS is primarily responsible for arousing the body, the _____ branch for quieting it.
44. Sudden death due to prolonged and intense emotion is probably related to _____ rebound (excess activity). Heart attacks caused by sudden intense emotion are more likely due to _____ arousal.
45. The _____, or "lie detector," measures emotional arousal by monitoring heart rate, blood pressure, breathing rate, and the _____ skin response (GSR).
46. Asking a series of _____ and _____ questions may allow the detection of lies, but overall, the accuracy of the lie detector has been challenged by many researchers.

● *How accurately are emotions expressed by "body language" and the face?*

47. Basic emotional _____, such as smiling or baring one's teeth when angry, appear to be unlearned.

48. _____ expressions of fear, anger, disgust, sadness, and happiness are recognized by people of all cultures.

49. Body _____ and movements (body language) also express feelings, mainly by communicating emotional tone.

50. Three dimensions of emotional expressions are pleasantness-unpleasantness, attention-rejection, and _____.

51. The study of body language is known as _____.

● *How do psychologists explain emotions?*

52. The _____-Lange theory of emotion says that emotional experience follows an awareness of the bodily reactions of emotion.

53. In contrast, the _____-Bard theory says that bodily reactions and emotional experience occur at the same time and that emotions are organized in the brain.

54. Schachter's _____ theory of emotion emphasizes the importance of labels, or interpretations, applied to feelings of bodily _____.

55. Also important is the process of _____, in which bodily arousal is attributed to a particular person, object, or situation.

56. The _____ _____ hypothesis holds that sensations and information from emotional expressions help define what emotion a person is feeling.

57. Contemporary views of emotion place greater emphasis on how situations are _____ (evaluated). Also, all of the elements of emotion are seen as interrelated and interacting.

● *What does it mean to have "emotional intelligence"?*

58. Emotional _____ involves the following skills: self-awareness, _____, self-control, and an understanding of how to use emotions.

59. Emotionally intelligent people are good at reading _____ expressions, tone of _____, and other signs of emotion.

60. They also use their feelings to enhance _____ and _____ making.

61. Positive emotions are not just a luxury. They tend to encourage personal _____ and _____ connection.

● *What is the nature of love?*

62. Sternberg's _____ theory describes love as a combination of passion, _____, and commitment.

63. Combinations of these three factors produce nonlove, liking, infatuation, _____ love, fatuous love, _____ love, empty love, and consummate love.

MASTERY TEST

1. Which of the following is NOT one of the signs of emotional arousal recorded by a polygraph?
   a. heart rate   b. blood pressure   c. pupil dilation   d. breathing rate

2. Plain water is most satisfying when a person has _____ thirst.
   a. intracellular   b. hypothalamic   c. extracellular   d. homeostatic

3. We have a biological tendency to associate an upset stomach with foods eaten earlier. This is the basis for the development of
   a. taste aversions   b. yo-yo dieting   c. bulimia   d. frequent weight cycling

4. Strong external rewards tend to undermine
   a. extrinsic motivation   b. intrinsic motivation   c. prepotent motivation   d. stimulus motivation

5. Activity in the ANS is directly responsible for which element of emotion?
   a. emotional feelings   b. emotional expressions   c. physiological changes   d. misattributions

6. Empathy is a major element of
   a. nAch   b. intrinsic motivation   c. emotional intelligence   d. the sensation-seeking personality

7. Motivation refers to the ways in which activities are initiated, sustained, and
   a. acquired   b. valued   c. directed   d. aroused

8. The psychological state or feeling we call thirst corresponds to which element of motivation?
   a. need   b. drive   c. deprivation   d. incentive value

9. People who score high on the SSS generally prefer
   a. low levels of arousal   b. moderate levels of arousal   c. high levels of arousal
   d. the middle of the V function

10. Which facial expression is NOT recognized by people of all cultures?
    a. anger   b. disgust   c. optimism   d. fear

11. Learning to weaken eating cues is useful in
    a. self-selection feeding   b. yo-yo dieting   c. rapid weight cycling   d. behavioral dieting

12. People who score high on tests of the need for achievement tend to be:
    a. motivated by power and prestige   b. attracted to longshots   c. sensation seekers
    d. moderate risk takers

13. Which theory holds that emotional feelings, arousal, and behavior are generated simultaneously in the brain?
    a. James-Lange   b. Cannon-Bard   c. cognitive   d. attribution

14. Compared with people in North America, people in Asian cultures are less likely to express which emotion?
    a. anger   b. jealousy   c. curiosity   d. fear

15. Binge eating is most associated with
    a. bulimia nervosa   b. bait shyness   c. low levels of NPY   d. anorexia nervosa

16. Goals that are desirable are high in
    a. need reduction   b. incentive value   c. homeostatic valence   d. motivational "push"

17. _____ is to pain avoidance as _____ is to the sex drive.
    a. Non-homeostatic, episodic   b. Episodic, non-homeostatic   c. Non-homeostatic, cyclic
    d. Cyclic, non-homeostatic

18. A specialist in kinesics could be expected to be most interested in
    a. facial blends   b. circadian rhythms   c. sensation seeking   d. primary motives

19. Coping statements are a way to directly correct which part of test anxiety?
    a. overpreparation   b. under-arousal   c. excessive worry   d. compulsive rehearsal

20. Drives for exploration and activity are categorized as
    a. primary motives   b. secondary motives   c. stimulus motives   d. extrinsic motives

21. Sudden death following a period of intense fear may occur when _____ slows the heart to a stop.
    a. a sympathetic overload   b. adrenaline poisoning   c. opponent-process feedback
    d. a parasympathetic rebound

22. People who enjoy skydiving and ski jumping are very likely high in
    a. parasympathetic arousal   b. extrinsic motivation   c. their desires to meet meta-needs
    d. the trait of sensation seeking

23. You could induce eating in a laboratory rat by activating the
    a. lateral hypothalamus   b. corpus callosum   c. rat's set point   d. ventromedial hypothalamus

24. People think cartoons are funnier if they see them while holding a pen crosswise in their teeth. This observation supports
    a. the James-Lange theory   b. the Cannon-Bard theory   c. Schachter's cognitive theory
    d. the facial feedback hypothesis

25. Basic biological motives are closely related to
    a. nAch   b. homeostasis   c. activity in the thalamus   d. levels of melatonin in the body

26. Self-actualization is to _____ needs as safety and security are to _____ needs.
    a. growth, basic   b. basic, meta-   c. prepotent, basic   d. meta-, extrinsic

27. Which of the following is NOT a core element of emotion?
    a. physiological changes   b. emotional expressions   c. emotional feelings   d. misattributions

28. The effects of a "supermarket diet" on eating are related to the effects of _____ on eating.
    a. anxiety   b. incentive value   c. metabolic rates   d. stomach distention

29. According to the Yerkes-Dodson law, optimum performance occurs at _____ levels of arousal for simple tasks and _____ levels of arousal for complex tasks.
    a. higher, lower   b. lower, higher   c. minimum, high   d. average, high

30. Contemporary models of emotion place greater emphasis on _____, or the way situations are evaluated.
    a. appraisal   b. attribution   c. feedback   d. emotional tone

ANSWERS

Recite and Review

1. initiate, activities
2. need, goal
3. push, pull
4. goal, need
5. secondary
6. primary, steady
7. stomach, blood, liver
8. start, stop
9. feeding, satiety
10. fat, diet
11. taste, taste
12. starvation, gorging
13. anxiety
14. habits
15. dieting
16. bodily, brain
17. fluid, cells, fluid, cells
18. cycles
19. learned
20. females, arousal
21. drive
22. sensory
23. physical arousal
24. arousal
25. moderate
26. simple, complex
27. rhythms, sleep
28. change, schedule
29. sleep, hormone
30. Social
31. emotions, emotion
32. need
33. success, risk
34. motivation, effort, persist
35. basic
36. Lower, higher
37. Self, needs
38. external
39. behaviors
40. feelings

41. sadness, anger
42. hormone, nervous system
43. branch, branch
44. rebound, arousal
45. emotional arousal
46. relevant, lying
47. unlearned
48. fear, sadness
49. feelings, tone
50. facial
51. body language
52. follows
53. at the same time
54. labels
55. arousal
56. expressions
57. situations
58. self, self, emotions
59. emotion
60. feelings (or emotions)
61. Positive
62. passion
63. liking, empty

Connections

1. h
2. g
3. d
4. a
5. j
6. e
7. c
8. i
9. f
10. b
11. c
12. j
13. d
14. a
15. i
16. b
17. h
18. f
19. e
20. g
21. d
22. a

23. h
24. b
25. j
26. c
27. i
28. f
29. g
30. e

Check Your Memory

1. F
2. T
3. T
4. T
5. F
6. T
7. F
8. T
9. T
10. F
11. T
12. F
13. F
14. T
15. T
16. T
17. T
18. F
19. F
20. T
21. T
22. T
23. T
24. F
25. T
26. F
27. T
28. F
29. T
30. F
31. F
32. T
33. T
34. T
35. F
36. T
37. F

38. F
39. T
40. F
41. F
42. F
43. T
44. T
45. F
46. T
47. T
48. F
49. F
50. T
51. T
52. T
53. T
54. F
55. T
56. F
57. F
58. F
59. F
60. F
61. T
62. T
63. F
64. T
65. T
66. F
67. T
68. F
69. T
70. T
71. T
72. T
73. F
74. T
75. T
76. T
77. T

Final Survey and Review

1. sustain, direct
2. drive, attainment
3. needs, goals
4. incentive value

5. primary, stimulus, secondary
6. homeostasis
7. distention, hypoglycemia
8. hypothalamus, satiety
9. lateral, ventromedial, nucleus
10. set point, cues
11. aversions, bait shyness
12. Anorexia, bulimia
13. self-image
14. eating
15. Behavioral, self
16. hypothalamus
17. intracellular, extracellular
18. episodic, cyclic
19. avoidance, tolerance
20. estrus, homeostatic
21. androgens
22. stimulus, exploration
23. arousal theory
24. *Sensation-Seeking*
25. inverted U
26. Yerkes-Dodson
27. Circadian, time zones
28. preadapt
29. melatonin, pineal
30. socialization
31. Opponent-process
32. achievement
33. High, moderate
34. Self-confidence
35. hierarchy, growth
36. prepotent
37. actualization, meta
38. extrinsic, intrinsic
39. adaptive
40. expressions
41. primary
42. adrenaline, autonomic
43. sympathetic, parasympathetic
44. parasympathetic, sympathetic
45. polygraph, galvanic
46. relevant, irrelevant
47. expressions
48. Facial
49. gestures
50. activation
51. kinesics
52. James
53. Cannon
54. cognitive, arousal
55. attribution
56. facial feedback
57. appraised
58. intelligence, empathy
59. facial, voice
60. thinking, decision
61. personal, social
62. triangular, intimacy
63. romantic, companionate

Mastery Test

1. c (p. 457)
2. a (p. 441)
3. a (p. 438)
4. b (p. 452)
5. c (p. 455)
6. c (p. 467)
7. c (p. 431)
8. b (p. 431)
9. c (p. 443)
10. c (p. 459)
11. d (p. 436)
12. b (p. 448)
13. b (p. 463)
14. a (p. 459)
15. a (p. 439)
16. b (p. 432)
17. b (p. 441-442)
18. a (p. 459)
19. c (p. 445)
20. c (p. 432)
21. d (p. 456)
22. d (p. 443)
23. a (p. 434)
24. d (p. 465)
25. b (p. 432)
26. a (p. 450-451)
27. d (p. 453)
28. b (p. 432, 437)
29. a (p. 444)
30. a (p. 465)

Chapter 13
Gender and Sexuality

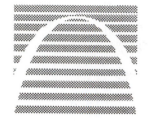

CHAPTER OVERVIEW

A person's sex is determined by a combination of genetic sex, gonadal sex, hormonal sex, genital sex, and gender identity. The development of primary and secondary sexual characteristics is influenced by androgens and estrogens. Prenatal hormones may exert a biological biasing effect that combines with social factors to influence psychosexual development.

On most psychological dimensions, men and women are more alike than they are different. Social factors are especially apparent in learned gender identity and the effects of gender roles. Gender role socialization accounts for most observed male/female differences. Psychological androgyny is related to greater personal adaptability.

"Normal" sexual behavior is defined differently by various cultures. There is little difference in male and female sexual responsiveness. Sexual orientation refers to whether a person is heterosexual, homosexual, or bisexual. A combination of hereditary, biological, social, and psychological influences combine to produce one's sexual orientation.

Human sexual response can be divided into four phases: (1) excitement; (2) plateau; (3) orgasm; and (4) resolution, which apply to both males and females.

Atypical sexual behavior can produce troubling sexual disorders such as pedophilia and fetishism. Such disorders are called paraphilias.

Attitudes toward sexual behavior have grown more liberal, but actual changes in behavior have been more gradual. During the last 20 years there has been a steady increase in the incidence of sexually transmitted diseases, which has altered patterns of sexual behavior.

The principal problems in sexual adjustment are desire disorders, arousal disorders, orgasm disorders, and sexual pain disorders. Behavioral methods and counseling techniques can alleviate each problem. However, communication skills that foster and maintain intimacy are the real key to successful relationships.

Patterns of touching vary from culture to culture, and they depend on the nature of the relationship between two people. Touch can therefore have a variety of meanings, most of which are nonsexual.

LEARNING OBJECTIVES

To demonstrate mastery of this chapter you should be able to:

1. Distinguish between the terms *sex* and *gender*. Differentiate primary from secondary sex characteristics and state (in general) what causes them.

2. Define or describe the following terms or concepts:
- a. menarche
- b. ovulation
- c. menopause
- d. gonads
- e. estrogens
- f. androgens
- g. testosterone

3. List and describe the five dimensions of sex.

4. Explain how a person's sex develops. Include in your discussion a description of these conditions:
- a. androgen insensitivity
- b. intersexual person
- c. androgenital syndrome
- d. biological biasing effect

5. Differentiate gender identity from gender role and explain how gender identity is formed. Include the concept of gender role stereotypes and cultural variations in gender roles.

6. Describe the effects of socialization on gender roles and include a discussion of instrumental and expressive behaviors.

7. Explain the meaning of the term *androgyny* and its relationship to masculinity, femininity, and adaptability.

8. Define *erogenous zone,* and explain what a sexual script is and how it relates to sexual behavior.

9. Discuss the differences between males and females in their degree of arousal to erotic stimuli.

10. Explain what causes differences in sex drives in males and females. Define the term *nocturnal orgasm.*

11. Describe the effects of alcohol, castration, and aging on the sex drive.

12. Discuss the normality and acceptability of masturbation.

13. Define the term *sexual orientation* and discuss the various types of sexual orientation. Discuss the combination of influences that appears to produce homosexuality. Characterize the emotional adjustment of homosexuals versus heterosexuals.

14. List in order and briefly describe the four phases of sexual response in men and women.

15. Describe the basic female and male sexual responses, and state the basic differences in sexual response styles of men and women.

16. Explain the difference between public and private standards of sexual behavior and what sets true sexual deviations apart from other sexual activity.

17. List and define eight behavior patterns (paraphilias) that fit the definition of sexual deviation.

18. Describe exhibitionism, including who the offenders are, why they do it, and how one's reactions may encourage them.

19. Describe pedophilia (child molestation) including who does it, what the offenders are like, and the factors that affect the seriousness of the molestation. Explain how parents should react to an incident of molestation.

20. List seven ways to recognize molestation from a child's behavior.

21. List six tactics of molesters, and discuss the impact of repeated molestations on the victims.

22. Describe the changes that have taken place in sexual attitudes and behavior in the last 50 years. Include a brief discussion of how the pace of the "revolution" seems to have slowed recently.

23. Explain what is meant by the phrase "slow death of the double standard."

24. Define *acquaintance* or *"date" rape* and discuss its effects.

25. Explain how gender role stereotyping may encourage the act of rape.

26. Differentiate forcible rape from date rape, and explain why rape is not viewed by experts as primarily a sexual act.

27. Explain the cause, methods of transmission, and ways of preventing AIDS.

The following objectives are related to the material in the "Psychology in Action" and "A Step Beyond" sections of your text.

28. Describe the following sexual problems including the nature, cause, and treatment of each:
    a. desire disorders
        1. hypoactive sexual desire
        2. sexual aversion
    b. arousal disorders
        1. male erectile disorder
        2. female sexual arousal disorder
    c. orgasm disorders
        1. female orgasmic disorder
        2. male orgasmic disorder
        3. premature ejaculation
    d. sexual pain disorders
        1. dyspareunia
        2. vaginismus

29. List four elements of a healthy sexual relationship.

30. List seven guidelines that can be followed to encourage effective communication between husbands and wives.

31. Discuss the cultural limitations of nonsexual touching.

RECITE AND REVIEW

● *What are the basic dimensions of sex?*

Recite and Review: Pages 474-478

1. Physical differences between males and females can be divided into _____ and _____ sexual characteristics.

2. Primary sexual characteristics are the _____ and internal reproductive organs.

3. Secondary sexual characteristics are bodily features such as breast development, body _____, and facial hair.

4. Reproductive maturity in females is signaled by menarche (the onset of _____). Soon after, ovulation (the release of _____, or eggs) begins.

5. The development of sexual characteristics is influenced by androgens (_____ sex hormones) and estrogens (_____ sex hormones) secreted by the gonads (sex _____).

6. A person's sex can be broken down into genetic sex, gonadal sex, _____ sex, genital sex, and _____ identity.

7. Sexual development begins with _____ sex (*XX* or *XY* chromosomes). Two *X* chromosomes normally produce a _____; an *X* plus a *Y* produces a _____.

8. During prenatal sexual development, the presence of testosterone produces _____ genitals; an absence of testosterone produces _____ genitals.

9. Androgen insensitivity, exposure to progestin, and the androgenital _____ result in _____ ambiguities called intersexualism.

10. Many researchers believe that prenatal _____ can exert a biological biasing _____ that combines with social factors present after birth to influence psychosexual development.

11. On most psychological dimensions, men and women are more _____ than they are _____.

● *How does one's sense of maleness or femaleness develop?*

Recite and Review: Pages 478-481

12. Social factors are especially apparent in learned gender identity (a private sense of _____ or _____) and the effect of gender roles (patterns of behavior defined as male or female within a particular culture).

13. Gender identity, which is based to a large extent on labeling, usually becomes stable by age ____ or ____ years.

14. Gender roles contribute to the development of _____ _____ stereotypes (oversimplified beliefs about the nature of men and women) that often distort perceptions about the kinds of occupations for which men and women are suited.

15. _____ _____ socialization (learning gender roles) seems to account for most observed male/female differences.

16. Parents tend to encourage _____ in instrumental behaviors and _____ in expressive behaviors.

● *What is psychological androgyny (and is it contagious)?*

Recite and Review: Pages 481-483

17. Research conducted by Sandra Bem indicates that roughly one third of all persons are androgynous (they possess both _____ and _____ traits).

18. Androgyny is measured with the *Bem* _____ _____ *Inventory* (BSRI).

19. Being _____ means that a person is independent and assertive.

20. Being _____ means that a person is nurturant and interpersonally oriented.

21. Psychological _____ appears related to greater adaptability or flexibility in behavior.

● *What are the most typical patterns of human sexual behavior?*

Recite and Review: Pages 483-488

22. Sexual behavior, including orgasm (sexual _____) is apparent soon after birth and expressed in various ways throughout life.

23. Sexual arousal is related to stimulation of the body's erogenous zones (areas that produce erotic _____), but cognitive elements such as _____ and images are equally important.

24. "Normal" sexual behavior is defined differently by various _____. Also, each person uses learned sexual scripts (plots or mental plans) to guide sexual behavior.

25. There is little difference in sexual _____ between males and females.

26. Evidence suggests that the sex drive peaks at a _____ age for females than it does for males, although this difference is diminishing.

27. Sex _____ in both males and females may be related to bodily levels of androgens.

28. Nocturnal _____ are a normal, but relatively minor, form of sexual release.

29. _____ (removal of the gonads) may or may not influence sex drive in humans, depending on how sexually experienced a person is. Sterilization (a vasectomy or tubal ligation) does not alter sex drive.

30. There is a gradual _____ in the frequency of sexual intercourse with increasing age.

31. Masturbation is a normal, harmless behavior practiced by a large percentage of the population. For many, masturbation is an important part of sexual self-_____.

32. Sexual orientation refers to one's degree of emotional and erotic attraction to members of the same _____, opposite _____, or both _____.

33. A person may be heterosexual, _____, or bisexual.

34. A combination of hereditary, biological, social, and psychological influences combine to produce one's _____ _____.

35. As a group, homosexual men and women do not differ psychologically from _____.

36. However, gay men and lesbians are frequently affected by homophobia (fear of _____) and heterosexism (the belief that heterosexuality is more natural than homosexuality).

● *To what extent do males and females differ in sexual response?*

Recite and Review: Pages 489-491

37. In a series of landmark studies, William _____ and Virginia Johnson directly observed sexual response in a large number of adults.

38. Human sexual response can be divided into four phases: (1) _____; (2) plateau; (3) _____; and (4) resolution.

39. Both males and females may go through all four stages in ____ or ____ minutes. But during lovemaking, most females typically take longer than this, averaging from 10 to 20 minutes.

40. Males experience a refractory period after _____ and ejaculation. Only 5 percent of men are _____-orgasmic.

41. Fifteen percent of women are consistently _____ -orgasmic, and at least 48 percent are capable of _____ orgasm.

42. There do not appear to be any differences between "vaginal _____" and "clitoral _____" in the female.

43. Mutual _____ has been abandoned by most sex counselors as the ideal in lovemaking.

● *What are the most common sexual disorders?*

Recite and Review: Pages 491-492

44. Definitions of sexual deviance are highly _____. Many "sexually deviant" behaviors are acceptable in private or in some _____.

45. Sexual _____ that often cause difficulty are called paraphilias.

46. Some paraphilias include: pedophilia (sex with children), _____ (sexual arousal associated with inanimate objects), voyeurism (viewing the genitals of others without their permission), and _____ (displaying the genitals to unwilling viewers).

47. Other paraphilias are: transvestic fetishism (achieving sexual arousal by wearing clothing of the opposite sex), sexual _____ (deriving sexual pleasure from inflicting pain), sexual _____ (desiring pain as part of the sex act), and frotteurism (sexually touching or rubbing against a nonconsenting person).

48. Exhibitionists are rarely dangerous and can best be characterized as sexually _____ and immature.

49. The effects of child molestation vary greatly, depending on the _____ of the molestation and the child's relationship to the molester.

● *Have recent changes in attitudes affected sexual behavior?*

Recite and Review: Pages 492-494

50. Attitudes toward sexual behavior, especially the behavior of others, have become more liberal, but actual changes in sexual _____ have been more gradual.

51. Another change has been _____ and more frequent sexual activity among adolescents and young adults, including larger percentages of people who have premarital _____.

52. Also evident are a greater acceptance of _____ sexuality and a narrowing of differences in male and female patterns of sexual _____. In other words, the double standard is fading.

53. Acquaintance (_____) rape and _____-supportive myths and attitudes remain major problems.

54. _____ is primarily a violent crime of aggression rather than a sex crime.

● *What impacts have sexually transmitted diseases had on sexual behavior?*

Recite and Review: Pages 494-498

55. During the last 20 years there has been a steady increase in the incidence of sexually transmitted _____ (STDs).

56. Part of this increase is due to the emergence of _____ _____ deficiency syndrome (AIDS) caused by the human immunodeficiency _____ (HIV).
57. STDs have had a sizable impact on patterns of sexual behavior, including increased awareness of high-_____ behaviors and some curtailment of _____ taking.

● *What are the most common sexual adjustment problems? How are they treated?*

Recite and Review: PSYCHOLOGY IN ACTION

58. The principal problems in sexual adjustment are _____ disorders, arousal disorders, orgasm disorders, and sexual _____ disorders.
59. Desire disorders include hypoactive _____ _____ (a loss of sexual desire) and _____ aversion (fear or disgust about engaging in sex).
60. Arousal disorders include _____ erectile disorder and _____ sexual arousal disorder.
61. Orgasm disorders are male orgasmic disorder (retarded _____), premature _____, and female orgasm disorder (an inability to reach orgasm during lovemaking).
62. Sexual pain disorders are dyspareunia (_____ intercourse) and vaginismus (_____ _____ of the vagina).
63. Behavioral methods such as sensate _____ and the squeeze technique have been developed to alleviate each problem. In addition, counseling can be quite helpful.
64. However, most sexual adjustment problems are closely linked to the general health of a couple's _____.
65. For this reason, communication skills that foster and maintain _____ are the key to successful relationships.

● *What is the role of touching in personal relationships?*

Recite and Review: A STEP BEYOND

66. Patterns of touching vary from culture to culture, and they depend on the nature of the _____ between two people.
67. During childhood, girls are touched more by _____ than boys are.
68. The vast majority of touching takes place between _____.
69. However, touch has a variety of meanings, most of which are nonsexual. A lack of human contact is one of the consequences of equating touch with _____.

CONNECTIONS

1. _____ pelvic bone
2. _____ urethra
3. _____ labia minora
4. _____ ovary
5. _____ vagina
6. _____ uterus
7. _____ rectum
8. _____ fallopian tube
9. _____ clitoris
10. _____ labia majora
11. _____ urinary bladder
12. _____ cervix

13. _____ androgen
14. _____ estrogen
15. _____ genetic sex
16. _____ gonadal sex
17. _____ intersexual person
18. _____ gender identity
19. _____ gender role
20. _____ androgyny
21. _____ STD
22. _____ dyspareunia

a. ovaries or testes
b. cultural pattern
c. self-perception
d. AIDS
e. female hormone
f. man-woman
g. pain disorder
h. *XX* or *XY*
i. androgenital syndrome
j. testosterone

23. _____ Cowper's gland

24. _____ glans penis

25. _____ urethra

26. _____ seminal vesicle

27. _____ vas deferens

28. _____ pelvic bone

29. _____ urinary bladder

30. _____ testis

31. _____ rectum

32. _____ urethral orifice

33. _____ epididymis

34. _____ prostate

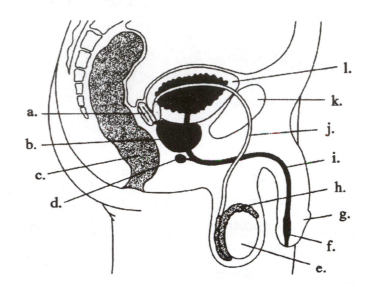

CHECK YOUR MEMORY

Check Your Memory: Pages 474-478

1. Primary sexual characteristics involve differences in the reproductive organs and the breasts. T or F?
2. The term menarche refers to the ending of regular monthly fertility cycles in females. T or F?
3. The female gonads are the ovaries. T or F?
4. Cowper's glands are female reproductive structures. T or F?
5. All individuals normally produce both androgens and testosterones. T or F?
6. Transsexuals are persons who have had their genetic sex altered medically. T or F?
7. Without testosterone, a human embryo will develop into a female. T or F?
8. Androgen insensitivity results in the development of female genitals. T or F?
9. Differences in male and female scores on the SAT have declined in recent years. T or F?
10. Observed differences in the abilities of males and females are based on averages; they tell nothing about a particular person. T or F?

Check Your Memory: Pages 478-481

11. Gender identity refers to all the behaviors that are defined as male or female by one's culture. T or F?
12. Babies are perceived differently and treated differently when they are labeled as males than when they are labeled as females. T or F?
13. Women continue to receive unequal pay for work comparable to that of men. T or F?
14. Even though their culture is quite different, the sex roles of Tchambuli men and women are almost identical to those in North America. T or F?
15. Boys are allowed to roam over wider areas than girls are. T or F?

16. Expressive behaviors are those that directly express a person's desire to attain a goal. T or F?

Check Your Memory: Pages 481-483

17. The BSRI consists of 20 masculine traits and 20 feminine traits. T or F?
18. About 50 percent of all people who take the BSRI are scored as androgynous. T or F?
19. Masculine men and feminine women consistently choose to engage in sex-appropriate activities. T or F?
20. Masculine men find it difficult to accept support from others. T or F?
21. Androgynous persons tend to be more satisfied with their lives than non-androgynous persons are. T or F?

Check Your Memory: Pages 483-488

22. Sexual scripts determine when, where, and with whom we are likely to express sexual feelings. T or F?
23. Women are less physically aroused by erotic stimuli than men are. T or F?
24. Women may engage in sexual activity at any time during their menstrual cycles. T or F?
25. More women than men have sexual dreams that result in orgasm. T or F?
26. Drunkenness lowers sexual arousal and performance. T or F?
27. Sterilization tends to abolish the sex drive in the sexually inexperienced. T or F?
28. Masturbation typically ends soon after people get married. T or F?
29. The average frequency of sexual intercourse declines dramatically between the ages of 30 and 39. T or F?
30. Your sexual orientation is revealed, in part, by who you have erotic fantasies about. T or F?
31. Gay males are converted to homosexuality during adolescence by other homosexuals. T or F?
32. Sexual orientation is a very stable personal characteristic. T or F?
33. Sexual orientation is influenced by heredity. T or F?
34. Hormone imbalances cause most instances of homosexuality and bisexuality. T or F?
35. Homosexual persons tend to discover their sexual orientation at a later age than heterosexual persons do. T or F?

Check Your Memory: Pages 489-491

36. Masters and Johnson's data on human sexuality was restricted to questionnaires and interviews. T or F?
37. During the excitement phase of sexual response, the nipples become erect in both males and females. T or F?
38. In males, orgasm is always accompanied by ejaculation. T or F?
39. Almost all women experience a short refractory period after ejaculation. T or F?
40. Both orgasm and resolution tend to last longer in females than they do in males. T or F?
41. Contemporary research has confirmed that clitoral orgasms are an inferior form of sexual response. T or F?
42. Women tend to go through the phases of sexual response more slowly than men do. T or F?
43. One woman in 3 does not experience orgasm during the first year of marriage. T or F?

Check Your Memory: Pages 491-492

44. Oral sex and masturbation are formally classified as paraphilias. T or F?
45. Frotteurism refers to sex with children. T or F?

46. Most exhibitionists are male and married. T or F?

47. An exhibitionist who approaches closer than arm's length may be dangerous. T or F?

48. In the majority of cases of child molesting, the offender is an acquaintance or relative of the child. T or F?

49. Child molesting is especially likely to be harmful if the molester is someone the child deeply trusts. T or F?

Check Your Memory: Pages 492-494

50. In recent decades the gap between sexual values and actual behavior has narrowed. T or F?

51. A majority of young adults continue to believe that premarital sex is unacceptable. T or F?

52. The incidence of extramarital sex has not changed much in the last 40 years. T or F?

53. The majority of men and women have sexual experiences before marriage. T or F?

54. About 12 percent of all adult Americans are sexually abstinent. T or F?

55. Women who are raped usually asked for trouble by wearing sexy clothes. T or F?

56. One woman in 70 will be raped in her lifetime. T or F?

57. The majority of rapists are friends or acquaintances of the victim. T or F?

58. Males high in sex role stereotyping are more aroused by stories about rape than males low in sex role stereotyping. T or F?

Check Your Memory: Pages 494-498

59. The first symptoms of AIDS may not appear for up to 7 years. T or F?

60. HIV infections are spread by direct contact with body fluids. T or F?

61. The AIDS epidemic has dramatically altered the sexual behavior of college students. T or F?

62. Most women who contract the HIV virus today do so through intravenous drug use. T or F?

63. It is unwise to count on a partner for protection from HIV infection. T or F?

64. Gonorrhea can be prevented by vaccination. T or F?

65. Hepatitis B can be prevented by vaccination. T or F?

66. Chlamydia is now the most common STD among men. T or F?

67. Many people suffering from STDs are asymptomatic. T or F?

Check Your Memory: PSYCHOLOGY IN ACTION

68. In a desire disorder the person desires sex, but does not become sexually aroused. T or F?

69. A person who is repelled by sex and seeks to avoid it suffers from a sexual aversion. T or F?

70. Men suffering from primary erectile dysfunction have never had an erection. T or F?

71. The squeeze technique is the most commonly recommended treatment for erectile disorders. T or F?

72. The majority of erectile dysfunctions are psychogenic. T or F?

73. Treatment for female sexual arousal disorder usually involves sensate focus. T or F?

74. Female orgasmic disorder is the female equivalent of premature ejaculation in the male. T or F?

75. Both males and females can experience dyspareunia. T or F?

76. Masters and Johnson regard all sexual problems as mutual, or shared by both parties. T or F?

77. Gunnysacking is an important communication skill that all couples should master. T or F?

78. Rather than telling your partner what he or she thinks, you should ask her or him. T or F?

Check Your Memory: A STEP BEYOND

79. Very limited body contact is all that occurs outside of strictly sexual contexts. T or F?
80. College students are touched mainly on the head and arms by their parents. T or F?
81. Most regions of the body remain untouched unless one has a romantic partner. T or F?

FINAL SURVEY AND REVIEW

● *What are the basic dimensions of sex?*

1. Physical differences between males and females can be divided into primary and secondary
_____ _____.

2. _____ refers to the genitals and internal _____ organs.

3. _____ refers to bodily features such as _____ development in females, body shape, and facial _____.

4. Reproductive maturity in females is signaled by _____ (the onset of menstruation). Soon after, _____ (the release of eggs) begins.

5. The development of sexual characteristics is influenced by _____ (male sex hormones) and _____ (female sex hormones) secreted by the _____ (sex glands).

6. A person's sex can be broken down into _____ sex, _____ sex, hormonal sex, _____ sex, and gender identity.

7. Sexual development begins with genetic sex (*XX* or *XY* _____). Two ___s normally produce a female ___ plus a ___ produces a male.

8. During prenatal sexual development, the presence of _____ produces male _____; its absence produces female _____.

9. _____ insensitivity, exposure to progestin, and the androgenital syndrome result in sexual ambiguities called _____.

10. Many researchers believe that _____ hormones can exert a biological _____ effect that combines with social factors present after birth to influence psychosexual development.

11. On most _____ dimensions, men and women are more alike than they are different.

● *How does one's sense of maleness or femaleness develop?*

12. Social factors are especially apparent in learned _____ _____ (a private sense of maleness or femaleness) and the effect of _____ _____ (patterns of behavior defined as male or female within a particular culture).

13. Gender identity, which is based to a large extent on _____, usually becomes stable by age 3 or 4 years.

14. Gender roles contribute to the development of gender role _____ (oversimplified beliefs about the nature of men and women) that often distort perceptions about the kinds of occupations for which men and women are suited.

15. Gender role _____ (learning gender roles) seems to account for most observed male/female differences.

16. Parents tend to encourage boys in _____ behaviors (goal-directed actions) and girls in _____ (emotional) behaviors.

● *What is psychological androgyny (and is it contagious)?*

17. Research conducted by Sandra Bem indicates that roughly one _____ of all persons are _____ (they possess both masculine and feminine traits).

18. Androgyny is measured with the _____ *Sex Role* _____ (BSRI).

19. Being masculine means that a person is _____ and assertive.

20. Being feminine means that a person is _____ (helpful and comforting) and interpersonally oriented.

21. Psychological androgyny appears related to greater _____ or flexibility in behavior.

● *What are the most typical patterns of human sexual behavior?*

22. Sexual behavior, including _____ (sexual climax), is apparent soon after birth and expressed in various ways throughout life.

23. Sexual arousal is related to stimulation of the body's _____ zones (areas that produce erotic pleasure), but _____ elements such as thoughts and images are equally important.

24. "Normal" sexual behavior is defined differently by various cultures. Also, each person uses learned sexual _____ (plots or mental _____) to guide sexual behavior.

25. There is little _____ in sexual behavior between males and females.

26. Evidence suggests that the sex drive peaks at a later age for _____ than it does for _____, although this difference is diminishing.

27. Sex drive in both males and females may be related to bodily levels of _____.

28. _____ orgasms, which occur during sleep, are a normal form of sexual release.

29. Castration (removal of the gonads) may or may not influence sex drive in humans, depending on how sexually experienced a person is. _____ (a vasectomy or tubal ligation) does not alter sex drive.

30. There is a gradual decline in the _____ of sexual intercourse with increasing _____. However, many elderly persons remain sexually active and great variations exist at all ages.

31. _____ (sexual self-stimulation) is a normal, harmless behavior practiced by a large percentage of the population. For many, it is an important part of sexual self-discovery.

32. Sexual _____ refers to one's degree of emotional and erotic attraction to members of the same sex, opposite sex, or both sexes.

33. A person may be _____, homosexual, or _____.

34. A combination of _____, biological, _____, and psychological influences combine to produce one's sexual orientation.

35. As a group, _____ men and women do not differ psychologically from _____.

36. However, gay men and lesbians are frequently affected by _____ (fear of homosexuality) and _____ (the belief that heterosexuality is better than homosexuality).

● *To what extent do males and females differ in sexual response?*

37. In a series of landmark studies, William Masters and Virginia _____ directly observed sexual response in a large number of adults.

38. Human sexual response can be divided into four phases: (1) excitement; (2) _____; (3) orgasm; and (4) _____.

39. Both males and females may go through all four stages in 4 or 5 minutes. But during lovemaking, most _____ typically take longer than this, averaging from 10 to 20 minutes.

40. Males experience a _____ period after orgasm and ejaculation. Only 5 percent of men are multi-_____.

41. _____ percent of women are consistently _____, and at least 48 percent are capable of multiple orgasm.

42. There do not appear to be any differences between "_____ orgasms" and "_____ orgasms" in the female.

43. _____ orgasm has been abandoned by most sex counselors as the ideal in lovemaking.

● *What are the most common sexual disorders?*

44. Definitions of _____ _____ are highly subjective. Many publicly disapproved sexual behaviors are acceptable in private or in some cultures.

45. Sexual deviations that often cause difficulty are called _____ (destructive deviations in sexual preferences or behavior).

46. Some of these problems include: _____ (sex with children), fetishism (sexual arousal associated with inanimate objects), _____ (viewing the genitals of others without their permission), and exhibitionism (displaying the genitals to unwilling viewers).

47. Others are: _____ fetishism (achieving sexual arousal by wearing clothing of the opposite sex), sexual sadism (deriving sexual pleasure from inflicting pain), sexual masochism (desiring pain as part of the sex act), and _____ (sexually touching or rubbing against a nonconsenting person).

48. _____ ("flashers") are rarely dangerous and can best be characterized as sexually inhibited and immature.

49. The effects of child molestation vary greatly, depending on the severity of the _____ and the child's _____ to the molester.

● *Have recent changes in attitudes affected sexual behavior?*

50. _____ toward sexual behavior, especially the behavior of others, have become more _____, but actual changes in sexual behavior have been more gradual.

51. Another change has been earlier and more frequent sexual activity among adolescents and young adults, including larger percentages of people who have _____ intercourse.

52. Also evident are a greater acceptance of female sexuality and a narrowing of differences in male and female patterns of sexual behavior. In other words, the _____ _____ is fading.

53. _____ (date) rape and rape-supportive _____ (false beliefs) and attitudes remain major problems.

54. Rape is primarily a violent crime of _____ rather than a sex crime.

● *What impacts have sexually transmitted diseases had on sexual behavior?*

55. During the last 20 years there has been a steady increase in the incidence of _____ _____ diseases (STDs).

56. Part of this increase is due to the emergence of acquired immune _____ syndrome (AIDS) caused by the human _____ virus (HIV).

57. _____ have had a sizable impact on patterns of sexual behavior, including increased awareness of high-risk behaviors and some curtailment of risk taking.

● *What are the most common sexual adjustment problems? How are they treated?*

58. The principal problems in sexual adjustment are desire disorders, _____ disorders, _____ disorders, and sexual pain disorders.

59. Desire disorders include _____ sexual desire (a loss of sexual desire) and sexual _____ (fear or disgust about engaging in sex).

60. Arousal disorders include male _____ disorder and female sexual _____ disorder.

61. Orgasm disorders are male orgasmic disorder (_____ ejaculation), _____ ejaculation, and female _____ disorder (an inability to reach orgasm during lovemaking).

62. Sexual pain disorders are _____ (painful intercourse) and _____ (muscle spasms of the vagina).

63. Behavioral methods such as _____ focus and the _____ technique for premature ejaculation have been developed to alleviate each problem. In addition, counseling can be quite helpful.

64. However, most sexual _____ problems are closely linked to the general health of a couple's relationship.

65. For this reason, _____ skills that foster and maintain intimacy are the key to successful relationships.

● *What is the role of touching in personal relationships?*

66. Patterns of touching vary in different _____, and they depend on the nature of the relationship between two people.
67. During childhood, _____ are touched more by parents than _____ are.
68. The _____ of touching takes place between lovers.
69. However, touch has a variety of meanings, most of which are non-_____. A lack of human contact is one of the consequences of equating touch with sexuality.

MASTERY TEST

1. The strength of the sex drive in both men and women increases when _____ levels are higher in the body.
   a. testosterone   b. progestin   c. ovulin   d. androgenin

2. Worldwide, the main source of HIV infection is
   a. heterosexual sex   b. homosexual sex   c. intravenous drug use   d. blood transfusions

3. Boys are encouraged to be strong, aggressive, dominant, and achieving through the process of
   a. biological biasing   b. sexual orienting   c. gender adaptation   d. gender role socialization

4. Before birth, a genetic male will develop as a female if which condition exists?
   a. excessive progestin   b. an androgen insensitivity   c. the androgenital syndrome
   d. the testes produce testosterone

5. Concerning masturbation, it can be concluded that
   a. masturbation typically ceases after marriage   b. after age 30, women masturbate more than men do
   c. those who are most sexually active masturbate the most   d. masturbation slows psychosexual development

6. One of the greatest changes in attitudes toward sex is a tolerance for
   a. teenage pregnancies   b. the sexual behavior of others   c. the double standard   d. STDs

7. The squeeze technique is typically used to treat
   a. dyspareunia   b. vaginismus   c. female sexual arousal disorder   d. premature ejaculation

8. In a female, gonadal sex is determined by the presence of
   a. estrogens   b. androgens   c. ovaries   d. a vagina and uterus

9. A policeman who accepts emotional support from others, especially from women, would most likely be scored as _____ on the BSRI.
   a. masculine   b. feminine   c. androgynous   d. expressive-nurturant

10. Which of the following is POOR advice for couples who want to communicate effectively and maintain intimacy?
    a. Avoid gunnysacking.   b. Avoid expressing anger.   c. Don't try to win.   d. Don't be a mind-reader.

11. The aspect of sex that is essentially formed by age 4 is
    a. gender identity   b. gender roles   c. sexual scripting   d. psychological androgyny

12. In a female, broadening of the hips and breast development are
    a. primary sexual characteristics   b. secondary sexual characteristics   c. caused by the release of androgens   d. associated with the presence of a *Y* chromosome

13. The first two phases of the sexual response cycle are
    a. excitement, arousal   b. arousal, orgasm   c. excitement, plateau   d. stimulation, arousal

14. A special danger in the transmission of STDs is that many people are _____ at first.
    a. not infectious   b. androgynous   c. androgenital   d. asymptomatic

15. The presence of a *Y* chromosome is associated with
    a. intersexualism   b. prenatal testosterone   c. menarche   d. the presence of progestin

16. With respect to the behaviors parents encourage in their children, which is a correct match?
    a. controlling-female   b. goal-oriented-female   c. expressive-male   d. instrumental-male

17. Which condition is LEAST likely to lower sexual performance?
    a. sterilization   b. castration   c. extreme alcohol intoxication   d. sexual aversion

18. Prenatally masculinized females tend to be tomboys during childhood, and observation that supports the
    a. biological biasing effect   b. estrogen paradox   c. view that gender is genetically determined
    d. idea that gender role socialization is dominant

19. Which of the following increases the likelihood that a man will commit rape?
    a. drinking alcohol   b. being high in gender role stereotyping   c. belief in rape myths
    d. all of the preceding

20. Gender role _____ treat learned gender role differences as if they were real gender differences.
    a. labels   b. behavior patterns   c. stereotypes   d. templates

21. Regarding sexual response it can be said that
    a. orgasm and resolution tend to last longer in women   b. a short refractory period occurs just before orgasm in males   c. some women skip the arousal phase of the cycle   d. men are incapable of having second orgasms

22. The decline of the double standard refers to abandoning different standards for
    a. risky sex and "safe" sex   b. heterosexual relationships and homosexual relationships   c. sexuality before and after marriage   d. male and female sexual behavior

23. Declines in the differences in male and female scores on the SAT call into question which concept?
    a. the androgenital syndrome   b. the biological biasing effect   c. gender role socialization
    d. gender identity

24. When expectations of a friendly first date clash with an attempted seduction the problem can be attributed to differences in
    a. gender roles   b. erogenous confrontation   c. gender myths   d. sexual scripts

25. Which statement concerning sexual orientation is TRUE?
    a. Sexual orientation is partly hereditary.   b. Homosexuality is caused by a hormone imbalance.
    c. Sexual orientation can be changed fairly easily.   d. Heterosexual persons tend to discover their sexual orientation at a later date than homosexual persons do.

26. Patterns of touching by same-sex friends primarily avoid the
    a. head   b. torso   c. hands   d. legs

27. Pedophilia, fetishism, and sadism are classified as
    a. the three basic forms of child molestation   b. STDs   c. paraphilias   d. hormonal disorders

28. All but one of the following is a rape myth. Which is NOT a myth?
    a. Women who get raped ask for it in one way or another.   b. A majority of rapes are committed by a friend or acquaintance of the victim.   c. Women who are sexually active are usually lying if they say they were raped.   d. Many women who are raped secretly enjoy it.

29. Which of the following diseases is currently untreatable?
    a. gonorrhea   b. chlamydia   c. syphilis   d. hepatitis B

30. The male sexual disorder that corresponds most closely to female sexual arousal disorder is
    a. sexual aversion   b. erectile disorder   c. premature ejaculation   d. dyspareunia

ANSWERS

Recite and Review

1. primary, secondary
2. genitals
3. shape
4. menstruation, ova
5. male, female, glands
6. hormonal, gender
7. genetic, female, male
8. male, female
9. syndrome, sexual
10. hormones, effect
11. alike, different
12. maleness, femaleness
13. 3, 4

14. gender role
15. Gender role
16. boys, girls
17. masculine, feminine
18. *Sex Role*
19. masculine
20. feminine
21. androgyny
22. climax
23. pleasure, thoughts
24. cultures
25. responsiveness
26. later
27. drive
28. orgasms
29. Castration
30. decline (or decrease)
31. discovery
32. sex, sex, sex
33. homosexual
34. sexual orientation
35. heterosexuals
36. homosexuality
37. Masters
38. excitement, orgasm
39. 4, 5
40. orgasm, multi
41. multi, multiple
42. orgasms, orgasms
43. orgasm
44. subjective, cultures
45. deviations
46. fetishism, exhibitionism
47. sadism, masochism
48. inhibited
49. severity
50. behavior
51. earlier, intercourse
52. female, behavior
53. date, rape
54. Rape
55. diseases
56. acquired immune, virus
57. risk, risk
58. desire, pain
59. sexual desire, sexual
60. male, female
61. ejaculation, ejaculation
62. painful, muscle spasms

63. focus
64. relationship
65. intimacy
66. relationship
67. parents
68. lovers
69. sexuality

Connections

1. d
2. h
3. f
4. b
5. j
6. l
7. i
8. a
9. e
10. g
11. c
12. k
13. j
14. e
15. h
16. a
17. i
18. c
19. b
20. f
21. d
22. g
23. d
24. g
25. i
26. a
27. j
28. k
29. l
30. e
31. c
32. f
33. h
34. b

Check Your Memory

1. F
2. F
3. T
4. F
5. F
6. F
7. T
8. T
9. T
10. T
11. F
12. T
13. T
14. F
15. T
16. F
17. F
18. F
19. T
20. T
21. T
22. T
23. F
24. T
25. F
26. T
27. F
28. F
29. F
30. T
31. F
32. T
33. T
34. F
35. T
36. F
37. T
38. F
39. F
40. T
41. F
42. T
43. T
44. F
45. F
46. T
47. T

48. T
49. T
50. T
51. F
52. T
53. T
54. T
55. F
56. F
57. T
58. T
59. T
60. T
61. F
62. F
63. T
64. F
65. T
66. F
67. T
68. F
69. T
70. T
71. F
72. T
73. T
74. F
75. T
76. T
77. F
78. T
79. T
80. T
81. T

Final Survey and Review

1. sexual characteristics
2. Primary, reproductive
3. Secondary, breast, hair
4. menarche, ovulation
5. androgens, estrogens, gonads
6. genetic, gonadal, genital
7. chromosomes, *X, X, Y*
8. testosterone, genitals, genitals
9. Androgen, intersexualism
10. prenatal, biasing
11. psychological
12. gender identity, gender roles
13. labeling
14. stereotypes
15. socialization
16. instrumental, expressive
17. third, androgynous
18. *Bem, Inventory*
19. independent
20. nurturant
21. adaptability
22. orgasm
23. erogenous, cognitive
24. scripts, plans
25. difference
26. females, males
27. androgens
28. Nocturnal
29. Sterilization
30. frequency, age
31. Masturbation
32. orientation
33. heterosexual, bisexual
34. hereditary, social
35. homosexual, heterosexuals
36. homophobia, heterosexism
37. Johnson
38. plateau, resolution
39. females
40. refractory, orgasmic
41. Fifteen, multi-orgasmic
42. vaginal, clitoral
43. Mutual
44. sexual deviance
45. paraphilias
46. pedophilia, voyeurism
47. transvestic, frotteurism
48. Exhibitionists
49. molestation, relationship
50. Attitudes, liberal
51. premarital
52. double standard
53. Acquaintance, myths
54. aggression
55. sexually transmitted
56. deficiency, immunodeficiency
57. STDs
58. arousal, orgasm
59. hypoactive, aversion
60. erectile, arousal
61. retarded, premature, orgasm
62. dyspareunia, vaginismus
63. sensate, squeeze
64. adjustment
65. communication
66. cultures
67. girls, boys
68. majority
69. sexual

Mastery Test

1. a (p. 485)
2. a (p. 497)
3. d (p. 480)
4. b (p. 477)
5. c (p. 486)
6. b (p. 492)
7. d (p. 501)
8. c (p. 476)
9. c (p. 482)
10. b (p. 503)
11. a (p. 478)
12. b (p. 475)
13. c (p. 489)
14. d (p. 495)
15. b (p. 477)
16. d (p. 481)
17. a (p. 486)
18. a (p. 478)
19. d (p. 493-494)
20. c (p. 480)
21. a (p. 489-490)
22. d (p. 493)
23. b (p. 479)
24. d (p. 484)
25. a (p. 488)
26. b (p. 505)
27. c (p. 491)
28. b (p. 494)
29. d (p. 495)
30. b (p. 499)

Chapter 14
Personality

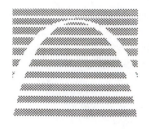

CHAPTER OVERVIEW

Personality refers to unique and enduring behavior patterns. Character is personality evaluated. Temperament refers to the hereditary and physiological aspects of one's emotional nature. Personality traits are lasting personal qualities. Personality types are categories defined by groups of shared traits. Behavior is also influenced by self-concept. Personality theories combine various ideas and principles to explain personality.

Allport's trait theory classifies traits as common, individual, cardinal, central, or secondary. Cattell's trait theory attributes visible surface traits to the existence of 16 underlying source traits. The five-factor model reduces traits to 5 dimensions. Traits appear to interact with situations to determine behavior. Behavioral genetics suggests that heredity influences personality traits.

Like other psychodynamic approaches, Sigmund Freud's psychoanalytic theory emphasizes unconscious forces and conflicts within the personality. The neo-Freudian theorists retained many of Freud's basic ideas, but modified some of them or added to them. Behavioral theories of personality emphasize learning, conditioning, and the immediate effects of the environment. Social learning theory adds cognitive elements, such as perception, thinking, expectancies, and understanding, to the behavioral view. Humanistic theory emphasizes subjective experiences and needs for self-actualization.

Techniques typically used to assess personality are interviews, direct observation, rating scales, questionnaires, and projective tests.

Shyness is a mixture of social inhibition and social anxiety. It is marked by heightened public self-consciousness and a tendency to regard one's shyness as a lasting trait. Shyness can be lessened by changing self-defeating beliefs and by improving social skills.

People vary in their degree of self-monitoring. High self-monitoring persons try to fit their public image to various situations. Low self-monitors are interested in accurately expressing their feelings, beliefs, and values, regardless of the situation.

LEARNING OBJECTIVES

To demonstrate mastery of this chapter you should be able to:

1. Define the term *personality* and explain how personality differs from character and temperament.
2. Define the term *trait*. Discuss the stability of personality.

3. Describe the trait approach and the type approach to personality, and explain the shortcoming of the type approach.

4. Explain the terms *self-concept* and *self-esteem*. Briefly discuss how they affect behavior and personal adjustment.

5. Briefly discuss the differences in the basis of self-esteem in Eastern and Western cultures.

6. Define the term *personality theory*. List and describe the five broad perspectives covered in your text.

7. Describe the general approach that trait theorists take in the study of personality.

8. Distinguish common traits from individual traits.

9. Define, differentiate, and give examples of Allport's cardinal traits, central traits, and secondary traits.

10. Distinguish between surface traits and source traits, and state how Cattell measures source traits.

11. Explain how Cattell's approach to personality traits differed from Allport's approach.

12. Discuss the five-factor model of personality.

13. Explain what a trait-situation interaction is.

14. Define behavioral genetics and explain how twin studies are used to assess the relative contribution of heredity and environment to a person's personality. Discuss how the similarities in the personalities of twins can be explained.

15. Assess the relative contributions of heredity and environment to the makeup of personality.

16. Explain why Freud became interested in personality.

17. List and describe the three parts of the personality according to Freud.

18. Describe the dynamic conflict between the three parts of the personality and relate neurotic and moral anxiety to the conflict.

19. Describe the relationships among the three parts of the personality (according to Freud) and the three levels of awareness.

20. List and describe Freud's four psychosexual stages. In your answer include an explanation of fixation and the corresponding age range for each stage.

21. Discuss the positive and the negative aspects of Freud's developmental theory.

22. Define the term *neo-Freudian* and explain why many of Freud's followers eventually disagreed with him.

23. Describe Adler's view of personality, including the concept of compensation.

24. Describe Horney's view of neurosis and emotional health including the concept of basic anxiety.

25. Describe Jung's view of personality by defining or explaining the following terms:
   - a. persona
   - b. introversion/extroversion
   - c. personal unconscious
   - d. collective unconscious
   - e. archetype
        - 1. anima   2. animus   3. self archetype

26. Explain how behaviorists view personality.

27. Explain how learning theorists view the structure of personality. Include in your discussion the terms situational determinants, habit, drive, cue, response, and reward.

28. Explain how learning theory and social learning theory differ. Include in your discussion a description of the terms *psychological situation, expectancy, reinforcement value, self-efficacy,* and *self-reinforcement.*

29. Describe the role of social reinforcement in personality development.

30. Using the behavioristic view of development, explain why feeding, toilet training, sex training, and learning to express anger or aggression may be particularly important to personality formation.

31. Describe the role of imitation and identification in personality development and sex training.

32. Briefly explain how the humanists set themselves apart from the Freudian and behaviorist viewpoints of personality.

33. Describe the development of Maslow's interest in self-actualization.

34. Using at least five of the characteristics of self-actualizers listed in your text, describe a self-actualizing person. From the original list of eleven, evaluate yourself and explain what may be helping or hindering your self-actualization.

35. List and briefly explain or describe (where applicable) eight steps to promote self-actualization.

36. Differentiate Freud's and Rogers' views of the normal or fully functioning individual.

37. Describe Rogers' view of the self, self-concept, and incongruence.

38. Describe an incongruent person in Rogers' view, and discuss the concept of ideal self.

39. Explain how possible selves help translate our hopes, dreams, and fears and ultimately direct our future behavior.

40. Explain how conditions of worth, organismic valuing, positive self-regard, and unconditional positive regard may affect personality formation.

41. Compare and contrast in general terms the strengths and weaknesses of the trait, psychoanalytic, behavioristic, social learning, and humanistic theories of personality.

42. Discuss the following assessment techniques in terms of purpose, method, advantages, and limitations:

   a. structured, unstructured, and diagnostic interviews (include the halo effect)
   b. direct observation (combined with rating scales, behavioral assessment and situational testing)
   c. personality questionnaires (include the MMPI-2)
   d. honesty tests
   e. projective tests (include the Rorschach and TAT)

43. Describe the personality characteristics of sudden murderers, and explain how their characteristics are related to the nature of their homicidal actions.

The following objectives are related to the material in the "Psychology in Action" and "A Step Beyond" sections of your text.

44. List and describe the three elements of shyness. State what usually causes shyness.

45. Compare the personality of the shy and not-shy. Include the terms *labeling* and *self-esteem.*

46. List and discuss the four self-defeating beliefs that can lead to shyness and possible ways to counteract these beliefs.

47. Define the term *self-monitoring* and differentiate high self-monitoring behavior from low self-monitoring behavior. Explain the advantages and disadvantages of each.

RECITE AND REVIEW

● *How do psychologists use the term* personality?

Recite and Review: Pages 508-510

1. Personality is made up of one's unique and relatively stable _____ patterns.

2. Character is personality that has been judged or _____. That is, it is the possession of desirable qualities.

3. Temperament refers to the _____ and physiological aspects of one's emotional nature.

● *What core concepts make up the psychology of personality?*

Recite and Review: Pages 510-512

4. Personality traits are lasting personal qualities that are inferred from _____.

5. A personality type is a style of personality defined by having a group of related _____ or similar characteristics.

6. Two widely recognized personality _____ are an introvert (shy, self-centered person) and an extrovert (bold, outgoing person).

7. Behavior is influenced by self-concept, which is a person's perception of his or her own _____ traits.

8. _____ theories combine interrelated assumptions, ideas, and principles to explain personality.

9. Five major types of personality theories are: _____, psychodynamic, behavioristic, _____ learning, and humanistic.

● *Are some personality traits more basic or important than others?*

Recite and Review: Pages 512-518

10. Trait _____ attempt to specify qualities of personality that are most lasting or characteristic of a person.

11. Gordon Allport made useful distinctions between common traits (which are shared by most members of a culture) and _____ traits (characteristics of a single person).

12. Allport also identified cardinal traits (a trait that influences nearly all of a person's activities), central traits (core traits of personality), and _____ traits (superficial traits).

13. The theory of Raymond Cattell attributes visible _____ traits to the existence of 16 underlying source traits (which he identified using factor _____).

14. Source traits are measured by the *Sixteen* _____ _____ *Questionnaire* (16 PF).

15. The outcome of the 16 PF and other personality tests may be graphically presented as a _____ profile.

16. The five-factor model of personality reduces traits to 5 _____ dimensions of personality.

17. The five factors are: extroversion, _____, conscientiousness, neuroticism, and openness to _____.

18. _____ interact with situations to determine behavior.

19. Behavioral genetics is the study of _____ behavioral traits.

20. Studies of separated _____ twins suggest that heredity contributes significantly to adult personality traits. Overall, however, personality is shaped as much, or more by differences in environment.

● *How do psychodynamic theories explain personality?*

Recite and Review: Pages 518-524

21. Psychodynamic theories focus on the inner workings of personality, especially hidden or _____ forces and internal conflicts.

22. According to Sigmund Freud's psychoanalytic theory, personality is made up of the id, _____, and superego.

23. The id operates on the pleasure _____. The ego is guided by the reality _____.

24. The _____ is made up of the conscience and the ego ideal.

25. Libido, derived from the _____ instincts, is the primary _____ running the personality.

26. Conflicts within the personality may cause neurotic _____ or moral _____ and motivate use of ego-defense mechanisms.

27. The personality operates on three levels, the _____, preconscious, and unconscious.

28. The id is completely _____; the ego and superego can operate at all three levels of awareness.

29. The Freudian view of personality development is based on a series of psychosexual _____: the _____, anal, phallic, and genital.

30. Fixations (unresolved emotional conflicts) at any stage can leave a lasting imprint on _____.

31. Personality theorists who altered or revised Freud's ideas are called neo-_____. Three prominent members of this group are Alfred Adler, Karen Horney, and Carl Jung.

● *What do behaviorists emphasize in their approach to personality?*

Recite and Review: Pages 524-528

32. Behavioral theories of personality emphasize _____, conditioning, and immediate effects of the environment.

33. Learning theorists generally stress the effects of prior learning and _____ determinants of behavior.

34. Learning theorists John Dollard and Neal Miller consider _____ the basic core of personality. _____ express the combined effects of drive, cue, response, and _____.

35. _____ learning theory adds cognitive elements, such as perception, thinking, and understanding to the behavioral view of personality.

36. Examples of social learning concepts are the _____ situation (the situation as it is perceived), expectancies (expectations about what effects a response will have), and reinforcement _____ (the subjective value of a reinforcer or activity).

37. Albert Bandura believes that self-efficacy beliefs influence the _____ and situations we choose to get into.

38. Some social learning theorists treat "conscience" as a case of _____-reinforcement.

39. The behavioristic view of personality development holds that social reinforcement in four situations is critical. The critical situations are _____, toilet or cleanliness training, sex training, and _____ or aggression training.

40. Identification (feeling emotionally connected to a person) and _____ (mimicking another person's behavior) are of particular importance in sex (or gender) training.

● *How do humanistic theories differ from other perspectives?*

Recite and Review: Pages 529-532

41. Humanistic theory views human nature as _____, and emphasizes subjective experience, _____ choice, and needs for self-actualization.

42. Abraham Maslow's study of self-actualizers identified characteristics they share, ranging from efficient perceptions of reality to frequent _____ _____ (temporary moments of self-actualization).

43. Carl Rogers' theory views the _____ as an entity that emerges when experiences that match the self-_____ are symbolized (admitted to consciousness), while those that are incongruent are excluded.

44. The incongruent person has a highly unrealistic _____ and/or a mismatch between the _____ and the ideal self.

45. The congruent or _____ functioning person is flexible and open to experiences and feelings.

46. In the development of personality, humanists are primarily interested in the emergence of a _____ and in self-evaluations.

47. As parents apply conditions of _____ (standards used to judge thoughts, feelings, and actions) to a child, the child begins to do the same.

48. Internalized conditions of worth contribute to incongruence, they damage _____ self-regard, and they disrupt the organismic _____ process.

● *How do psychologists measure personality?*

Recite and Review: Pages 534-541

49. Techniques typically used for personality assessment are _____, observation, questionnaires, and projective _____.

50. Structured and unstructured _____ provide much information, but they are subject to _____ bias and misperceptions. The halo effect may also _____ accuracy.

51. Direct observation, sometimes involving situational tests, behavioral assessment, or the use of _____ scales, allows evaluation of a person's actual _____.

52. Personality questionnaires, such as the _____ _____ *Personality Inventory-2* (MMPI-2), are objective and _____, but their validity is open to question.

53. Honesty tests, which are essentially personality _____, are widely used by businesses to make hiring decisions. Their validity is hotly debated.

54. Projective tests ask a subject to project thoughts or feelings onto an ambiguous _____ or unstructured situation.

55. The *Rorschach*, or _____ test, is a well-known projective technique. A second is the _____ *Apperception Test* (TAT).

56. The validity and objectivity of projective tests are quite _____. Nevertheless, projective techniques are considered useful by many clinicians, particularly as part of a _____ battery.

● *What causes shyness? What can be done about it?*

Recite and Review: PSYCHOLOGY IN ACTION

57. Shyness is a mixture of _____ inhibition and _____ anxiety.

58. Shy persons tend to lack social skills and they feel social anxiety (because they believe they are being _____ by others).

59. Shy persons also have a self-defeating bias in their _____ (they tend to blame _____ for social failures).

60. Shyness is marked by heightened _____ self-consciousness (awareness of oneself as a _____ object) and a tendency to regard shyness as a lasting trait.

61. Shyness can be lessened by changing self-defeating _____ and by improving _____ skills.

● *How does self-monitoring affect behavior?*

Recite and Review: A STEP BEYOND

62. People vary in their degree of _____-monitoring or desire to control the impression they make on others.

63. _____ self-monitoring persons try to fit their public image to various situations.

64. _____ self-monitors are interested in accurately expressing their feelings, beliefs, and values, regardless of the situation.

CONNECTIONS

1. _____	character	a. heart-attack risk
2. _____	trait	b. hot-tempered
3. _____	Type A	c. personality judged
4. _____	melancholic	d. cheerful
5. _____	choleric	e. source traits
6. _____	phlegmatic	f. culturally typical
7. _____	sanguine	g. sluggish
8. _____	16 PF	h. universal dimensions
9. _____	common traits	i. sad, gloomy
10. _____	Big Five	j. lasting personal quality

11. _____	trait-situation	a. mouth
12. _____	Thanatos	b. pride
13. _____	Eros	c. genitals
14. _____	conscience	d. female conflict
15. _____	ego ideal	e. interaction
16. _____	oral stage	f. male conflict
17. _____	anal stage	g. death instinct
18. _____	phallic stage	h. elimination
19. _____	Oedipus	i. life instinct
20. _____	Electra	j. guilt

21. _____	Horney	a. interview problem
22. _____	Jung	b. evaluation fears
23. _____	Maslow	c. shoot-don't-shoot
24. _____	Rogers	d. personality questionnaire
25. _____	social learning	e. faking good
26. _____	halo effect	f. fully functioning person
27. _____	MMPI	g. self-actualization
28. _____	validity scale	h. archetypes
29. _____	social anxiety	i. cognitive behaviorism
30. _____	situational test	j. basic anxiety

CHECK YOUR MEMORY

Check Your Memory: Pages 508-510

1. The term personality refers to charisma or personal style. T or F?
2. Personality is a person's relatively stable pattern of attitudes. T or F?
3. Character refers to the inherited "raw material" from which personality is formed. T or F?
4. In Asian cultures, self-esteem is strongly tied to personal achievement, rather than group success. T or F?

Check Your Memory: Pages 510-512

5. Traits are stable or lasting qualities of personality, displayed in most situations. T or F?
6. Personality traits typically become quite stable by age 30. T or F?
7. Paranoid, dependent, and antisocial personalities are regarded as personality types. T or F?
8. Two major dimensions of Eysenck's personality theory are stable-unstable and calm-moody. T or F?
9. Trait theories of personality stress subjective experience and personal growth. T or F?

Check Your Memory: Pages 512-518

10. Extroverted students tend to study in noisy areas of the library. T or F?
11. Nearly all of a person's activities can be traced to one or two common traits. T or F?
12. Roughly 7 central traits are needed, on the average, to describe an individual's personality. T or F?
13. Allport used factor analysis to identify central traits. T or F?
14. The 16 PF is designed to measure surface traits. T or F?
15. Judging from scores on the 16 PF, airline pilots have traits that are similar to creative artists. T or F?
16. As one of the Big Five factors, neuroticism refers to having negative, upsetting emotions. T or F?
17. Extreme perfectionism typically lowers performance at school and elsewhere. T or F?
18. The expression of personality traits tends to be influenced by external situations. T or F?
19. Intelligence, some mental disorders, temperament, and personality traits are all influenced by heredity. T or F?
20. Studies of identical twins show that personality traits are approximately 70 percent hereditary. T or F?
21. Some of the coincidences shared by identical twins appear to be based on the fallacy of positive instances. T or F?

Check Your Memory: Pages 518-524

22. The id is totally unconscious. T or F?
23. The ego is guided by the pleasure principle. T or F?
24. The superego is the source of feelings of guilt and pride. T or F?
25. Threats of punishment from the Thanatos cause moral anxiety. T or F?
26. Oral-dependent persons are gullible. T or F?
27. Vanity and narcissism are traits of the anal-retentive personality. T or F?
28. The genital stage occurs between the ages of 3 and 6, just before latency. T or F?
29. Boys are more likely to develop a strong conscience if their fathers are affectionate and accepting. T or F?

30. Alfred Adler believed that we are driven by basic anxiety to move toward, against, or away from others. T or F?

31. According to Jung, people strive for superiority by creating a unique style of life. T or F?

32. Jung called the male principle the animus. T or F?

Check Your Memory: Pages 524-528

33. Behaviorists view personality as a collection of learned behavior patterns. T or F?

34. Behaviorists attribute our actions to prior learning and specific situations. T or F?

35. According to Dollard and Miller, habits are acquired through observational learning. T or F?

36. Cues are signals from the environment that guide responses. T or F?

37. An expectancy refers to the anticipation that making a response will lead to reinforcement. T or F?

38. People who are depressed tend to engage in a high rate of self-reinforcement to make themselves feel better. T or F?

39. Social reinforcement is based on attention and approval from others. T or F?

40. In elementary school, boys typically get more attention from teachers than girls do. T or F?

Check Your Memory: Pages 529-532

41. Humanists believe that humans are capable of free choice. T or F?

42. To investigate self-actualization, Maslow studied eminent men and women exclusively. T or F?

43. Self-actualizers usually try to avoid task centering. T or F?

44. Personal autonomy is a characteristic of the self-actualizing person. T or F?

45. Information inconsistent with one's self-image is described as incongruent. T or F?

46. Poor self-knowledge is associated with high self-esteem because people do not have to think about their own faults. T or F?

47. Congruence represents a close correspondence between self-image, the ideal self, and the true self. T or F?

48. Images of possible selves typically cause feelings of incongruence. T or F?

49. Rogers believed that organismic valuing is healthier than trying to meet someone else's conditions of worth. T or F?

Check Your Memory: Pages 534-541

50. Planned questions are used in a structured interview. T or F?

51. Computers are sometimes used to do diagnostic interviews at psychological clinics. T or F?

52. The halo effect may involve either a positive or a negative impression. T or F?

53. Personality questionnaires are used to do behavioral assessments. T or F?

54. Judgmental firearms training is a type of honesty test. T or F?

55. Items on the MMPI-2 were selected for their ability to identify persons with psychiatric problems. T or F?

56. The validity scale of the MMPI-2 is used to rate Type A behavior. T or F?

57. The psychasthenia scale of the MMPI-2 detects the presence of phobias and compulsive actions. T or F?

58. It is very easy to fake responses to a projective test. T or F?

59. The TAT is a situational test. T or F?

60. Habitually violent prison inmates are aggressive and over-controlled. T or F?

Check Your Memory: PSYCHOLOGY IN ACTION

61. Shyness is closely related to private self-consciousness. T or F?
62. Not-shy persons believe that external situations cause their occasional feelings of shyness. T or F?
63. The odds of meeting someone interested in socializing are about the same wherever you are. T or F?
64. Open-ended questions help keep conversations going. T or F?

Check Your Memory: A STEP BEYOND

65. Self-monitoring refers to how much attention you pay to your ideal self. T or F?
66. High self-monitors would probably agree that they would make good actors. T or F?
67. High self-monitors vary their behavior, depending on who they are speaking to. T or F?
68. Low self-monitors tend to have friends who are all pretty much alike. T or F?

FINAL SURVEY AND REVIEW

● *How do psychologists use the term* personality?

1. _____ is made up of one's unique and relatively stable behavior _____.

2. _____ is personality that has been judged or evaluated. That is, it is the possession of desirable qualities.

3. _____ refers to the hereditary and physiological aspects of one's emotional nature.

● *What core concepts make up the psychology of personality?*

4. Personality _____ are lasting personal qualities that are inferred from behavior.
5. A personality _____ is a style of personality defined by having a group of related traits or similar characteristics.
6. Two widely recognized personality types are an _____ (shy, self-centered person) and an _____ (bold, outgoing person).
7. Behavior is influenced by _____, which is a person's perception of his or her own personality traits.
8. Personality _____ combine interrelated assumptions, ideas, and principles to explain personality.
9. Four major types of personality theories are: trait, _____, behavioristic, social learning, and _____.

● *Are some personality traits more basic or important than others?*

10. _____ theories attempt to specify qualities of personality that are most lasting or characteristic of a person.

11. Gordon _____ made useful distinctions between _____ traits (which are shared by most members of a culture) and individual traits (characteristics of a single person).

12. He also identified _____ traits (a trait that influences nearly all of a person's activities), _____ traits (core traits of personality), and secondary traits (superficial traits).

13. The theory of Raymond _____ attributes visible surface traits to the existence of 16 underlying _____ traits (which he identified using _____ analysis).

14. _____ _____ are measured by the *Sixteen Personality Factor Questionnaire* (16 PF).

15. The outcome of the 16 PF and other personality tests may be graphically presented as a trait _____.

16. The _____ model of personality reduces traits to 5 universal dimensions of personality.

17. They are: _____, agreeableness, conscientiousness, _____, and openness to experience.

18. Traits _____ with _____ to determine behavior.

19. _____ _____ is the study of inherited behavioral traits.

20. Studies of separated identical twins suggest that _____ contributes significantly to adult personality traits. Overall, however, personality is shaped as much, or more by differences in _____.

● *How do psychodynamic theories explain personality?*

21. Psychodynamic theories focus on the inner workings of _____, especially hidden or unconscious forces and internal _____.

22. According to Sigmund Freud's _____ theory, personality is made up of the _____, ego, and _____.

23. The id operates on the _____ principle. The ego is guided by the _____ principle.

24. The superego is made up of the _____ and the _____ ideal.

25. _____, derived from the life _____, is the primary energy running the personality.

26. Conflicts within the personality may cause _____ anxiety or _____ anxiety and motivate use of ego-defense mechanisms.

27. The personality operates on three levels, the conscious, _____, and _____.

28. The _____ is completely unconscious; the _____ and _____ can operate at all three levels of awareness.

29. The Freudian view of personality development is based on a series of _____ stages: the oral, anal, _____, and genital.

30. _____ (unresolved emotional conflicts) at any stage can leave a lasting imprint on personality.

31. Personality theorists who altered or revised Freud's ideas are called _____-Freudians. Three prominent members of this group are Alfred _____, Karen Horney, and Carl _____.

● *What do behaviorists emphasize in their approach to personality?*

32. _____ theories of personality emphasize learning, conditioning, and immediate effects of the environment.

33. Learning theorists generally stress the effects of prior learning and situational _____ of behavior.

34. Learning theorists John Dollard and Neal Miller consider habits the basic core of personality. Habits express the combined effects of _____, _____, response, and reward.

35. Social learning theory adds _____ elements, such as perception, thinking, and understanding to the behavioral view of personality.

36. Examples of social learning concepts are the psychological situation (the situation as it is perceived), _____ (expectations about what effects a response will have), and _____ value (the subjective value of a reinforcer or activity).

37. Albert Bandura believes that _____ beliefs influence the activities and situations we choose to get into.

38. Some social learning theorists treat "conscience" as a case of self-_____.

39. The behavioristic view of personality development holds that social reinforcement in four situations is critical. The critical situations are feeding, _____ _____, sex training, and anger or _____ training.

40. _____ (feeling emotionally connected to a person) and imitation (mimicking another person's behavior) are of particular importance in sex (or gender) training.

● *How do humanistic theories differ from other perspectives?*

41. Humanistic theory views human nature as good, and emphasizes _____ experience, free choice, and needs for self-_____.

42. Abraham _____ study of _____ identified characteristics they share, ranging from efficient perceptions of reality to frequent peak experiences.

43. Carl Rogers' theory views the self as an entity that emerges when experiences that match the self-image are _____ (admitted to consciousness), while those that are _____ are excluded.

44. The _____ person has a highly unrealistic self-image and/or a mismatch between the self-image and the _____ self.

45. The _____, or fully functioning person, is flexible and open to experiences and feelings.

46. In the development of personality, humanists are primarily interested in the emergence of a self-image and in _____.

47. As parents apply _____ of worth (standards used to judge thoughts, feelings, and actions) to a child, the child begins to do the same.

48. Internalized _____ ____ _____ contribute to incongruence, they damage positive self-regard, and they disrupt the _____ valuing process.

● *How do psychologists measure personality?*

49. Techniques typically used for personality assessment are interviews, direct _____, questionnaires, and _____ tests.

50. Structured and _____ interviews provide much information, but they are subject to interviewer _____ and misperceptions. The halo effect may also lower the accuracy of an interview.

51. Direct observation, sometimes involving _____ tests, _____ assessment, or the use of rating scales, allows evaluation of a person's actual behavior.

52. Personality questionnaires, such as the *Minnesota Multiphasic* _____ _____-2 (MMPI-2), are objective and reliable, but their _____ is open to question.

53. _____ tests, which are essentially personality questionnaires, are widely used by businesses to measure integrity and make hiring decisions.

54. _____ tests ask subjects to react to an ambiguous stimulus or unstructured situation.

55. The _____, or inkblot test, is a well-known projective technique. A second is the *Thematic* _____ *Test* (TAT).

56. The _____ and objectivity of projective tests are quite low. Nevertheless, projective techniques are considered useful by many clinicians, particularly as part of a test _____.

● *What causes shyness? What can be done about it?*

57. Shyness is a mixture of social _____ and social anxiety.

58. Shy persons tend to lack social _____ and they feel social anxiety (because they believe they are being evaluated by others).

59. Shy persons also have a _____ bias in their thinking (they tend to blame themselves for social failures).

60. Shyness is marked by heightened public self-_____ (awareness of oneself as a _____ object) and a tendency to regard shyness as a lasting _____.

61. Shyness can be lessened by changing _____ beliefs and by improving social _____.

● *How does self-monitoring affect behavior?*

62. People vary in their degree of self-monitoring or desire to control the _____ they make on _____.

63. High self-monitoring persons try to fit their _____ _____ to various situations.

64. Low self-monitors are interested in _____ expressing their feelings, beliefs, and values, regardless of the situation.

MASTERY TEST

1. The hereditary aspects of a person's emotional nature define his or her
   a. character   b. personality   c. cardinal traits   d. temperament

2. Two parts of the psyche that operate on all three levels of awareness are the
   a. id and ego   b. ego and superego   c. id and superego   d. id and ego ideal

3. The four critical situations Miller and Dollard consider important in the development of personality are feeding, toilet training,
   a. sex, and aggression   b. cleanliness, and language   c. attachment, and imitation   d. social learning

4. Scales that rate a person's tendencies for depression, hysteria, paranoia, and mania are found on the
   a. MMPI-2   b. Rorschach   c. TAT   d. 16 PF

5. In the five-factor model, people who score high on openness to experience are
   a. intelligent   b. extroverted   c. choleric   d. a personality type

6. Jung regarded mandalas as symbols of the
   a. animus   b. anima   c. self archetype   d. persona

7. Maslow used the term _____ to describe the tendency to make full use of personal potentials.
   a. full functionality   b. self-potentiation   c. ego-idealization   d. self-actualization

8. Studies of reunited identical twins support the idea that
   a. personality traits are 70 percent hereditary and 30 percent learned   b. childhood fixations influence the expression of personality traits in adulthood   c. personality traits are altered by selective mating
   d. personality is shaped at least as much by environment as by heredity

9. A person's perception of his or her own personality is the core of
   a. temperament   b. source traits   c. self-concept   d. trait-situation interactions

10. Which of the following concepts is NOT part of Dollard and Miller's behavioral model of personality?
    a. drive   b. expectancy   c. cue   d. reward

11. The terms structured and unstructured apply most to
    a. the halo effect   b. interviews   c. questionnaires   d. honesty tests

12. Persons low in self-monitoring usually
    a. are concerned with outer appearances   b. make a good actors   c. prefer jobs where they can be themselves   d. have different friends for various activities

13. Feelings of pride come from the _____, a part of the _____.
    a. libido, conscience   b. ego ideal, superego   c. reality principle, superego   d. superego, ego

14. Four types of temperament recognized by the early Greeks are: melancholic, choleric, phlegmatic and
    a. sanguine   b. sardonic   c. sagittarian   d. sagacious

15. Freud believed that boys identify with their fathers in order to resolve the _____ conflict.
    a. Animus   b. Electra   c. Oedipus   d. Persona

16. Maslow regarded peak experiences as temporary moments of
    a. task-centering   b. congruent selfhood   c. self-actualization   d. organismic valuing

17. Ambiguous stimuli are used primarily in the
    a. MMPI-2   b. Shoot-Don't-Shoot Test   c. Rorschach   d. 16 PF

18. A person who is generally extroverted is more outgoing in some situations than in others. This observation supports the concept of
    a. trait-situation interactions   b. behavioral genetic determinants   c. situational fixations
    d. possible selves

19. Allport's concept of central traits is most closely related to Cattell's
    a. surface traits   b. source traits   c. secondary traits   d. cardinal traits

20. According to Freud, tendencies to be orderly, obstinate, and stingy are formed during the _____ stage.
    a. genital   b. anal   c. oral   d. phallic

21. Which of the following is NOT part of Carl Rogers' view of personality?
    a. possible selves   b. organismic valuing   c. conditions of worth   d. congruence

22. Rating scales are primarily used in which approach to personality assessment?
    a. projective testing   b. direct observation   c. questionnaires   d. the TAT technique

23. Which theory of personality places the greatest emphasis on the effects of the environment?
    a. trait   b. psychodynamic   c. behavioristic   d. humanistic

24. Freudian psychosexual stages occur in the order:
    a. oral, anal, genital, phallic   b. oral, phallic, anal, genital   c. genital, oral, anal, phallic
    d. oral, anal, phallic, genital

25. Rogers described mismatches between one's self-image and reality as a state of
    a. moral anxiety   b. incongruence   c. basic anxiety   d. negative symbolization

26. All but one of the following are major elements of shyness; which does not apply?
a. private self-consciousness b. social anxiety c. self-defeating thoughts d. belief that shyness is a lasting trait

27. People who all grew up in the same culture would be most likely to have the same _____ traits.
a. cardinal b. common c. secondary d. source

28. A trait profile is used to report the results of
a. the 16 PF b. situational tests c. the TAT d. the inkblot test

29. An emphasis on the situational determinants of actions is a key feature of _____ theories of personality.
a. psychodynamic b. projective c. behaviorist d. humanist

30. The behavioral concept most closely related to the superego is
a. psychological situation b. self-reinforcement c. reinforcement value d. self-concept

ANSWERS

Recite and Review

1. behavior
2. evaluated
3. hereditary
4. behavior
5. traits
6. types
7. personality
8. Personality
9. trait, social
10. theories
11. individual
12. secondary
13. surface, analysis
14. *Personality Factor*
15. trait
16. universal
17. agreeableness, experience
18. Traits
19. inherited
20. identical
21. unconscious
22. ego

23. principle, principle
24. superego
25. life, energy
26. anxiety, anxiety
27. conscious
28. unconscious
29. stages, oral
30. personality
31. Freudians
32. learning
33. situational
34. habits, Habits, reward
35. Social
36. psychological, value
37. activities
38. self
39. feeding, anger
40. imitation
41. good, free
42. peak experiences
43. self, image
44. self-image, self-image
45. fully
46. self-image

47. worth
48. positive, valuing
49. interviews, tests
50. interviews, interviewer, lower
51. rating, behavior
52. *Minnesota, Multiphasic,* reliable
53. questionnaires
54. stimulus
55. inkblot, *Thematic*
56. low, test
57. social, social
58. evaluated
59. thinking, themselves
60. public, social
61. beliefs, social
62. self
63. High
64. Low

Connections

1. c
2. j
3. a
4. i
5. b
6. g
7. d
8. e
9. f
10. h
11. e
12. g
13. i
14. j
15. b
16. a
17. h
18. c
19. f
20. d
21. j
22. h
23. g
24. f
25. i
26. a
27. d
28. e
29. b
30. c

Check Your Memory

1. F
2. F
3. F
4. F
5. T
6. T
7. T
8. F
9. F
10. T
11. F
12. T
13. F
14. F
15. F
16. T
17. T
18. T
19. T
20. F
21. T
22. T
23. F
24. T
25. F
26. T
27. F
28. F
29. T
30. F
31. F
32. T
33. T
34. T
35. F
36. T
37. T
38. F
39. T
40. T
41. T
42. F
43. F
44. T
45. T
46. F
47. T
48. F
49. T
50. T
51. T
52. T
53. F
54. F
55. T
56. F
57. T
58. F
59. F
60. F
61. F
62. T
63. F
64. T
65. F
66. T
67. T
68. T

Final Survey and Review

1. Personality, patterns
2. Character
3. Temperament
4. traits
5. type
6. introvert, extrovert
7. self-concept
8. theories
9. psychodynamic, humanistic
10. Trait
11. Allport, common
12. cardinal, central
13. Cattell, source, factor
14. Source traits
15. profile
16. five-factor
17. extroversion, neuroticism
18. interact, situations
19. Behavioral genetics
20. heredity, environment
21. personality, conflicts
22. psychoanalytic, id, superego
23. pleasure, reality
24. conscience, ego
25. Libido, instincts
26. neurotic, moral
27. preconscious, unconscious
28. id, ego, superego
29. psychosexual, phallic
30. Fixations
31. neo, Adler, Jung
32. Behavioral
33. determinants
34. drive, cue
35. cognitive

36. expectancies, reinforcement
37. self-efficacy
38. reinforcement
39. toilet training, aggression
40. Identification
41. subjective, actualization
42. Maslow's, self-actualizers
43. symbolized, incongruent
44. incongruent, ideal
45. congruent
46. self-evaluations
47. conditions
48. conditions of worth, organismic
49. observation, projective
50. unstructured, bias
51. situational, behavioral
52. *Personality Inventory,* validity
53. Honesty
54. Projective
55. *Rorschach, Apperception*

56. validity, battery
57. inhibition
58. skills
59. self-defeating
60. consciousness, social, trait
61. self-defeating, skills
62. impression, others
63. public image
64. accurately

Mastery Test

1. d (p. 509)
2. b (p. 520)
3. a (p. 527)
4. a (p. 537)
5. a (p. 515)
6. c (p. 523)
7. d (p. 529)
8. d (p. 518)
9. c (p. 511)
10. b (p. 525)

11. b (p. 534)
12. c (p. 545)
13. b (p. 520)
14. a (p. 513)
15. c (p. 521)
16. c (p. 530)
17. c (p. 539)
18. a (p. 516)
19. b (p. 514)
20. b (p. 521)
21. a (p. 531-532)
22. b (p. 535)
23. c (p. 534)
24. d (p. 521-522)
25. b (p. 531)
26. a (p. 542)
27. b (p. 514)
28. a (p. 514)
29. c (p. 525)
30. b (p. 526)

Chapter 15
Health, Stress, and Coping

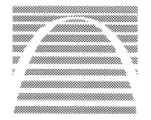

CHAPTER OVERVIEW

Health psychologists study behavioral risk factors and health-promoting behaviors. Various "lifestyle" diseases are directly related to unhealthy personal habits. Stress is also a major risk factor. At work, prolonged stress can lead to burnout. Emotional appraisals greatly affect our stress reactions and coping attempts. Traumatic stressors, such as violence, torture, or natural disasters, tend to produce severe stress reactions.

Frustration and conflict are common sources of stress. Major behavioral reactions to frustration include persistence, more vigorous responding, circumvention, direct aggression, displaced aggression, and escape or withdrawal. Five major types of conflict are approach-approach, avoidance-avoidance, approach-avoidance, double approach-avoidance, and multiple approach-avoidance.

Anxiety, threat, or feelings of inadequacy frequently lead to the use of defense mechanisms. Common defense mechanisms include compensation, denial, fantasy, intellectualization, isolation, projection, rationalization, reaction formation, regression, repression, and sublimation. Learned helplessness explains some depression and some failures to cope with threat. Mastery training acts as an antidote to helplessness.

A large number of life changes can increase susceptibility to illness. However, immediate health is more closely related to the severity of daily hassles or microstressors. Intense or prolonged stress may cause psychosomatic problems. Biofeedback may be used to combat stress and psychosomatic illnesses. People with Type A personalities run a heightened risk of suffering a heart attack. People with hardy personality traits are resistant to stress. The body reacts to stress in a pattern called the general adaptation syndrome (G.A.S.). In addition, stress may lower the body's immunity to disease.

The *College Life Stress Inventory*, which is similar to the SRRS, can be used to rate the amount of stress an undergraduate student has experienced. A number of coping skills can be applied to manage stress. Most focus on bodily effects, ineffective behaviors, and upsetting thoughts. Meditation can also be used to reduce stress. Two benefits of meditation are its ability to interrupt anxious thoughts and its ability to elicit the relaxation response.

LEARNING OBJECTIVES

To demonstrate mastery of this chapter, you should be able to:

1. Define the terms *health psychology* and *behavioral medicine.*

2. List twelve behavioral risk factors that can adversely affect one's health.

3. Describe the disease-prone personality.

4. Briefly describe the relationship between health-promoting behaviors and longevity.

5. Explain how health psychologists work to lessen behavioral risks to health. Describe the impact of refusal-skills training and community health programs on illness prevention.

6. Define the term *wellness* and list five characteristics of wellness.

7. Explain the similarity between your body's stress reaction and emotion.

8. List five aspects of stress that make it more intense and damaging.

9. Describe burnout. List and describe the three aspects of the problem. Describe three things that can be done to help reduce burnout.

10. Give an example of how primary and secondary appraisal is used in coping with a threatening situation.

11. Explain how the perception of control of a stressor influences the amount of threat felt.

12. Differentiate problem-focused coping from emotion-focused coping and explain how they may help or hinder each other.

13. Describe the impact of traumatic stress and list five ways to cope with reactions to traumatic stress.

14. List and describe the two different kinds of frustration.

15. List four factors that increase frustration.

16. List and describe five common reactions to frustration (see Figure 15.3).

17. Explain how scapegoating is a special form of displaced aggression.

18. Describe and give an example of each of the following four types of conflict:
    a. approach-approach
    b. avoidance-avoidance
    c. approach-avoidance (include the terms *ambivalence* and *partial approach*)
    d. double approach-avoidance (include the term *vacillation*)

19. Define the term *defense mechanism.* Discuss the positive value of defense mechanisms.

20. Describe the following defense mechanisms and give an example of each:

a. denial	d. regression	g. compensation
b. repression	e. projection	h. sublimation
c. reaction formation	f. rationalization	

21. Describe the development of learned helplessness and relate this concept to attribution and depression. Explain how helplessness may be unlearned.

22. Describe the six problems that typically contribute to depression among college students.

23. List the five conditions of depression and describe how it can be combated.

24. Discuss the relationship between life changes and long-term health. Describe the SRRS.
25. Explain how hassles are related to immediate health and how acculturative stress can cause problems.
26. Distinguish between psychosomatic disorders and hypochondria. List the causes of psychosomatic disorders.
27. Discuss biofeedback in terms of the process involved and its possible applications.
28. Differentiate between Type A and Type B personalities. Note the twelve strategies for reducing hostility that apply to you.
29. Describe what a hardy personality is and list the three ways such people view the world.
30. Explain the concept of the General Adaptation Syndrome. List and describe its three stages.
31. Explain how stress affects the immune system.

The following objectives are related to the material in the "Psychology in Action" and "A Step Beyond" sections of the text.

32. Define the term *stress management*. Briefly discuss the College Life Stress Inventory.
33. List the three responses that are triggered by stress
34. Discuss the stress management techniques that can be used to diminish or break the cycle of stress responses.
35. Define *stereotyped response* and how it differs from persistence.
36. Discuss three effective ways to avoid frustration and four strategies for coping with conflict.
37. Distinguish between concentrative and receptive meditation.
38. Discuss how concentrative meditation can be used as a self-control technique in reducing stress.

RECITE AND REVIEW

● *What is health psychology? How does behavior affect health?*

Recite and Review: Pages 548-553

  1. Health psychologists are interested in _____ that helps maintain and promote health. The related field of behavioral medicine applies psychology to _____ treatment and problems.
  2. Most people today die from lifestyle diseases caused by unhealthy personal _____.
  3. Studies have identified a number of behavioral risk factors, which increase the chances of _____ or injury.
  4. A general disease-prone personality pattern also raises the risk of _____.
  5. Health-promoting _____ tend to maintain good health. They include practices such as getting regular exercise, controlling _____ and alcohol use, maintaining a balanced _____, getting good medical care, avoiding _____ deprivation, and managing stress.

6. Health psychologists attempt to promote wellness (a positive state of _____) through community health _____ that educate people about risk factors and healthful behaviors.

● *What is stress? What factors determine its severity?*

Recite and Review: Pages 554-558

7. Stress occurs when we are forced to _____ or adapt to external demands.

8. Stress is more damaging in situations involving pressure (responding at full capacity for long periods), a lack of _____, unpredictability of the stressor, and _____ or repeated emotional shocks.

9. _____ is intensified when a situation is perceived as a threat and when a person does not feel competent to cope with it.

10. In _____ settings, prolonged stress can lead to burnout, marked by emotional _____, depersonalization (detachment from others), and reduced personal accomplishment.

11. The _____ (initial) appraisal of a situation greatly affects our emotional response to it. Stress reactions, in particular, are related to an appraisal of _____.

12. During a _____ appraisal some means of coping with a situation is selected. Coping may be either problem-focused (managing the situation) or emotion-focused (managing one's emotional reactions) or both.

13. Traumatic _____, such as violence, torture, or natural disasters, tend to produce severe _____ reactions.

14. Traumatic _____ leave people feeling threatened, vulnerable, and with the sense that they are losing control over their _____.

15. Severe or _____ traumatic _____ can leave people with lasting emotional handicaps called stress disorders.

● *What causes frustration and what are typical reactions to it?*

Recite and Review: Pages 558-559

16. Frustration is the negative emotional state that occurs when progress toward a _____ is _____. Sources of frustration may be external or personal.

17. External frustrations are based on delay, failure, rejection, loss, and other direct blocking of motives. Personal frustration is related to _____ characteristics over which one has little control.

18. Frustrations of all types become more _____ as the strength, urgency, or importance of the blocked motive increases.

19. Major behavioral reactions to frustration include persistence, more _____ responding, and circumvention of barriers.

20. Other reactions to frustration are _____ aggression, displaced aggression (including scapegoating), and escape, or _____.

● *Are there different types of conflict? How do people react to conflict?*

Recite and Review: Pages 560-561

21. _____ occurs when we must choose between contradictory alternatives.
22. Three basic types of conflict are approach-approach (choice between two _____
alternatives), avoidance-avoidance (both alternatives are _____), and approach-avoidance
(a goal or activity has both positive and negative aspects).
23. More complex conflicts are: double approach-avoidance (both alternatives have
_____ and _____ qualities) and multiple approach-avoidance (several
alternatives each have good and bad qualities).
24. Approach-approach conflicts are usually the _____ to resolve.
25. Avoidance conflicts are _____ to resolve and are characterized by inaction,
indecision, freezing, and a desire to escape (called _____ the field).
26. People usually remain in approach-avoidance conflicts, but fail to fully resolve them. Approach-
avoidance conflicts are associated with ambivalence (_____ feelings) and _____
approach.
27. Vacillation (wavering between choices) is the most common reaction to double
_____ conflicts.

● *What are defense mechanisms?*

Recite and Review: Pages 562-564

28. Anxiety, threat, or feelings of _____ frequently lead to the use of psychological
defense mechanisms. These are habitual strategies used to avoid or reduce anxiety.
29. A number of defense mechanisms have been identified, including denial, fantasy, intellectualization,
isolation, projection, rationalization, _____ formation, regression, and
_____ (motivated forgetting).
30. Two defense mechanisms that have some _____ qualities are compensation and
sublimation.

● *What do we know about coping with feelings of helplessness and depression?*

Recite and Review: Pages 564-567

31. Learned helplessness is a learned inability to overcome obstacles or to _____ punishment.
32. Learned helplessness explains the failure to cope with some threatening situations. The symptoms of
learned helplessness and depression are nearly _____ .
33. Mastery _____ and hope act as antidotes to helplessness.
34. Depression (a state of deep sadness or despondency) is a serious emotional problem. Actions and
thoughts that counter feelings of helplessness tend to _____ depression.

● *How is stress related to health and disease?*

Recite and Review: Pages 568-575

35. Work with the *Social Readjustment Rating Scale* (SRRS) indicates that a large number of life
_____ units (LCUs) can increase susceptibility to _____ or illness.
36. Immediate health is more closely related to the intensity and severity of daily annoyances, known as
_____ or microstressors.
37. Intense or prolonged stress may damage the body in the form of psychosomatic disorders (illnesses in
which _____ factors play a part).
38. Psychosomatic (mind-body) disorders have no connection to hypochondria, the tendency to imagine that
one has a _____.
39. During biofeedback training, bodily processes are _____ and converted to a signal
that indicates what the body is doing.
40. Biofeedback allows alteration of many bodily activities. It shows promise for promoting
_____, self-regulation, and for treating some psychosomatic illnesses.
41. People with Type A (_____ attack prone) personalities are competitive, striving, and frequently
angry or hostile, and they have a chronic sense of _____ urgency.
42. _____ and hostility are especially likely to increase the chances of heart attack.
43. People who have traits of the hardy personality seem to be resistant to _____, even if they
also have Type A traits.
44. The body reacts to stress in a series of stages called the _____ adaptation syndrome
(G.A.S.).
45. The stages of the G.A.S. are alarm, resistance, and exhaustion. The G.A.S. contributes to the
development of _____ disorders.
46. Stress weakens the immune system and lowers the body's resistance to _____.

● *What are the best strategies for managing stress?*

Recite and Review: PSYCHOLOGY IN ACTION

47. Most stress management skills focus on one of three areas: bodily effects, ineffective
_____, and upsetting _____.
48. Bodily effects can be managed with exercise, meditation, progressive _____, and
guided _____.
49. The impact of ineffective behavior can be remedied by slowing down, getting organized, striking a
balance between "good stress" and _____, accepting your limits, and seeking social
support.
50. A good way to control upsetting thoughts is to replace negative self-statements with
_____ coping statements.

● *Is meditation useful for coping with stress?*

Recite and Review: A STEP BEYOND

51. Meditation is a self-control technique that can be used to reduce _____.

52. In receptive meditation, attention is _____ to include an awareness of one's entire moment-by-moment experience.

53. In concentrative meditation, attention is focused on a _____ object or thought.

54. Two major benefits of meditation are its ability to interrupt anxious thoughts and its ability to elicit the relaxation response (the pattern of changes that occur in the body at times of deep _____).

CONNECTIONS

1. _____	risk factors	a. leading cause of death
2. _____	tobacco	b. ANS arousal
3. _____	refusal skills	c. blocked motive
4. _____	stress reaction	d. lifestyle diseases
5. _____	burnout	e. psychological escape
6. _____	primary appraisal	f. scapegoat
7. _____	frustration	g. approach-avoidance
8. _____	displaced aggression	h. "Am I in trouble?"
9. _____	apathy	i. job stress
10. _____	ambivalence	j. smoking prevention

11. _____ compensation
12. _____ denial
13. _____ fantasy
14. _____ intellectualization
15. _____ isolation
16. _____ projection
17. _____ rationalization
18. _____ reaction formation
19. _____ regression
20. _____ repression
21. _____ sublimation

a. Fulfilling unmet desires in imagined activities.
b. Separating contradictory thoughts into "logic-tight" mental compartments.
c. Preventing actions by exaggerating opposite behavior.
d. Justifying your behavior by giving reasonable but false reasons for it.
e. Unconsciously preventing painful thoughts from entering awareness.
f. Counteracting a real or imagined weakness by seeking to excel.
g. Retreating to an earlier level of development.
h. Attributing one's own shortcomings or unacceptable impulses to others.
i. Protecting oneself from an unpleasant reality by refusing to perceive it.
j. Working off unacceptable impulses in constructive activities.
k. Thinking about threatening situations in impersonal terms.

22. _____	learned helplessness	a.	LCU
23. _____	mastery training	b.	stress resistant
24. _____	SRRS	c.	mind-body
25. _____	hassle	d.	self-regulation
26. _____	hardy personality	e.	cardiac personality
27. _____	psychosomatic	f.	alarm reaction
28. _____	biofeedback	g.	microstressor
29. _____	Type A	h.	hope
30. _____	G.A.S.	i.	shuttle box

CHECK YOUR MEMORY

Check Your Memory: Pages 548-553

1. Heart disease, lung cancer, and stroke are typical lifestyle diseases. T or F?

2. Illicit use of drugs is the second most common cause of death in the United States, after smoking. T or F?

3. People with disease-prone personalities are depressed, anxious, and hostile. T or F?

4. Unhealthy lifestyles typically involve multiple risks. T or F?

5. A major community study done in California found that eating breakfast and not eating between meals are two of the most important health-promoting behaviors. T or F?

6. Community health campaigns provide refusal skills training to large numbers of people. T or F?

7. Wellness can be described as an absence of disease. T or F?

Check Your Memory: Pages 554-558

8. Unpleasant activities produce stress, whereas pleasant activities do not. T or F?

9. Initial reactions to stressors are similar to those that occur during strong emotion. T or F?

10. Short-term stresses rarely do any damage to the body. T or F?

11. Unpredictable demands increase stress. T or F?

12. Pressure occurs when we are faced with a stressor we can control. T or F?

13. Burnout is especially a problem in helping professions. T or F?

14. The opposite of burnout is positive job engagement. T or F?

15. Stress is often related to the meaning a person places on events. T or F?

16. The same situation can be a challenge or a threat, depending on how it is appraised. T or F?

17. In a secondary appraisal, we decide if a situation is relevant or irrelevant, positive or threatening. T or F?

18. When confronted by a stressor, it is best to choose one type of coping—problem focused or emotion focused. T or F?

19. Emotion-focused coping is best suited to managing stressors you cannot control. T or F?

20. Nightmares, grief, flashbacks, nervousness, and depression are common reactions to traumatic stress. T or F?

21. It is possible to have stress symptoms from merely witnessing traumatically stressful events on television. T or F?

22. An excellent way to cope with traumatic stress is to stop all of your daily routines and isolate yourself from others. T or F?

Check Your Memory: Pages 558-559

23. Delays, rejections, and losses are good examples of personal frustrations. T or F?

24. Varied responses and circumvention attempt to directly destroy or remove barriers that cause frustration. T or F?

25. Scapegoating is a good example of escape or withdrawal. T or F?

26. Abuse of drugs can be a way of psychologically escaping frustration. T or F?

Check Your Memory: Pages 560-561

27. Approach-approach conflicts are fairly easy to resolve. T or F?

28. Indecision, inaction, and freezing are typical reactions to approach-approach conflicts. T or F?

29. People find it difficult to escape approach-avoidance conflicts. T or F?

30. Wanting to eat, but not wanting to be overweight, creates an approach-approach conflict. T or F?

31. People are very likely to vacillate when faced with a double approach-avoidance conflict. T or F?

Check Your Memory: Pages 562-564

32. Defense mechanisms are used to avoid or distort sources of threat or anxiety. T or F?

33. Denial is a common reaction to bad news, such as learning that a friend has died. T or F?

34. In reaction formation, a person fulfills unmet desires in imagined achievements. T or F?

35. A child who becomes homesick while visiting relatives may be experiencing a mild regression. T or F?

36. Denial and repression are the two most positive of the defense mechanisms. T or F?

Check Your Memory: Pages 564-567

37. The deep depression experienced by prisoners of war appears to be related to learned helplessness. T or F?

38. Learned helplessness occurs when events appear to be uncontrollable. T or F?

39. Attributing failure to lasting, general factors, such as personal characteristics, tends to create the most damaging feelings of helplessness.

40. Mastery training restores feelings of control over the environment. T or F?

41. At any given time, 52 to 61 percent of all college students are experiencing the symptoms of depression. T or F?

42. Depression is more likely when students find it difficult to live up to idealized images of themselves. T or F?

43. Writing rational answers to self-critical thoughts can help counteract feelings of depression.

Check Your Memory: Pages 568-575

44. Scores on the SRRS are expressed as life control units. T or F?

45. A score of 300 LCUs on the SRRS is categorized as a major life crisis. T or F?

46. According to the SRRS, being fired at work involves more LCUs than divorce does. T or F?

47. Microstressors tend to predict changes in health 1 to 2 years after the stressful events took place. T or F?
48. Psychosomatic disorders involve actual damage to the body or damaging changes in bodily functioning. T or F?
49. A person undergoing biofeedback can sleep if he or she desires—the machine does all the work. T or F?
50. Type B personalities are more than twice as likely to suffer heart attacks as Type A personalities. T or F?
51. People with the hardy personality type tend to see life as a series of challenges. T or F?
52. In the stage of resistance of the G.A.S., people have symptoms of headache, fever, fatigue, upset stomach, and the like. T or F?
53. Serious health problems tend to occur when a person reaches the stage of exhaustion in the G.A.S. T or F?
54. Stress management training can actually boost immune system functioning. T or F?

Check Your Memory: PSYCHOLOGY IN ACTION

55. Concern about being pregnant is the most stressful item listed on the *College Life Stress Inventory*. T or F?
56. Exercising for stress management is most effective when it is done daily. T or F?
57. Guided imagery is used to reduce anxiety and promote relaxation. T or F?
58. Merely writing down thoughts and feelings about daily events can provide some of the benefits of social support. T or F?
59. To get the maximum benefits, coping statements should be practiced in actual stressful situations. T or F?
60. Persistence must be flexible before it is likely to aid a person trying to cope with frustration. T or F?

Check Your Memory: A STEP BEYOND

61. Receptive meditation is typically harder to do than concentrative meditation. T or F?
62. A mantra is used as a focus for attention during receptive meditation. T or F?
63. Herbert Benson states that the physical benefits of meditation are based on evoking the body's relaxation response. T or F?
64. The harder you try to meditate the more likely you arc to succeed. T or F?

FINAL SURVEY AND REVIEW

● *What is health psychology? How does behavior affect health?*

1. Health psychologists are interested in behavior that helps maintain and promote health. The related field of _____ _____ applies psychology to medical treatment and problems.
2. Most people today die from _____ diseases caused by unhealthy personal habits.
3. Studies have identified a number of behavioral _____ _____, which increase the chances of disease or injury.

4. A general _____ personality pattern also raises the risk of illness.
5. Health-_____ behaviors tend to maintain good health. They include practices such as getting regular exercise, controlling smoking and alcohol use, maintaining a balanced diet, getting good medical care, avoiding sleep _____, and managing _____.
6. Health psychologists attempt to promote _____ (a positive state of health) through _____ _____ campaigns that educate people about risk factors and healthful behaviors.

● *What is stress? What factors determine its severity?*

7. Stress occurs when we are forced to adjust or _____ to external _____.
8. Stress is more damaging in situations involving _____ (responding at full capacity for long periods), a lack of control, unpredictability of the _____, and intense or repeated emotional shocks.
9. Stress is intensified when a situation is perceived as a _____ and when a person does not feel _____ to cope with it.
10. In work settings, prolonged stress can lead to _____, marked by emotional exhaustion, _____ (detachment from others), and reduced personal accomplishment.
11. The primary _____ of a situation greatly affects our emotional response to it. Stress reactions, in particular, are related to an _____ of threat.
12. During a secondary appraisal some means of coping with a situation is selected. Coping may be either _____-focused (managing the situation) or _____-focused (managing one's emotional reactions) or both.
13. _____ stressors, such as violence, torture, or natural disasters, tend to produce severe stress reactions.
14. Traumatic stresses leave people feeling threatened, vulnerable, and with the sense that they are losing _____ over their lives.
15. Severe or repeated traumatic stress can leave people with lasting emotional handicaps called _____ _____.

● *What causes frustration and what are typical reactions to it?*

16. _____ is the negative emotional state that occurs when progress toward a goal is blocked. Sources of frustration may be external or _____.
17. _____ frustrations are based on delay, failure, rejection, loss, and other direct blocking of motives. _____ frustration is related to personal characteristics over which one has little control.
18. Frustrations of all types become more intense as the strength, urgency, or importance of the _____ _____ increases.
19. Major behavioral reactions to frustration include _____, more vigorous responding, and _____ of barriers.
20. Other reactions to frustration are direct aggression, _____ aggression (including _____), and escape, or withdrawal.

● *Are there different types of conflict? How do people react to conflict?*

21. Conflict occurs when we must choose between _____ alternatives.
22. Three basic types of conflict are _____ (choice between two positive alternatives), _____ (both alternatives are negative), and approach-avoidance (a goal or activity has both positive and negative aspects).
23. More complex conflicts are: _____ approach-avoidance (both alternatives have positive and negative qualities) and _____ approach-avoidance (several alternatives each have good and bad qualities).
24. _____ conflicts are usually the easiest to resolve.
25. _____ conflicts are difficult to resolve and are characterized by inaction, indecision, freezing, and a desire to escape (called leaving the field).
26. People usually remain in approach-avoidance conflicts but fail to fully resolve them. Approach-avoidance conflicts are associated with _____ (mixed feelings) and partial approach.
27. _____ (wavering between choices) is the most common reaction to double approach-avoidance conflicts.

● *What are defense mechanisms?*

28. Anxiety, threat, or feelings of inadequacy frequently lead to the use of psychological _____ _____. These are habitual strategies used to avoid or reduce _____.
29. A number of defense mechanisms have been identified, including _____ (refusing to perceive an unpleasant reality), fantasy, intellectualization, isolation, projection, _____ (justifying one's behavior), reaction formation, regression, and repression.
30. Two defense mechanisms that have some positive qualities are _____ and _____.

● *What do we know about coping with feelings of helplessness and depression?*

31. Learned _____ is a learned inability to overcome obstacles or to avoid _____.
32. The symptoms of learned helplessness and _____ are nearly identical.
33. _____ training and hope act as antidotes to helplessness.
34. _____ (a state of deep sadness or despondency) is a serious emotional problem. Actions and thoughts that counter feelings of _____ tend to reduce depression.

● *How is stress related to health and disease?*

35. Work with the _____ _____ _____ *Scale* (SRRS) indicates that a large number of life change units (LCUs) can increase susceptibility to accident or illness.
36. Immediate health is more closely related to the intensity and severity of daily annoyances, known as hassles or _____.

37. Intense or prolonged stress may damage the body in the form of _____
disorders (illnesses in which psychological factors play a part).

38. _____ (mind-body) disorders have no connection to
_____, the tendency to imagine that one has a disease.

39. During _____ training, bodily processes are monitored and converted to a
_____ that indicates what the body is doing.

40. Biofeedback allows alteration of many bodily activities. It shows promise for promoting relaxation, self-
_____, and for treating some psychosomatic illnesses.

41. People with _____ _____ (heart attack prone) personalities are competitive, striving, and
frequently _____ or hostile, and they have a chronic sense of time urgency.

42. Anger and hostility are especially likely to increase the chances of _____ _____.

43. People who have traits of the _____ personality seem to be resistant to stress, even if they
also have Type A traits.

44. The body reacts to stress in a series of stages called the general _____
_____ (G.A.S.).

45. The stages of the G.A.S. are _____, resistance, and _____. The G.A.S.
contributes to the development of psychosomatic disorders.

46. Stress weakens the _____ system and lowers the body's resistance to illness.

● *What are the best strategies for managing stress?*

47. Most stress management skills focus on one of three areas: bodily effects,
_____ behavior, and _____ thoughts.

48. Bodily effects can be managed with exercise, meditation, _____ relaxation, and
_____ imagery.

49. The impact of ineffective behavior can be remedied by slowing down, getting organized, striking a
balance between "good stress" and relaxation, accepting your _____, and seeking
_____ support.

50. A good way to control upsetting thoughts is to replace _____ self-statements with
positive _____ statements.

● *Is meditation useful for coping with stress?*

51. _____ is a self-control technique that can be used to reduce stress.

52. In _____ meditation, attention is broadened to include an awareness of one's entire
moment-by-moment experience.

53. In _____ meditation, attention is focused on a single object or thought.

54. Two major benefits of meditation are its ability to interrupt anxious thoughts and its ability to elicit the
_____ _____ (the pattern of changes that occur in the body at times of
deep relaxation).

MASTERY TEST

1. When stressful events appear to be uncontrollable, two common reactions are
   a. apathy and double-approach conflict   b. helplessness and depression
   c. assimilation and marginalization   d. psychosomatic disorders and hypochondria

2. The *College Life Stress Inventory* is most closely related to the
   a. SRRS   b. G.A.S.   c. K.I.S.   d. *Disease-Prone Personality Scale*

3. We answer the question "Am I okay or in trouble" when making
   a. negative self-statements   b. coping statements   c. a primary appraisal   d. a secondary appraisal

4. Which of the following is NOT a major symptom of burnout?
   a. emotional exhaustion   b. depersonalization   c. reduced accomplishment
   d. dependence on co-workers

5. A child who displays childish speech and infantile play after his parents bring home a new baby shows signs of
   a. compensation   b. reaction formation   c. regression   d. sublimation

6. Persistent but inflexible responses to frustration can become
   a. stereotyped behaviors   b. imagined barriers   c. negative self-statements
   d. sublimated and depersonalized

7. The leading cause of death in the United States is
   a. tobacco   b. diet/inactivity   c. alcohol   d. infection

8. Both mountain climbing and marital strife
   a. are behavioral risk factors   b. are appraised as secondary threats   c. cause stress reactions
   d. produce the condition known as pressure

9. LCUs are used to assess
   a. burnout   b. social readjustments   c. microstressors   d. what stage of the G.A.S. a person is in

10. Sujata is often ridiculed by her boss, who also frequently takes advantage of her. Deep inside, Sujata has come to hate her boss, yet on the surface she acts as if she likes him very much. It is likely that Sujata is using the defense mechanism called
    a. reaction formation   b. Type B appraisal   c. problem-focused coping   d. sublimation

11. Lifestyle diseases are of special interest to _____ psychologists.
    a. health   b. community   c. wellness   d. psychosomatic

12. Which of the following is NOT characteristic of the hardy personality?
    a. commitment   b. a sense of control   c. accepting challenge   d. repression

13. Unhealthy lifestyles are marked by the presence of a number of
    a. health refusal factors   b. behavioral risk factors   c. cultural stressors
    d. Type B personality traits

14. The most effective response to a controllable stressor is
    a. problem-focused coping   b. emotion-focused coping   c. leaving the field   d. depersonalization

15. Delay, rejection, failure, and loss are all major causes of
    a. pressure   b. frustration   c. conflict   d. helplessness

16. There is evidence that the core lethal factor of Type A behavior is
    a. time urgency   b. anger and hostility   c. competitiveness and ambition
    d. accepting too many responsibilities

17. According to Herbert Benson, the one thing that all types of meditation have in common is
    a. use of a mantra   b. the relaxation response   c. that meditation replaces sleep   d. that you should
    end meditation if distracting thoughts occur

18. A person is caught between "the frying pan and the fire" in an _____ conflict.
    a. approach-approach   b. avoidance-avoidance   c. approach-avoidance   d. double appraisal

19. Which of the following is NOT one of the major health-promoting behaviors listed in the text?
    a. do not smoke   b. get adequate sleep   c. get regular exercise   d. avoid eating between meals

20. Ambivalence and partial approach are very common reactions to what type of conflict?
    a. approach-approach   b. avoidance-avoidance   c. approach-avoidance   d. multiple avoidance

21. Which of the following terms does not belong with the others?
    a. Type A personality   b. stage of exhaustion   c. displaced aggression   d. psychosomatic disorder

22. Coping statements are a key element in
    a. stress inoculation   b. the K.I.S. technique   c. guided imagery   d. refusal skills training

23. Which of the following factors typically minimizes the amount of stress experienced?
    a. predictable stressors   b. repeated stressors   c. uncontrollable stressors   d. intense stressors

24. Scapegoating is closely related to which response to frustration?
    a. leaving the field   b. displaced aggression   c. circumvention   d. reaction formation

25. The study of the ways in which stress and the immune system affect susceptibility to disease is called
    a. neuropsychosymptomology   b. immunohypochondrology   c. psychosomatoneurology
    d. psychoneuroimmunology

26. Refusal skills training is typically used to teach young people how to
    a. avoid drug use   b. cope with burnout   c. resist stressors at home and at school   d. avoid forming habits that lead to heart disease

27. Which combination is most relevant to managing bodily reactions to stress?
    a. social support, self pacing   b. exercise, social support   c. exercise, negative self-statements
    d. progressive relaxation, guided imagery

28. Stress reactions are most likely to occur when a stressor is viewed as a _____ during the _____.
    a. pressure, primary appraisal   b. pressure, secondary appraisal   c. threat, primary appraisal
    d. threat, secondary appraisal

29. External symptoms of the body's adjustment to stress are least visible in which stage of the G.A.S?
    a. alarm   b. regulation   c. resistance   d. exhaustion

30. A perceived lack of control creates a stressful sense of threat when combined with a perceived
    a. sense of time urgency   b. state of sublimation   c. need to change secondary risk factors
    d. lack of competence

ANSWERS

Recite and Review

1. behavior, medical
2. habits
3. disease (or illness)
4. illness (or disease)
5. behaviors, smoking, diet, sleep
6. health, campaigns
7. adjust
8. control, intense
9. Stress
10. work, exhaustion
11. primary, threat
12. secondary
13. stressors, stress
14. stresses, lives
15. repeated, stress
16. goal, blocked
17. personal
18. intense
19. vigorous
20. direct, withdrawal
21. Conflict
22. positive, negative
23. positive, negative
24. easiest
25. difficult, leaving
26. mixed, partial
27. approach-avoidance
28. inadequacy
29. reaction, repression
30. positive
31. avoid
32. identical
33. training
34. reduce
35. change, accident
36. hassles
37. psychological
38. disease
39. monitored
40. relaxation
41. heart, time
42. Anger
43. stress
44. general
45. psychosomatic
46. disease (or illness)
47. behavior, thoughts
48. relaxation, imagery
49. relaxation
50. positive
51. stress
52. widened
53. single
54. relaxation

Connections

1. d
2. a
3. j
4. b
5. i
6. h
7. c
8. f
9. e
10. g
11. f
12. i
13. a
14. k
15. b
16. h
17. d
18. c
19. g
20. e
21. j
22. i
23. h
24. a
25. g
26. b
27. c
28. d
29. e
30. f

Check Your Memory

1. T
2. F
3. T
4. T
5. F
6. F
7. F
8. F
9. T
10. T
11. T
12. F
13. T
14. T
15. T
16. T
17. F
18. F
19. T
20. T
21. T
22. F
23. F
24. F
25. F
26. T
27. T
28. F
29. T
30. F
31. T
32. T
33. T
34. F
35. T
36. F
37. T
38. T
39. T
40. T
41. F
42. T
43. T
44. F
45. T
46. F
47. F
48. T
49. F
50. F
51. T
52. F
53. T
54. T
55. F
56. T
57. T
58. T
59. T
60. T
61. T
62. F
63. T
64. F

Final Survey and Review

1. behavioral medicine
2. lifestyle
3. risk factors
4. disease-prone
5. promoting, deprivation, stress
6. wellness, community health
7. adapt, demands
8. pressure, stressor
9. threat, competent
10. burnout, depersonalization
11. appraisal, appraisal
12. problem, emotion
13. Traumatic
14. control
15. stress disorders
16. Frustration, personal
17. External, Personal
18. blocked motive
19. persistence, circumvention
20. displaced, scapegoating
21. contradictory
22. approach-approach, avoidance-avoidance
23. double, multiple
24. Approach-approach
25. Avoidance
26. ambivalence
27. Vacillation
28. defense mechanisms, anxiety
29. denial, rationalization
30. compensation, sublimation
31. helplessness, punishment
32. depression
33. Mastery
34. Depression, helplessness
35. *Social Readjustment Rating*
36. microstressors
37. psychosomatic
38. Psychosomatic, hypochondria

39. biofeedback, signal
40. regulation
41. Type A, angry
42. heart attack
43. hardy
44. adaptation syndrome
45. alarm, exhaustion
46. immune
47. ineffective, upsetting
48. progressive, guided
49. limits, social
50. negative, coping
51. Meditation
52. receptive
53. concentrative
54. relaxation response

Mastery Test

1. b (p. 565)
2. a (p. 576)
3. c (p. 556)
4. d (p. 555)
5. c (p. 562)
6. a (p. 580)
7. a (p. 550)
8. c (p. 554)
9. b (p. 568)
10. a (p. 562)
11. a (p. 549)
12. d (p. 574)
13. b (p. 549)
14. a (p. 557)
15. b (p. 558)
16. b (p. 572)
17. b (p. 582)
18. b (p. 560)
19. d (p. 551)
20. c (p. 561)
21. c (p. 571-572, 574)
22. a (p. 579)
23. a (p. 554)
24. b (p. 559)
25. d (p. 575)
26. a (p. 551)
27. d (p. 577-578)
28. c (p. 556)
29. c (p. 574)
30. d (p. 556)

Chapter 16
Psychological Disorders

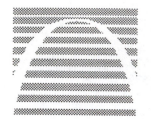

CHAPTER OVERVIEW

Abnormal behavior is defined by subjective discomfort, deviation from statistical norms, social nonconformity, and cultural or situational contexts. Disordered behavior is also maladaptive. Major types of psychopathology are described by DSM-IV-TR. Insanity is a legal term, not a mental disorder.

Personality disorders are deeply ingrained maladaptive personality patterns, such as the antisocial personality. Anxiety disorders, dissociative disorders, and somatoform disorders are characterized by high levels of anxiety, rigid defense mechanisms, and self-defeating behavior patterns.

Anxiety disorders include generalized anxiety disorder, panic disorder (with or without agoraphobia), agoraphobia, specific phobia, social phobia, obsessive-compulsive disorders, and posttraumatic or acute stress disorders. Dissociative disorders may take the form of amnesia, fugue, or identity disorder (multiple personality). Somatoform disorders center on physical complaints that mimic disease or disability.

Psychodynamic explanations of anxiety disorders emphasize unconscious conflicts. The humanistic approach emphasizes faulty self-images. The behavioral approach emphasizes the effects of learning, particularly avoidance learning. The cognitive approach stresses maladaptive thinking patterns.

Psychosis is a break in contact with reality. Persons suffering from delusional disorders have delusions of grandeur, persecution, infidelity, romantic attraction, or physical disease. The most common delusional disorder is paranoid psychosis.

Schizophrenia is the most common psychosis. Four types of schizophrenia are: disorganized, catatonic, paranoid, and undifferentiated. Explanations of schizophrenia emphasize environmental stress, inherited susceptibility, and biochemical abnormalities.

Mood disorders involve disturbances of emotion. Two moderate mood disorders are dysthymic disorder and cyclothymic disorder. Major mood disorders include bipolar disorders and major depressive disorder. Seasonal affective disorder is another common form of depression. Biological, psychoanalytic, cognitive, and behavioral theories of depression have been proposed. Heredity is clearly a factor in susceptibility to mood disorders.

Two basic approaches to treating major disorders are psychotherapy and medical therapies.

Suicide is statistically related to such factors as age, sex, and marital status. However, in individual cases the potential for suicide is best identified by a desire to escape, unbearable psychological pain, frustrated psychological needs, and a constriction of options. Suicide can sometimes be prevented by the efforts of family, friends, and mental health professionals.

In Western law, the insanity defense evolved from the M'Naghten rule. Insanity is closely related to claims of diminished capacity or irresistible impulses. Inconsistencies in the application of the insanity defense have fueled debate about its validity.

Thomas Szasz has raised challenging questions about the nature of the medical model, abnormal behavior, personal responsibility, and civil rights. Public policies concerning treatment of the mentally ill continue to evolve, as authorities try to strike a balance between providing help and taking away personal freedoms.

LEARNING OBJECTIVES

To demonstrate mastery of this chapter, you should be able to:

1. Present information to indicate the magnitude of mental health problems in this country.
2. Define *psychopathology.*
3. Describe the following ways of viewing normality, including the shortcoming(s) of each:
   a. subjective discomfort
   b. statistical definitions
   c. social nonconformity
   d. situational context
   e. cultural relativity
4. Explain why more women than men are treated for psychological problems.
5. Name and explain the two core features of abnormal behavior.
6. Explain why caution is necessary when using psychiatric labels. Briefly describe Rosenhan's pseudo-patient study, and explain how his observations relate to the idea of labeling.
7. Generally describe each of the following categories of mental disorders found in the DSM-IV-TR:
   a. psychotic disorders
   b. organic mental disorders
   c. substance related disorders
   d. mood disorders
   e. anxiety disorders
   f. somatoform disorders
   g. dissociative disorders
   h. personality disorders
   i. sexual and gender-identity disorders
8. List the four general risk factors for mental disorders.
9. Briefly discuss ethnic group membership as a factor in mental disorders.
10. Distinguish the term *insanity* from a mental disorder.
11. List and briefly describe the ten different types of personality disorders. (See Table 16.4.)
12. Describe the distinctive characteristics, causes, and treatment of the antisocial personality.
13. Differentiate anxiety from fear.
14. Outline the general features and characteristics of anxiety-related problems.
15. State what is usually meant when the term *nervous breakdown* is used. Differentiate this category from an anxiety disorder.
16. Define the key element of most anxiety disorders.
17. Differentiate generalized anxiety disorders from panic disorders.
18. Describe the following conditions:
    a. agoraphobia
    b. specific phobia

   c. social phobia
   d. obsessive-compulsive disorder
   e. stress disorder
      1.. acute stress disorder
      2. posttraumatic stress disorder
   f. dissociative disorders
      1. amnesia
      2. fugue
      3. dissociative identity disorder
   g. somatoform disorders
      1. hypochondriasis
      2. somatization disorder
      3. pain disorder
      4. conversion disorder
19. Discuss how each of the four major perspectives view anxiety disorders.
   a. psychodynamic
   b. humanistic-existential (include the terms *self-image* and *existential anxiety*)
   c. behavioral (include the terms *self-defeating, paradox, avoidance learning,* and *anxiety reduction hypothesis*)
   d. cognitive
20. Define *psychosis*. List and explain the five major characteristics of psychotic disorders.
21. Define *delusion*. List and describe the six different types of delusions.
22. Define *hallucination* and name the most common type.
23. Define the terms *organic psychosis* and *dementia*.
24. Briefly describe Alzheimer's disease, including its incidence, symptoms, and neurological concomitants.
25. Describe the main feature of *delusional disorders* and discuss five types of delusional disorders.
26. Describe a paranoid psychosis, including its characteristics and treatment.
27. Generally describe schizophrenia, including its frequency, typical age of onset, and symptoms.
28. List and describe the four major types of schizophrenia.
29. Explain how paranoid delusional disorder and paranoid schizophrenia differ.
30. Describe the general relationship between psychosis and violence.
31. Describe the roles of the following three areas as causes of schizophrenia:
   a. environment
      1. prenatal problems and birth complications
      2. psychological trauma
      3. disturbed family environment
      4. deviant communication patterns
   b. heredity

    c. brain chemistry

        1. dopamine

        2. glutamate

32. Explain how CT, MRI, and PET scans contribute to the study of abnormal brain activity.

33. Describe the stress-vulnerability model of psychosis.

34. State the incidence and characteristics of mood disorders, especially depression, in the general population.

35. Describe the characteristics of moderate mood disorders. Include a description of dysthymia and cyclothymia.

36. List and describe the three major mood disorders.

37. Explain the difference between major mood disorders and dysthymia and cyclothymia.

38. Describe the possible explanations for depression.

39. Define and briefly discuss the symptoms of *maternity blues* and *postpartum depression*.

40. Define *seasonal affective disorder* (SAD), list five major symptoms, and briefly describe the treatment of SAD.

41. List and describe the two basic kinds of treatment for psychosis.

The following objectives are related to the material in the "Psychology in Action" and "A Step Beyond" sections of your text.

42. Discuss how each of the following factors affects suicide rates: season, sex, age, income, and marital status.

43. List the conditions that typically precede suicide. Discuss why people try to kill themselves.

44. Name the twelve warning signs of suicide.

45. List four common characteristics of suicidal thoughts and feelings.

46. Explain how you can help prevent suicide.

47. Briefly discuss the history of the insanity defense, including the concept of expert testimony.

48. Describe Thomas Szasz's view of mental illness and its treatment.

RECITE AND REVIEW

● *How is normality defined, and what are the major psychological disorders?*

Recite and Review: Pages 586-595

  1. *Psychopathology* refers to mental _____ themselves or to psychologically _____ behavior.

  2. Formal definitions of abnormality usually take into account subjective _____ (private feelings of suffering or unhappiness).

  3. Statistical definitions define abnormality as an extremely _____ or _____ score on some dimension or measure.

4. Social nonconformity is a failure to follow societal _____ for acceptable conduct.

5. Frequently, the _____ or situational context that a behavior takes place in affects judgments of normality and abnormality.

6. _____ of the preceding definitions are relative standards.

7. A key element in judgments of disorder is that a person's _____ must be maladaptive (it makes it difficult for the person to _____ to the demands of daily life.

8. A _____ disorder is a significant impairment in psychological functioning.

9. Major disorders and categories of psychopathology are described in the *Diagnostic and Statistical _____ of _____ Disorders* (DSM-IV-TR).

10. Psychotic disorders are characterized by a retreat from _____, by hallucinations and delusions, and by _____ withdrawal.

11. Organic mental disorders are problems caused by _____ injuries and _____.

12. Substance related disorders are defined as abuse of or dependence on _____- or behavior-altering _____.

13. Mood disorders involve disturbances in affect, or _____.

14. Anxiety disorders involve high levels of fear or _____ and distortions in behavior that are _____ related.

15. Somatoform disorders involve physical symptoms that mimic physical _____ or injury for which there is no identifiable _____.

16. Dissociative disorders include cases of sudden amnesia, multiple _____, or episodes of depersonalization.

17. Personality disorders are deeply ingrained, unhealthy _____ patterns.

18. Sexual and gender disorders include _____ identity disorders, paraphilias, and _____ dysfunctions.

19. In the past, the term *neurosis* was used to describe milder, _____ related disorders. However, the term is fading from use.

20. Insanity is a _____ term defining whether a person may be held responsible for his or her actions. Sanity is determined in _____ on the basis of testimony by expert witnesses.

● *What is a personality disorder?*

Recite and Review: Pages 595-597

21. Personality disorders are deeply ingrained _____ personality patterns.

22. The personality disorders are: antisocial, avoidant, _____, dependent, histrionic, narcissistic, obsessive-_____, paranoid, schizoid, and schizotypal.

23. Antisocial persons (sociopaths) seem to lack a _____. They are _____ shallow and manipulative.

● *What problems result when a person suffers high levels of anxiety?*

Recite and Review: Pages 597-602

24. Anxiety disorders, dissociative disorders, and somatoform disorders all involve high levels of _____, rigid _____ mechanisms, and self-defeating behavior patterns.

25. The term *nervous breakdown* has no formal meaning. However, "emotional breakdowns" do correspond somewhat to adjustment disorders, in which the person is overwhelmed by ongoing _____ _____.

26. Anxiety disorders include generalized anxiety disorder (chronic _____ and worry) and panic disorder (anxiety attacks, panic, free-_____ anxiety).

27. Panic disorder may occur with or without agoraphobia (fear of _____ places, unfamiliar situations, or leaving the _____).

28. Other anxiety disorders are agoraphobia and _____ phobia (irrational fears of specific objects or situations).

29. In the anxiety disorder called social phobia, the person fears being _____, evaluated, embarrassed, or humiliated by others in _____ situations.

30. Obsessive-compulsive disorders (obsessions and compulsions), and posttraumatic stress disorder or acute stress disorder (emotional disturbances triggered by severe _____) are also classified as _____ disorders.

31. Dissociative disorders may take the form of dissociative amnesia (loss of _____ and personal identity) or _____ fugue (flight from familiar surroundings).

32. A more dramatic problem is dissociative identity disorder, in which a person develops _____ personalities.

33. Somatoform disorders center on physical complaints that mimic _____ or disability.

34. In hypochondriasis, persons think that they have specific diseases, when they are, in fact _____.

35. In a somatization disorder, the person has numerous _____ complaints. The person repeatedly seeks medical _____ for these complaints, but no organic problems can be found.

36. Somatoform pain refers to discomfort for which there is no identifiable _____ cause.

37. In conversion disorders, actual symptoms of disease or disability develop but their causes are really _____.

● *How do psychologists explain anxiety-based disorders?*

Recite and Review: Pages 602-604

38. The psychodynamic approach emphasizes _____ conflicts within the personality as the cause of disabling anxiety.

39. The humanistic approach emphasizes the effects of a faulty _____.

40. The behavioral approach emphasizes the effects of previous _____, particularly avoidance _____.

41. Some patterns in anxiety disorders can be explained by the _____ reduction hypothesis, which states that immediate _____ from anxiety rewards self-defeating behaviors.

42. According to the cognitive view, distorted _____ patterns cause anxiety disorders.

● *What are the general characteristics of psychotic disorders?*

Recite and Review: Pages 604-607

43. Psychosis is a _____ in contact with reality.

44. Psychosis is marked by delusions, _____ (false sensations), and sensory changes.

45. Other symptoms of psychosis are disturbed emotions, disturbed communication, and _____ disintegration.

46. An organic psychosis is based on known injuries or _____ of the brain.

47. The most common _____ problem is dementia, a serious mental impairment in old age caused by deterioration of the _____.

48. One of the common causes of _____ is Alzheimer's disease.

● *How do delusional disorders differ from other forms of psychosis?*

Recite and Review: Page 607-608

49. A diagnosis of delusional disorder is based primarily on the presence of _____.

50. Delusions may concern grandeur, _____ (harassment or threat), infidelity, _____ attraction, or physical disease.

51. The most common delusional disorder is paranoid psychosis. Because they often have intense and irrational delusions of _____, paranoids may be violent if they believe they are threatened.

● *What forms does schizophrenia take? What causes it?*

Recite and Review: Pages 608-614

52. Schizophrenia is distinguished by a _____ between _____ and emotion, and by delusions, hallucinations, and communication difficulties.

53. Disorganized schizophrenia is marked by extreme _____ disintegration and silly, bizarre, or obscene behavior. _____ impairment is usually extreme.

54. Catatonic schizophrenia is associated with stupor, _____ (inability to speak), _____ flexibility, and odd postures. Sometimes violent and agitated behavior also occurs.

55. In paranoid schizophrenia (the most common type), outlandish delusions of grandeur and _____ are coupled with psychotic symptoms and personality breakdown.

56. Undifferentiated schizophrenia is the term used to indicate a _____ of clear-cut patterns of disturbance.

57. Current explanations of schizophrenia emphasize a combination of environmental _____, inherited susceptibility, and biochemical _____ in the body or brain.

58. A number of environmental factors appear to increase the risk of developing schizophrenia. These include viral _____ during the mother's pregnancy and _____ complications.

59. Early psychological _____ (psychological injury or shock) and a disturbed
_____ environment, especially one marked by deviant communication, also increase the risk
of schizophrenia.

60. Studies of _____ and other close relatives strongly support heredity as a major factor in
schizophrenia.

61. Recent biochemical studies have focused on abnormalities in brain _____
substances, especially glutamate, dopamine, and their receptor sites.

62. Additional abnormalities in brain structure or _____ have been detected in
schizophrenic brains by the use of CT scans, MRI scans, and PET scans.

63. The dominant explanation of schizophrenia is the _____-vulnerability model.

● *What are mood disorders? What causes depression?*

Recite and Review: Pages 614-618

64. Mood disorders primarily involve disturbances of mood or _____.

65. Long-lasting, though relatively moderate, _____ is called a dysthymic disorder.

66. Chronic, though moderate, swings in mood between _____ and _____ are
called a cyclothymic disorder.

67. In a bipolar I disorder the person alternates between extreme mania and _____.

68. In a bipolar II disorder the person is mostly _____, but has had at least one episode of
hypomania (mild _____).

69. The problem known as major depressive disorder involves extreme sadness and despondency, but no
evidence of _____.

70. Postpartum depression is a mild to moderate depressive disorder that affects many women after they give
birth. Postpartum depression is more serious than the more common _____
_____.

71. Major mood disorders more often appear to be endogenous (produced from _____) rather
than reactions to _____ events.

72. _____ affective disorder (SAD), which occurs during the _____ months,
is another common form of depression. SAD is typically treated with phototherapy.

73. Biological, psychoanalytic, cognitive, and _____ theories of depression have been
proposed. Heredity is clearly a factor in susceptibility to mood disorders.

74. Psychotherapy is any psychological treatment for behavioral or emotional problems. _____
_____ disorders are more often treated medically, rather than with psychotherapy.

● *Why do people commit suicide? Can suicide be prevented?*

Recite and Review: PSYCHOLOGY IN ACTION

75. _____ is statistically related to such factors as age, sex, and marital status.

76. Major risk factors for suicide include _____ or _____ abuse, a prior attempt, depression, hopelessness, antisocial behavior, suicide by relatives, shame, failure, or rejection, and the availability of a _____ .

77. In individual cases the potential for suicide is best identified by a desire to _____, unbearable psychological pain, frustrated psychological needs, and a constriction of _____ .

78. Suicidal _____ usually precede suicide threats, which progress to suicide attempts.

79. Suicide can often be prevented by the efforts of family, friends, and mental health professionals to establish _____ and rapport with the person, and by gaining day-by-day commitments from her or him.

● *What does it mean to be "crazy"? What should be done about it?*

Recite and Review: A STEP BEYOND

80. In Western law, the _____ defense evolved from the M'Naghten rule.

81. Insanity is closely related to claims of diminished _____ (impaired ability to control actions) or claims that a person had an irresistible _____ (uncontrollable urge to act).

82. Insanity is determined by courts of law, usually on the basis of _____ by expert witnesses (psychiatrists or psychologists).

83. Inconsistencies in applying the insanity defense have fueled debate about its _____ .

84. Thomas Szasz has raised challenging questions about the nature of abnormal behavior and its relationship to personal _____ and civil rights.

85. Szasz rejects the medical model of mental illness that treats emotional problems as _____ with symptoms that can be cured.

86. Public policies concerning treatment of the chronically mentally ill continue to evolve as authorities try to strike a balance between providing help and taking away personal _____ .

CONNECTIONS

1.	_____	DSM-IV-TR	a. culturally recognized disorder
2.	_____	drapetomania	b. physical symptoms
3.	_____	psychosis	c. legal problem
4.	_____	mood disorder	d. outdated term
5.	_____	somatoform disorder	e. sexual deviation
6.	_____	insanity	f. diagnostic manual
7.	_____	organic disorder	g. retreat from reality
8.	_____	neurosis	h. fear of germs
9.	_____	paraphilia	i. brain pathology
10.	_____	amok	j. mania or depression

11. _____	dependent personality	a.	self-importance
12. _____	histrionic personality	b.	rigid routines
13. _____	narcissistic personality	c.	submissiveness
14. _____	antisocial personality	d.	little emotion
15. _____	obsessive-compulsive	e.	attention seeking
16. _____	schizoid personality	f.	unstable self-image
17. _____	avoidant personality	g.	odd, disturbed thinking
18. _____	borderline personality	h.	suspiciousness
19. _____	paranoid personality	i.	fear of social situations
20. _____	schizotypal personality	j.	no conscience

21. _____	adjustment disorder	a.	afraid to leave the house
22. _____	generalized anxiety	b.	fears being observed
23. _____	panic disorder	c.	conversion disorder
24. _____	agoraphobia	d.	one month after extreme stress
25. _____	specific phobia	e.	dissociation
26. _____	social phobia	f.	within weeks after extreme stress
27. _____	PTSD	g.	sudden attacks of fear
28. _____	acute stress disorder	h.	normal life stress
29. _____	glove anesthesia	i.	chronic worry
30. _____	fugue	j.	fears objects or activities

31. _____	schizotypal	a.	incoherence, bizarre thinking
32. _____	catatonic type	b.	false belief
33. _____	paranoid type	c.	personality disorder
34. _____	disorganized type	d.	depression and hypomania
35. _____	psychological trauma	e.	stuporous or agitated
36. _____	twin studies	f.	severe mania and depression
37. _____	dopamine	g.	genetics of schizophrenia
38. _____	delusion	h.	grandeur or persecution
39. _____	bipolar I	i.	chemical messenger
40. _____	bipolar II	j.	risk factor for schizophrenia

CHECK YOUR MEMORY

Check Your Memory: Pages 586-595

1. Psychopathology refers to the study of mental disorders and to disorders themselves. T or F?
2. One out of every 10 persons will require mental hospitalization during his or her lifetime. T or F?
3. Statistical definitions do not automatically tell us where to draw the line between normality and abnormality. T or F?

4. All cultures classify people as abnormal if they fail to communicate with others. T or F?

5. Gender is a common source of bias in judging normality. T or F?

6. Being a persistent danger to oneself or others is regarded as a clear sign of disturbed psychological functioning. T or F?

7. Poverty, abusive parents, low intelligence, and head injuries are risk factors for mental disorder. T or F?

8. "Organic mental disorders" is one of the major categories in DSM-IV-TR. T or F?

9. *Koro, locura,* and *zar* are brain diseases that cause psychosis. T or F?

10. Multiple personality is a dissociative disorder. T or F?

11. Neurosis is a legal term, not a type of mental disorder. T or F?

Check Your Memory: Pages 595-597

12. Histrionic persons are preoccupied with their own self-importance. T or F?

13. Personality disorders usually appear suddenly in early adulthood. T or F?

14. The schizoid person shows little emotion and is uninterested in relationships with others. T or F?

15. "Psychopath" is another term for the borderline personality. T or F?

16. Sociopaths usually have a childhood history of emotional deprivation, neglect, and abuse. T or F?

17. Antisocial behavior typically declines somewhat after age 20. T or F?

Check Your Memory: Pages 597-602

18. Anxiety is an emotional response to an ambiguous threat. T or F?

19. Adjustment disorders occur when severe stresses outside the normal range of human experience push people to their breaking points. T or F?

20. Sudden, unexpected episodes of intense panic are a key feature of generalized anxiety disorder. T or F?

21. A person who fears he or she will have a panic attack in public places or unfamiliar situations suffers from acrophobia. T or F?

22. Arachnophobia, claustrophobia, and pathophobia are all specific phobias. T or F?

23. Many people who have an obsessive-compulsive disorder are checkers or cleaners. T or F?

24. PTSD is a psychological disturbance lasting more than one month after exposure to severe stress. T or F?

25. Multiple personality is the most common form of schizophrenia. T or F?

26. Depersonalization and fusion are the goals of therapy for dissociative identity disorders. T or F?

27. The word somatoform means "body form." T or F?

28. An unusual lack of concern about the appearance of a sudden disability is a sign of a conversion reaction. T or F?

Check Your Memory: Pages 602-604

29. Anxiety disorders appear to be partly hereditary. T or F?

30. The psychodynamic approach characterizes anxiety disorders as a product of id impulses that threaten a loss of control. T or F?

31. Carl Rogers interpreted emotional disorders as the result of a loss of meaning in one's life. T or F?

32. Disordered behavior is paradoxical, because it makes the person more anxious and unhappy in the long run. T or F?

33. The cognitive view attributes anxiety disorders to distorted thinking that leads to avoidance learning. T or F?

Check Your Memory: Pages 604-607

34. The most common psychotic delusion is hearing voices. T or F?
35. Even a person who displays flat affect may continue to privately feel strong emotion. T or F?
36. Extremely psychotic behavior tends to occur in brief episodes. T or F?
37. Severe brain injuries or diseases sometimes cause psychoses. T or F?
38. Children must eat leaded paint flakes before they are at risk for lead poisoning. T or F?
39. Roughly 80 percent of all cases of Alzheimer's disease are genetic. T or F?

Check Your Memory: Page 607-608

40. In delusional disorders, people have auditory hallucinations of grandeur or persecution. T or F?
41. Delusions of persecution are a key symptom of paranoid psychosis. T or F?
42. A person who believes that his body is diseased and rotting has a erotomanic type of delusional disorder. T or F?

Check Your Memory: Pages 608-614

43. One person out of 100 will become schizophrenic. T or F?
44. Schizophrenia is the most common dissociative psychosis. T or F?
45. Silliness, laughter, and bizarre behavior are common in disorganized schizophrenia. T or F?
46. Periods of immobility and odd posturing are characteristic of paranoid schizophrenia. T or F?
47. At various times, patients may shift from one type of schizophrenia to another. T or F?
48. Exposure to influenza during pregnancy produces children who are more likely to become schizophrenic later in life. T or F?
49. If one identical twin is schizophrenic, the other twin has a 46 percent chance of also becoming schizophrenic. T or F?
50. Excess amounts of the neurotransmitter substance PCP are suspected as a cause of schizophrenia. T or F?
51. The brains of schizophrenics tend to be more responsive to dopamine than the brains of normal persons. T or F?
52. PET scans show that activity in the frontal lobes of schizophrenics tends to be abnormally low. T or F?

Check Your Memory: Pages 614-618

53. The two most basic types of mood disorder are bipolar I and bipolar II. T or F?
54. In bipolar disorders, people experience both mania and depression. T or F?
55. If a person is moderately depressed for at least two weeks, a dysthymic disorder exists. T or F?
56. A cyclothymic disorder is characterized by moderate levels of depression and manic behavior. T or F?
57. Endogenous depression appears to be generated from within, with little connection to external events. T or F?
58. Behavioral theories of depression emphasize the concept of learned helplessness. T or F?

59. Overall, women are twice as likely as men are to become depressed. T or F?
60. SAD is most likely to occur during the winter, in countries lying near the equator. T or F?
61. Postpartum depression typically lasts from about two months to a year after giving birth. T or F?
62. At least three schizophrenic patients out of four are completely recovered 10 years after being diagnosed. T or F?

Check Your Memory: PSYCHOLOGY IN ACTION

63. The greatest number of suicides during a single day takes place at New Year's. T or F?
64. More men than women complete suicide. T or F?
65. Suicide rates steadily decline after young adulthood. T or F?
66. Most suicides involve despair, anger, and guilt. T or F?
67. People who threaten suicide rarely actually attempt it—they're just crying wolf. T or F?
68. Only a minority of people who attempt suicide really want to die. T or F?
69. The risk of attempted suicide is high if a person has a concrete, workable plan for doing it. T or F?

Check Your Memory: A STEP BEYOND

70. The insanity defense has been used in Western law for over 130 years. T or F?
71. The M'Naghten rule says that a person must intentionally harm others before he or she has committed a crime. T or F?
72. The "Twinkie defense" in the Dan White case was essentially a plea of diminished capacity. T or F?
73. In most cases, persons declared insane are hospitalized longer than they would have been imprisoned for the same crime. T or F?
74. Thomas Szasz regards mental illness as the greatest problem facing our society today. T or F?
75. Szasz believes that mental illness is a moral judgment, not a medical reality. T or F?
76. According to Szasz, the only legitimate reason for depriving a person of freedom is for breaking the law. T or F?
77. Recently, several states in the U.S. have made it easier to force the mentally ill into hospitals. T or F?

FINAL SURVEY AND REVIEW

● *How is normality defined, and what are the major psychological disorders?*

1. _____ refers to mental disorders themselves or to psychologically unhealthy behavior.
2. Formal definitions of abnormality usually take into account _____ discomfort (private feelings of suffering or unhappiness).
3. _____ definitions define abnormality as an extremely high or low score on some dimension or measure.
4. _____ _____ is a failure to follow societal standards for acceptable conduct.

5. Frequently, the cultural or situational _____ that a behavior takes place in affects judgments of normality and abnormality.
6. All of the preceding definitions are _____ standards.
7. A key element in judgments of disorder is that a person's behavior must be _____ (it makes it difficult for the person to adapt to the environment).
8. A mental disorder is a significant impairment in _____ functioning.
9. Major disorders and categories of psychopathology are described in the _____ and _____ *Manual of Mental Disorders* (DSM-IV-TR).
10. _____ disorders are characterized by a retreat from reality, by _____ and delusions, and by social withdrawal.
11. _____ mental disorders are problems caused by brain injuries and diseases.
12. _____ _____ disorders are defined as abuse of or dependence on mood- or behavior-altering drugs.
13. _____ disorders involve disturbances in _____ or emotion.
14. _____ disorders involve high levels of fear or anxiety and distortions in behavior that are anxiety related.
15. _____ disorders involve physical symptoms that mimic physical disease or injury for which there is no identifiable cause.
16. _____ disorders include cases of sudden _____, multiple personality, or episodes of depersonalization.
17. _____ disorders are deeply ingrained, unhealthy personality patterns.
18. Sexual and gender disorders include gender _____ disorders, paraphilias, and sexual - _____.
19. In the past, the term _____ was used to describe milder, anxiety related disorders. However, the term is fading from use.
20. _____ is a legal term defining whether a person may be held responsible for his or her actions. Sanity is determined in court on the basis of testimony by expert witnesses.

● *What is a personality disorder?*

21. Personality disorders are deeply _____ maladaptive personality patterns.
22. The personality disorders are: antisocial, avoidant, borderline, _____, histrionic, narcissistic, obsessive-compulsive, _____, schizoid, and _____.
23. _____ persons (sociopaths) seem to lack a conscience. They are emotionally shallow and _____.

● *What problems result when a person suffers high levels of anxiety?*

24. Anxiety disorders, _____ disorders, and _____ disorders are characterized by high levels of anxiety, rigid defense mechanisms, and self-defeating behavior patterns.
25. The term nervous _____ has no formal meaning. However, people do experience _____ disorders, in which the person is overwhelmed by ongoing life stresses.

26. Anxiety disorders include _____ anxiety disorder (chronic anxiety and worry) and _____ disorder (anxiety attacks, panic, free-floating anxiety).

27. Panic disorder may occur with or without _____ (fear of public places or leaving the home).

28. Other anxiety disorders are _____ (fear of public places, _____ situations, or leaving the home) and specific phobia (irrational fears of specific objects or situations).

29. In the anxiety disorder called _____ _____, the person fears being observed, _____, embarrassed, or humiliated by others in social situations.

30. _____-compulsive disorders, and _____ stress disorder (PTSD) or _____ stress disorder (emotional disturbances triggered by severe stress) are also classified as anxiety disorders.

31. Dissociative disorders may take the form of dissociative _____ (loss of memory and personal identity) or dissociative _____ (confused identity and flight from familiar surroundings).

32. A more dramatic problem is dissociative _____ _____, in which a person develops multiple personalities.

33. _____ disorders center on physical complaints that mimic disease or disability.

34. In _____, persons think that they have specific diseases, when they are, in fact healthy.

35. In a _____ disorder, the person has numerous physical complaints. The person repeatedly seeks medical treatment for these complaints, but no organic problems can be found.

36. _____ _____ refers to discomfort for which there is no identifiable physical cause.

37. In _____ disorders, actual symptoms of disease or disability develop but their causes are actually psychological.

● *How do psychologists explain anxiety-based disorders?*

38. The _____ approach emphasizes unconscious conflicts within the personality as the cause of disabling anxiety.

39. The _____ approach emphasizes the effects of a faulty self-image.

40. The _____ approach emphasizes the effects of previous learning, particularly _____ learning.

41. Some patterns in anxiety disorders can be explained by the anxiety _____ hypothesis, which states that immediate relief from anxiety rewards _____ behaviors.

42. According to the _____ view, distorted thinking patterns cause anxiety disorders.

● *What are the general characteristics of psychotic disorders?*

43. _____ is a break in contact with _____.

44. Psychosis is marked by _____ (false beliefs), hallucinations, and _____ changes.

45. Other symptoms of psychosis are disturbed emotions, disturbed _____, and personality _____ .

46. An _____ psychosis is based on known injuries or diseases of the brain.

47. The most common organic problem is _____, a serious mental impairment in old age caused by deterioration of the brain.

48. One of most common causes of dementia is _____ disease.

● *How do delusional disorders differ from other forms of psychosis?*

49. A _____ of _____ disorder is based primarily on the presence of delusions.

50. Delusions may concern _____ (personal importance), persecution, infidelity, romantic attraction, or physical _____ .

51. The most common delusional disorder is _____ psychosis. Because they often have intense and irrational delusions of persecution, afflicted persons may be _____ if they believe they are threatened.

● *What forms does schizophrenia take? What causes it?*

52. Schizophrenia is distinguished by a split between thought and _____, and by delusions, hallucinations, and _____ difficulties.

53. _____ schizophrenia is marked by extreme personality _____ and silly, bizarre, or obscene behavior. Social impairment is usually extreme.

54. _____ schizophrenia is associated with stupor, mutism, waxy _____, and odd postures. Sometimes violent and agitated behavior also occurs.

55. In _____ schizophrenia (the most common type), outlandish delusions of _____ and persecution are coupled with psychotic symptoms and personality breakdown.

56. _____ schizophrenia is the term used to indicate a lack of clear-cut patterns of disturbance.

57. Current explanations of schizophrenia emphasize a combination of _____ stress, inherited susceptibility, and _____ abnormalities in the body or brain.

58. A number of _____ factors appear to increase the risk of developing schizophrenia. These include viral infection during the mother's pregnancy and birth complications.

59. Early _____ trauma and a disturbed family environment, especially one marked by _____ communication, also increase the risk of schizophrenia.

60. Studies of twins and other close relatives strongly support _____ as a major factor in schizophrenia.

61. Recent biochemical studies have focused on abnormalities in brain transmitter substances, especially glutamate, _____ and their _____ sites.

62. Additional abnormalities in brain structure or function have been detected in schizophrenic brains by the use of _____ scans, _____ scans, and _____ scans.

63. The dominant explanation of schizophrenia is the stress-_____ model.

● *What are mood disorders? What causes depression?*

64. Mood disorders primarily involve disturbances of _____ or emotion.
65. Long-lasting, though relatively moderate, depression is called a _____ disorder.
66. Chronic, though moderate, swings in mood between depression and elation are called a
_____ disorder.
67. In a _____ ____ disorder the person alternates between extreme _____ and
depression.
68. In a _____ ____ disorder the person is mostly depressed, but has had at least one episode
of _____ (mild mania).
69. The problem known as _____ _____ disorder involves extreme sadness and
despondency, but no evidence of mania.
70. _____ depression is a mild to moderate depressive disorder that affects many
women after they give birth. It is more serious than the more common maternity blues.
71. Major mood disorders more often appear to be _____ (produced from within) rather
than reactions to external events.
72. Seasonal _____ disorder (SAD), which occurs during the winter months, is another
common form of depression. SAD is typically treated with _____ (exposure to bright
light).
73. _____, psychoanalytic, _____, and behavioral theories of
depression have been proposed. Heredity is clearly a factor in susceptibility to mood disorders.
74. _____ is any psychological treatment for behavioral or emotional problems.
Major mental disorders are more often treated medically.

● *Why do people commit suicide? Can suicide be prevented?*

75. Suicide is _____ related to such factors as age, sex, and marital status.
76. Major _____ _____ for suicide include drug or alcohol abuse, a prior attempt,
depression, hopelessness, _____ behavior, suicide by relatives, shame, failure, or
rejection, and the availability of a firearm.
77. In individual cases the potential for suicide is best identified by a desire to escape, unbearable
psychological _____, _____ psychological needs, and a constriction of options.
78. Suicidal thoughts usually precede suicide _____, which progress to suicide
_____.
79. Suicide can often be prevented by the efforts of family, friends, and mental health professionals to
establish communication and _____ with the person, and by gaining day-by-day
_____ from her or him.

● *What does it mean to be "crazy"? What should be done about it?*

80. In Western law, the insanity defense evolved from the _____ rule.

81. Insanity is closely related to claims of _____ capacity (impaired ability to control actions) or claims that a person had an _____ impulse (uncontrollable urge to act).

82. Insanity is determined by courts of law, usually on the basis of testimony by _____ _____ .

83. _____ in applying the insanity defense have fueled debate about its validity.

84. Thomas Szasz has raised challenging questions about the nature of _____ behavior and its relationship to personal responsibility and _____ rights.

85. Szasz rejects the _____ model of mental illness that treats emotional problems as diseases with _____ that can be cured.

86. Public policies concerning treatment of the chronically _____ _____ continue to evolve as authorities try to strike a balance between providing help and taking away personal freedom.

MASTERY TEST

1. The difference between an acute stress disorder and PTSD is
   a. how long the disturbance lasts   b. the severity of the stress   c. whether the anxiety is free-floating
   d. whether dissociative behavior is observed

2. A person is at greatest risk of becoming schizophrenic if he or she has
   a. schizophrenic parents   b. a schizophrenic fraternal twin   c. a schizophrenic mother
   d. a schizophrenic sibling

3. A core feature of all abnormal behavior is that it is
   a. statistically extreme   b. associated with subjective discomfort   c. ultimately maladaptive
   d. marked by a loss of contact with reality

4. Excess amounts of dopamine in the brain, or high sensitivity to dopamine provides one major explanation for the problem known as
   a. PTSD   b. schizophrenia   c. major depression   d. SAD

5. The descriptions "acro," and "claustro," and "pyro" refer to
   a. common obsessions   b. specific phobias   c. free-floating anxieties   d. hypochondriasis

6. Glove anesthesia strongly implies the existence of a _____ disorder.
   a. organic   b. depersonalization   c. somatization   d. conversion

7. In the stress-vulnerability model of psychosis, vulnerability is primarily attributed to
   a. heredity   b. exposure to influenza   c. psychological trauma   d. disturbed family life

8. A patient believes that she has a mysterious disease that is causing her body to "rot away." What type of symptom is she suffering from?
   a. bipolar b. delusion c. neurosis d. cyclothymic

9. Phototherapy is used primarily to treat
   a. postseasonal depression b. SAD c. catatonic depression d. affective psychoses

10. Psychopathology is defined as an inability to behave in ways that
    a. foster personal growth and happiness b. match social norms c. lead to personal achievement
    d. do not cause anxiety

11. Which of the following is NOT characteristic of suicidal thinking?
    a. desires to escape b. psychological pain c. frustrated needs d. too many options

12. Fear of using the rest room in public is
    a. a social phobia b. an acute stress disorder c. a panic disorder d. an adjustment disorder

13. A person who displays personality disintegration, waxy flexibility, and delusions of persecution suffers
    from _____ schizophrenia.
    a. disorganized b. catatonic c. paranoid d. undifferentiated

14. You find yourself in an unfamiliar town and you can't remember your name or address. It is likely that
    you are suffering from
    a. paraphilia b. Alzherimer's disease c. a borderline personality disorder d. a dissociative disorder

15. A major problem with statistical definitions of abnormality is
    a. calculating the normal curve b. choosing dividing lines c. that they do not apply to groups of
    people d. that they do not take norms into account

16. DSM-IV-TR primarily describes and classifies _____ disorders.
    a. mental b. organic c. psychotic d. cognitive

17. A person who is a frequent "checker" may have which disorder?
    a. agoraphobia b. somatization c. free-floating fugue d. obsessive-compulsive

18. The most direct explanation for the anxiety reducing properties of self-defeating behavior is found in
    a. an overwhelmed ego b. avoidance learning c. the loss of meaning in one's life d. the concept of
    existential anxiety

19. A person with a(an) _____ personality disorder might be described as "charming" by
    people who don't know the person well.
    a. avoidant b. schizoid c. antisocial d. dependent

20. One of the most powerful situational contexts for judging the normality of behavior is
    a. culture b. gender c. statistical norms d. private discomfort

21. A person who is manic most likely suffers from a(an) _____ disorder.
    a. anxiety b. somatoform c. organic d. mood

22. The principal problem in paranoid psychosis is
    a. delusions b. hallucinations c. disturbed emotions d. personality disintegration

23. A problem that may occur with or without agoraphobia is
    a. dissociative disorder b. somatoform disorder c. panic disorder d. obsessive-compulsive disorder

24. Hearing voices that do not exist is an almost sure sign of a _____ disorder.
    a. psychotic b. dissociative c. personality d. delusional

25. A conversion reaction is a type of _____ disorder.
    a. somatoform b. dissociative c. obsessive-compulsive d. postpartum

26. The existence, in the past, of "disorders" such as "drapetomania" and "nymphomania" suggests that judging normality is greatly affected by
    a. gender b. cultural disapproval c. levels of functioning d. subjective discomfort

27. Which of the following terms does NOT belong with the others?
    a. neurosis b. somatoform disorder c. personality disorder d. dissociative disorder

28. Threats to one's self-image are a key element in the _____ approach to understanding anxiety and disordered functioning.
    a. Freudian b. humanistic c. existential d. behavioral

29. Which of the following is NOT classified as an anxiety disorder?
    a. adjustment disorder b. panic disorder c. agoraphobia d. obsessive-compulsive disorder

30. Cyclothymic disorder is most closely related to
    a. neurotic depression b. major depressive disorder c. bipolar disorder d. SAD

ANSWERS

Recite and Review

1. disorders, unhealthy
2. discomfort
3. high, low
4. standards
5. cultural
6. All
7. behavior, adapt
8. mental
9. *Manual, Mental*
10. reality, social
11. brain, diseases
12. mood, drugs
13. emotion
14. anxiety, anxiety
15. disease, cause
16. personality
17. personality
18. gender, sexual
19. anxiety
20. legal, court
21. maladaptive
22. borderline, compulsive
23. conscience, emotionally
24. anxiety, defense
25. life stresses
26. anxiety, floating
27. public, home
28. specific
29. observed, social
30. stress, anxiety
31. memory, dissociative
32. multiple
33. disease
34. healthy
35. physical, treatment
36. physical
37. psychological
38. unconscious
39. self-image
40. learning, learning
41. anxiety, relief
42. thinking
43. break

44. hallucinations
45. personality
46. diseases
47. organic, brain
48. dementia
49. delusions
50. persecution, romantic
51. persecution
52. split, thought
53. personality, Social
54. mutism, waxy
55. persecution
56. lack
57. stress, abnormalities
58. infection, birth
59. trauma, family
60. twins
61. transmitter
62. activity
63. stress
64. emotion
65. depression
66. depression, elation
67. depression
68. depressed, mania
69. mania
70. maternity blues
71. within, external
72. Seasonal, winter
73. behavioral
74. Major mental
75. Suicide
76. alcohol, drug, firearm
77. escape, options
78. thoughts
79. communication
80. insanity
81. capacity, impulse
82. testimony
83. validity
84. responsibility
85. diseases
86. freedom

Connections

1. f
2. a
3. g
4. j
5. b
6. c
7. i
8. d
9. e
10. h
11. c
12. e
13. a
14. j
15. b
16. d
17. i
18. f
19. h
20. g
21. h
22. i
23. g
24. a
25. j
26. b
27. d
28. f
29. c
30. e
31. c
32. e
33. h
34. a
35. j
36. g
37. i
38. b
39. f
40. d

Check Your Memory

1. T
2. F
3. T
4. T
5. T
6. T
7. T
8. F
9. F
10. T
11. F
12. F
13. F
14. T
15. F
16. T
17. F
18. T
19. F
20. F
21. F
22. T
23. T
24. T
25. F
26. F
27. T
28. T
29. T
30. T
31. F
32. T
33. F
34. F
35. T
36. T
37. T
38. F
39. F
40. F
41. T
42. F
43. T
44. F
45. T
46. F
47. T

48. T
49. T
50. F
51. T
22. T
53. F
54. T
55. F
56. T
57. T
58. T
59. T
60. F
61. T
62. F
63. T
64. T
65. F
66. T
67. F
68. T
69. T
70. T
71. F
72. T
73. T
74. F
75. T
76. T
77. T

Final Survey and Review

1. *Psychopathology*
2. subjective
3. Statistical
4. Social nonconformity
5. context
6. relative
7. maladaptive
8. psychological
9. *Diagnostic, Statistical*
10. Psychotic, hallucinations
11. Organic
12. Substance related
13. Mood, affect
14. Anxiety
15. Somatoform
16. Dissociative, amnesia
17. Personality
18. identity, dysfunctions
19. neurosis
20. Insanity
21. ingrained
22. dependent, paranoid, schizotypal
23. Antisocial, manipulative
24. dissociative, somatoform
25. breakdown, adjustment
26. generalized, panic
27. agoraphobia
28. agoraphobia, unfamiliar
29. social phobia, evaluated
30. Obsessive, posttraumatic, acute
31. amnesia, fugue
32. identity disorder
33. Somatoform
34. hypochondriasis
35. somatization
36. Somatoform pain
37. conversion
38. psychodynamic
39. humanistic
40. behavioral, avoidance
41. reduction, self-defeating
42. cognitive
43. Psychosis, reality
44. delusions, sensory
45. communication, disintegration
46. organic
47. dementia
48. Alzheimer's
49. diagnosis, delusional
50. grandeur, disease
51. paranoid, violent
52. emotion, communication
53. Disorganized, disintegration
54. Catatonic, flexibility
55. paranoid, grandeur
56. Undifferentiated
57. environmental, biochemical
58. environmental
59. psychological, deviant
60. heredity

61. dopamine, receptor
62. CT, MRI, PET
63. vulnerability
64. mood
65. dysthymic
66. cyclothymic
67. bipolar I, mania
68. bipolar II, hypomania
69. major depressive
70. postpartum
71. endogenous
72. affective, phototherapy
73. Biological, cognitive
74. Psychotherapy
75. statistically
76. risk factors, antisocial
77. pain, frustrated
78. threats, attempts
79. rapport, commitments
80. M'Naghten

81. diminished, irresistible
82. expert witnesses
83. Inconsistencies
85. abnormal, civil
85. medical, symptoms
86. mentally ill

Mastery Test

1. a (p. 600)
2. a (p. 611)
3. c (p. 589)
4. b (p. 612)
5. b (p. 599)
6. d (p. 602)
7. a (p. 614)
8. b (p. 605)
9. b (p. 617)
10. a (p. 587)
11. d (p. 621)
12. a (p. 599)
13. d (p. 608-610)
14. d (p. 601)
15. b (p. 588)
16. a (p. 591)
17. d (p. 600)
18. b (p. 604)
19. c (p. 596)
20. a (p. 588)
21. d (p. 592)
22. a (p. 607)
23. c (p. 598)
24. a (p. 605)
25. a (p. 602)
26. b (p. 589)
27. a (p. 593)
28. b (p. 603)
29. a (p. 598)
30. c (p. 615)

Chapter 17
Therapies

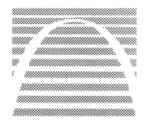

CHAPTER OVERVIEW

Psychotherapies may be classified as individual, group, insight, action, directive, nondirective, or supportive, and combinations of these. Primitive and superstitious approaches to mental illness have included trepanning and demonology. More humane treatment began in 1793 with the work of Philippe Pinel in Paris.

Freudian psychoanalysis seeks to release repressed thoughts and emotions from the unconscious. Brief psychodynamic therapy has largely replaced traditional psychoanalysis.

Client-centered (or person-centered) therapy is a nondirective humanistic technique dedicated to creating an atmosphere of growth. Existential therapies focus on the meaning of life choices. Gestalt therapy attempts to rebuild thinking, feeling, and acting into connected wholes.

Behavior therapists use behavior modification techniques such as aversion therapy, systematic desensitization, operant shaping, extinction, and token economies.

Cognitive therapists attempt to change troublesome thought patterns. In rational-emotive behavior therapy, clients learn to recognize and challenge their own irrational beliefs.

Group therapies, such as psychodrama and family therapy, may be based on individual therapy methods or special group techniques. Sensitivity groups, encounter groups, and large-group awareness trainings also try to promote constructive changes.

All psychotherapies offer a caring relationship, emotional rapport, a protected setting, catharsis, explanations for one's problems, a new perspective, and a chance to practice new behaviors. Many basic counseling skills underlie the success of therapies.

Three medical approaches to the treatment of psychological disorders are pharmacotherapy, electroconvulsive therapy, and psychosurgery.

Mental hospitalization can serve as a treatment for psychological disorders. Prolonged hospitalization has been discouraged by deinstitutionalization and by partial-hospitalization policies. Community mental health centers attempt to prevent mental health problems before they become serious.

Cognitive and behavioral techniques such as covert sensitization, thought stopping, covert reinforcement, and desensitization can aid self-management. In most communities, competent therapists can be located through public sources or by referrals.

Many cultural barriers to effective counseling and therapy have been identified. Aware therapists are beginning to seek out the knowledge and skills needed to intervene successfully in the lives of clients from diverse cultural backgrounds.

LEARNING OBJECTIVES

To demonstrate mastery of this chapter, you should be able to:

1. Define *psychotherapy*.
2. Describe each of the following approaches to therapy:

a. individual therapy   d. action therapy   g. time-limited therapy

b. group therapy   e. directive therapy   h. supportive therapy

c. insight therapy   f. nondirective therapy

3. Discuss what a person can expect as possible outcomes from psychotherapy.
4. Briefly describe the history of the treatment of psychological problems, including in your description trepanning, demonology, exorcism, ergotism, and Pinel.
5. Explain why the first formal psychotherapy was developed.
6. List the four basic techniques used in psychoanalysis and explain their purpose.
7. Name and describe the therapy that is frequently used today instead of psychoanalysis. Describe the criticism that helped prompt the switch, including the concept of spontaneous remission.
8. Contrast client-centered (humanistic) therapy and psychoanalysis.
9. Describe client-centered therapy including the four conditions that should be maintained for successful therapy.
10. Explain the approach of existential therapy and compare and contrast it with client-centered therapy. Name and describe one example of existential therapy, including its key aspect.
11. Briefly describe Gestalt therapy, including its main emphasis.
12. Discuss the limitations of media phone-in psychologists and describe what the APA recommends should be the extent of their activities.
13. Discuss the advantages and disadvantages of telephone therapy, cybertherapy, and videoconferencing therapy.
14. Contrast the goal of behavior therapy with the goal of insight therapies.
15. Define *behavior modification* and state its basic assumption.
16. Explain the relationship of aversion therapy to classical conditioning.
17. Describe aversion therapy and explain how it can be used to stop smoking and drinking.
18. Explain how relaxation, reciprocal inhibition, and use of a hierarchy are combined to produce systematic desensitization.
19. State what desensitization is used for and give an example of desensitization therapy or vicarious desensitization therapy.
20. Explain how virtual reality exposure may be used to treat phobias.
21. Very briefly describe eye-movement desensitization and reprocessing.
22. List and briefly describe the seven operant principles most frequently used by behavior therapists.

23. Explain how nonreinforcement and time out can be used to bring about extinction of a maladaptive behavior.

24. Describe a token economy including its advantages and possible disadvantages. Include the terms *token* and *target behavior* in your description.

25. Describe what sets cognitive therapists apart from behavior therapists.

26. List and describe three thinking errors that underlie depression and explain what can be done to correct such thinking.

27. Describe the effectiveness of cognitive therapy for depression.

28. Describe rational-emotive behavior therapy. List the three core ideas that serve as the basis of most irrational beliefs.

29. Describe the advantages of group therapy.

30. Briefly describe each of the following group therapies:
   a. psychodrama (include role-playing, role reversal, and the mirror technique)
   b. family therapy
   c. group awareness training (include sensitivity groups, encounter groups, and large group awareness training)

31. Evaluate the effectiveness of encounter groups and sensitivity groups. Include the concept of the therapy placebo effect.

32. Discuss the effectiveness of psychotherapy. Describe the rate at which doses of therapy help people improve.

33. List the eight goals of psychotherapy, and state the four means used to accomplish the goals.

34. List ten characteristics of effective therapists.

35. List and briefly describe the nine points or tips that can help a person when counseling a friend.

36. List the three main types of somatic therapy.

37. Define *pharmacotherapy*. Discuss the advantages and disadvantages of the use of pharmacotherapy in the treatment of psychosis.

38. List the three major classes of drugs used in pharmacotherapy, including their effects and the types of disorders for which they are each most useful.

39. Describe the risk-benefit controversy for drugs such as Clozaril and Risperdal.

40. Briefly describe the risks associated with self-medication with herbal extracts.

41. Describe the advantages and disadvantages of electroconvulsive therapy. Include a discussion of how the ECT debate is resolved.

42. Describe the past and current uses of psychosurgery in the treatment of psychosis. Include a description of prefrontal lobotomy and deep lesioning techniques.

43. Describe the role of hospitalization and partial hospitalization in the treatment of psychological disorders.

44. Explain what deinstitutionalization is and how halfway houses have attempted to help in the treatment of mental health.

45. Discuss the role of community mental health centers in mental health.

The following objectives are related to the material in the "Psychology in Action" and "A Step Beyond" sections of your text.

46. Describe how covert sensitization, thought-stopping, and covert reinforcement can be used to reduce unwanted behavior.

47. Give an example of how you can overcome a common fear or break a bad habit using the steps given for desensitization.

48. List and describe four indicators that may signal the need for professional psychological help.

49. List six methods a person can use for finding a therapist.

50. Describe how one can choose a psychotherapist. Include the concepts of paraprofessionals, peer counselors, and self-help groups.

51. Summarize what is known about the importance of the personal qualities of the therapist and the client for successful therapy.

52. List six psychotherapy danger signals.

53. List the four main cultural barriers to effective counseling discussed by Sue and Sue.

54. List and explain the seven characteristics of culturally skilled counselors.

RECITE AND REVIEW

● *How do psychotherapies differ? How did modern therapies originate?*

Recite and Review: Pages 628-632

1. Psychotherapy is any psychological technique used to facilitate _____ changes in a person's personality, _____, or adjustment.

2. _____ therapies seek to produce personal understanding. Action therapies try to directly change troublesome thoughts, feelings, or behaviors.

3. Directive therapists provide strong _____. Nondirective therapists assist, but do not _____ their clients.

4. Supportive therapies provide on-going support, rather than actively promoting personal _____.

5. Therapies may be conducted either individually or in groups, and they may be _____ limited (restricted to a set number of sessions).

6. Primitive approaches to mental illness were often based on _____.

7. Trepanning involved boring a hole in the _____.

8. Demonology attributed mental disturbance to supernatural forces and prescribed _____ as the cure.

9. In some instances, the actual cause of bizarre behavior may have been ergotism or _____ fungus _____.

10. More humane treatment began in 1793 with the work of Philippe Pinel who created the first _____ _____ in Paris.

● *Is Freudian psychoanalysis still used?*

Recite and Review: Pages 632-633

11. Sigmund Freud's psychoanalysis was the first formal _____.

12. Psychoanalysis was designed to treat cases of hysteria (physical symptoms without known _____ causes).

13. Psychoanalysis seeks to release repressed thoughts, memories, and emotions from the _____ and resolve _____ conflicts.

14. The psychoanalyst uses _____ association, _____ analysis, and analysis of resistance and transference to reveal health-producing insights.

15. Some critics have argued that traditional psychoanalysis may frequently receive credit for _____ remissions of symptoms. However, psychoanalysis has been shown to be better than no treatment at all.

16. _____ psychodynamic therapy (which relies on psychoanalytic theory but is brief and focused) is as effective as other major therapies.

● *What are the major humanistic therapies?*

Recite and Review: Pages 633-637

17. _____ therapies try to help people live up to their potentials and to give tendencies for mental health to emerge.

18. Carl Rogers' client-centered (or _____-centered) therapy is nondirective and is dedicated to creating an atmosphere of _____.

19. In client-centered therapy, unconditional _____ regard, _____ (feeling what another is feeling), authenticity, and reflection are combined to give the client a chance to solve his or her own problems.

20. Existential therapies focus on the end result of the _____ one makes in life.

21. Clients in existential therapy are encouraged through confrontation and encounter to exercise free _____, to take responsibility for their _____, and to find _____ in their lives.

22. Frederick Perls' Gestalt therapy emphasizes immediate _____ of thoughts and feelings.

23. The goal of Gestalt therapy is to rebuild thinking, feeling, and acting into connected _____ and to help clients break through emotional blocks.

24. Media psychologists, such as those found on the radio, are supposed to restrict themselves to _____ listeners, rather than actually doing _____.

25. Telephone therapists and cybertherapists working on the _____ may or may not be competent. Even if they are, their effectiveness may be severely limited.

26. In an emerging approach called telehealth, _____ is being done at a distance, through the use of videoconferencing (two-way _____ links).

● *What is behavior therapy?*

Recite and Review: Pages 637-639

27. Behavior therapists use various behavior modification techniques that apply _____ principles to change human behavior.
28. Classical conditioning is a basic form of _____ in which existing reflex responses are _____ with new conditioned stimuli.
29. In aversion therapy, classical conditioning is used to associate maladaptive behavior with _____ or other aversive events in order to inhibit undesirable responses.
30. To be most effective, aversive _____ must be response-contingent (closely connected with responses).

● *How is behavior therapy used to treat phobias, fears, and anxieties?*

Recite and Review: Pages 639-642

31. Classical conditioning also underlies _____ desensitization, a technique used to reduce fears, phobias, and anxieties.
32. In desensitization, gradual _____ and reciprocal inhibition break the link between fear and particular situations.
33. Typical steps in desensitization are: Construct a fear hierarchy; learn to produce total _____; and perform items on the hierarchy (from least to most disturbing).
34. Desensitization may be carried out in real settings or it may be done by vividly _____ scenes from the fear hierarchy.
35. Desensitization is also effective when it is administered vicariously; that is, when clients watch _____ perform the feared responses.
36. In a newly developed technique, virtual _____ exposure is used to present _____ stimuli to patients undergoing desensitization.
37. Another new technique called eye-movement desensitization shows promise as a treatment for traumatic _____ and _____ disorders.

● *What role does reinforcement play in behavior therapy?*

Recite and Review: Pages 642-644

38. Behavior modification also makes use of operant principles, such as positive reinforcement, nonreinforcement, extinction, punishment, shaping, stimulus _____, and _____ out.
39. Nonreward can extinguish troublesome behaviors. Often this is done by simply identifying and eliminating _____.
40. Time out is an extinction technique in which attention and approval are withheld following undesirable _____.
41. Time out can also be done by _____ a person from the setting in which misbehavior occurs, so that it will not be reinforced.
42. To apply positive reinforcement and operant shaping, symbolic rewards known as tokens are often used. Tokens allow _____ reinforcement of selected target _____.
43. Full-scale use of _____ in an institutional setting produces a token economy.

44. Toward the end of a token economy program, patients are shifted to social rewards such as recognition and _____.

● Can therapy change thoughts and emotions?

Recite and Review: Pages 644-646

45. Cognitive therapy emphasizes changing _____ patterns that underlie emotional or behavioral problems.

46. The goals of cognitive therapy are to correct distorted thinking and/or teach improved coping _____.

47. Aron Beck's cognitive therapy for depression corrects major distortions in thinking, including _____ perception, overgeneralization, and all-or-nothing _____.

48. In a variation of cognitive therapy called rational-emotive behavior therapy (REBT), clients learn to recognize and challenge their own irrational _____, which lead to upsetting consequences.

● Can psychotherapy be done with groups of people?

Recite and Review: Pages 647-648

49. Group therapy may be a simple extension of _____ methods or it may be based on techniques developed specifically for groups.

50. In psychodrama, individuals use _____ playing, _____ reversals, and the mirror technique to gain insight into incidents resembling their real-life problems.

51. In family therapy, the family group is treated as a _____ so that the entire _____ system is changed for the better.

52. Although they are not literally _____, sensitivity groups and encounter groups attempt to encourage positive personality change.

53. In recent years, commercially offered large-group awareness _____ have become popular.

54. The therapeutic benefits of large-group techniques are questionable and may reflect nothing more than a _____ placebo effect.

● What do various therapies have in common?

Recite and Review: Pages 649-652

55. To alleviate personal problems, all psychotherapies offer a caring relationship and _____ rapport in a protected _____.

56. All therapies encourage catharsis and they provide explanations for the client's _____.

57. In addition, psychotherapy provides a new perspective and a chance to practice new _____.

58. Many basic _____ skills are used in therapy. These include listening actively and helping to clarify the problem.

59. Effective therapists also focus on feelings and avoid giving unwanted _____.

60. It helps to accept the person's perspective, to reflect thoughts and feelings, and to be patient during _____.

61. In counseling it is important to use _____ questions when possible and to maintain confidentiality.

● *How do psychiatrists treat psychological disorders?*

Recite and Review: Pages 652-655

62. Three _____ (bodily) approaches to treatment of psychosis are pharmacotherapy (use of _____), electroconvulsive therapy (ECT) (brain shock for the treatment of depression), and psychosurgery (surgical alteration of the _____).

63. Pharmacotherapy is done with _____ tranquilizers (anti-anxiety drugs), antipsychotics (which reduce delusions and _____), and antidepressants (_____ elevators).

64. All psychiatric drugs involve a trade-off between _____ and benefits.

65. _____ hospitalization is considered a form of treatment for mental disorders.

66. Prolonged hospitalization has been discouraged by deinstitutionalization (reduced use of commitment to treat mental disorders) and by _____-hospitalization policies.

67. Half-way _____ within the community can help people make the transition from a hospital or institution to _____ living.

68. Community mental health centers were created to help avoid or minimize _____.

69. Community mental health centers also have as their goal the prevention of mental health problems through education, consultation, and _____ intervention.

● *How are behavioral principles applied to everyday problems? How would a person go about finding professional help?*

Recite and Review: PSYCHOLOGY IN ACTION

70. In covert sensitization, aversive _____ are used to discourage unwanted behavior.

71. Thought stopping uses mild _____ to prevent upsetting thoughts.

72. Covert reinforcement is a way to encourage desired _____ by mental rehearsal.

73. Desensitization pairs _____ with a hierarchy of upsetting images in order to lessen fears.

74. In most communities, a competent and reputable therapist can usually be located through public sources of information or by a _____.

75. Practical considerations such as _____ and qualifications enter into choosing a therapist. However, the therapist's personal characteristics are of equal importance.

76. Self-help _____, made up of people who share similar problems, can sometimes add valuable support to professional treatment.

● *Do cultural differences affect counseling and psychotherapy?*

Recite and Review: A STEP BEYOND

77. Many _____ barriers to effective counseling and therapy exist.
78. Culturally skilled _____ have the knowledge and skills needed to intervene successfully in the lives of clients from diverse cultural backgrounds.
79. The culturally skilled counselor must be able to establish rapport with a person from a _____ cultural background and adapt traditional theories and techniques to meet the needs of clients from non-European ethnic or racial groups.

CONNECTIONS

1. _____	trepanning	a. tainted rye
2. _____	exorcism	b. old relationships
3. _____	ergotism	c. hysteria
4. _____	Pinel	d. reflection
5. _____	Freud	e. waiting list control
6. _____	dream analysis	f. client-centered
7. _____	transference	g. Bicêtre
8. _____	spontaneous remission	h. latent content
9. _____	Rogers	i. possession
10. _____	rephrasing	j. release of evil spirits

11. _____	authenticity	a. telehealth
12. _____	existentialist	b. operant extinction
13. _____	distance therapy	c. no facades
14. _____	Gestalt therapy	d. thinking error
15. _____	rapid smoking	e. being in the world
16. _____	desensitization	f. token economy
17. _____	time out	g. whole experiences
18. _____	target behaviors	h. aversion therapy
19. _____	overgeneralization	i. irrational beliefs
20. _____	REBT	j. fear hierarchy

21. _____	psychodrama	a. public education
22. _____	family therapy	b. enhanced self-awareness
23. _____	sensitivity group	c. emotional release
24. _____	encounter group	d. positive imagery
25. _____	media psychologist	e. shared problems
26. _____	therapeutic alliance	f. systems approach
27. _____	catharsis	g. aversive imagery
28. _____	covert sensitization	h. role reversals
29. _____	covert reinforcement	i. caring relationship
30. _____	self-help group	j. intense interactions

CHECK YOUR MEMORY

Check Your Memory: Pages 628-632

1. A particular psychotherapy could be both insight- and action-oriented. T or F?
2. With the help of psychotherapy, chances of improvement are fairly good for phobias and low self-esteem. T or F?
3. Psychotherapy is sometimes used to encourage personal growth for people who are already functioning well. T or F?
4. Personal autonomy, a sense of identity, and feelings of personal worth are elements of mental health. T or F?
5. Trepanning was really an excuse to kill people since none of the patients survived. T or F?
6. Exorcism sometimes took the form of physical torture. T or F?
7. Trepanning was the most common treatment for ergotism. T or F?
8. Pinel was the first person to successfully treat ergotism. T or F?
9. The problem Freud called hysteria is now called a somatoform disorder. T or F?

Check Your Memory: Pages 632-633

10. During free association, patients try to remember the earliest events in their lives. T or F?
11. Freud called transference "the royal road to the unconscious." T or F?
12. The manifest content of a dream is its surface or visible meaning. T or F?
13. In an analysis of resistance, the psychoanalyst tries to understand a client's resistance to forming satisfying relationships. T or F?
14. Therapists use direct interviewing as part of brief psychodynamic therapy. T or F?
15. If members of a waiting list control group improve at the same rate as people in therapy, it demonstrates that the therapy is effective. T or F?

Check Your Memory: Pages 633-637

16. Through client-centered therapy, Carl Rogers sought to explore unconscious thoughts and feelings. T or F?

17. The client-centered therapist does not hesitate to react with shock, dismay, or disapproval to a client's inappropriate thoughts or feelings. T or F?

18. In a sense, the person-centered therapist acts as a psychological mirror for clients. T or F?

19. Existential therapy emphasizes our ability to freely make choices. T or F?

20. According to the existentialists, our choices must be courageous. T or F?

21. Existential therapy emphasizes the integration of fragmented experiences into connected wholes. T or F?

22. Fritz Perls was an originator of telehealth. T or F?

23. Gestalt therapy may be done individually or in a group. T or F?

24. Gestalt therapists urge clients to intellectualize their feelings. T or F?

25. The APA suggests that media psychologists should discuss only problems of a general nature. T or F?

26. The problem with doing therapy by videoconferencing is that facial expressions are not available to the therapist or the client. T or F?

Check Your Memory: Pages 637-639

27. Aversion therapy is based primarily on operant conditioning. T or F?

28. For many children, the sight of a hypodermic needle becomes a conditioned stimulus for fear because it is often followed by pain. T or F?

29. Rapid smoking creates an aversion because people must hyperventilate to smoke at the prescribed rate. T or F?

30. About one half of all people who quit smoking begin again. T or F?

31. In aversion therapy for alcohol abuse, the delivery of shock must appear to be response-contingent to be most effective. T or F?

32. Poor generalization of conditioned aversions to situations outside of therapy can be a problem. T or F?

Check Your Memory: Pages 639-642

33. During desensitization, the steps of a hierarchy are used to produce deep relaxation. T or F?

34. Relaxation is the key ingredient of reciprocal inhibition. T or F?

35. Clients typically begin with the most disturbing item in a desensitization hierarchy. T or F?

36. Desensitization is most effective when people are directly exposed to feared stimuli. T or F?

37. Live or filmed models are used in vicarious desensitization. T or F?

38. During eye-movement desensitization, clients concentrate on pleasant, calming images. T or F?

Check Your Memory: Pages 642-644

39. Operant punishment is basically the same thing as nonreinforcement. T or F?

40. Shaping involves reinforcing ever closer approximations to a desired response. T or F?

41. An undesirable response can be extinguished by reversing stimulus control. T or F?

42. Misbehavior tends to decrease when others ignore it. T or F?

43. To be effective, tokens must be tangible rewards, such as slips of paper or poker chips. T or F?

44. The value of tokens is based on the fact that they can be exchanged for other reinforcers. T or F?

45. A goal of token economies is to eventually switch patients to social reinforcers.

Check Your Memory: Pages 644-646

46. Cognitive therapy is especially successful in treating depression. T or F?
47. Depressed persons tend to magnify the importance of events. T or F?
48. Cognitive therapy is as effective as drugs for treating many cases of depression. T or F?
49. Stress inoculation is a form of rational-emotive behavior therapy. T or F?
50. The A in the ABC analysis of REBT stands for "anticipation." T or F?
51. The C in the ABC analysis of REBT stands for "consequence." T or F?

Check Your Memory: Pages 647-648

52. The mirror technique is the principal method used in family therapy. T or F?
53. Family therapists try to meet with the entire family unit during each session of therapy. T or F?
54. A "trust walk" is a typical sensitivity group exercise. T or F?
55. Sensitivity groups attempt to tear down defenses and false fronts. T or F?
56. Large-group awareness training has been known to create emotional crises where none existed before. T or F?

Check Your Memory: Pages 649-652

57. Half of all people who begin psychotherapy feel better after 8 sessions. T or F?
58. Emotional rapport is a key feature of the therapeutic alliance. T or F?
59. Therapy gives clients a chance to practice new behaviors. T or F?
60. Regarding the future of psychotherapy, experts predict that the use of psychoanalysis will increase. T or F?
61. Regarding the future of psychotherapy, experts predict that there will be an increase in the use of short-term therapy. T or F?
62. Competent counselors do not hesitate to criticize clients, place blame when it is deserved, and probe painful topics. T or F?
63. "Why don't you . . . Yes, but . . ." is a common game used to avoid taking responsibility in therapy. T or F?
64. Closed questions tend to be most helpful in counseling another person. T or F?

Check Your Memory: Pages 652-655

65. Major mental disorders are primarily treated with psychotherapy. T or F?
66. When used for long periods of time, major tranquilizers can cause a neurological disorder. T or F?
67. Two percent of all patients taking clozaril suffer from a serious blood disease. T or F?
68. ECT treatments are usually given in a series of 20 to 30 sessions, occurring once a day. T or F?
69. ECT is most effective when used to treat depression. T or F?
70. The prefrontal lobotomy is the most commonly performed type of psychosurgery today. T or F?
71. Psychosurgeries performed by deep lesioning can be reversed if necessary. T or F?
72. In the approach known as partial hospitalization, patients live at home. T or F?
73. Deinstitutionalization increased the number of homeless persons living in many communities. T or F?
74. Most half-way houses are located on the grounds of mental hospitals. T or F?
75. Crisis intervention is typically one of the services provided by community mental health centers. T or F?

Check Your Memory: PSYCHOLOGY IN ACTION

76. Disgusting images are used in thought stopping. T or F?
77. To do covert sensitization, you must first learn relaxation exercises. T or F?
78. Covert reinforcement should be visualized before performing steps in a fear hierarchy. T or F?
79. The tension-release method is used to produce deep relaxation. T or F?
80. Significant changes in your work, relationships, or use of drugs or alcohol can be signs that you should seek professional help. T or F?
81. Marital problems are the most common reason for seeing a mental health professional. T or F?
82. For some problems, paraprofessional counselors and self-help groups are as effective as professional psychotherapy. T or F?
83. All major types of psychotherapy are about equally successful. T or F?

Check Your Memory: A STEP BEYOND

84. Cultural barriers to effective counseling include differences in language, social class, and nonverbal communication. T or F?
85. A necessary step toward becoming a culturally skilled counselor is to adopt the culture of your clients as your own. T or F?
86. Multicultural counselors must be aware of their clients' degree of acculturation. T or F?
87. Cultural barriers to successful counseling include differences in age, sexual orientation, handicaps, and religion. T or F?

FINAL SURVEY AND REVIEW

● *How do psychotherapies differ? How did modern therapies originate?*

1. _____ is any psychological technique used to facilitate positive changes in a person's _____, behavior, or adjustment.
2. Insight therapies seek to produce personal understanding. _____ therapies try to directly change troublesome thoughts, feelings, or behaviors.
3. _____ therapists provide strong guidance. _____ therapists assist, but do not guide their clients.
4. _____ therapies provide on-going assistance, rather than actively promoting personal change.
5. Therapies may be conducted either _____ or in _____, and they may be time _____ (restricted to a set number of sessions).
6. _____ approaches to mental illness were often based on superstition.
7. _____ involved boring a hole in the skull.
8. _____ attributed mental disturbance to supernatural forces and prescribed exorcism as the cure.
9. In some instances, the actual cause of bizarre behavior may have been _____, a type of _____ poisoning.

10. More humane treatment began in 1793 with the work of Philippe _____ who created the first mental hospital in _____ .

● *Is Freudian psychoanalysis still used?*

11. Sigmund _____ _____ was the first formal psychotherapy.

12. Psychoanalysis was designed to treat cases of _____ (physical symptoms without known physical causes).

13. Psychoanalysis seeks to release _____ thoughts, memories, and emotions from the unconscious and resolve unconscious conflicts.

14. The psychoanalyst uses free _____, dream analysis, and analysis of _____ and transference to reveal health-producing insights.

15. Some critics have argued that traditional psychoanalysis may frequently receive credit for spontaneous _____ of symptoms. However, psychoanalysis has been shown to be better than no treatment at all.

16. Brief _____ therapy (which relies on _____ theory but is brief and focused) is as effective as other major therapies.

● *What are the major humanistic therapies?*

17. Humanistic therapies try to help people live up to their _____ and to give tendencies for mental health to emerge.

18. Carl _____ client-centered (or person-centered) therapy is _____ and is dedicated to creating an atmosphere of growth.

19. In client-centered therapy, _____ positive regard, empathy, authenticity, and _____ (restating thoughts and feelings) are combined to give the client a chance to solve his or her own problems.

20. _____ therapies focus on the end result of the choices one makes in life.

21. Clients in existential therapy are encouraged through _____ and _____ to exercise free will, to take responsibility for their choices, and to find meaning in their lives.

22. Frederick Perls' _____ therapy emphasizes immediate awareness of thoughts and feelings.

23. The goal of Perls' approach is to rebuild thinking, feeling, and acting into connected wholes and to help clients break through _____ _____ .

24. _____ psychologists, such as those found on the radio, are supposed to restrict themselves to educating listeners, rather than actually doing therapy.

25. Telephone therapists and _____ working on the Internet may or may not be competent. Even if they are, their effectiveness may be severely limited.

26. In an emerging approach called _____, therapy is being done at a distance, through the use of _____ (two-way audio-video links).

● *What is behavior therapy?*

27. _____ therapists use various behavior _____ techniques that apply learning principles to change human behavior.

28. _____ conditioning is a basic form of learning in which existing _____ responses are associated with new conditioned stimuli.

29. In _____ therapy, classical conditioning is used to associate maladaptive behavior with pain or other unpleasant events in order to inhibit undesirable responses.

30. To be most effective, aversive stimuli must be _____ (closely connected with responses).

● *How is behavior therapy used to treat phobias, fears, and anxieties?*

31. Classical conditioning also underlies systematic _____, a technique used to reduce fears, phobias, and anxieties.

32. In this approach, gradual adaptation and reciprocal _____ break the link between fear and particular situations.

33. Typical steps are: Construct a fear _____; learn to produce total relaxation; and perform items on the _____ (from least to most disturbing).

34. Desensitization may be carried out in real settings or it may be done by vividly imagining scenes from the _____ _____.

35. Desensitization is also effective when it is administered _____; that is, when clients watch models perform the feared responses.

36. In a newly developed technique, _____ reality _____ is used to present fear stimuli to patients undergoing desensitization.

37. Another new technique called _____ desensitization shows promise as a treatment for traumatic memories and stress disorders.

● *What role does reinforcement play in behavior therapy?*

38. Behavior modification also makes use of _____ principles, such as positive reinforcement, nonreinforcement, _____ (eliminating responses), punishment, _____ (molding responses), stimulus control, and time out.

39. _____ can extinguish troublesome behaviors. Often this is done by simply identifying and eliminating reinforcers.

40. Time out is an _____ technique in which attention and approval are withheld following undesirable responses.

41. Time out can also be done by removing a person from the _____ in which misbehavior occurs, so that it will not be _____.

42. To apply positive reinforcement and operant shaping, symbolic rewards known as _____ are often used. These allow immediate reinforcement of selected _____ behaviors.

43. Full-scale use of symbolic rewards in an institutional setting produces a _____ _____.

44. Toward the end of such programs, patients are shifted to _____ rewards such as recognition and approval.

● *Can therapy change thoughts and emotions?*

45. _____ therapy emphasizes changing thinking patterns that underlie emotional or behavioral problems.

46. Its goals are to correct distorted thinking and/or teach improved _____ skills.

47. Aron _____ therapy for depression corrects major distortions in thinking, including selective perception, _____ , and all-or-nothing thinking.

48. In a variation called _____ _____ therapy (REBT), clients learn to recognize and challenge their own irrational beliefs that lead to upsetting consequences.

● *Can psychotherapy be done with groups of people?*

49. _____ therapy may be a simple extension of individual methods or it may be based on techniques developed specifically for _____.

50. In _____, individuals use role playing, role _____, and the mirror technique to gain insight into incidents resembling real-life problems.

51. In _____ therapy, the _____ group is treated as a unit so that the entire family system is changed for the better.

52. Although they are not literally psychotherapies, sensitivity groups and _____ groups attempt to encourage positive personality change.

53. In recent years, commercially offered large-group _____ trainings have become popular.

54. The therapeutic benefits of large-group techniques are questionable and may reflect nothing more than a therapy _____ effect.

● *What do various therapies have in common?*

55. To alleviate personal problems, all psychotherapies offer a caring relationship and emotional _____ in a _____ setting.

56. All therapies encourage _____ (emotional release) and they provide explanations for the client's problems.

57. In addition, psychotherapy provides a new _____ and a chance to practice new behaviors.

58. Many basic counseling skills are used in therapy. These include listening _____ and helping to _____ the problem.

59. Effective therapists also focus on _____ and avoid giving unwanted advice.

60. It helps to accept the person's _____, to _____ thoughts and feelings, and to be patient during silences.

61. In counseling it is important to use open questions when possible and to maintain _____.

● *How do psychiatrists treat psychological disorders?*

62. Three somatic approaches to treatment of psychosis are _____ (use of drugs), _____ therapy (ECT), and psychosurgery.

63. Pharmacotherapy is done with minor tranquilizers (anti-anxiety drugs), _____ (which control delusions and hallucinations), and _____ (mood elevators).

64. All psychiatric drugs involve a trade-off between risks and _____.

65. Psychiatric _____ is considered a form of treatment for mental _____.

66. Prolonged hospitalization has been discouraged by _____ (reduced use of commitment to treat mental disorders) and by partial-hospitalization policies.

67. _____ houses within the community can help people make the transition from a hospital or institution to independent living.

68. _____ _____ health centers were created to help avoid or minimize hospitalization.

69. These centers also have as their goal the _____ of mental health problems through education, consultation, and crisis _____.

● *How are behavioral principles applied to everyday problems?*

70. In _____ sensitization, aversive images are used to discourage unwanted behavior.

71. _____ _____ uses mild punishment to prevent upsetting thoughts.

72. Covert _____ is a way to encourage desired responses by mental rehearsal.

73. _____ pairs relaxation with a hierarchy of upsetting images in order to lessen fears.

● *How would a person go about finding professional help?*

74. In most communities, a _____ and reputable therapist can usually be located through public sources of information or by a referral.

75. Practical considerations such as cost and qualifications enter into choosing a therapist. However, the therapist's _____ _____ are of equal importance.

76. _____ groups made up of people who share similar _____ can sometimes add valuable support to professional treatment.

● *Do cultural differences affect counseling and psychotherapy?*

77. Many cultural _____ to effective counseling and therapy exist.

78. _____ _____ counselors have the knowledge and skills needed to intervene successfully in the lives of clients from diverse cultural backgrounds.

79. The aware counselor must be able to establish _____ with a person from a different cultural background and _____ traditional theories and techniques to meet the needs of clients from non-European ethnic or racial groups.

MASTERY TEST

1. To demonstrate that spontaneous remissions are occurring, you could use a
   a. patient-defined hierarchy   b. waiting list control group   c. target behavior group
   d. short-term dynamic correlation

2. In desensitization, relaxation is induced to block fear, a process known as
   a. systematic adaptation   b. vicarious opposition   c. stimulus control   d. reciprocal inhibition

3. Role reversals and the mirror technique are methods of
   a. psychodrama   b. person-centered therapy   c. family therapy   d. brief psychodynamic therapy

4. One thing that both trepanning and exorcism have in common is that both were used
   a. to treat ergotism   b. by Pinel in the Bicêtre Asylum   c. to remove spirits
   d. to treat cases of hysteria

5. Unconditional positive regard is a concept particularly associated with
   a. Beck   b. Frankl   c. Perls   d. Rogers

6. Many of the claimed benefits of large-group awareness trainings appear to represent a therapy
   _____ effect.
   a. remission   b. education   c. placebo   d. transference

7. Personal change is LEAST likely to be the goal of
   a. supportive therapy   b. action therapy   c. desensitization   d. humanistic therapy

8. Inducing seizures is a standard part of using
   a. Gestalt therapy   b. antidepressants   c. ECT   d. cybertherapy

9. Which counseling behavior does not belong with the others listed here?
   a. paraphrasing   b. judging   c. reflecting   d. active listening

10. In psychoanalysis, the process most directly opposite to free association is
    a. resistance   b. transference   c. symbolization   d. remission

11. Identification of target behaviors is an important step in designing
    a. a desensitization hierarchy   b. activating stimuli   c. token economies   d. encounter groups

12. A person who wants to lose weight looks at a dessert and visualizes maggots crawling all over it. The person is obviously using
    a. systematic adaptation   b. covert sensitization   c. stress inoculation   d. systematic desensitization

13. Which of the following is NOT a humanistic therapy?
    a. client-centered   b. Gestalt   c. existential   d. cognitive

14. Not many emergency room doctors drive without using their seatbelts. This observation helps explain the effectiveness of
a. systematic desensitization b. aversion therapy c. covert reinforcement d. the mirror technique

15. Telephone counselors have little chance of using which element of effective psychotherapy?
a. empathy b. nondirective reflection c. the therapeutic alliance d. accepting the person's frame of reference

16. Which of the following is a self-management technique?
a. thought stopping b. vicarious reality exposure c. REBT d. EMDR

17. A good example of a nondirective insight therapy is _____ therapy.
a. client-centered b. Gestalt c. psychoanalytic d. brief psychodynamic

18. Which statement about psychotherapy is true?
a. Most therapists are equally successful. b. Most techniques are equally successful.
c. Therapists and clients need not agree about the goals of therapy. d. Effective therapists instruct their clients not to discuss their therapy with anyone else.

19. Analysis of resistances and transferences is a standard feature of
a. client-centered therapy b. Gestalt therapy c. REBT d. psychoanalysis

20. Both classical and operant conditioning are the basis for
a. desensitization b. token economies c. behavior therapy d. aversion therapy

21. Rational-emotive behavior therapy is best described as
a. insight, nondirective, individual b. insight, supportive, individual c. action, supportive, group
d. action, directive, individual

22. Deep lesioning is a form of
a. ECT b. psychosurgery c. pharmacotherapy d. PET

23. Identifying and removing rewards is a behavioral technique designed to bring about
a. operant shaping b. extinction c. respondent aversion d. token inhibition

24. Culturally skilled counselors must be aware of their own cultural backgrounds, as well as
a. the percentage of ethnic populations in the community b. that of their clients c. the importance of maintaining confidentiality d. the life goals of minorities

25. A behavioral therapist would treat acrophobia with
a. desensitization b. aversion therapy c. covert sensitization d. cybertherapy

26. Which technique most closely relates to the idea of nondirective therapy?
a. confrontation b. dream analysis c. role reversal d. reflection

27. Fifty percent of psychotherapy patients say they feel better after the first _____ sessions.
    a. 4   b. 8   c. 12   d. 20

28. Overgeneralization is a thinking error that contributes to
    a. depression   b. somatization   c. phobias   d. emotional reprocessing

29. Death, freedom, and meaning are special concerns of
    a. REBT   b. cognitive therapy   c. existential therapy   d. psychodrama

30. An intense awareness of present experience and breaking through emotional impasses is the heart of
    a. action therapy   b. Gestalt therapy   c. time-limited therapy   d. REBT

31. The ABCs of REBT stand for
    a. anticipation, behavior, conduct   b. action, behavior, conflict   c. activating experience,
    belief, consequence   d. anticipation, belief, congruent experience

32. Which of the following in NOT a "distance therapy"?
    a. REBT   b. telephone therapy   c. cybertherapy   d. telehealth

33. Virtual reality exposure is a type of
    a. psychodrama   b. ECT therapy   c. cognitive therapy   d. desensitization

34. ECT is most often used to treat
    a. psychosis   b. anxiety   c. hysteria   d. depression

35. Which of the following is most often associated with community mental health programs?
    a. pharmacotherapy   b. covert reinforcement   c. crisis intervention   d. REBT

ANSWERS

Recite and Review

1. positive, behavior
2. Insight
3. guidance, guide
4. change
5. time
6. superstition
7. skull
8. exorcism
9. ergot, poisoning
10. mental hospital
11. psychotherapy
12. physical
13. unconscious, unconscious
14. free, dream
15. spontaneous
16. Brief
17. Humanistic
18. person, growth
19. positive, empathy
20. choices
21. will, choices, meaning
22. awareness
23. wholes
24. educating, therapy
25. Internet
26. therapy, audio-video
27. learning
28. learning, associated

29. pain
30. stimuli
31. systematic
32. adaptation
33. relaxation
34. imagining
35. models
36. reality, fear
37. memories, stress
38. control, time
39. reinforcers
40. responses
41. removing
42. immediate, behaviors
43. tokens
44. approval
45. thinking
46. skills
47. selective, thinking
48. beliefs
49. individual
50. role, role
51. unit, family
52. psychotherapies
53. trainings
54. therapy
55. emotional, setting
56. problems
57. behaviors
58. counseling
59. advice
60. silences
61. open
62. somatic, drugs, brain
63. minor, hallucinations, mood
64. risks
65. Mental or Psychiatric
66. partial
67. houses, independent
68. hospitalization
69. crisis
70. images
71. punishment
72. responses
73. relaxation
74. referral
75. cost (or fees)
76. groups

77. cultural
78. counselors
79. different

Connections

1. j
2. i
3. a
4. g
5. c
6. h
7. b
8. e
9. f
10. d
11. c
12. e
13. a
14. g
15. h
16. j
17. b
18. f
19. d
20. i
21. h
22. f
23. b
24. j
25. a
26. i
27. c
28. g
29. d
30. e

Check Your Memory

1. T
2. T
3. T
4. T
5. F
6. T
7. F
8. F

9. T
10. F
11. F
12. T
13. F
14. T
15. F
16. F
17. F
18. T
19. T
20. T
21. F
22. F
23. T
24. F
25. T
26. F
27. F
28. T
29. F
30. T
31. T
32. T
33. F
34. T
35. F
36. T
37. T
38. F
39. F
40. T
41. F
42. T
43. F
44. T
45. T
46. T
47. T
48. T
49. F
50. F
51. T
52. F
53. F
54. T
55. F
56. T
57. T

58. T
59. T
60. F
61. T
62. F
63. T
64. F
65. F
66. T
67. T
68. F
69. T
70. F
71. F
72. T
73. T
74. F
75. T
76. F
77. F
78. F
79. T
80. T
81. F
82. T
83. T
84. T
85. F
86. T
87. T

Final Survey and Review

1. Psychotherapy, personality
2. Action
3. Directive, Nondirective
4. Supportive
5. individually, groups, limited
6. Primitive
7. Trepanning
8. Demonology
9. ergotism, fungus
10. Pinel, Paris
11. Freud's, psychoanalysis
12. hysteria
13. repressed
14. association, resistance
15. remissions
16. psychodynamic, psychoanalytic
17. potentials
18. Rogers', nondirective
19. unconditional, reflection
20. Existential
21. confrontation, encounter
22. Gestalt
23. emotional blocks
24. Media
25. cybertherapists
26. telehealth, videoconferencing
27. Behavior, modification
28. Classical, reflex
29. aversion
30. response-contingent
31. desensitization
32. inhibition
33. hierarchy, hierarchy
34. fear hierarchy
35. vicariously
36. virtual, exposure
37. eye-movement
38. operant, extinction, shaping
39. Nonreward (or nonreinforcement)
40. extinction
41. setting, reinforced
42. tokens, target
43. token economy
44. social
45. Cognitive
46. coping
47. Beck's, overgeneralization
48. rational-emotive behavior
49. Group, groups
50. psychodrama, reversals
51. family, family
52. encounter
53. awareness
54. placebo
55. rapport, protected
56. catharsis
57. perspective
58. actively, clarify
59. feelings
60. perspective, reflect
61. confidentiality
62. pharmacotherapy, electroconvulsive
63. antipsychotics, antidepressants
64. benefits
65. hospitalization, disorders
66. deinstitutionalization
67. Half-way
68. Community mental
69. prevention, intervention
70. covert
71. Thought stopping
72. reinforcement
73. Desensitization
74. competent
75. personal characteristics
76. Self-help, problems
77. barriers
78. Culturally skilled
79. rapport, adapt

Mastery Test

1. b (p. 633)
2. d (p. 639)
3. a (p. 647)
4. c (p. 630-631)
5. d (p. 634)
6. c (p. 648)
7. a (p. 630)
8. c (p. 652)
9. b (p. 650)
10. a (p. 632)
11. c (p. 643)
12. b (p. 657)
13. d (p. 634-635)
14. b (p. 638)
15. c (p. 636. 649)
16. a (p. 657)
17. a (p. 634)
18. b (p. 660)
19. d (p. 632)
20. c (p. 638)
21. d (p. 629, 645)
22. b (p. 653)
23. b (p. 642)
24. b (p. 662)

25. a (p. 639)

26. d (p. 634)

27. b (p. 649)

28. a (p. 645)

29. c (p. 635)

30. b (p. 635)

31. c (p. 645)

32. a (p. 636-637)

33. d (p. 641)

34. d (p. 653)

35. c (p. 655)

Chapter 18
Social Behavior

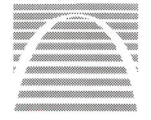

CHAPTER OVERVIEW

Social psychology is the study of individual behavior in social situations. Social roles, status, group structure, norms, and group cohesiveness influence interpersonal behavior.

Attribution theory summarizes how we make inferences about behavior. The fundamental attributional error is to ascribe the actions of others to internal causes. Because of an actor-observer bias, we tend to attribute our own behavior to external causes.

The need to affiliate is related to needs for approval, support, friendship, information, and desires to reduce anxiety or uncertainty. Social comparison theory holds that we affiliate to evaluate our actions, feelings, and abilities. Interpersonal attraction is increased by physical proximity, frequent contact, physical attractiveness, competence, and similarity. Self-disclosure, which follows a reciprocity norm, occurs more when two people like one another. According to social exchange theory, we tend to maintain relationships that are profitable. Romantic love can be distinguished from liking by the use of attitude scales. Adult love relationships tend to mirror patterns of emotional attachment observed in infancy and early childhood. Evolutionary psychology attributes human mating patterns to the reproductive challenges faced by men and women since the dawn of time.

Social influence refers to alterations in behavior brought about by the behavior of others. Examples are conformity, groupthink, and obedience to authority. Social influence is also related to five types of social power: reward power, coercive power, legitimate power, referent power, and expert power. Compliance with direct requests is another means by which behavior is influenced.

Self-assertion, as opposed to aggression, involves clearly stating one's wants and needs to others. Learning to be assertive is accomplished by role-playing, rehearsing assertive actions, overlearning, and use of specific techniques, such as the "broken record."

A social trap is a social situation in which immediately rewarded actions have undesired effects in the long run.

LEARNING OBJECTIVES

To demonstrate mastery of this chapter you should be able to:

1. Define *social psychology*.
2. Define the following terms:

    a. culture   b. social roles   c. ascribed role
    d. achieved role   e. role conflict   f. group structure
    g. group cohesiveness   h. status   i. norm

3. Explain how norms are formed using the idea of the autokinetic effect.

4. Define *personal space* and *proxemics*.

5. List and describe the four basic interpersonal zones and describe the nature of the interactions that occur in each.

6. Define *attribution* and state the difference between external and internal causes.

7. Explain how the consistency and distinctiveness of a person's behavior affects the attributions others make about the person. Include six other factors affecting attribution.

8. Explain how self-handicapping protects a person who has a fragile self-image.

9. Explain what the fundamental attribution error is. Include the concept of the actor-observer bias in making attributions.

10. State the needs that appear to be satisfied by affiliation and describe research indicating humans have a need to affiliate.

11. Describe social comparison theory.

12. List and describe the factors that affect interpersonal attraction. Include a description of homogamy.

13. Explain self-disclosure and discuss the effects of varying degrees of disclosure on interpersonal relationships. Explain the difference in gendered friendships.

14. Describe the social exchange theory as it relates to interpersonal relationships.

15. Describe Rubin's studies of romantic love. Discuss the differences between loving and liking and between male and female friendships (including the term *mutual absorption* and the three different love/attachment styles).

16. Define the term *evolutionary psychology* and describe how it explains the different mating preferences of males and females.

17. State the meaning of *social influence*.

18. Describe Asch's experiment on conformity.

19. Define *groupthink* and explain how it may contribute to poor decision-making.

20. Describe six ways to prevent groupthink.

21. Explain how group sanctions and unanimity affect conformity.

22. List and describe the five sources of social power.

23. Describe Milgram's study of obedience.

24. Identify the factors that affect the degree of obedience.

25. Explain how compliance differs from simple conformity.

26. Describe the following methods of gaining compliance:
    a. foot-in-the-door   b. door-in-the-face   c. low-ball technique

27. Describe the research that deals with passive compliance and briefly explain how it applies to everyday behavior.

The following objectives are related to the material in the "Psychology in Action" and "A Step Beyond" sections of your text.

28. Describe assertiveness training, including the concept of self-assertion and contrasting it with aggression.

29. Describe how a person can learn to be more assertive using rehearsal, role playing, overlearning, and the broken record technique.

30. Explain what social traps, collective social traps, and the tragedy of the commons are. Explain how they can be avoided or escaped.

RECITE AND REVIEW

● *How does group membership affect individual behavior?*

Recite and Review: Pages 666-669

1. Social psychology studies how individuals behave, think, and feel in _____ situations.

2. Culture provides a broad social context for our behavior. One's position in _____ defines a variety of roles to be played.

3. _____ _____, which may be achieved or ascribed, are particular behavior patterns associated with social positions.

4. When two or more _____ roles are held, role conflict may occur.

5. The Stanford _____ experiment showed that destructive roles may override individual motives for behavior.

6. Positions within _____ typically carry higher or lower levels of status. High status is associated with special privileges and respect.

7. Group structure refers to the organization of _____, communication pathways, and power within a group.

8. Group cohesiveness is basically the degree of _____ among group members.

9. Norms are _____ of conduct enforced (formally or informally) by _____.

10. The autokinetic effect (the illusion of _____ in a stationary light in a darkened room) has been used to demonstrate that norms rapidly form even in _____ groups.

● *What unspoken rules govern the use of personal space?*

Recite and Review: Pages 669-671

11. The study of _____ _____ is called proxemics.

12. Four basic spatial zones around each person's body are intimate distance (0-18 inches), _____ distance (1.5-4 feet), _____ distance (4-12 feet), and public distance (12 feet or more).

13. Norms for the use of personal space vary considerably in various _____.

● *How do we perceive the motives of others, and the causes of our own behavior?*

Recite and Review: Pages 671-673

14. Attribution theory is concerned with how we make inferences about the _____ of behavior.
15. Behavior can be attributed to internal _____ or external _____.
16. To infer _____ we take into account the _____, the object of the action, and the setting in which the action occurs.
17. The _____ of behavior on different occasions and its distinctiveness (whether it occurs only in certain circumstances) affect the attributions we make.
18. Situational demands tend to cause us to discount _____ causes as explanations of someone's behavior.
19. Consensus in behavior (in which many people act alike) implies that their behavior has an _____ cause.
20. The fundamental attributional _____ is to ascribe the actions of others to _____ causes. This is part of the actor-observer bias, in which we ascribe the behavior of others to _____ causes, and our own behavior to _____ causes.
21. Self-handicapping involves arranging excuses for poor _____ as a way to protect your self-image or self-esteem.

● *Why do people affiliate?*

Recite and Review: Pages 674-675

22. The need to affiliate is tied to needs for _____, support, friendship, and _____.
23. Additionally, research indicates that we sometimes affiliate to _____ anxiety and uncertainty.
24. Social comparison theory holds that we affiliate to _____ our actions, feelings, and abilities.
25. Social _____ are also made for purposes of self-protection and self-enhancement.
26. Downward _____ are sometimes used to make us feel better when faced with a threat. Upward _____ may be used for self-improvement.

● *What factors influence interpersonal attraction?*

Recite and Review: Pages 675-681

27. Interpersonal attraction is increased by physical proximity (_____) and frequent _____.
28. Initial acquaintance and _____ are influenced by physical attractiveness (beauty), competence (high ability), and _____ (being alike).
29. A large degree of _____ on many dimensions is characteristic of _____ selection, a pattern called homogamy.
30. Self-disclosure (_____ oneself to others) occurs to a greater degree if two people like one another.

31. Self-disclosure follows a reciprocity _____: Low levels of self-disclosure are met with low levels in return, whereas moderate self-disclosure elicits more personal replies.

32. Overdisclosure tends to inhibit _____ by others.

33. According to social exchange theory, we tend to maintain relationships that are profitable; that is, those for which perceived _____ exceed perceived _____.

34. Romantic love can be distinguished from liking by the use of attitude scales. Dating couples _____ and _____ their partners but only _____ their friends.

35. Romantic love is also associated with greater _____ absorption between people.

36. Adult _____ relationships tend to mirror patterns of emotional attachment observed in infancy and early childhood.

37. _____, avoidant, and ambivalent patterns can be defined on the basis of how a person approaches romantic and affectionate relationships with others.

38. Evolutionary psychology attributes human _____ patterns to the differing reproductive challenges faced by men and women since the dawn of time.

● *What have social psychologists learned about conformity, social power, obedience, and compliance?*

Recite and Review: Pages 681-689

39. Social influence refers to alterations in _____ brought about by the behavior of _____.

40. Conformity to group pressure is a familiar example of social influence. Virtually everyone _____ to a variety of broad social and cultural _____.

41. Conformity pressures also exist within small _____. The famous Asch experiments demonstrated that various _____ sanctions encourage conformity.

42. Groupthink refers to compulsive conformity in group _____ _____. Victims of groupthink seek to maintain each other's approval, even at the cost of critical thinking.

43. Social influence is also related to five types of _____ _____: reward power, coercive power, legitimate power, referent power, and expert power.

44. Obedience to _____ has been investigated in a variety of experiments, particularly those by Stanley Milgram.

45. _____ in Milgram's studies decreased when the victim was in the same room, when the victim and subject were face to face, when the authority figure was absent, and when others refused to obey.

46. Compliance with direct _____ by a person who has little or no social _____ is another means by which behavior is influenced.

47. Three strategies for inducing compliance are the _____-in-the-door technique, the door-in-the-_____ approach, and the low-ball technique.

48. Recent research suggests that in addition to excessive obedience to _____, many people show a surprising passive compliance to unreasonable _____.

● *How does self-assertion differ from aggression?*

Recite and Review: PSYCHOLOGY IN ACTION

49. Self-assertion involves clearly stating one's _____ and _____ to others.
50. Aggression expresses one's feelings and desires, but it _____ others.
51. Non-assertive behavior is self-_____ and inhibited.
52. Learning to be _____ is accomplished by role-playing and rehearsing assertive actions.
53. Self-assertion is also aided by overlearning (practice that _____ after initial mastery of a skill) and use of specific techniques, such as the "broken record" (_____ a request until it is acknowledged).

● *What is a social trap?*

Recite and Review: A STEP BEYOND

54. A social trap is a social situation in which immediately rewarded actions have _____ effects in the long run.
55. One prominent social trap occurs when limited public _____ are overused, a problem called the tragedy of the commons.

CONNECTIONS

1. _____	culture	a.	privilege and importance
2. _____	ascribed role	b.	rule or standard
3. _____	achieved role	c.	0-18 inches
4. _____	status	d.	way of life
5. _____	cohesiveness	e.	self-moving
6. _____	norm	f.	12 feet plus
7. _____	autokinetic	g.	use of space
8. _____	proxemics	h.	1.5-4 feet
9. _____	intimate distance	i.	assigned role
10. _____	personal distance	j.	4-12 feet
11. _____	social distance	k.	degree of attraction
12. _____	public distance	l.	voluntary role

13. _____	attribution	a. relating self to others
14. _____	self-handicapping	b. honest expression
15. _____	need to affiliate	c. following authority
16. _____	social comparison	d. generalized impression
17. _____	social exchange	e. yielding to requests
18. _____	halo effect	f. rewards and punishments
19. _____	conformity	g. delayed harm
20. _____	group sanctions	h. desire to associate
21. _____	obedience	i. matching behavior
22. _____	compliance	j. impairing performance
23. _____	assertiveness	k. rewards minus costs
24. _____	social trap	l. social inference

CHECK YOUR MEMORY

Check Your Memory: Pages 666-669

1. The average number of first-name acquaintance links needed to connect two widely separated strangers is about 70 people. T or F?
2. Language and marriage customs are elements of culture. T or F?
3. *Son, husband,* and *teacher* are achieved roles. T or F?
4. The Stanford prison experiment investigated the impact of the roles "prisoner" and "guard." T or F?
5. Persons of higher status are more likely to touch persons of lower status than the reverse. T or F?
6. Women are more likely to touch men than men are to touch women. T or F?
7. A group could have a high degree of structure but low cohesiveness. T or F?
8. The more trash that is visible in public places, the more likely people are to litter. T or F?
9. An autokinetic light appears to move about the same distance for everyone who observes it. T or F?

Check Your Memory: Pages 669-671

10. Most people show signs of discomfort when someone else enters their personal space without permission. T or F?
11. The Dutch sit closer together when talking than the English do. T or F?
12. Social distance basically keeps people within arm's reach. T or F?
13. Formal interactions tend to take place in the 4 to 12 foot range. T or F?

Check Your Memory: Pages 671-673

14. The deliberateness of another person's behavior affects the attributions we make about it. T or F?
15. If someone always salts her food before eating, it implies that her behavior has an external cause. T or F?

16. Situational demands lead us to discount claims that a person's behavior is externally caused. T or F?
17. A strong consensus in the behavior of many people implies that their behavior is externally caused. T or F?
18. Getting drunk is a common form of self-handicapping. T or F?
19. Attributing the actions of others to external causes is the most common attributional error. T or F?
20. Good performances by women are more often attributed to luck than skill. T or F?

Check Your Memory: Pages 674-675

21. The need to affiliate is a basic human characteristic. T or F?
22. People who are frightened prefer to be with others who are in similar circumstances. T or F?
23. Social comparisons are used to confirm objective evaluations and measurements. T or F?
24. Useful social comparisons are usually made with persons similar to ourselves. T or F?
25. Some social comparisons are made for self-protection. T or F?
26. Downward social comparisons are typically made for self-improvement. T or F?

Check Your Memory: Pages 675-681

27. Nearness has a powerful impact on forming friendships. T or F?
28. Physical proximity leads us to think of people as competent, and therefore worth knowing. T or F?
29. The halo effect is the tendency to generalize a positive or negative first impression to other personal characteristics. T or F?
30. Physical attractiveness is closely associated with intelligence, talents, and abilities. T or F?
31. Physical attractiveness has more influence on women's fates than men's. T or F?
32. The risk of divorce is higher than average for couples who have large differences in age and education. T or F?
33. In choosing mates, women rank physical attractiveness as the most important feature. T or F?
34. Self-disclosure is a major step toward friendship. T or F?
35. Overdisclosure tends to elicit maximum self-disclosure from others. T or F?
36. Male friendships tend to be activity-based; women's friendships tend to be based on shared feelings and confidences. T or F?
37. The personal standard used to judge the acceptability of a social exchange is called the comparison level. T or F?
38. The statement, "I find it easy to ignore _____'s faults" is an item on the Liking Scale. T or F?
39. People with an avoidant attachment style tend to form relationships that are marked by mixed emotions. T or F?
40. Where their mates are concerned, men tend to be more jealous over a loss of emotional commitment than they are over sexual infidelities. T or F?

Check Your Memory: Pages 681-689

41. Conformity situations occur when a person becomes aware of differences between his or her own behavior and that of a group. T or F?
42. Most subjects in the Asch conformity experiments suspected that they were being deceived in some way. T or F?

43. Seventy-five percent of Asch's subjects yielded to the group at least once. T or F?

44. People who are anxious are more likely to conform to group pressure. T or F?

45. Groupthink is more likely to occur when people emphasize the task at hand, rather than the bonds between group members. T or F?

46. Rejection, ridicule, and disapproval are group norms that tend to enforce conformity. T or F?

47. A unanimous majority of 3 is more powerful than a majority of 8 with 1 person dissenting. T or F?

48. If you identify with a particular person, that person has referent power with respect to your behavior. T or F?

49. Milgram's famous shock experiment was done to study compliance and conformity. T or F?

50. Over half of Milgram's "teachers" went all the way to the maximum shock level. T or F?

51. Being face-to-face with the "learner" had no effect on the number of subjects who obeyed in the Milgram experiments. T or F?

52. People are less likely to obey an unjust authority if they have seen others disobey. T or F?

53. The foot-in-the-door effect is a way to gain compliance from another person. T or F?

54. The low-ball technique involves changing the terms that a person has agreed to, so that they are less desirable from the person's point of view. T or F?

Check Your Memory: PSYCHOLOGY IN ACTION

55. Many people have difficulty asserting themselves because they have learned to be obedient and "good." T or F?

56. Self-assertion involves the rights to request, reject, and retaliate. T or F?

57. Aggression does not take into account the rights of others. T or F?

58. Overlearning tends to lead to aggressive responses. T or F?

59. In order to be assertive, you should never admit that you were wrong. T or F?

60. If someone insults you, an assertive response should include getting the person to accept responsibility for his or her aggression. T or F?

Check Your Memory: A STEP BEYOND

61. Panic during a theater fire is an example of a social trap. T or F?

62. In social traps, behavior that seems to make sense from an individual point of view ends up doing harm to the group. T or F?

63. Under-use of natural resources is called the tragedy of the commodities. T or F?

64. In a social trap, people are more likely to restrain their own behavior if they believe others will too. T or F?

FINAL SURVEY AND REVIEW

● *How does group membership affect individual behavior?*

1. _____ _____ studies how individuals behave, think, and feel in social situations.

2. _____ provides a broad social context for our behavior. One's position in groups defines a variety of _____ to be played.

3. Social roles, which may be _____ or _____, are particular behavior patterns associated with social positions.

4. When two or more contradictory roles are held, role _____ may occur.

5. The _____ prison experiment showed that destructive _____ may override individual motives for behavior.

6. Positions within groups typically carry higher or lower levels of _____. _____ is associated with special privileges and respect.

7. Group _____ refers to the organization of roles, _____ pathways, and power within a group.

8. Group _____ is basically the degree of attraction among group members.

9. _____ are standards of conduct enforced (formally or informally) by groups.

10. The _____ effect (the illusion of movement in a _____ light in a darkened room) has been used to demonstrate that _____ rapidly form even in temporary groups.

● *What unspoken rules govern the use of personal space?*

11. The study of personal space is called _____.

12. Four basic spatial zones around each person's body are _____ distance (0-18 inches), personal distance (1.5-4 feet), social distance (4-12 feet), and _____ distance (12 feet or more).

13. _____ for the use of personal space vary considerably in various cultures.

● *How do we perceive the motives of others and the causes of our own behavior?*

14. _____ theory is concerned with how we make inferences about the causes of behavior.

15. Behavior can be attributed to _____ causes or _____ causes.

16. To infer causes we take into account the actor, the _____ of the action, and the _____ in which the action occurs.

17. The consistency of behavior on different occasions and its _____ (whether it occurs only in certain circumstances) affect the attributions we make.

18. _____ demands tend to cause us to _____ (downgrade) internal causes as explanations of someone's behavior.

19. _____ in behavior (in which many people act alike) implies that their behavior has an external cause.

20. The _____ _____ error is to ascribe the actions of others to internal causes. This is part of an _____ bias, in which we ascribe the behavior of others to internal causes, and our own behavior to external causes.

21. _____ involves arranging excuses for poor performance as a way to protect your self-image or self-esteem.

● *Why do people affiliate?*

22. The _____ to _____ is tied to additional needs for approval, support, friendship, and information.

23. Additionally, research indicates that we sometimes affiliate to reduce _____ and uncertainty.

24. Social _____ theory holds that we affiliate to evaluate our actions, feelings, and abilities.

25. Social comparisons are also made for purposes of self-_____ and self-enhancement.

26. _____ comparisons are sometimes used to make us feel better when faced with a threat. _____ comparisons may be used for self-improvement.

● *What factors influence interpersonal attraction?*

27. Interpersonal attraction is increased by physical _____ (nearness) and frequent contact.

28. Initial acquaintance and attraction are influenced by _____ attractiveness (beauty), _____ (high ability), and similarity.

29. A large degree of similarity on many dimensions is characteristic of mate selection, a pattern called _____.

30. _____ (revealing oneself to others) occurs to a greater degree if two people like one another.

31. Self-disclosure follows a _____ norm: Low levels of self-disclosure are met with low levels in return, whereas moderate self-disclosure elicits more personal replies.

32. _____ (excessive) tends to inhibit self-disclosure by others.

33. According to social _____ theory, we tend to maintain relationships that are _____; that is, those for which perceived rewards exceed perceived costs.

34. Romantic love can be distinguished from liking by the use of _____ _____. Dating couples love and like their partners but only like their friends.

35. Romantic love is also associated with greater mutual _____ between people.

36. Adult love relationships tend to mirror patterns of emotional _____ observed in infancy and early childhood.

37. Secure, _____ (noncommittal), and _____ (conflicted) patterns can be defined on the basis of how a person approaches romantic and affectionate relationships with others.

38. _____ psychology attributes human mating patterns to the differing _____ challenges faced by men and women since the dawn of time.

● *What have social psychologists learned about conformity, social power, obedience, and compliance?*

39. _____ _____ refers to alterations in behavior brought about by the behavior of others.

40. _____ to group pressure is a familiar example of social influence. Virtually everyone conforms to a variety of broad social and _____ norms.

41. Conformity pressures also exist within small groups. The famous _____ experiments demonstrated that various group _____ encourage conformity.

42. _____ refers to compulsive conformity in group decision making. Its victims seek to maintain each other's _____, even at the cost of critical thinking.

43. Social influence is also related to five types of social power: _____ power, _____ power (based on an ability to punish), legitimate power, referent power, and expert power.

44. _____ to authority has been investigated in a variety of experiments, particularly those by Stanley _____.

45. Obedience in his studies _____ when the victim was in the same room, when the victim and subject were face to face, when the _____ figure was absent, and when others refused to obey.

46. _____ with direct requests by a person who has little or no social power is another means by which behavior is influenced.

47. Three strategies for getting people to comply are the foot-in-the-_____ technique, the _____-in-the-face approach, and the _____ technique.

48. Recent research suggests that in addition to excessive obedience to authority, many people show a surprising _____ compliance to unreasonable requests.

● *How does self-assertion differ from aggression?*

49. _____ involves clearly stating one's wants and needs to others.

50. _____ expresses one's feelings and desires, but it hurts others.

51. _____ behavior is self-denying and inhibited.

52. Learning to be assertive is accomplished by _____ and rehearsing assertive actions.

53. Self-assertion is also aided by _____ (practice that continues after initial mastery of a skill) and use of specific techniques, such as the _____ _____ (repeating a request until it is acknowledged).

● *What is a social trap?*

54. A social trap is a social situation in which _____ _____ actions have undesired effects in the long run.

55. One prominent social trap occurs when limited public resources are _____, a problem called the _____ of the _____.

MASTERY TEST

1. Homogamy is directly related to which element of interpersonal attraction?
   a. competence   b. similarity   c. beauty   d. proximity

2. Being an agent of an accepted social order is the basis for _____ power.
   a. coercive   b. legitimate   c. referent   d. compliant

3. Suspicion and reduced attraction are associated with
   a. reciprocity   b. self-disclosure   c. competence and proximity   d. overdisclosure

4. We expect people to be respectful and polite at funerals because of
   a. situational demands   b. the door-in-the-face effect   c. attributional discounting
   d. self-handicapping

5. Conflicting feelings of anger, affection, doubt, and attraction are characteristic of what attachment style?
   a. avoidant   b. ambivalent   c. compliant   d. kinetic

6. Which of the following is an assertiveness technique?
   a. foot-in-the-door   b. calm absorption   c. door-in-the-face   d. broken record

7. Using social comparison for self-protection typically involves
   a. external attributions   b. comparisons with group norms   c. downward comparisons
   d. comparison with a person of higher ability

8. "President of the United States" is
   a. an ascribed role   b. an achieved role   c. a structural norm   d. a cohesive role

9. Where attribution is concerned, wants, needs, motives, or personal characteristics are perceived as
   a. external causes   b. situational attributions   c. discounted causes   d. internal causes

10. Asch is to _____ experiments as Milgram is to _____ experiments.
    a. compliance, assertion   b. conformity, obedience   c. autokinetic, social power
    d. groupthink, authority

11. Social psychology is the scientific study of how people
    a. behave in the presence of others   b. form into groups and organizations   c. form and maintain
    interpersonal relationships   d. make inferences about the behavior of others

12. "A person who first agrees with a small request is later more likely to comply with a larger demand."
    This summarizes the
    a. low-ball technique   b. set-the-hook technique   c. door-in-the-face effect   d. foot-in-the-door effect

13. Large desks in business offices almost ensure that interactions with others take place at
    a. ascribed distance b. social distance c. personal distance d. public distance

14. Comparison level is an important concept in
    a. social comparison theory b. social exchange theory c. evolutionary psychology
    d. social compliance theory

15. The _____ is a classic social trap.
    a. error of misattribution b. compulsion for unanimity c. tragedy of the commons
    d. downward comparison dilemma

16. Group structure involves all but one of the following elements. Which does NOT belong?
    a. roles b. communication pathways c. allocation of power d. social comparisons

17. A "guard" in the Stanford prison experiment who discovers that one of the "prisoners" is a friend would very likely experience
    a. role conflict b. a change in status c. groupthink d. a shift to coercive power

18. Groupthink is a type of _____ that applies to decision making in groups.
    a. conformity b. social comparison c. social power d. obedience

19. If procrastinating on school assignments helps protect your self-image, you have used procrastination as a type of
    a. double standard b. attributional error c. self-handicapping d. situational demand

20. When two people view an autokinetic light at the same time, their estimates of movement
    a. polarize b. normalize c. cohere d. converge

21. In Milgram's studies, the smallest percentage of subjects followed orders when
    a. the teacher and learner were in the same room b. the teacher received orders by phone
    c. the teacher and learner were face to face d. the experiment was conducted off campus

22. The most basic attributional error is to attribute the behavior of others to _____ causes, even when they are caused by _____ causes.
    a. inconsistent, consistent b. internal, external c. random, distinctive d. situational, personal

23. In an experiment, most women waiting to receive a shock preferred to wait with others who
    a. were about to be shocked b. did not share their fears c. were trained to calm them
    d. had been shocked the day before

24. Evolutionary theories attribute mate selection, in part, to the _____ of past generations.
    a. food-gathering habits b. tribal customs c. maternal instincts d. reproductive success

25. The "what is beautiful is good" stereotype typically does NOT include the assumption that physically attractive people are more
    a. likable b. intelligent c. honest d. mentally healthy

26. Which of the following gives special privileges to a member of a group?
    a. convergent norms b. high cohesiveness c. actor-observer bias d. high status

27. When situational demands are strong we tend to discount _____ causes as a way of explaining another person's behavior.
    a. public b. internal c. legitimate d. external

28. When we are subjected to conformity pressures, the _____ of a majority is more important the number of people in it.
    a. unanimity b. cohesion c. proximity d. comparison level

29. Distressed couples tend to _____ their partner's actions to negative motives.
    a. discount b. compare c. coerce d. attribute

30. Which of the following factors does NOT increase interpersonal attraction?
    a. competence b. overdisclosure c. proximity d. similarity

ANSWERS

Recite and Review

1. social
2. groups
3. Social roles
4. contradictory
5. prison
6. groups
7. roles
8. attraction
9. standards, groups
10. movement, temporary
11. personal space
12. personal, social
13. cultures
14. causes
15. causes, causes
16. causes, actor
17. consistency
18. internal
19. external
20. error, internal, internal, external
21. performance
22. approval, information
23. reduce
24. evaluate
25. comparisons
26. comparisons, comparisons
27. nearness, contact
28. attraction, similarity
29. similarity, mate
30. revealing
31. norm
32. self-disclosure
33. rewards, costs
34. like, love, like
35. mutual
36. love
37. Secure
38. mating
39. behavior, others
40. conforms, norms
41. groups, group
42. decision making
43. social power
44. authority
45. Obedience
46. requests, power
47. foot, face
48. authority, requests
49. wants, needs
50. hurts
51. denying
52. assertive
53. continues, repeating
54. undesired

55. resources

Connections

1. d
2. i
3. l
4. a
5. k
6. b
7. e
8. g
9. c
10. h
11. j
12. f
13. l
14. j
15. h
16. a
17. k
18. d
19. i
20. f
21. c
22. e
23. b
24. g

Check Your Memory

1. F
2. T
3. F
4. T
5. T
6. F
7. T
8. T
9. F
10. T
11. F
12. F
13. F
14. F
15. F
16. F
17. T
18. T
19. F
20. T
21. T
22. T
23. F
24. T
25. T
26. F
27. T
28. F
29. T
30. F
31. T
32. T
33. F
34. T
35. F
36. T
37. T
38. F
39. F
40. F
41. T
42. F
43. T
44. T
45. F
46. F
47. T
48. T
49. F
50. T
51. F
52. T
53. T
54. T
55. T
56. F
57. T
58. F
59. F
60. T
61. T
62. T
63. F
64. T

Final Survey and Review

1. Social psychology
2. Culture, roles
3. achieved, ascribed
4. conflict
5. Stanford, roles
6. status, High status
7. structure, communication
8. cohesiveness
9. Norms
10. autokinetic, stationary, norms
11. proxemics
12. intimate, public
13. Norms
14. Attribution
15. internal, external
16. object, setting
17. distinctiveness
18. Situational, discount
19. Consensus
20. fundamental attributional, actor-observer
21. Self-handicapping
22. need, affiliate
23. anxiety
24. comparison
25. protection
26. Downward, Upward
27. proximity
28. physical, competence
29. homogamy
30. Self-disclosure
31. reciprocity
32. Overdisclosure
33. exchange, profitable
34. attitude scales
35. absorption
36. attachment
37. avoidant, ambivalent
38. Evolutionary, reproductive
39. Social influence
40. Conformity, cultural
41. Asch, sanctions
42. Groupthink, approval
43. reward, coercive
44. Obedience, Milgram

45. decreased, authority
46. Compliance
47. door, door, low-ball
48. passive
49. Self-assertion
50. Aggression
51. Non-assertive
52. role-playing
53. overlearning, "broken record"
54. immediately rewarded
55. overused, tragedy, commons

Mastery Test

1. b (p. 676-677)
2. b (p. 684)
3. d (p. 677)
4. a (p. 672)
5. b (p. 680)
6. d (p. 691)
7. c (p. 675)
8. b (p. 667)
9. d (p. 671)
10. b (p. 682, 685)
11. a (p. 667)
12. d (p. 687)
13. b (p. 670)
14. b (p. 678)
15. c (p. 692)
16. d (p. 668)
17. a (p. 667)
18. a (p. 683)
19. c (p. 672)
20. d (p. 669)
21. b (p. 686)
22. b (p. 673)
23. a (p. 674)
24. d (p. 680)
25. c (p. 676)
26. c (p. 668)
27. b (p. 672)
28. a (p. 683)
29. d (p. 673)
30. b (p. 675-677)

Chapter 19
Attitudes, Culture, and Human Relations

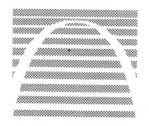

CHAPTER OVERVIEW

Attitudes have a belief component, an emotional component, and an action component. Attitudes may be formed by direct contact, interaction with others, child-rearing, group pressures, peer group influences, the mass media, and chance conditioning. Attitudes are measured by open-ended interviews, social distance scales, and attitude scales. Attitude change is related to reference group membership, to deliberate persuasion, and to personal experiences. Effective persuasion occurs when characteristics of the communicator, the message, and the audience are well matched. Cognitive dissonance theory explains how attitudes are maintained and changed. Brainwashing is forced attitude change. Many cults recruit new members with high-pressure techniques similar to brainwashing.

Prejudice is a negative attitude held toward out-group members. Prejudice can be attributed to scapegoating, personal prejudice, group norms, and authoritarian personality traits. Intergroup conflict leads to hostility and stereotyping. Status inequalities tend to build prejudices. Equal-status contact and superordinate goals tend to reduce these problems.

Ethologists blame aggression on instincts. Biological explanations emphasize brain mechanisms and physical factors. Aggression tends to follow frustration, especially when aggression cues are present. Social learning theory relates aggressive behavior to the influence of aggressive models.

Four decision points that must be passed before we give help to others are: noticing, defining an emergency, taking responsibility, and selecting a course of action. Helping is less likely at each point when other potential helpers are present. Giving help tends to encourage others to help too.

Multiculturalism is an attempt to give equal status to different ethnic, racial, and cultural groups. Cultural awareness is a key element in promoting greater social harmony.

Evolutionary psychology attempts to explain human social behavior by relating it to adaptations gained through natural selection during the course of human history.

LEARNING OBJECTIVES

To demonstrate mastery of this chapter you should be able to:

1. Define *attitude*. Describe the belief, emotional, and action components of an attitude.

2. List, describe, and give examples of six ways in which attitudes are acquired.

3. Explain three reasons why people may exhibit discrepancies between attitudes and behavior and how conviction affects attitudes.

4. Briefly describe the following techniques for measuring attitudes:
   a. open-ended interview   b. social distance scale   c. attitude scale

5. Differentiate between reference groups and membership groups.

6. Define *persuasion* and list three factors in understanding the success or failure of persuasion.

7. List nine conditions that encourage attitude change.

8. Describe consumer psychology and explain how marketing research and brand image are used to affect consumer behavior.

9. Describe the effects of role playing as a way to change attitudes.

10. Explain cognitive dissonance theory.

11. List five strategies for reducing dissonance.

12. Describe the effect of reward or justification on dissonance.

13. Differentiate between brainwashing and other persuasive techniques.

14. Explain how beliefs may unfreeze, change, and refreeze, and indicate how permanent the attitude changes brought about by brainwashing are.

15. Describe how cults are able to recruit, convert, and retain their members.

16. Define and differentiate between *prejudice* and *discrimination*.

17. Explain how scapegoating relates to prejudice.

18. Distinguish between personal and group prejudices.

19. Describe the characteristic beliefs (including ethnocentrism and dogmatism) and childhood experiences of the authoritarian personality.

20. Present the major characteristics of social stereotypes and indicate how they may lead to intergroup conflicts. Include a description of symbolic prejudice.

21. Explain how status inequalities may lead to the development of stereotypes and how equal-status contact may reduce intergroup tension. Give an example of each situation.

22. Define *superordinate goals*. Include an explanation of how they can reduce conflict and hostility.

23. Explain how a jigsaw classroom utilizes superordinate goals and helps reduce prejudice.

24. Define *aggression*. Discuss the roles of instincts and biology in terms of aggression.

25. State the frustration-aggression hypothesis, indicating why it may or may not be true.

26. Discuss how frustration, in the form of aversive stimuli, can encourage aggression.

27. Explain how the weapons effect encourages aggression.

28. Discuss how social learning theory explains aggression.

29. Briefly describe the results of studies on the relationship between aggressive pornography and aggression of males toward females.

30. Explain how television may serve as a disinhibiting factor with respect to aggression, and present evidence to support the viewpoint that watching television can cause a desensitization to violence.

31. Briefly list six ways in which parents can buffer the impact of television on children's behavior.

32. Explain how it is known that watching television can increase prosocial behavior.

33. Explain the basic principle of anger control and list five strategies for controlling anger.

34. List at least eight signs that indicate a student may be prone to school violence.

35. Give an example of bystander apathy, and indicate the major factor that determines whether or not help will be given.

36. Describe four conditions that need to exist before bystanders are likely to give help. Indicate how the presence of other people can influence apathy.

37. Discuss how heightened and empathic arousal affect helping behavior. Include the concept of the empathy-helping relationship.

38. State three ways in which prosocial behavior can be encouraged.

The following objectives are related to the material in the "Psychology in Action" and "A Step Beyond" sections of your text.

39. Define the term *multiculturalism.*

40. Discuss eight ways in which a person can become more tolerant.

41. Explain how a person can develop cultural awareness.

42. Explain what evolutionary psychologists mean when they use the term *adaptation.* Give at least three examples of human adaptations that aid survival.

43. Explain the basic idea behind sociobiology, differentiate it from evolutionary psychology, and evaluate it in terms of its strengths and weaknesses.

RECITE AND REVIEW

● *What are attitudes? How are they acquired?*

Recite and Review: Pages 696-700

  1. Attitudes are learned tendencies to respond in a _____ or _____ way.

  2. Attitudes are made up of a belief component, an emotional component, and an _____ component.

  3. Attitudes may be formed by _____ contact, interaction with others, the effects of _____-rearing practices, and social pressures from group membership.

  4. Peer group influences, the mass _____, and _____ conditioning (accidental learning) also appear to be important in attitude formation.

  5. The _____ consequences of actions, how we think others will _____ our actions, and habits all influence whether attitudes are converted to actions.

  6. Attitudes held with conviction are most likely to be _____ in behavior.

● *How are attitudes measured and changed? Under what conditions is persuasion most effective?*

Recite and Review: Pages 700-702

7. One way of measuring attitudes is the open-ended _____, in which a person freely states his or her views.

8. A social distance scale is a rating of the degree of _____ a person would be willing to have with a member of another _____.

9. Attitude scales are a collection of statements with which people express _____ or _____.

10. People tend to change their attitudes to match those of their reference group (a group the person _____ with and refers to for guidance).

11. Effective persuasion occurs when characteristics of the communicator, the _____, and the audience are well matched.

12. In general, a likable and believable communicator who repeats a credible message that arouses _____ in the audience and states clear-cut _____ will be persuasive.

13. Consumer psychologists study consumer behaviors such as selecting brands, _____, and deciding to _____.

14. Consumer psychologists often do marketing research, which is a type of public opinion _____ to aid the promotion of various products.

● *What is cognitive dissonance? What does it have to do with attitudes and behavior?*

Recite and Review: Pages 702-703

15. Significant personal experiences (which may be engineered through role-playing) tend to _____ attitudes.

16. One reason for this is that maintaining and changing attitudes is closely related to needs for _____ in thoughts and actions. Cognitive dissonance theory explains the dynamics of such needs.

17. Cognitive dissonance occurs when there is a _____ between thoughts or between thoughts and actions.

18. The amount of reward or justification (reasons) for one's actions influences whether _____ occurs.

19. We are motivated to _____ dissonance when it occurs, often by changing beliefs or attitudes.

● *Is brainwashing actually possible? How are people converted to cult membership?*

Recite and Review: Pages 703-705

20. Brainwashing is a form of _____ attitude change. It depends on control of the target person's total environment.

21. Three steps in brainwashing are unfreezing (loosening) old attitudes and beliefs, _____, and refreezing (rewarding and strengthening) new attitudes and beliefs.

22. Many cults recruit new members with high-pressure indoctrination techniques resembling
_____.

23. Cults attempt to catch people when they are vulnerable. Then they combine isolation, displays of
_____, discipline and rituals, intimidation, and escalating commitment to bring about
_____.

● *What causes prejudice and intergroup conflict? What can be done about these problems?*

Recite and Review: Pages 706-712

24. Prejudice is a _____ attitude held toward members of various out-groups.
25. Racism, ageism, and sexism are specific types of prejudice based on race, age, and
_____.

26. One theory attributes prejudice to scapegoating, which is a type of displaced
_____.

27. A second account says that prejudices may be held for personal reasons such as direct threats to a
person's well being (personal prejudice) or simply through adherence to group _____ (group
prejudice).

28. Prejudiced individuals tend to have an authoritarian or dogmatic _____,
characterized by rigidity, inhibition, intolerance, and _____-simplification.

29. Authoritarians tend to be very ethnocentric (they use their own _____ as a basis for judging all
others).

30. Intergroup _____ gives rise to hostility and the formation of social stereotypes (oversimplified images of members of various groups).

31. Symbolic prejudice, or prejudice expressed in _____ ways, is common today.

32. _____ inequalities (differences in power, prestige, or privileges) tend to build prejudices.

33. Equal-status contact (social interaction on an equal footing) tends to _____ prejudice.

34. Superordinate _____ (those that rise above all others) usually reduce intergroup conflict.

35. On a small scale, jigsaw _____ (which encourage cooperation through
_____ interdependence) have been shown to be an effective way of combating prejudice.

● *How do psychologists explain human aggression?*

Recite and Review: Pages 713-718

36. Ethologists explain aggression as a natural expression of inherited _____.

37. Biological explanations emphasize brain mechanisms and physical factors that _____ the
threshold (trigger point) for aggression.

38. According to the frustration-_____ hypothesis, frustration and
_____ are closely linked.

39. Frustration is only one of many aversive _____ that can arouse a person and make
aggression more likely. Aggression is especially likely to occur when _____ cues
(stimuli associated with aggression) are present.

40. Social learning theory has focused attention on the role of aggressive _____ in the
development of aggressive behavior.

41. Aggressive _____ on television encourage aggression because they desensitize (lower the sensitivity of) _____ to violence and disinhibit (remove restraints against) aggressive impulses.

● *Why are bystanders so often unwilling to help in an emergency?*

Recite and Review: Pages 718-721

42. Prosocial behavior is _____, constructive, or altruistic toward others.
43. Bystander apathy is the unwillingness of bystanders to offer _____ to others during emergencies.
44. Four decision points that must be passed before a person gives help are: _____, defining an emergency, taking responsibility, and selecting a course of action.
45. Helping is _____ likely at each point when other potential helpers are present.
46. Helping is encouraged by general arousal, empathic _____, being in a good mood, low effort or _____, and perceived similarity between the victim and the helper.

● *What can be done to lower prejudice and promote social harmony?*

Recite and Review: PSYCHOLOGY IN ACTION

47. Multiculturalism is an attempt to give _____ status to different ethnic, racial, and cultural groups.
48. Greater tolerance can be encouraged by neutralizing stereotypes with individuating information (which helps see others as _____).
49. Tolerance comes from looking for commonalties with others and by avoiding the effects of just-world _____, self-fulfilling prophecies, and _____ competition.
50. _____ awareness is a key element in promoting greater social harmony.

● *How do evolutionary psychologists explain social behavior?*

Recite and Review: A STEP BEYOND

51. Evolutionary psychology attempts to explain human _____ behavior by relating it to natural _____ and human adaptations.
52. Evolutionary psychologists believe humans developed various mental modules, or specialized _____ circuits, that guide behavior.
53. Sociobiology is a more extreme view that attempts to explain human social behavior by relating it to adaptations that aided _____ survival, as well as individual survival.
54. Sociobiology relies heavily on the idea of biological determinism (belief that behavior is controlled by _____ processes).

CONNECTIONS

1. _____	Mrs. Keech	a.	belief plus strong emotion
2. _____	misdirected letter	b.	standard for comparison
3. _____	mean world	c.	unequal treatment
4. _____	conviction	d.	doomsday group
5. _____	social distance	e.	thought reform
6. _____	reference group	f.	aggression target
7. _____	dissonance	g.	uncomfortable clash
8. _____	brainwashing	h.	attitude-behavior test
9. _____	discrimination	i.	allowed contact
10. _____	scapegoat	j.	television perspective

11. _____	authoritarianism	a.	modern bias
12. _____	ethnocentric	b.	above all others
13. _____	dogmatism	c.	F scale
14. _____	stereotype	d.	instincts
15. _____	symbolic prejudice	e.	group-centered
16. _____	superordinate	f.	altruistic
17. _____	ethology	g.	aggression cue
18. _____	weapons effect	h.	group rivalry
19. _____	prosocial	i.	unwarranted certainty
20. _____	social competition	j.	simplified image

CHECK YOUR MEMORY

Check Your Memory: Pages 696-700

1. Attitudes predict and direct future actions. T or F?

2. The misdirected letter technique was used to measure the belief component of attitudes toward the Irish. T or F?

3. What you think about the object of an attitude makes up its belief component. T or F?

4. If both parents belong to the same political party, their child probably will too. T or F?

5. A person who deviates from the majority opinion in a group tends to be excluded from conversation. T or F?

6. Heavy TV viewers feel safer than average because they spend so much time in security at home. T or F?

7. The combination of music and antisocial behavior in rock videos can make antisocial behavior seem more acceptable. T or F?

8. An attitude held with conviction is more likely to be acted upon. T or F?

Check Your Memory: Pages 700-702

9. In an open-ended interview, people respond to a series of statements for and against a particular issue. T or F?

10. A social distance scale is used to measure attitudes toward members of various social groups. T or F?

11. Five-point rating scales are frequently used in open-ended attitude interviews. T or F?

12. Our attitudes are more likely to match those held by members of our reference groups than our membership groups. T or F?

13. Persuasion refers to a deliberate attempt to change a person's reference groups. T or F?

14. Persuasion is less effective if the message appeals to the emotions. T or F?

15. For a poorly informed audience, persuasion is more effective if only one side of the argument is presented. T or F?

16. A persuasive message should not be repeated; doing so just weakens its impact. T or F?

Check Your Memory: Pages 702-703

17. Emotional experiences can alter attitudes, even if the experience is created by role-playing. T or F?

18. Acting contrary to one's attitudes or self-image causes cognitive dissonance. T or F?

19. Public commitment to an attitude or belief makes it more difficult to change. T or F?

20. Romantic couples reduce the dissonance caused by their partner's faults by ignoring them. T or F?

21. The greater the reward or justification for acting contrary to one's beliefs, the greater the cognitive dissonance felt. T or F?

22. Dissonance is especially likely to be felt when a person causes an undesired event to occur. T or F?

Check Your Memory: Pages 703-705

23. Roughly 16 percent of American POWs in the Korean war signed false confessions. T or F?

24. True brainwashing requires a captive audience. T or F?

25. In brainwashing, the target person is housed with other people who hold the same attitudes and beliefs that he or she does. T or F?

26. In most cases, the effects of brainwashing are very resistant to further change. T or F?

27. A cult is a group in which the belief system is more important than the leader who espouses it. T or F?

28. Cults play on emotions and discourage critical thinking. T or F?

29. Cult members are typically isolated from former reference groups. T or F?

Check Your Memory: Pages 706-712

30. Sexism is a type of prejudice. T or F?

31. The term *racial profiling* refers to giving preferential treatment to some students seeking admission to college. T or F?

32. Scapegoating is a prime example of discrimination. T or F?

33. A person who views members of another group as competitors for jobs displays group prejudice. T or F?

34. Authoritarian persons tend to be prejudiced against all out-groups. T or F?

35. The *F* in F scale stands for fanatic. T or F?

36. An authoritarian would agree that people can be divided into the weak and the strong. T or F?

37. Dogmatic personalities are found at both ends of the political spectrum. T or F?

38. Social stereotypes can be positive as well as negative. T or F?

39. People who feel they are being evaluated in terms of a stereotype tend to become anxious, which can lower their performance and seemingly confirm the stereotype. T or F?
40. Symbolic prejudice is the most obvious and socially unacceptable form of bigotry. T or F?
41. Images of national enemies tend to humanize the inhabitants of other countries, making them seem less threatening. T or F?
42. The key to creating prejudice in Jane Elliot's experiment was her use of scapegoating to cause group conflict. T or F?
43. Equal-status contact tends to reduce prejudice and stereotypes. T or F?
44. Superordinate groups help people of opposing groups to see themselves as members of a single larger group. T or F?
45. The term nuclear winter refers to widespread crop failures following the Chernobyl Nuclear Power Plant disaster. T or F?
46. Prejudice tends to be reduced when members of groups that have higher status offer to reward members of other groups for cooperating. T or F?

Check Your Memory: Pages 713-718

47. Over 75 percent of all married persons physically attack their spouses at one time or another. T or F?
48. Ethologists argue that humans learn to be aggressive by observing aggressive behavior in lower animals. T or F?
49. Specific areas of the brain are capable of initiating or ending aggression. T or F?
50. Intoxication tends to raise the threshold for aggression, making it more likely. T or F?
51. Higher levels of the hormone testosterone are associated with more aggressive behavior by both men and women. T or F?
52. The frustration-aggression hypothesis says that being aggressive is frustrating. T or F?
53. People exposed to aversive stimuli tend to become less sensitive to aggression cues. T or F?
54. Murders are less likely to occur in homes where guns are kept. T or F?
55. Social learning theorists assume that instinctive patterns of human aggression are modified by learning. T or F?
56. The erotic content of pornography is usually more damaging than the aggressive content. T or F?
57. Aggressive crimes in TV dramas occur at a much higher rate than they do in real life. T or F?
58. Preferring violent TV programs at age 8 predicts higher levels of violent behavior at age 19. T or F?
59. Prosocial TV programs have little effect on viewer behavior. T or F?
60. An important element of anger control is looking at upsetting situations as problems to be solved. T or F?
61. A student who is easily frustrated and reacts with extreme anger to criticism or disappointments has a heightened risk of engaging in school violence. T or F?
62. Children who see violence in the community tend to be less likely to engage in violence themselves. T or F?

Check Your Memory: Pages 718-721

63. In the Kitty Genovese murder, no one called the police until after the attack was over. T or F?
64. In an emergency, the more potential helpers present, the more likely a person is to get help. T or F?
65. The first step in giving help is to define the situation as an emergency. T or F?
66. Emotional arousal, especially empathic arousal, lowers the likelihood that one person will help

another. T or F?

67. You are more likely to help a person who seems similar to yourself. T or F?

68. In many emergency situations it can be more effective to shout "Fire!" rather than "Help!" T or F?

Check Your Memory: PSYCHOLOGY IN ACTION

69. Multiculturalism is an attempt to blend multiple ethnic backgrounds into one universal culture. T or F?

70. The emotional component of prejudicial attitudes may remain even after a person intellectually renounces prejudice. T or F?

71. Both prejudiced and nonprejudiced people are equally aware of social stereotypes. T or F?

72. Individuating information forces us to focus mainly on the labels attached to a person. T or F?

73. From a scientific point of view, "race" is a matter of social labeling, not a biological reality. T or F?

74. People who hold just-world beliefs assume that people generally get what they deserve. T or F?

75. Every major ethnic group rates itself better than other groups. T or F?

Check Your Memory: A STEP BEYOND

76. Evolutionary psychologists believe that human social behavior is influenced by adaptations that were shaped by natural selection. T or F?

77. Evolutionary psychologists believe that humans have a brain module for detecting cheaters in social groups. T or F?

78. The fact that humans tend to be poor at recognizing faces is an example of an evolutionary adaptation. T or F

79. Sociobiology explains altruistic suicide as an action that may help close kin survive. T or F?

80. Sociobiologists assume that species with highly evolved brains and high intelligence do not need any genetically programmed social behaviors to survive. T or F?

FINAL SURVEY AND REVIEW

● *What are attitudes? How are they acquired?*

1. Attitudes are _____ _____ to respond in a positive or negative way.

2. Attitudes are made up of a _____ component, an _____ component, and an action component.

3. Attitudes may be formed by direct _____, interaction with others, the effects of child-rearing practices, and social pressures from _____ _____.

4. _____ group influences, the mass media, and chance _____ (accidental learning) also appear to be important in attitude formation.

5. The immediate _____ of actions, how we think others will evaluate our actions, and _____ all influence whether attitudes are converted to actions.

6. Attitudes held with _____ are most likely to be expressed in behavior.

● *How are attitudes measured and changed? Under what conditions is persuasion most effective?*

7. One way of measuring attitudes is the _____ interview, in which a person freely states his or her views.

8. A _____ _____ scale is a rating of the degree of contact a person would be willing to have with a member of another group.

9. _____ _____ are a collection of statements with which people express agreement or disagreement.

10. People tend to change their attitudes to match those of their _____ group (a group the person identifies with and refers to for guidance).

11. Effective persuasion occurs when characteristics of the _____, the message, and the _____ are well matched.

12. In general, a likable and believable _____ who repeats a credible message that arouses emotion in the _____ and states clear-cut conclusions will be persuasive.

13. _____ psychologists study behaviors such as selecting _____, shopping, and deciding to purchase.

14. They often do _____ _____, which is a type of public opinion polling to aid the promotion of various products.

● *What is cognitive dissonance? What does it have to do with attitudes and behavior?*

15. Significant personal experiences (which may be engineered through _____) tend to change attitudes.

16. One reason for this is that maintaining and changing attitudes is closely related to needs for consistency in thoughts and actions. Cognitive _____ theory explains the dynamics of such needs.

17. Cognitive _____ occurs when there is a clash between _____ or between thoughts and actions.

18. The amount of _____ or _____ (reasons) for one's actions influences whether dissonance occurs.

19. We are motivated to reduce dissonance when it occurs, often by changing _____ or _____, rather than behavior.

● *Is brainwashing actually possible? How are people converted to cult membership?*

20. Brainwashing is a form of forced attitude change. It depends on _____ of the target person's total _____.

21. Three steps in brainwashing are _____ (loosening) old attitudes and beliefs, change, and _____ (rewarding and strengthening) new attitudes and beliefs.

22. Many cults recruit new members with high-pressure _____ techniques resembling brainwashing.

23. Cults attempt to catch people when they are vulnerable. Then they combine isolation, displays of affection, discipline and _____, intimidation, and escalating _____ to bring about conversion.

24. Prejudice is a negative attitude held toward members of various _____.

25. _____, _____, and _____ are specific types of prejudice based on race, age, and gender.

26. One theory attributes prejudice to _____, which is a type of _____ aggression.

27. A second account says that prejudices may be held for personal reasons such as direct threats to a person's well being (_____ prejudice) or simply through adherence to group norms (_____ prejudice).

28. Prejudiced individuals tend to have an _____ or _____ personality, characterized by rigidity, inhibition, intolerance, and over-simplification.

29. Authoritarians tend to be very _____ (they use their own group as a basis for judging all others).

30. Intergroup conflict gives rise to hostility and the formation of _____ _____ (over-simplified images of members of various groups).

31. _____ prejudice, or prejudice expressed in disguised ways, is common today.

32. Status _____ (differences in power, prestige, or privileges) tend to build prejudices.

33. _____ contact (social interaction on an equal footing) tends to reduce prejudice.

34. _____ goals (those that rise above all others) usually reduce intergroup conflict.

35. On a small scale, _____ classrooms (which encourage cooperation through mutual _____) have been shown to be an effective way of combating prejudice.

36. _____ explain aggression as a natural expression of inherited instincts.

37. Biological explanations emphasize brain mechanisms and physical factors that lower the _____ (trigger point) for aggression.

38. According to the _____-aggression hypothesis, _____ and aggression are closely linked.

39. Frustration is only one of many _____ stimuli that can arouse a person and make aggression more likely. Aggression is especially likely to occur when aggression _____ (stimuli associated with aggression) are present.

40. _____ _____ theory has focused attention on the role of aggressive models in the development of aggressive behavior.

41. Aggressive models on television encourage aggression because they _____ (lower the sensitivity of) viewers to violence and _____ (remove restraints against) aggressive impulses.

● *Why are bystanders so often unwilling to help in an emergency?*

42. Prosocial behavior is helpful, constructive, or _____ toward others.
43. Bystander _____ is the unwillingness of bystanders to offer help to others during emergencies.
44. Four decision points that must be passed before a person gives help are: noticing, defining an _____, taking _____, and selecting a course of action.
45. Helping is less likely at each point when other _____ _____ are present.
46. Helping is encouraged by general arousal, _____ arousal, being in a good mood, low effort or risk, and perceived _____ between the victim and the helper.

● *What can be done to lower prejudice and promote social harmony?*

47. _____ is an attempt to give equal status to different ethnic, racial, and cultural groups.
48. Greater tolerance can be encouraged by neutralizing stereotypes with _____ information (which helps see others as individuals).
49. Tolerance comes from looking for commonalties with others and by avoiding the effects of _____ beliefs, _____ prophecies, and social competition.
50. Cultural _____ is a key element in promoting greater social harmony.

● *How do evolutionary psychologists explain social behavior?*

51. Evolutionary psychology attempts to explain human social behavior by relating it to _____ _____ and human _____.
52. Evolutionary psychologists believe humans developed various _____ _____, or specialized brain circuits, that guide behavior.
53. _____ is a more extreme view that attempts to explain human social behavior by relating it to adaptations that aided group survival, as well as individual survival.
54. Sociobiology relies heavily on the idea of _____ _____ (belief that behavior is controlled by biological processes.)

MASTERY TEST

1. The weapons effect refers to the fact that weapons can serve as aggression
   a. thresholds b. cues c. models d. inhibitors

2. The Seekers' renewed conviction and interest in persuading others after the world failed to end can be explained by the
   a. social competition hypothesis b. frustration-persuasion hypothesis c. group's just-world beliefs
   d. theory of cognitive dissonance

3. One thing that reduces the chances that a bystander will give help in an emergency is
   a. heightened arousal   b. empathic arousal   c. others who could help   d. similarity to the victim

4. The misdirected letter technique is a way to demonstrate the _____ component of an attitude.
   a. emotional   b. belief   c. action   d. reactive

5. One consequence of seeing aggression portrayed on TV is a loss of emotional response, called
   a. disinhibition   b. disassociation   c. deconditioning   d. desensitization

6. If you are speaking to a well-informed audience, it is important to _____ if you want to persuade them.
   a. repeat your message   b. give both sides of the argument   c. be likable   d. appeal to their emotions

7. Which view of human aggression is most directly opposed to that of the ethologists?
   a. social learning   b. brain mechanisms   c. sociobiological   d. innate releaser

8. Development of a mean world view is usually associated with which source of attitudes?
   a. child rearing   b. mass media   c. chance conditioning   d. group membership

9. Research suggests that the most damaging element of pornography is the
   a. erotic content   b. nudity   c. aggressive content   d. impersonality

10. Creating superordinate goals is an important way to
    a. reduce group conflict   b. break the frustration-aggression link   c. promote bystander intervention
    d. reverse self-fulfilling prophecies

11. Children who learn good manners by watching television demonstrate that TV can promote
    a. disinhibition   b. prosocial behavior   c. deconditioning   d. superordinate behavior

12. A person who is dogmatic and politically conservative would be most likely to score high on the
    a. R Scale   b. Individuation Inventory   c. Social Competition Scale   d. F Scale

13. A major problem with the ethological view of human aggression is that
    a. labeling a behavior does not explain it   b. aversive stimuli alter the threshold for aggression
    c. it assumes that aggression begets aggression   d. it assumes that aggression is related to biological processes

14. The Bennington College study showed that attitudes are not affected very much by
    a. membership groups   b. child-rearing   c. reference groups   d. chance conditioning

15. Students who were paid to lie about a boring task experienced the most dissonance and changed their ratings the most when they were
    a. paid $1   b. paid $10   c. paid $20   d. asked to help lure other students into the experiment

16. A key element in the effectiveness of jigsaw classrooms is
    a. deindividuation   b. the promotion of self-fulfilling prophecies   c. mutual interdependence
    d. selecting competent student leaders

17. A good antidote for social stereotyping is
    a. adopting just-world beliefs   b. creating self-fulfilling prophecies   c. accepting status inequalities
    d. seeking individuating information

18. A learned tendency to respond to people and objects in positive or negative ways. This defines a(an)
    a. opinion   b. belief   c. attitude   d. social distance scale

19. An important difference between brainwashing and other types of persuasion is that brainwashing
    a. requires a captive audience   b. is almost always permanent   c. changes actions, not attitudes
    and beliefs   d. is reversed during the refreezing phase

20. The effects of frustration on aggression are most like the effects of _____ on aggression.
    a. social learning   b. prosocial models   c. defining an emergency   d. aversive stimuli

21. Evolutionary psychologists argue that many basic patterns of social behavior ultimately help us to
    a. inhibit natural instincts for aggression   b. survive and reproduce   c. benefit from culture
    d. make full use of our potential for learning

22. A negative attitude toward eggplant would be best explained by _____ if you were ill the first
    time you tried it.
    a. chance conditioning   b. attitudinal freezing   c. scapegoating   d. dogmatic association

23. The top three categories on which social stereotypes are based are
    a. employment, age, race   b. age, race, income   c. race, national origin, income   d. gender, age, race

24. Status inequalities are to _____ as equal-status contact is to _____.
    a. dependence, independence   b. discrimination, stereotyping   c. prejudice, tolerance
    d. aggression, individuation

25. Your actions are most likely to agree with one of your attitudes when
    a. the actions reverse an old habit   b. the attitude is held with conviction   c. you know that others
    disagree with your position   d. you score high on an attitude scale

26. Conversion to membership in a cult usually involves
    a. depression, disorientation, and intimidation   b. a series of emotional disturbances similar to
    post-traumatic stress   c. loyalty tests and unfreezing   d. a progression from small to large
    commitments

27. If it is easier for Anglo Americans to get automobile insurance than it is for African Americans, then African Americans have experienced
    a. discrimination b. scapegoating c. ethnocentrism d. personal prejudice

28. The presence of other potential helpers reduces the likelihood that a bystander will offer help in an emergency during which decision point?
    a. all of the decision points b. noticing c. defining an emergency d. taking responsibility

29. You mark a 5-point scale after reading a series of statements on the issue of rent control. Obviously you are completing an
    a. attitude differential b. attitude scale c. R scale d. attitudinal distance test

30. Racism expressed in a disguised form, so that it appears to be socially acceptable, is called _____ prejudice.
    a. secondary b. subjective c. silent d. symbolic

31. According to evolutionary psychology, our sensitivity to cheaters is based on the existence of a specific
    a. prosocial instinct b. mental module c. aversion cue d. ethological adaptation

ANSWERS

Recite and Review

1. positive, negative
2. action
3. direct, child
4. media, chance
5. immediate, evaluate
6. expressed
7. interview
8. contact, group
9. agreement, disagreement
10. identifies
11. message
12. emotion, conclusions
13. shopping, purchase
14. polling
15. change
16. consistency
17. clash
18. dissonance
19. reduce
20. forced
21. changing
22. brainwashing
23. affection, conversion
24. negative
25. gender (or sex)
26. aggression
27. norms
28. personality, over
29. group
30. conflict
31. disguised
32. Status
33. reduce
34. goals
35. classrooms, mutual
36. instincts
37. lower
38. aggression, aggression
39. stimuli, aggression
40. models
41. models, viewers
42. helpful
43. help
44. noticing
45. less
46. arousal, risk
47. equal
48. individuals
49. beliefs, social
50. Cultural
51. social, selection
52. brain
53. group
54. biological

Connections

1. d
2. h
3. j
4. a
5. i
6. b

7. g
8. e
9. c
10. f
11. c
12. e
13. i
14. j
15. a
16. b
17. d
18. g
19. f
20. h

Check Your Memory

1. T
2. F
3. T
4. T
5. T
6. F
7. T
8. T
9. F
10. T
11. F
12. T
13. F
14. F
15. T
16. F
17. T
18. T
19. T
20. F
21. F
22. T
23. T
24. T
25. F
26. F
27. F
28. T
29. T
30. T
31. F

32. F
33. F
34. T
35. F
36. T
37. T
38. T
39. T
40. F
41. F
42. F
43. T
44. T
45. F
46. F
47. F
48. F
49. T
50. F
51. T
52. F
53. F
54. F
55. F
56. F
57. T
58. T
59. F
60. T
61. T
62. F
63. T
64. F
65. F
66. F
67. T
68. T
69. F
70. T
71. T
72. F
73. T
74. T
75. T
76. T
77. T
78. F
79. T
80. F

Final Survey and Review

1. learned tendencies
2. belief, emotional
3. contact, group membership
4. Peer, conditioning
5. consequences, habits
6. conviction
7. open-ended
8. social distance
9. Attitude scales
10. reference
11. communicator, audience
12. communicator, audience
13. Consumer, brands
14. marketing research
15. role-playing
16. dissonance
17. dissonance, thoughts
18. reward, justification
19. beliefs, attitudes
20. control, environment
21. unfreezing, refreezing
22. indoctrination
23. rituals, commitment
24. out-groups
25. Racism, ageism, sexism
26. scapegoating, displaced
27. personal, group
28. authoritarian, dogmatic
29. ethnocentric
30. social stereotypes
31. Symbolic
32. inequalities
33. Equal-status
34. Superordinate
35. jigsaw, interdependence
36. Ethologists
37. threshold
38. frustration, frustration
39. aversive, cues
40. Social learning
41. desensitize, disinhibit
42. altruistic
43. apathy
44. emergency, responsibility
45. potential helpers
46. empathic, similarity

47. Multiculturalism
48. individuating
49. just-world, self-fulfilling
50. awareness
51. natural selection,
adaptations
52. mental modules
53. Sociobiology
54. biological determinism

Mastery Test

1. b (p. 715)
2. d (p. 702)
3. c (p. 720)

4. c (p. 697)
5. d (p. 716)
6. b (p. 700)
7. a (p. 713, 715)
8. b (p. 698)
9. c (p. 715)
10. a (p. 711)
11. b (p. 717)
12. d (p. 707)
13. a (p. 713)
14. a (p. 700)
15. a (p. 703)
16. c (p. 712)
17. d (p. 722)
18. c (p. 697)
19. a (p. 703)

20. d (p. 714)
21. b (p. 724)
22. a (p. 698)
23. d (p. 708)
24. c (p. 712)
25. b (p. 699)
26. d (p. 704)
27. a (p. 706)
28. a (p. 719-720)
29. b (p. 700)
30. d (p. 708)
31. b (p. 724)

Chapter 20
Applied Psychology

OVERVIEW

Applied psychologists attempt to solve practical problems. Some major applied specialties are: clinical and counseling, industrial-organizational, environmental, educational, legal, and sports psychology.

Industrial-organizational psychologists are interested in the problems people face at work. They specialize in personnel psychology and human relations at work. Personnel psychologists try to match people with jobs by combining job analysis with various tests and selection procedures. Two basic approaches to business and industrial management are scientific management and human relations approaches.

Environmental psychologists study the effects of behavioral settings, physical or social environments, and human territoriality, among many other major topics. Over-population is a major world problem, often reflected at an individual level in crowding. Environmental psychologists are solving many practical problems—from noise pollution to architectural design.

Educational psychologists seek to understand how people learn and teachers instruct. They are particularly interested in teaching styles and teaching strategies.

The psychology of law includes courtroom behavior and other topics that pertain to the legal system. Psychologists serve various consulting and counseling roles in legal, law enforcement, and criminal justice settings.

Sports psychologists seek to enhance sports performance and the benefits of sports participation. A careful task analysis of sports skills is a major tool for improving coaching and performance. The psychological dimension contributes greatly to peak performance.

Communication at work can be improved by following a few simple guidelines for effective speaking and listening.

Space psychologists study the behavioral challenges that accompany space flight, space habitats, and life in restricted environments.

LEARNING OBJECTIVES

To demonstrate mastery of this chapter you should be able to:

1. Define the term *applied psychology.*
2. List the two main areas of interest of industrial-organizational psychology.

3. Describe the activities of personnel psychologists by defining or describing the following areas and related concepts:
   a. job analysis (include the concept of critical incidents)
   b. biodata (include the concepts of personal interviews and the halo effect)
   c. vocational interest test
   d. aptitude test (include multi-media computerized tests)
   e. assessment center (include situational judgment tests, in-basket tests, and leaderless group discussions)
4. Differentiate scientific management styles (Theory X) from human relations approaches (Theory Y) to management, including work efficiency and psychological efficiency.
5. Define the terms *participative management, management by objectives, self-managed teams,* and *quality circles.*
6. List eight factors that seem to contribute the most to job satisfaction.
7. Explain the purpose and results of job enrichment.
8. Explain what is meant by *organizational culture* and *organizational citizenship.*
9. Explain the goals of environmental psychology, including the three types of environments or settings of interest.
10. Describe the four basic coping styles in making career decisions.
11. Describe how people exhibit territoriality.
12. Discuss the results of animal experiments on the effects of overcrowding, and state the possible implications for humans.
13. Differentiate between crowding and density.
14. Discuss the concept of attentional overload.
15. Briefly discuss the effects of noise pollution on school children.
16. List and describe four ways people can be encouraged to preserve the environment.
17. Explain how environmental assessments and architectural psychology can be used to solve environmental problems.
18. Describe the goals of educational psychology. Include a brief description of a teaching strategy and differentiate direct instruction from open teaching in your answer.
19. Discuss the psychology of law and identify topics of special interest.
20. List several problems in jury behavior. Describe the process of scientific jury selection.
21. Explain the ways in which a sports psychologist might contribute to peak performance by an athlete.
22. Define the terms *motor skill* and *motor program.* List and explain six rules that can aid skill learning.
23. Define the term *peak performance.*

The following objectives are related to the material in the "Psychology in Action" and "A Step Beyond" sections of your text.

24. List and explain ten ways to improve communication skills.

25. List and describe six ways to be a good listener.

26. Define *space psychologist* and describe the major human factors concerns that will have an impact on the success of future space missions and habitats.

RECITE AND REVIEW

● *How is psychology applied in business and industry?*

Recite and Review: Pages 728-736

1. Applied psychology refers to the use of psychological principles and research methods to solve _____ _____.

2. Major applied specialties include clinical and _____ psychology.

3. Other applied areas are related to business, such as _____/organizational psychology.

4. Psychology is also applied to problems that arise in the environment, in education, in law, and in _____.

5. Industrial-organizational psychologists are interested in the problems people face at _____ and within organizations.

6. Typically they specialize in personnel psychology and human _____ at work.

7. Personnel psychologists try to match people with _____ by combining _____ analysis with a variety of selection procedures.

8. To effectively match people with jobs, it is important to identify critical incidents (situations with which _____ employees must be able to cope).

9. Personnel selection is often based on gathering biodata (detailed _____ information about an applicant).

10. The traditional _____ interview is still widely used to select people for jobs. However, interviewers must be aware of the halo effect and other sources of _____.

11. Standardized psychological _____, such as vocational interest inventories, aptitude tests, and multi-media _____ tests, are mainstays of personnel selection.

12. In the assessment center approach, in-depth _____ of job candidates are done by observing them in simulated _____ situations.

13. Two popular assessment center techniques are the in-basket test, and leaderless _____ discussions.

14. Two basic approaches to business and industrial management are scientific management (Theory ___) and human relations approaches (Theory ___).

15. Theory ___ is most concerned with work efficiency (productivity), whereas, Theory ___ emphasizes psychological efficiency (good human relations).

16. Two common Theory ___ methods are participative management and _____ by objectives.

17. Recently, many companies have given employees more autonomy and responsibility by creating self-managed _____.

18. Below the management level, employees may be encouraged to become more involved in their work by participating in _____ circles.
19. Job satisfaction is related to _____, and it usually affects absenteeism, morale, employee turnover, and other factors that affect overall business efficiency.
20. Job satisfaction is usually enhanced by _____ ___ oriented job enrichment.
21. An active, vigilant coping style is most likely to produce good _____ decisions.
22. Workers who fit comfortably within the _____ of a business typically show good organizational citizenship.

● *What have psychologists learned about the effects of our physical and social environments?*

Recite and Review: Pages 737-745

23. Environmental psychologists are interested in the effects of behavioral _____, physical or _____ environments, and human territoriality, among many other major topics.
24. Territorial behavior involves defining a space as one's own, frequently by placing _____ markers (signals of ownership) in it.
25. Over-population is a major world problem, often reflected at an individual level in _____.
26. Animal experiments indicate that excessive crowding can be unhealthy and lead to _____ and pathological behaviors.
27. However, human research shows that psychological feelings of _____ do not always correspond to density (the number of people in a given space).
28. One major consequence of _____ is attentional overload (stress caused when too many demands are placed on a person's attention).
29. Toxic or poisoned environments, pollution, excess consumption of natural resources, and other types of environmental _____ pose serious threats to future _____.
30. In many cases, solutions to environmental problems are the result of doing a careful _____ assessment (an analysis of the effects environments have on behavior).
31. Architectural psychology is the study of the effects _____ have on behavior and the design of _____ using _____ principles.
32. Recycling can be encouraged by monetary _____, removing barriers, persuasion, obtaining public commitment, _____ setting, and giving feedback.

● *How has psychology improved education?*

Recite and Review: Pages 745-746

33. Educational psychologists seek to understand how people _____ and teachers _____.
34. An effective teaching strategy involves _____ preparation, stimulus presentation, the learner's _____, reinforcement, evaluation of the learner' progress, and periodic review.
35. They are particularly interested in teaching styles, such as direct instruction (_____ and demonstrations) and open teaching (active student-teacher _____).

● *What does psychology reveal about juries and court verdicts?*

Recite and Review: Pages 747-749

36. The psychology of law includes studies of courtroom behavior and other topics that pertain to the _____ system.
37. Studies of mock juries (_____ juries) show that jury decisions are often far from _____.
38. Psychologists are sometimes involved in jury _____. Demographic information, a community survey, nonverbal behavior, and looking for authoritarian _____ traits may be used to select jurors.

● *Can psychology enhance athletic performance?*

Recite and Review: Pages 749-751

39. Sports psychologists seek to enhance sports performance and the benefits of sports _____.
40. A careful task analysis breaks _____ _____ into their subparts.
41. Motor skills are the core of many sports performances. Motor skills are nonverbal _____ chains assembled into a smooth sequence.
42. Motor skills are guided by internal _____ plans or models called motor programs.
43. _____ performances are associated with the flow experience, an unusual mental state.
44. Top athletes typically _____ their arousal level so that it is appropriate for the task. They also focus _____ on the task and mentally rehearse it beforehand.
45. Most top athletes use various self-regulation strategies to _____ their performances and make necessary adjustments.

● *What can be done to improve communication at work?*

Recite and Review: PSYCHOLOGY IN ACTION

46. To improve communication at work you should state your message _____ and precisely.
47. Try to avoid overuse of obscure vocabulary, jargon, _____, and loaded words.
48. Learn and use people's _____. Be polite, but not servile.
49. Be expressive when you _____. Pay attention to nonverbal cues and the messages they send.
50. To be a good listener, you should _____ pay attention.
51. Try to identify the speaker's purpose and core _____.
52. Suspend evaluation while listening but check your _____ frequently and note nonverbal information.

● *How is psychology being applied in space missions?*

Recite and Review: A STEP BEYOND

53. Space psychologists study the many behavioral challenges that accompany space flight and life in restricted _____.

54. Space habitats (living areas) must be designed with special attention to environmental stressors, such as noise, control of the environment, _____ cycles, and _____ restriction.

55. Psychological issues, such as _____ isolation, _____ resolution, privacy, cultural differences, and maintaining mental health are equally important.

CONNECTIONS

1. _____	community psychology	a. simulated trial
2. _____	I-O psychology	b. mental health
3. _____	flextime	c. communication barrier
4. _____	biodata	d. vocational interests
5. _____	mock jury	e. essential work problem
6. _____	feedback	f. variable schedule
7. _____	jargon	g. work efficiency
8. _____	critical incident	h. personal history
9. _____	Kuder	i. information about effects
10. _____	in-basket test	j. work and organizations
11. _____	Theory X	k. psychological efficiency
12. _____	Theory Y	l. typical work problems

13. _____	quality circle	a. persons in area
14. _____	territorial marker	b. better for thinking
15. _____	density	c. better for facts
16. _____	noise pollution	d. movement plan
17. _____	cognitive map	e. flow
18. _____	direct instruction	f. strong emotional meaning
19. _____	open teaching	g. ownership signal
20. _____	School of the Future	h. discussion group
21. _____	loaded word	i. micro-society
22. _____	motor program	j. full service institution
23. _____	peak performance	k. mental area plan
24. _____	space habitat	l. intrusive sounds

CHECK YOUR MEMORY

Check Your Memory: Pages 728-736

1. Applied psychology can be defined as the use of learning principles to change undesirable human behavior. T or F?
2. Psychological research has shown that the best fire alarm is a recorded voice. T or F?
3. During a fire in a high-rise building, you should use the elevators, rather than the stairwell, so that you can leave as quickly as possible. T or F?
4. Personnel psychology is a specialty of I-O psychologists. T or F?
5. The basic idea of flextime is that employees can work as many or as few hours a week as they choose. T or F?
6. One way of doing a job analysis is to interview expert workers. T or F?
7. Critical incidents are serious employee mistakes identified by doing a job analysis. T or F?
8. Use of biodata is based on the idea that past behavior predicts future behavior. T or F?
9. Because of their many shortcomings, personal interviews are fading from use as a way of selecting job applicants. T or F?
10. The halo effect is a major problem in aptitude testing. T or F?
11. Excessive self-promotion tends to lower the ratings candidates receive in job interviews. T or F?
12. "I would prefer to read a good book," is the kind of statement typically found on aptitude tests. T or F?
13. Multi-media computerized tests seek to present realistic work situations to job candidates. T or F?
14. Leaderless quality circles are a typical task applicants face in assessment centers. T or F?
15. Theory X assumes that workers enjoy autonomy and accept responsibility. T or F?
16. The main benefit of a Theory X management style is a high level of psychological efficiency among workers. T or F?
17. Participative management aims to make work a cooperative effort. T or F?
18. Quality circles are typically allowed to choose their own methods of achieving results as long as the group is effective. T or F?
19. Job satisfaction comes from a good fit between work and a person's interests, needs, and abilities. T or F?
20. Job enrichment involves assigning workers a large number of new tasks. T or F?
21. A hypervigilant style usually leads to the best career decisions. T or F?
22. People who display organizational citizenship tend to contribute in ways that are not part of their job description. T or F?
23. "Desk rage" at work is associated with job stresses, threats to one's self-esteem, and conflicts with other workers. T or F?

Check Your Memory: Pages 737-745

24. A study of the pace of life found that the three fastest cities in the U.S. are Boston, New York, and Los Angeles. T or F?
25. Environmental psychologists study physical environments rather than social environments. T or F?
26. A dance is a behavioral setting. T or F?
27. Saving a place at a theater is a type of territorial behavior. T or F?

28. Burglars tend to choose houses to break into that have visible territorial markers. T or F?
29. World population doubled between 1950 and 1987. T or F?
30. In Calhoun's study of overcrowding in a rat colony, food and water rapidly ran out as the population increased. T or F?
31. High densities invariably lead to subjective feelings of crowding. T or F?
32. Stress is most likely to result when crowding causes a loss of control over a person's immediate social environment. T or F?
33. People suffering from attentional overload tend to ignore nonessential events and their social contacts are superficial. T or F?
34. Exposure to toxic hazards increases the risk of mental disease, as well as physical problems. T or F?
35. Long-corridor dormitories reduce feelings of crowding and encourage friendships. T or F?
36. Providing feedback about energy consumption tends to promote conservation of resources. T or F?
37. Direct monetary rewards have little or no effect on whether or not people recycle. T or F?

Check Your Memory: Pages 745-746

38. Reinforcement, evaluation, and spaced review are elements of a teaching strategy. T or F?
39. Students of direct instruction do a little better on achievement tests than students of open teaching do. T or F?
40. Students of open instruction tend to be better at thinking and problem solving than students of direct instruction. T or F?
41. One feature of the School of the Future was that children were evaluated and sent to appropriate agencies around the community for help. T or F?
42. The School of the Future model is based on a very high level of teacher, parent, and community involvement in children's education and welfare. T or F?

Check Your Memory: Pages 747-749

43. In court, attractive defendants are less likely to be found guilty than unattractive persons. T or F?
44. Jurors are supposed to take into account the severity of the punishment that a defendant faces, but many don't. T or F?
45. Scientific jury selection is only used in laboratory studies—the practice isn't allowed in real jury trials. T or F?
46. Demographic information consists of the most prominent personality traits a person displays. T or F?
47. All members of a death-qualified jury must be opposed to the death penalty. T or F?

Check Your Memory: Pages 749-751

48. Peak performances in sports require both mental and physical training. T or F?
49. Distance running tends to reduce anxiety, tension, and depression. T or F?
50. The most accurate marksmen are those who learn to pull the trigger just as their heart beats. T or F?
51. Motor programs adapt complex movements to changing conditions. T or F?
52. Verbal rules add little to learning a sports skill; you should concentrate on lifelike practice. T or F?
53. To enhance motor skill learning, feedback should call attention to correct responses. T or F?
54. Mental practice refines motor programs. T or F?

55. The top athletes in most sports are the ones who have learned how to force the flow experience to occur. T or F?

56. Better athletes often use imagery, relaxation techniques, and fixed routines to control their arousal levels. T or F?

Check Your Memory: PSYCHOLOGY IN ACTION

57. Effective communication addresses the who, what, when, where, how, and why of events. T or F?

58. Ambiguous messages are desirable because they leave others room to disagree. T or F?

59. Jargon is an acceptable means of communication as long as you are sure that listeners are familiar with it. T or F?

60. True politeness puts others at ease. T or F?

61. To add credibility to your message, you should learn to speak very slowly and deliberately. T or F?

62. Arriving late for meetings is a form of communication. T or F?

63. To be a good listener, learn to evaluate each sentence as it is completed. T or F?

64. Good listening improves communication as much as effective speaking does. T or F?

Check Your Memory: A STEP BEYOND

65. Many of the social and psychological problems of space flight can be prevented by carefully selecting astronauts before they leave Earth. T or F?

66. In space, astronauts have no preference for rooms with an obvious top or bottom. T or F?

67. Sleep cycles are best allowed to run freely in space since there are no real light and dark cycles. T or F?

68. The need for privacy in space habitats can be met, in part, by defining private territories for each astronaut. T or F?

69. Most people in restricted environments prefer games and other interactive pastimes as a way to break the monotony. T or F?

70. In the specialized environment of a space station, differences in culture no longer seem important. T or F?

71. Fifteen percent of space inhabitants are expected to experience a serious psychological disturbance. T or F?

72. Most major problems facing the world today are behavioral. T or F?

FINAL SURVEY AND REVIEW

● *How is psychology applied in business and industry?*

1. Applied psychology refers to the use of psychological _____ and _____ methods to solve practical problems.

2. Major applied specialties include _____ and _____ psychology.

3. Other applied areas are related to business, such as industrial/_____ psychology.

4. Psychology is also applied to problems that arise in the natural and social _____, in _____, in law, and in sports.

5. _____ psychologists are interested in the problems people face at work and within organizations.

6. Typically they specialize in _____ psychology (testing, selecting, and promoting employees) and human relations at work.

7. _____ psychologists try to match people with jobs by combining job _____ with a variety of selection procedures.

8. To effectively match people with jobs, it is important to identify _____ incidents (situations with which competent employees must be able to cope).

9. Personnel selection is often based on gathering _____ (detailed biographical information about an applicant).

10. The traditional personal _____ is still widely used to select people for jobs. However, interviewers must be aware of the _____ effect and other sources of bias.

11. Standardized psychological tests, such as _____ interest inventories, _____ tests, and multi-media computerized tests, are mainstays of personnel selection.

12. In the _____ _____ approach, in-depth evaluations of job candidates are done by observing them in simulated work situations.

13. Two popular assessment center techniques are the in-_____ test, and _____ group discussions.

14. Two basic approaches to business and industrial management are _____ management (Theory X) and _____ _____ approaches (Theory Y).

15. Theory X is most concerned with work _____ (productivity), whereas, Theory Y emphasizes _____ efficiency (good human relations).

16. Two common Theory Y methods are _____ management and management by _____.

17. Recently, many companies have given employees more autonomy and responsibility by creating _____ teams.

18. Below the management level, employees may be encouraged to become more involved in their work by participating in _____ _____.

19. Job _____ is related to productivity, and it usually affects absenteeism, _____, employee turnover, and other factors that affect overall business efficiency.

20. Comfort with one's work is usually enhanced by Theory Y-oriented job _____.

21. An active, _____ coping style is most likely to produce good career decisions.

22. Workers who fit comfortably within the culture of a business typically show good organizational _____.

● *What have psychologists learned about the effects of our physical and social environments?*

23. _____ psychologists are interested in the effects of _____ settings, physical or social environments, and human territoriality, among many other major topics.

24. Territorial behavior involves defining a space as one's own, frequently by placing territorial _____ (signals of ownership) in it.

25. _____ is a major world problem, often reflected at an individual level in crowding.

26. Animal experiments indicate that excessive _____ can be unhealthy and lead to abnormal and pathological behaviors.

27. However, human research shows that psychological feelings of crowding do not always correspond to _____ (the number of people in a given space).

28. One major consequence of crowding is _____ _____ (stress caused when too many demands are placed on a person's attention).

29. Toxic or poisoned environments, _____, excess consumption of natural _____, and other types of environmental damage pose serious threats to future generations.

30. In many cases, solutions to environmental problems are the result of doing a careful environmental _____ (an analysis of the effects environments have on behavior).

31. _____ psychology is the study of the effects buildings have on behavior and the design of buildings using psychological principles.

32. Recycling can be encouraged by _____ rewards, removing barriers, persuasion, obtaining public _____, goal setting, and giving feedback.

● *How has psychology improved education?*

33. _____ psychologists seek to understand how people learn and teachers instruct.

34. An effective teaching _____ involves learner preparation, stimulus presentation, the learner's response, _____, evaluation of the learner's progress, and periodic _____.

35. They are particularly interested in teaching styles, such as _____ _____ (lecture and demonstrations) and _____ teaching (active student-teacher _____).

● *What does psychology reveal about juries and court verdicts?*

36. The psychology of _____ includes studies of courtroom behavior and other topics that pertain to the legal system.

37. Studies of _____ juries (simulated juries) show that jury decisions are often far from objective.

38. Psychologists are sometimes involved in jury selection. _____ information (population data), a community survey, nonverbal behavior, and looking for _____ personality traits may be used to select jurors.

● *Can psychology enhance athletic performance?*

39. Sports psychologists seek to enhance sports _____ and the benefits of sports participation.

40. A careful _____ _____ breaks sports skills into their subparts.

41. _____ skills are the core of many sports performances. Such skills are nonverbal response _____ assembled into a smooth sequence.

42. Motor skills are guided by internal mental plans or models called _____ _____.

43. Peak performances are associated with the _____ experience, an unusual _____ state.

44. Top athletes typically adjust their _____ level so that it is appropriate for the task. They also focus attention on the task and mentally _____ it beforehand.
45. Most top athletes use various _____ strategies to evaluate their performances and make necessary adjustments.

● *What can be done to improve communication at work?*

46. To improve communication at work you should state your _____ clearly and precisely.
47. Try to avoid overuse of obscure _____, _____ (inside lingo), slang, and loaded words.
48. Learn and use people's names. Be _____, but not servile.
49. Be _____ when you speak. Pay attention to _____ cues and the messages they send.
50. To be a good _____, you should actively _____ _____.
51. Try to identify the speaker's _____ and core message.
52. Suspend _____ while listening but check your understanding frequently and note nonverbal information.

● *How is psychology being applied in space missions?*

53. _____ psychologists study the many behavioral challenges that accompany space flight and life in _____ environments.
54. Space _____ (living areas) must be designed with special attention to environmental _____, such as noise, control of the environment, sleep cycles, and sensory restriction.
55. Psychological issues, such as social _____, conflict _____, privacy, cultural _____, and maintaining mental health are equally important.

MASTERY TEST

1. Praise and feedback make up what part of a teaching strategy?
   a. learner preparation b. stimulus presentation c. reinforcement d. review

2. Which is POOR advice for learning motor skills?
   a. Observe a skilled model. b. Learn only nonverbal information. c. Get feedback.
   d. Avoid learning artificial parts of a task.

3. Which of the following would be a question for applied psychology?
   a. How does conditioning occur? b. How can eyewitness memory be improved? c. What are the most basic personality traits? d. Do athletes have unusual personality profiles?

4. Signs are placed on a recycling container each week showing how many aluminum cans were deposited during the previous week. This practice dramatically increases recycling, showing the benefits of using _____ to promote recycling.
   a. feedback   b. public commitment   c. consumer symbolization   d. persuasion

5. Psychological efficiency is promoted by
   a. scientific management   b. Theory Y   c. time-and-motion studies   d. progressive pay schedules

6. In court, being attractive does NOT help a defendant avoid being found guilty when
   a. a majority of jurors are also attractive   b. the defendant is a man   c. the defendant is over age 30
   d. being attractive helped the person commit a crime

7. The best antidote for social isolation on extended space missions is expected to be
   a. defining private social territories for crew members   b. coordinated sleep schedules   c. electronic contact with Earth   d. making conflict resolution teams part of all missions

8. Which of the following is NOT a specialty of I-O psychologists?
   a. personnel psychology   b. theories of management   c. human relations   d. architectural psychology

9. Dividing long-corridor dormitories into two living areas separated by a lounge
   a. makes residents feel more crowded, not less   b. decreases social contacts   c. increases energy consumption   d. decreases stress

10. You leave a book on a table in the library to save your place. The book is a territorial
    a. display   b. marker   c. strategy   d. control

11. When professional golfer Jack Nicklaus talks about "watching a movie" in his head before each shot, he is referring to the value of _____ for enhancing sports performance.
    a. mental practice   b. self-regulation   c. skilled modeling   d. task analysis

12. What cognitive maps, behavioral settings, and crowding have in common is that all
    a. are studied by community psychologists   b. produce attentional overload   c. are studied by environmental psychologists   d. are characteristics of Type A cities

13. Potentials for learning the skills used in various occupations are measured by
    a. interest tests   b. aptitude tests   c. in-basket tests   d. cognitive mapping

14. To encourage creative thinking by students, a teacher would be wise to use
    a. direct instruction   b. demonstrations as well as lectures   c. open teaching   d. spaced review

15. A good job analysis should identify
    a. critical incidents   b. compatible controls   c. motor programs   d. essential biodata

16. High _____ is experienced as crowding when it leads to a loss of _____ one's immediate environment.
    a. overload, attention to   b. density, control over   c. stimulation, interest in   d. arousal, contact with

17. Studies of flextime would most likely be done by a _____ psychologist.
    a. community   b. environmental   c. I-O   d. consumer

18. The halo effect is a problem in
    a. collecting biodata   b. scoring interest inventories   c. conducting interviews   d. aptitude testing

19. Mental practice is one way to improve
    a. motor programs   b. the flow experience   c. the accuracy of cognitive maps   d. job satisfaction

20. Joan has been given a specific sales total to meet for the month, suggesting that she works for a company that uses
    a. quality circles   b. job enrichment   c. flexi-quotas   d. management by objectives

21. Which of the following is NOT recommended for people who want to be effective listeners in the workplace?
    a. Identify the speaker's purpose.   b. Evaluate as you listen.   c. Check your understanding.
    d. Attend to nonverbal messages.

22. Planning, control, and orderliness are typical of _____ management.
    a. Theory X   b. participative   c. Theory Y   d. enriched

23. A psychologist who checks demographic information, does a community survey, and looks for authoritarian traits is most likely
    a. a personnel psychologist   b. doing a community mental health assessment   c. a consumer welfare advocate   d. a legal consultant

24. A very important element of job enrichment is
    a. switching to indirect feedback   b. increasing worker knowledge   c. use of bonuses and pay incentives   d. providing closer supervision and guidance

25. Procrastination, inaction, and indecision are most characteristic of the _____ style of career decision making.
    a. vigilant   b. complacent   c. defensive-avoidant   d. hypervigilant

ANSWERS

Recite and Review

1. practical problems
2. counseling
3. industrial
4. sports
5. work
6. relations
7. jobs, job
8. competent
9. biographical
10. personal, bias
11. tests, computerized
12. evaluations, work
13. group
14. X, Y
15. X, Y
16. Y, management
17. teams
18. quality
19. productivity
20. Theory Y
21. career
22. culture
23. settings, social
24. territorial
25. crowding
26. abnormal
27. crowding
28. crowding
29. damage, generations
30. environmental
31. buildings, buildings, behavioral
32. rewards, goal
33. learn, instruct
34. learner, response
35. lecture, discussion
36. legal
37. simulated, objective
38. selection, personality
39. participation
40. sports skills
41. response
42. mental
43. Peak
44. adjust, attention
45. evaluate
46. clearly
47. slang
48. names
49. speak
50. actively
51. message
52. understanding
53. environments
54. sleep, sensory
55. social, conflict

Connections

1. b
2. j
3. f
4. h
5. a
6. i
7. c
8. e
9. d
10. l
11. g
12. k
13. h
14. g
15. a
16. l
17. k
18. c
19. b
20. j
21. f
22. d
23. e
24. i

Check Your Memory

1. F
2. T
3. F
4. T
5. F
6. T
7. F
8. T
9. F
10. F
11. T
12. F
13. T
14. F
15. F
16. F
17. T
18. F
19. T
20. F
21. F
22. T
23. T
24. F
25. F
26. F
27. T
28. F
29. T
30. F
31. F
32. T
33. T
34. T
35. F
36. T
37. F
38. T
39. T
40. T
41. F
42. T
43. T

44. F
45. F
46. F
47. F
48. T
49. T
50. F
51. T
52. F
53. T
54. T
55. F
56. T
57. T
58. F
59. T
60. T
61. F
62. T
63. F
64. T
65. T
66. F
67. F
68. T
69. F
70. F
71. F
72. T

Final Survey and Review

1. principles, research
2. clinical, community
3. organizational
4. environment, education
5. Industrial-organizational
6. personnel
7. Personnel, analysis
8. critical
9. biodata
10. interview, halo
11. vocational, aptitude,
12. assessment center
13. basket, leaderless
14. scientific, human relations
15. efficiency, psychological
16. participative, objectives
17. self-managed
18. quality circles
19. satisfaction, morale
20. enrichment
21. vigilant
22. citizenship
23. Environmental, behavioral
24. markers
25. Over-population
26. crowding
27. density
28. attentional overload
29. pollution, resources
30. assessment
31. Architectural
32. monetary, commitment
33. Educational
34. strategy, reinforcement, review
35. direct instruction, open, discussion
36. law
37. mock
38. Demographic, authoritarian
39. performance
40. task analysis
41. Motor, chains
42. motor programs
43. flow, mental
44. arousal, rehearse
45. self-regulation
46. message
47. vocabulary, jargon
48. polite
49. expressive, nonverbal
50. listener, pay attention
51. purpose
52. evaluation
53. Space, restricted
54. habitats, stressors
55. isolation, resolution, differences

Mastery Test

1. c (p. 746)
2. b (p. 750)
3. b (p. 728)
4. a (p. 743)
5. b (p. 733)
6. d (p. 747)
7. c (p. 756)
8. d (p. 729)
9. d (p. 744)
10. b (p. 738)
11. a (p. 751)
12. c (p. 737)
13. b (p. 731)
14. c (p. 746)
15. a (p. 730)
16. b (p. 740)
17. c (p. 734)
18. c (p. 730)
19. a (p. 750)
20. d (p. 733)
21. b (p. 754)
22. a (p. 732)
23. d (p. 747)
24. b (p. 735)
25. c (p. 735)

Appendix
Statistics

OVERVIEW

Descriptive statistics are used to summarize data. Inferential statistics are used to make decisions and generalizations or to draw conclusions. Graphical statistics, such as histograms and frequency polygons, provide pictures (graphs) of groups of numbers. Measures of central tendency, such as the mean, median, and mode, supply a number describing an "average" or "typical" score in a group of scores. The range and standard deviation are measures of variability, or how spread-out scores are. Standard scores (z-scores) combine the mean and standard deviation in a way that tells how far above or below the mean a particular score lies. The normal curve is a bell-shaped distribution of scores that has useful and well known properties.

While psychologists are ultimately interested in entire populations, they must usually observe only a representative sample. Nevertheless, it is possible to tell if the results of an experiment are statistically significant (unlikely to be due to chance alone).

When measurements, scores, or observations come in pairs, it is possible to determine if they are correlated. The correlation coefficient tells if the relationship between two measures is positive or negative and how strong it is. While correlations are quite useful, correlation does not demonstrate causation.

LEARNING OBJECTIVES

To demonstrate mastery of this chapter, you should be able to:

1. Define and distinguish between the two major types of statistics, *descriptive* and inferential statistics.
2. List the three types of descriptive statistics.
3. Describe graphical statistics, including the terms *frequency distribution, histogram,* and *frequency polygon.*
4. Define measures of central tendency, including the terms *mean, median,* and *mode.*
5. Define measures of variability, including the range, standard deviation, and standard scores (z-score).
6. Describe the normal curve. Include its relationship to the standard deviation and z-scores.
7. Define *inferential statistics.*

8. Distinguish between a population and a sample, and include the concepts of representative samples and random samples.

9. Explain the concept of statistical significance.

10. Describe the concept of correlation, including scatter diagrams.

11. Distinguish among positive relationships, negative relationships, and zero correlations.

12. Define *coefficient of correlation*, and state the meaning of a perfect positive and perfect negative correlation.

13. Briefly discuss the value of correlations for making predictions. Include the concept of percent of variance.

14. Discuss the relationship between correlation and cause-and-effect determination.

RECITE AND REVIEW

● *What are descriptive statistics?*

Recite and Review: Pages A2-A3

1. Descriptive statistics are used to _____ data. Inferential statistics are used to make decisions and generalizations or to draw _____.

2. Three basic types of _____ statistics are graphical statistics, measures of central tendency, and measures of variability.

3. A frequency distribution organizes data by breaking an entire range of scores into _____ of equal size. Then, the number of scores falling in each _____ is recorded.

4. Graphical statistics provide _____ (graphs) of collections of numbers.

5. A histogram is drawn by placing _____ intervals on the abscissa (_____ line) and frequencies on the ordinate (_____ line) of a graph.

6. Next, vertical bars are drawn for each class interval, with the _____ of the bars being determined by the number of scores in each class.

7. A frequency polygon (line graph) results when points are plotted at the _____ of each class interval and connected by lines.

● *How are statistics used to identify an average score?*

Recite and Review: Pages A3-A4

8. Measures of central tendency are numbers describing an "_____" or "typical" score in a group of scores.

9. The mean is calculated by _____ all the scores for a group and then dividing by the total number of scores.

10. The median is found by arranging scores from the highest to the lowest and then selecting the _____ score.

11. The mode is the _____ _____ occurring score in a group of scores.

● *What statistics do psychologists use to measure how much scores differ from one another?*

Recite and Review: Pages A5-A8

12. Measures of variability tell how varied or widely _____ scores are.

13. The range is the _____ score minus the _____ score.

14. The standard deviation is calculated by finding the difference between each score and the _____. These differences are then _____. Then the squared deviations are totaled and their mean is found.

15. Standard scores (___-scores) are found by subtracting the _____ from a score. The resulting number is then divided by the standard deviation.

16. Standard scores tell how far above or below the _____ a particular score lies.

17. When they are collected from large groups of people, many psychological measures form a normal _____.

18. In a normal curve, 68 percent of all scores fall between plus and minus 1 standard deviations from the _____.

19. Ninety-five percent of all cases fall between plus and minus ___ standard deviations from the mean.

20. Ninety-nine percent of all cases fall between plus and minus ___ standard deviations from the mean.

● *What are inferential statistics?*

Recite and Review: Page A8-A9

21. The _____ _____ of subjects, objects, or events of interest in a scientific investigation is called a population.

22. When an entire population cannot be observed, a sample (smaller cross section) of the _____ is selected.

23. Samples must be representative (they must truly reflect the characteristics of the _____).

24. _____ drawn from representative samples are assumed to apply to the entire population.

25. Tests of statistical significance tell how often the results of an experiment could have occurred by _____ alone.

26. An experimental result that could have occurred only 5 times out of 100 (or less) by chance alone is considered _____.

● *How are correlations used in psychology?*

Recite and Review: Pages A9-A11

27. When measurements, scores, variables, or observations come in pairs, it is possible to determine if they are correlated (varying together in an _____ fashion).
28. The coefficient of correlation tells if the relationship between two measures is _____ or _____ and how strong it is.
29. While correlations are quite useful, correlation does not _____ causation.

CONNECTIONS

1. _____ frequency distribution   a. z-score
2. _____ histogram   b. subset
3. _____ mean   c. model distribution
4. _____ range   d. graphed correlation
5. _____ standard deviation   e. randomly selected
6. _____ standard score   f. correlation coefficient
7. _____ normal curve   g. no relationship
8. _____ population   h. central tendency
9. _____ sample   i. grouped scores
10. _____ representative   j. entire set
11. _____ zero correlation   k. percent of variance
12. _____ scatter diagram   l. average squared difference
13. _____ Pearson *r*   m. picture of frequencies
14. _____ *r* squared   n. spread of scores

CHECK YOUR MEMORY

Check Your Memory: Pages A2-A3

1. Descriptive statistics extract and summarize information. T or F?
2. Inferential statistics are used to make pictures (graphs) out of data. T or F?
3. Measures of variability are descriptive statistics. T or F?
4. A frequency distribution is made by recording the most frequently occurring score. T or F?
5. A frequency polygon is a graphical representation of a frequency distribution. T or F?
6. On a graph, the ordinate is the line that shows the frequency of scores at the center of each class interval. T or F?

Check Your Memory: Pages A3-A4

7. The mean, median, and mode are all averages. T or F?
8. The median is the most frequently occurring score in a group of scores. T or F?
9. To find the mode, you would have to know how many people obtained each possible score. T or F?

Check Your Memory: Pages A5-A8

10. The standard deviations can be different in two groups of scores even if their means are the same. T or F?
11. To find the range, you would have to know what the highest and lowest scores are. T or F?
12. To find a z-score you must know the median and the standard deviation. T or F?
13. A z-score of 1 means that a person scored exactly at the mean. T or F?
14. The majority of scores are found near the middle of a normal curve. T or F?
15. Fifty percent of all scores are found below the mean in a normal curve. T or F?

Check Your Memory: Page A8-A9

16. Psychologists prefer to study entire populations whenever it is practical to do so. T or F?
17. Random selection of subjects usually makes a sample representative. T or F?
18. A result that could have occurred by chance alone 25 times out of 100 is considered statistically significant. T or F?
19. A probability of .05 or less is statistically significant. T or F?

Check Your Memory: Pages A9-A11

20. A scatter diagram is a plot of two sets of unrelated measurements on the same graph. T or F?
21. In a positive relationship, increases in measure X are matched by increases in measure Y. T or F?
22. A correlation coefficient of .100 indicates a perfect positive relationship. T or F?
23. The Pearson r ranges from −.100 to +.100. T or F?
24. Correlations allow psychologists to make predictions. T or F?
25. Two correlated measures may be related through the influence of a third variable. T or F?
26. Correlation proves that one variable causes another if the correlation coefficient is significant. T or F?

FINAL SURVEY AND REVIEW

● *What are descriptive statistics?*

1. _____ statistics are used to summarize data. _____ statistics are used to make decisions and generalizations or to draw conclusions.
2. Three basic types of descriptive statistics are graphical statistics, measures of _____ tendency, and measures of _____.

3. A _____ _____ organizes data by breaking an entire range of scores into classes of equal size. Then, the number of scores falling in each class is recorded.

4. _____ statistics provide pictures of collections of numbers.

5. A _____ is drawn by placing class intervals on the _____ (horizontal line) and frequencies on the _____ (vertical line) of a graph.

6. Next, vertical bars are drawn for each _____ _____, with the height of the bars being determined by the number of scores in each class.

7. A _____ _____ (line graph) results when points are plotted at the center of each class interval and connected by lines.

● *How are statistics used to identify an average score?*

8. Measures of _____ _____ are numbers describing an "average" or "typical" score in a group of scores.

9. The _____ is calculated by adding all the scores for a group and then _____ by the total number of scores.

10. The _____ is found by arranging scores from the highest to the lowest and then selecting the middle score.

11. The _____ is the most frequently occurring score in a group of scores.

● *What statistics do psychologists use to measure how much scores differ from one another?*

12. Measures of _____ tell how varied or widely spread scores are.

13. The _____ is the highest score minus the lowest score.

14. The _____ _____ is calculated by finding the difference between each score and the mean. These differences are then squared. Then the squared deviations are totaled and their mean is found.

15. _____ scores (z-scores) are found by subtracting the mean from a score. The resulting number is then divided by the _____ _____.

16. _____ tell how far above or below the mean a particular score lies.

17. When they are collected from large groups of people, many psychological measures form a _____ curve.

18. In such curves, _____ percent of all scores fall between plus and minus 1 standard deviations from the mean.

19. _____ percent of all cases fall between plus and minus 2 standard deviations from the mean.

20. _____ percent of all cases fall between plus and minus 3 standard deviations from the mean.

● *What are inferential statistics?*

21. The entire set of subjects, objects, or events of interest in a scientific investigation is called a
_____.

22. When an entire set cannot be observed, a _____ (smaller cross section) is selected.

23. Samples must be _____ (they must truly reflect the characteristics of the population).

24. Conclusions drawn from _____ _____ are assumed to apply to the entire population.

25. Tests of statistical _____ tell how often the results of an experiment could have occurred by chance alone.

26. An experimental result that could have occurred only ____ times out of _____ (or less) by chance alone is considered significant.

● *How are correlations used in psychology?*

27. When measurements, scores, variables, or observations come in pairs, it is possible to determine if they are _____ (varying together in an orderly fashion).

28. The _____ of correlation tells if the relationship between two measures is positive or negative and how _____ it is.

29. While correlations are quite useful, correlation does not demonstrate _____.

MASTERY TEST

1. _____ statistics are especially valuable for decision making and drawing conclusions.
   a. Graphical b. Descriptive c. Inferential d. Significant

2. Measures of central tendency are _____ statistics.
   a. graphical b. descriptive c. inferential d. significant

3. Sorting scores into classes is a necessary step in creating a
   a. frequency distribution b. correlation c. scatter diagram d. variability plot

4. Vertical bars are used to indicate frequencies in a
   a. frequency polygon b. scatter diagram c. normal distribution d. histogram

5. Which is NOT a measure of central tendency?
   a. mean b. midst c. mode d. median

6. A group of scores must be arranged from the lowest to the highest in order to find the
   a. mean b. midst c. mode d. median

7. The _____ is sensitive to extremely high or low scores in a distribution.
   a. mean b. midst c. mode d. median

8. Which is a measure of variability?
   a. Pearson r b. z-score c. midst d. range

9. What two statistics are needed to calculate a standard score?
   a. range and midst b. mean and standard deviation c. range and mode
   d. standard deviation and z-score

10. If the mean on a test is 90, and the standard deviation is 10, a person with a z-score of –1 scored _____
    on the test.
    a. 70   b. 80   c. 100   d. 110

11. The largest percentage of scores falls between _____ SD in a normal curve.
    a. 0 and +1   b. +1 and –1   c. +2 and +3   d. –3 and –2

12. What percent of all cases are found between +3 SD and –3 SD in a normal curve?
    a. 50   b. 86   c. 95   d. 99

13. An effective way to make sure that a sample is representative is to
    a. use random selection b. calculate the correlation coefficient c. make sure that the standard
    deviation is low d. use a scatter diagram

14. Results of an experiment that have a chance probability of _____ are usually regarded as statistically
    significant.
    a. .5   b. .05   c. 1.5   d. 1.05

15. A good way to visualize a correlation is to plot a
    a. frequency histogram b. polygon coefficient c. scatter diagram d. normal ordinate

16. When measure X gets larger, measure Y gets smaller in a
    a. zero correlation b. positive relationship c. variable relationship d. negative relationship

17. When plotted as a graph, a zero correlation forms a cluster of points in the shape of a
    a. diagonal oval to the right b. diagonal oval to the left c. horizontal line d. circle

18. The largest possible correlation coefficient is
    a. 1   b. .001   c. 100   d. 10

19. To find the percent of variance in one measure accounted for by knowing another measure you should square the

a. mean   b. z-score   c. Pearson *r*   d. standard deviation

20. Correlations do not demonstrate whether

a. a relationship is positive or negative   b. a cause-and-effect connection exists

c. knowing one measure allows prediction of another   d. two events are really co-relating

ANSWERS

Recite and Review

1. summarize, conclusions
2. descriptive
3. classes, class
4. pictures
5. class, horizontal, vertical
6. height
7. center
8. average
9. adding
10. middle
11. most frequently
12. spread
13. highest, lowest
14. mean, squared
15. z, mean
16. mean
17. curve
18. mean
19. 2
20. 3
21. entire set
22. population
23. population
24. Conclusions
25. chance
26. significant
27. orderly
28. positive, negative
29. demonstrate

Connections

1. i
2. m
3. h
4. n
5. l
6. a
7. c
8. j
9. b
10. e
11. g
12. d
13. f
14. k

Check Your Memory

1. T
2. F
3. T
4. F
5. T
6. F
7. T
8. F
9. T
10. T
11. T
12. F
13. F

14. T
15. T
16. T
17. T
18. F
19. T
20. F
21. T
22. F
23. F
24. T
25. T
26. F

Final Survey and Review

1. Descriptive, Inferential
2. central, variability
3. frequency distribution
4. Graphical
5. histogram, abscissa, ordinate
6. class interval
7. frequency polygon
8. central tendency
9. mean, dividing
10. median
11. mode
12. variability
13. range
14. standard deviation

15. Standard, standard deviation
16. Z-scores (or standard scores)
17. normal
18. 68
19. Ninety-five
20. Ninety-nine
21. population
22. sample
23. representative
24. representative samples
25. significance
26. 5, 100
27. correlated

28. coefficient, strong
29. causation

Mastery Test

1. c (p. A-2, A-8)
2. b (p. A-4)
3. a (p. A-3)
4. d (p. A-3)
5. b (p. A-4, A-5)
6. d (p. A-5)
7. a (p. A-4)
8. d (p. A-5)
9. b (p. A-6)

10. b (p. A-6)
11. b (p. A-6)
12. d (p. A-7)
13. a (p. A-8)
14. b (p. A-9)
15. c (p. A-9)
16. d (p. A-9)
17. d (p. A-9)
18. a (p. A-10)
19. c (p. A-11)
20. b (p. A-11)